New East Asian Regionalism

Dedication

To Sonya and Calum
Charles Harvie

To Eriko, Viola and Keisei
Fukunari Kimura

To Myung-Hee, Suejin and Joonkyu
Hyun-Hoon Lee

New East Asian Regionalism

Causes, Progress and Country Perspectives

Edited by

Charles Harvie

Associate Professor and Co-Director, Centre for SME Research and Development, University of Wollongong, Australia

Fukunari Kimura

Professor, Keio University, Japan

Hyun-Hoon Lee

Professor, Kangwon National University, Korea

Edward Elgar

Cheltenham, UK • Northampton, MA, USA

Published by
Edward Elgar Publishing Limited
Glensanda House
Montpellier Parade
Cheltenham
Glos GL50 1UA
UK

Edward Elgar Publishing, Inc.
136 West Street
Suite 202
Northampton
Massachusetts 01060
USA

A catalogue record for this book
is available from the British Library

ISBN 1 84542 007 1

Printed and bound in Great Britain by MPG Books Ltd, Bodmin, Cornwall

Contents

Editors' Biographical Notes

Charles Harvie is Associate Professor of Economics at the University of Wollongong in Australia. He has published numerous journal articles, book chapters, and books on the economies of East Asia. He is the co-editor (with Dr Boon Chye-Lee) of a series of four books, currently in the process of completion with Edward Elgar Publishing, on the contribution of Small- and Medium sized Enterprises to the recovery of the East Asian economies in the wake of the financial crisis. He has also authored/edited a further four books with Macmillan (Palgrave). His areas of research interest include the economies of East Asia (in particular Korea, China, Vietnam and Indonesia), the economics of transition, and SMEs and entrepreneurialism.

Fukunari Kimura is Professor of Economics at Keio University in Japan. He was born in Tokyo in 1958 and received his Bachelor of Laws from the Faculty of Law, University of Tokyo in 1982 and his Ph.D. in economics from the Department of Economics, University of Wisconsin-Madison in 1991. He was Assistant Professor, Department of Economics, State University of New York at Albany from 1991-1994, joined the Faculty of Economics, Keio University as Associate Professor in 1994, and was promoted to Professor in 2000. His research specialities are in international trade and development economics. He has recently written a number of articles and book chapters on fragmentation and international production networks, trade issues related to WTO and regional trade arrangements, and development strategies of developing countries under globalization. He has also frequently acted as a consultant or advisor to the Government of Japan, various business associations, and international organizations.

Hyun-Hoon Lee graduated with a Ph.D. in Economics from the University of Oregon in 1989. He is currently Professor of Economics at Kangwon National University, Korea. During the first half of 2005 he worked as Environment Section Chief for UNESCAP (United Nations Economic and Social Commission for Asia and the Pacific). He has been visiting professor/scholar/fellow at the University of Oregon (USA), Keio University (Japan), the University of Melbourne (Australia) and the Bank of Korea. He has worked primarily on problems of intra-industry trade, international technology transfer and trade, and regional economic cooperation in East Asia and the Pacific. His research has been published in journals such as *Kyongjehak Yongu* (Korea), *The Korean Economic Review* (Korea), *Southern Economic Journal* (USA), *Japan and the World Economy,* (USA) *Weltwirtschaftliched Archiv* (Germany), *Canadian Journal of Economics* (Canada), and *Agenda* (Australia). He has also published several books with Palgrave Macmillan, and Edward Elgar Publishing among others, on intra-industry trade, the Korean economy and the Asian economy.

Other books published by Charles Harvie

Vietnam's Reforms and Economic Growth (co-authored with Tran Van Hoa),
Korea's Economic Miracle: Fading or Reviving? (co-authored with Hyun-Hoon Lee),
Causes and Impact of the Asian Financial Crisis (edited with Tran Van Hoa),
Contemporary Developments and Issues in China's Economic Transition (editor),
Globalisation and SMEs in East Asia, Studies of Small and Medium sized Enterprises in East Asia (co-edited with Boon-Chye Lee),
The Role of SMEs in National Economies in East Asia, Studies of Small and Medium sized Enterprises in East Asia (co-edited with Boon Chye Lee),
The Korean Economy, Post Crisis Policies, Issues and Prospects (co-edited with Hyun-Hoon Lee and Junggun Oh).

Other books published by Fukunari Kimura

Asia and Europe: Beyond Competing Regionalism (co-edited with Kiichiro Fukasaku and Shujiro Urata).

Other books published by Hyun-Hoon Lee

Korea's Economic Miracle: Fading or Reviving? (co-authored with Charles Harvie),
Frontiers of Research in Intra-Industry Trade (co-edited with Peter J. Lloyd),
The Korean Economy, Post Crisis Policies, Issues and Prospects (co-edited with Charles Harvie and Junggun Oh).

Contributors

Mitsuyo Ando is Assistant Professor, Graduate School of Economics, Hitotsubashi University, Tokyo, Japan (Email: m-ando@mbj.nifty.com).

Suthiphand Chirathivat is Associate Professor, Faculty of Economics, Chulalongkorn University, Thailand (Email: Suthiphand.C@Chula.ac.th).

Charles Harvie is Associate Professor and Co-Director, Centre for SME Research and Development, University of Wollongong, Australia (Email: charvie@uow.edu.au).

Tran Van Hoa is Associate Professor, Economics Discipline, School of Economics and Information Systems, University of Wollongong, Australia (Email: tvheco@uow.edu.au).

Kazuhiko Itoh is Coordinating Supervisor, New University Founding Office, Office of University Management, Tokyo Metropolitan Government, Japan (Email: Kazuhiko_1_Itou@member.metro.tokyo.jp).

Kentaro Kawasaki is Assistant Professor, Faculty of Business Administration, Toyo University, Japan (Email: kawasaki-k@toyonet.toyo.ac.jp).

Fukunari Kimura is Professor, Faculty of Economics, Keio University, Tokyo, Japan (Email: fkimura@econ.keio.ac.jp).

Hyun-Hoon Lee is Professor, Division of Economics and International Trade, Kangwon National University, Korea (Email:hhlee@mail.kangwon.ac.kr).

Zhao Lei is an Economist, Centre of Applied Statistics, Renmin University, China (Email: alexzhaolei@sohu.com).

Eiji Ogawa is Professor, Graduate School of Commerce and Management, Hitotsubashi University, Tokyo, Japan (Email: ogawa.eiji@srv.cc.hit-u.ac.jp).

David Roland-Holst is Director, Rural Development Research Consortium, University of California, Berkeley, USA (Email: dwrh@rdrc.net).

Robert Scollay is Associate Professor and Director of the APEC Study Centre, Department of Economics, University of Auckland Business School, New Zealand (Email: rscollay@auckland.ac.nz).

Chan-Hyun Sohn is Senior Fellow, Korea Institute for International Economic Policy and Visiting Professor at Yokohama National University, Japan (Email: chsohn@kiep.go.kr).

Seyed Komail Tayyebi is Associate Professor, Department of Economics, Faculty of Administrative Sciences and Economics, and Director of the International Scientific Cooperation Office, University of Isfahan, Iran (Email: komail@econ.ui.ac.ir).

Ryuhei Wakasugi is Professor, Faculty of Economics, Keio University, Japan (Email: wakasugi@econ.keio.ac.jp).

Yanyun Zhao is Professor and Director, The Centre for Research on Competitiveness and Assessment, Renmin University, China (Email: cas-kriu@mail.ruc.edu.cn).

Tang Zongming is Professor, Shanghai Jiao Tong University, China (Email: zmtang@mail.sjtu.edu.cn).

Acknowledgements

The economies of East Asia comprise the most dynamic region of the global economy. Rapid export growth and the attraction of foreign direct investment has lain at the core of the region's development strategy and underpinned its rapid economic growth and development since the 1970s. During this period support for a multilateral approach to trade liberalization was generally unequivocal, and seen as critical for further export oriented growth. However, more recently, the region has seen expanded interest in trade liberalization through the adoption of bilateral, plurilateral and other forms of free trade agreements. A key issue is whether such a development represents a building block that is consistent with the attainment of multilateral trade liberalization or whether it represents a stumbling block.

This volume consists of a collection of selected papers presented at the Asia Pacific Economic Forum (APEF) conference held at Keio University, Japan in September 2003, the theme of which was 'New East Asian Regionalism: Perspectives from Individual Countries'. Papers were presented by leading trade researchers from Australia, China, Iran, Japan, Korea, New Zealand and Thailand. The objectives of the conference were to identify and discuss the potential consequences from this recent trade policy phenomena.

The editors would like to extend their appreciation and gratitude first and foremost to the contributors to this book, without whose dedicated, timely, thought provoking and scholarly contributions this book would not have been possible. In addition, we would also like to extend our thanks to other conference attendees whose contributions assisted contributing authors to further fine-tune their chapters. At Edward Elgar Publishing we wish to thank Alexandra Minton and other staff for their patience and highly professional assistance. Last, but not least, we would like to thank our respective families and colleagues for their support and encouragement during the completion of this book.

Charles Harvie, Fukunari Kimura and Hyun-Hoon Lee
Wollongong, Australia, Tokyo, Japan and Seoul, Korea
December 2004

PART ONE

INTRODUCTION

1. Introduction

Charles Harvie, Fukunari Kimura and Hyun-Hoon Lee

1.1 OVERVIEW

Until the Asian crisis erupted in 1997 the East Asian economies pursued a multilateral approach to trade throughout the post-war period. In particular, Japan, China and South Korea were the world's only major economies that had yet to conclude a free trade agreement (FTA). The sole exception was the Association of South-East Asian Nations (ASEAN), which had been planning an FTA for several years. In recent years, however, a new regionalism has begun to emerge in East Asia that represents a clear break from the region's strong history of multilateralism. The countries of East Asia have been giving more attention to ways of expanding intra-regional trade that include: the establishment of regional trade agreements (RTAs) such as ASEAN+3; plans to establish a free trade area involving the economies of ASEAN and China; as well as moves towards bilateral trade agreements (BTAs).

A number of bilateral agreements have been concluded and are being negotiated or studied.[1] Singapore, the most trade-reliant ASEAN member, started the ball rolling by signing FTAs with 17 countries including New Zealand (2000), Japan (2002), Australia (2003), the United States (2003) and Jordan (2004). Singapore is currently negotiating/laying the groundwork for similar bilateral FTAs with Canada, India, Korea, Mexico, Sri Lanka, Bahrain, Egypt and Taiwan. Thailand is also one of the leading proponents of the creation of bilateral FTAs. Thailand signed an FTA with China in 2003, and signed a Closer Economic Relations (CER) Framework Agreement with India in 2003 and a Closer Economic Relations and free-trade agreement (CER-FTA) with Australia in 2004. Thailand has also negotiated similar FTA deals with the United States, Japan, Chile, New Zealand, Papua New Guinea, Peru, Bahrain and Australia. It also aims to reach bilateral FTAs with countries like Bangladesh, Qatar, Oman, Kuwait, the United Arab Emirates, Saudi Arabia, Malaysia, Taiwan and Singapore. The Philippines is also exploring the possibility of signing FTAs with countries outside of ASEAN. It is currently negotiating an FTA deal with Japan. Taiwan also signed its first FTA, with Panama in August 2003, and is exploring similar FTAs with a number of countries.

China has also been very active in pursuing FTA deals with countries in East Asia. It is now negotiating/studying FTAs with ASEAN and countries such as New Zealand, Australia, Japan and Korea. Japan signed an FTA in January 2002 with Singapore and another in September 2004 with Mexico. Japan is currently conducting official negotiations to conclude FTAs with Korea, Thailand, Malaysia and the Philippines, among which a basic agreement with the Philippines was reached in November 2004. Negotiations with Indonesia and ASEAN as a whole will be initiated in the first half of 2005. Korea also concluded an FTA with Chile in October 2002, for the first time in its history. In addition, Korea started formal government level talks with Japan for an FTA in December 2003, and with Singapore in February 2004. As both China and Japan have begun actively seeking FTAs with ASEAN, Korea also began a joint study with ASEAN in March 2004 for the feasibility of a Korea-ASEAN FTA. Korea has also been conducting a joint feasibility study of FTAs with New Zealand, Thailand, Mexico and a group of European countries (Switzerland, Norway, Iceland, Leichtenschtein). Korea has also considered concluding FTAs with Canada, India, New Zealand, Australia, the EU and the US.

Multi-country agreements are also being negotiated, proposed or studied in East Asia. ASEAN and CER countries discussed a link between the two free trade areas in November 2000. A Northeast Asian Free Trade Area consisting of China, Japan and Korea is also being studied. At the "ASEAN Plus Three" summit in November 1999, Japan, Korea and China agreed to launch a joint research project involving institutes from the three countries to discuss the possibility of forming an FTA among themselves in Northeast Asia. Since then, the three countries have held a summit every year at the ASEAN+3 meetings and have held regular meetings between their finance ministers.

During the summit of the ASEAN+3 countries in November 2001, China and ASEAN announced that they had decided to create an FTA within ten years. The Philippines has also proposed the East Asian Free Trade Area (EAFTA), an area covering the whole of East Asia. At the ASEAN+3 summit in November 2001, Korea also called for the formation of an East Asian economic community equivalent to the EAFTA.

Such a development is important given that an export led growth and development strategy provided the platform for the region's remarkable, and prolonged, period of high and sustained economic growth dating back to the 1960s, and that lies at the core of the East Asian Development Model. Export growth remains a key ingredient for the recovery of the region after the financial and economic crisis of 1997-98. The trend towards this new regionalism, the reasons for it, its impact upon the region, its future evolution and prospects are, therefore, of profound regional, and indeed global, significance.

While the recent regionalism of East Asia is not an altogether "new" idea, as Mahathir Mohamed the former Prime Minister of Malaysia proposed an East Asian Economic Group (EAEG) a decade ago, in practical terms it has only progressed rapidly more recently. Progress, however, has been proceeding more rapidly on financial issues than on trade, and there has been much discussion about creating an Asian Monetary Fund (AMF) and common currency baskets. Hong Kong and the Philippines have proposed the creation of the Asian Currency Unit (ACU). An Asian Bank for Reconstruction and Development and an Asian BIS (Bank for International Settlement) have also been discussed. A more concrete example of achievement in this area, however, is the Chiang Mai Initiative.

The important question is why have the East Asian countries changed their course of direction towards pursuing preferential arrangements? There are four main factors relating to the world economy that are relevant to this issue. The first factor is the slow process of liberalization under the WTO. Specifically, the failure of the WTO to begin a new round of multilateral negotiations in Seattle in 1999 as well as the more recent failure to make progress in Mexico in 2003, illustrate the difficulty of pushing through comprehensive multilateral liberalization. A second factor is the enlargements of the EU and growing Pan-American moves to increase free trade arrangements, such as expanding the North American Free Trade Agreement (NAFTA) into the proposed Free Trade Area of the Americas (FTAA) that includes the entire American continent except Cuba. Thus the EU process of economic integration has resulted in the proliferation of RTAs in the rest of the world.

The third factor is the East Asian financial crisis of 1997-98, which demonstrated the risk of contagion and investors' perception of the region as a "single market". This factor may have operated as a trigger, which explains the timing of the recent movement towards regionalism in East Asia, given the underlying changes outlined in the first two factors. In addition, cooperation among the East Asian countries during the crisis (such as in the provision of stand-by credit, the Miyazawa Fund, and China's no devaluation policy) nurtured mutual trust and the concept of "East Asia" as a natural entity heading for integration. The impotence of the Asia Pacific Economic Cooperation Forum (APEC) and ASEAN in the wake of the financial crisis also added to the urgency to consider alternative means to ensure the stability of future trading and financial arrangements in the region.

Finally, there is the *de facto* integration of the East Asian economy, symbolized by active cross-border production sharing. Hence, despite a complex historical/cultural background, people in East Asia are now increasingly sharing the view that East Asia is a natural economic entity heading for closer economic integration.

The region is currently standing at an important crossroads in terms of its economic development and growth, and a book such as this, with its focus on such a key contemporary issue for East Asia in the form of closer trade and monetary arrangements, is particularly opportune. The need to provide such an analysis, and discussion, stimulated the interest of the editors to produce this book. In addition, the participation of leading researchers on Asian trade and monetary cooperation in this project also provided a further major stimulus.

1.2 BOOK OUTLINE

The book consists, after an Introduction, of four parts: Background and Context; Issues in Trade and Investment Cooperation in East Asia; Country perspectives on Asian regionalism; and Monetary cooperation in East Asia.

Background and Context

This section of the book provides an overview of the expanding trade integration, and its various forms, and production networks among the economies of East Asia, that provide the basis for the increasing interest in, and logical expansion of, the further economic integration of the East Asian economies.

In Chapter 2 Robert Scollay conducts an extensive overview and stock-take of the evolution of preferential trading arrangements in East Asia and the Asia-Pacific region more generally. He provides a review and summary of the existing system and how it has evolved to this point in time, and the key factors that have contributed towards the movement to preferential trade agreements and away from further trade liberalization based on the WTOs principle of a non-discriminatory and fully consistent multilateral approach to trade liberalization. The author argues that recent changes in attitudes towards preferential trade agreements by Japan and Korea, in particular, marked a watershed for the East Asian region as a whole. An extensive review of the smorgasbord of trade agreements currently in effect, under consideration, or soon to become effective is presented.

The chapter also presents the results of simulations of a number of proposed Asia-Pacific preferential trade agreements (PTAs) using a modified version of the standard GTAP (Global Trade Analysis Project) model, to compare the potential relative welfare effects of different possible PTA configurations. The key implication from this exercise, not surprisingly, is that larger and more inclusive trade blocs produce more favourable outcomes for their members than smaller more limited arrangements. The larger the group the greater the potential for trade creation and reduced risk of trade diversion. Thus, an East Asian trade bloc is likely to yield more favourable welfare outcomes for the majority of its members than the more limited arrangements involving subsets of these economies. In turn, for APEC members as a group as well as for most individual APEC members, the prospective welfare outcomes from the implementation of one or other of the possible modes of APEC-wide liberalization are superior to those from an East Asian trading bloc, in some cases by a considerable margin. Hence, the author concludes, multilateral liberalization on a non-discriminatory basis will produce superior welfare outcomes to those from any regional initiative, including APEC. However, the reality is that this is not the direction along which the governments of the region are moving. The dominant trends are towards the continuing proliferation of bilateral agreements and the development of so-called "hub and spoke" configurations. The author then conducts a discussion of the implications of these results and then presents some observations on issues relating to the future evolution of PTAs involving East Asian economies.

In Chapter 3 David Roland-Holst presents a structural analysis of global supply networks and multilateral trade linkages in the context of the East Asian region. He argues that the movement towards a more open multilateral trading system resulted in a proliferation of supply chains in the region, with the role of private capital flows in the form of FDI being pivotal in this process as well as influencing patterns of regional production and trade. An important implication of the resulting supply chain decomposition is that the global network of value creation and income linkages is much more extensive and complex than would be suggested by bilateral trade statistics alone. The author argues for this reason that the significance of existing multilateral ties, as well as the gains from a more liberal trading environment, may be seriously underestimated.

To assess the significance of such global networks, and supply chain decomposition generally, the author compiles an international Social Accounting Matrix (SAM) using detailed international bilateral trade data. This international SAM is then used to conduct a multiplier decomposition analysis. The results obtained indicate that these network effects are complex, largely mediated by intermediate supply and intra-industry trade, and often represent the majority of value creation. They reach across geographic boundaries and sectors in ways that are impossible for policy makers or trade negotiators to anticipate by intuition alone. Open multilateralism is, therefore, a pervasive phenomenon that the conventional view of gains from trade seriously understates.

Issues in Trade and Investment Cooperation in East Asia

This section of the book further elaborates upon issues relating to the extent, nature, significance and performance of key trade and investment linkages among the economies of East Asia – production networks, trade relationships and their significance, and factors affecting FDI utilization and competitiveness.

In Chapter 4 Fukunari Kimura and Mitsuyo Ando further analyse the importance of international production and distribution networks in East Asia, but this time within the context of the prospective formation and establishment of regional free trade agreements. It reviews the nature and characteristics of international production/distribution networks in East Asia, discusses in detail the role of FTAs in rationalizing import-substituting industries, and proposes new elements of FTAs that will further activate international production/distribution networks. The authors argue that one of the reasons for the increasing interest in the region for further integration and the formation of free trade agreements bilaterally and for the region as a whole, has arisen from the formation of international production/distribution networks during the past decade. They also argue that there has been an important qualitative change in the East Asian economy during the last decade, with FDI playing a pivotal role in this process. Changes in FDI hosting policies contributed to an unprecedented formation of international production/distribution networks in East Asia along the lines of fragmentation theory. They further argue that regional FTAs should be designed in such a way as to be consistent with these new characteristics of the East Asian economy, enabling further facilitation of these international production/distribution networks. These networks will require new policy packages that recognize their breadth and complexity within the scheme of FTAs. If a region-wide integration is the aim then the contents of such an FTA must be designed with this in mind.

In Chapter 5 Ryuhei Wakasugi and Kazuhiko Itoh analyse the effect of regional trade agreements on non-member country exports and production. Specifically, they empirically examine how the bilateral trade flow and foreign production of a non-RTA member country is affected by the establishment of an RTA, and they take Japan as an example of a non-member country. Using estimates from a gravity equation they find that the formation of NAFTA and AFTA did not necessarily negatively affect Japan's trade with those member countries. They find that the growth in Japanese exports is largely caused by trade expansion between member and non-member countries rather than by trade expansion with member countries. Hence Japan benefited more from worldwide trade expansion than from regional trade expansion within RTA member countries. Similarly, with regard to the production of Japanese affiliates in foreign countries, their estimation results indicate that the formation of NAFTA and AFTA did not negatively affect the foreign production of Japanese firms in their member countries. However, the empirical examination again shows that growth in the foreign production of Japanese affiliates is largely caused by trade expansion between member and non-RTA member countries rather than by trade expansion within member countries, again suggesting that Japanese foreign production can be attributed mainly to global trade expansion rather than to regional trade expansion within RTA member countries.

These findings, therefore, reveal that the expansion of trade and the foreign production of Japan have been caused by worldwide trade expansion rather than by regional trade expansion, although RTAs did not necessarily affect Japanese trade and production in foreign countries negatively. Thus, global, rather than regional, trade liberalization is indispensable to the growth of Japanese exports to, and production of, Japanese affiliates in RTA member countries. These results suggest that Japanese trade policy should primarily be formulated on the basis of liberalizing the world trade system within the GATT/WTO framework, as well as deepening the regional free trade system through the introduction of RTAs.

In Chapter 6 Komail Tayyebi conducts an empirical investigation of the key factors determining export flows amongst some member countries of ASEAN (Singapore, Malaysia, Indonesia, Thailand and the Philippines). The econometric analysis uses the panel data method and relies on some of the main features belonging to trade gravity models, with the objective of testing the hypothesis of the extent to which trade integration affects the intra-trade flows of ASEAN members and their own volumes of imports and exports. The author also attempts to improve upon the technique by extending the range of topics these models may cover.

The estimation results indicate that trade integration between ASEAN members and their partners would increase the amount of trade flows between them. The larger the number of countries taking part in such an integration the more effective would cooperation be amongst its members. Hence the key implication of the current study is that most nations in the bloc are able to benefit from integrating their economic activities, and also benefit from economies of scale.

In Chapter 7 Yanyun Zhao and Zhao Lei use panel data to conduct a comparative analysis of the key factors influencing the utilization of FDI, and the relative importance of these different factors, between the ASEAN+3, ASEAN+1 and EU countries. They attempt to identify common and different factors affecting the utilization of FDI, emphasizing in which aspects the ASEAN+3 countries may be particularly lagging. Since the countries of ASEAN are at various stages of economic development they also conduct an empirical analysis of each ASEAN+3 country for FDI utilization using a Partial Least Squares (PLS) model, with the objective of identifying key differences between them.

Their results suggest that, generally speaking, more factors influence FDI utilization in ASEAN+3 than for the EU. For ASEAN+3 GDP per capita, economic strength and finance, international trade, and a safe social environment and stable political situation are particularly attractive for FDI utilization. The influential factors on the utilization of FDI for ASEAN+3 are almost the same as those of ASEAN+1, but the exclusion of Japan and Korea noticeably changes the relative importance of some of these variables.

Country Perspectives on Asian Regionalism

This section focuses upon developments in regional economic integration from the perspective of various individual countries and groups of countries.

In Chapter 8 Suthiphand Chirathivat presents an ASEAN perspective on movements towards East Asia wide regionalism, where the latter is considered to be ASEAN+3. The author suggests that the costs and benefits of reducing trade barriers for regional partners need to be assessed properly. China is shown to be the most heavily protected country compared to ASEAN-6,[2] Korea and Japan, and with trade liberalization it seems likely to gain most in terms of GDP and trade. ASEAN, however, could also make GDP gains, and these are likely to be relatively larger than for Japan and Korea. ASEAN, Japan and Korea are likely to emphasize exporting their products to supply China's vast market, which could result in slight trade diversion especially with those developed countries outside the region.

The author argues that a more integrated Asia-wide region will multiply the difficulties in terms of current developments and future challenges, however it must be hoped that the current proliferation of bilateral deals in the region will support, and not substitute, efforts towards Asia-wide regionalism. He also argues that the policy framework to assist this initiative must be market-driven and carried out with a view to increasing economic efficiency, better resource allocation, and openness for more competition. On the other hand there is a need to develop in parallel a long-term end goal of an Asia-wide regionalism that fits the present economic development needs of the East Asian economies, and is consistent with their further integration into the global economy.

In Chapter 9 Chan Hyun Sohn and Hyun-Hoon Lee discuss developments in East Asian Regionalism from a Korean perspective. In doing so they review recent movements toward regionalism in East Asia and discuss how Korea, and the other countries of East Asia, have responded to these developments and are likely to respond in the future in both plurilateral and bilateral contexts. The authors also highlight six important selection criteria that could be useful in determining eligible FTA partners for Korea.

Based on the selection criteria the authors suggest that among the various options for plurilateral trade arrangements, three options are plausible for Korea. The first option is that Korea and a subset of countries form a sub-regional agreement within APEC. Specifically, OECD member countries within APEC (such as the US, Japan, Canada, Australia and Korea), and some other advanced open economies (such as Singapore, New Zealand and Chile) could agree on forming an FTA among themselves. The second option is to pursue an ASEAN+5 FTA. A third option is to establish a Northeast Asian Free Trade Area. On the other hand, Japan, China and Singapore could be bilateral FTA partners for Korea, entailing large trade creation effects and lesser degrees of trade-induced adjustment costs. Lastly, the authors argue that it is important for Korea to ensure that any FTA initiatives are consistent with multilateral trade rules.

In Chapter 10 Tang Zongming and Tran Van Hoa provide insights into the implications for China's economic development arising from the growth of regional trade agreements in East Asia. The chapter analyses the performance and describes the key features of China's recent rapid economic growth. It then examines the importance of the Chinese economy for the other economies of East Asia, and the potential impact of regional integration, such as ASEAN+3 or its subset ASEAN+China, on China's economic development.

The authors argue that while China does compete against its neighbouring countries, such as ASEAN and Korea, the negative influence of competition would be offset by the benefits that China offers to these nations as their key-trading partner. China's trade liberalization, as a result of its accession to the WTO and the formation of an ASEAN-China FTA, the authors argue, would provide an important opportunity for expanding current trade and investment activities between the East and South East Asian countries and China. China will continue to provide East and South East Asian nations with considerable opportunities to expand their economic development, due to its low labour costs and a sizable domestic market. According to the authors, future closer economic integration between China and the economies of ASEAN will, therefore, be of considerable mutual benefit.

In Chapter 11 Tran Van Hoa outlines the development of new Asian regionalism and ASEAN+3. He also provides a linkage between ASEAN+3 and gravity theory, and outlines a new approach, the extended gravity theory, used in this study for analysis of the impact of ASEAN+3 on Asia-Australia trade and growth. A simple trade-growth model is also introduced and results from its estimation are reported. An analysis of these empirical findings and implications for policy regarding Asia-Australia trade, growth and economic policy are also presented.

The resulting trade-growth models using an extended gravity theory for ASEAN-Australia, Asia 3-Australia and ASEAN+3-Australia and their empirical findings appear to support the premise that trade does cause growth among the trading partners, but the evidence is weak statistically and in magnitude. More important to growth, however, are the economic, financial and other external or domestic crises, and trade and economic relations policies that promote regional cooperation to avoid, or to manage better, future similar crises. The author argues that trade and economic relations between ASEAN+3 and Australia should be encouraged, because it will strengthen bilateral cooperation and result in mutual benefits.

Monetary Cooperation in East Asia

The final section of the book explores some key issues involved in the process of developing closer monetary integration in East Asia. This is a logical extension to the closer economic and trade integration focused upon in the previous sections. In particular, the issue of the potential advantages and disadvantages of closer monetary integration for country and regional stability, and the possibility of establishing a common currency basket are emphasized.

In Chapter 12 Charles Harvie presents a conceptual framework for analysing the policy coordination benefits and costs for a small country whose macro-economy is strongly influenced by a large country, or bloc of countries. A simple Dornbusch (1976) type model is developed for both the small and large countries. The impact of external shocks emanating from the large country, and their impact upon the small country is then analysed by means of a numerical algorithm. Emphasis is given to their impact upon the small country price level, exchange rate, interest rate and output. Three exogenous shocks emanating from the large country are focused upon – interest rate, output and price level.

In analysing each of these shocks individually, the results tended to suggest that the adoption of an independent policy stance (involving a no policy response) produced more desirable macroeconomic outcomes for the small economy. However, in a simulation scenario involving external shocks arising from all of these variables the results obtained were less clear-cut. Indeed, the author finds that taking these shocks as a group, a coordinated monetary response by the small country could be best. However, if the aim of the small country was upon attaining price and output stability, the no response option could still be preferable.

Finally, in Chapter 13, Eiji Ogawa and Kentaro Kawasaki investigate the prospects and key issues involved in creating a common currency basket in East Asia according to optimal currency area theory. In doing so they conduct an empirical analysis of an optimal currency area in East Asia using a Generalized Purchasing Power Parity (G-PPP) model. In particular, they investigate which East Asian countries are conducive to the establishment of a common currency area. The empirical results presented suggest that the ASEAN-5[3] countries, Korea and China are able to form a common currency area, and that a common currency basket will be more applicable as an anchor currency rather than that of the US dollar. They emphasize that a common currency basket is more applicable as an anchor currency than the US dollar in forming a common currency area in the region. Policy implications arising from these results are also discussed.

The authors argue that it is necessary to create a common currency basket for the East Asian countries in order to resolve a coordination failure in exchange rate policies amongst them. In addition, they also suggest that the

European experience with the European Currency Unit (ECU) could provide useful information in establishing a common currency unit in East Asia. Since the East Asian countries have international trade relationships with Japan, the United States and the European countries, a possible common currency unit in East Asia would consist of the US dollar, the Japanese yen and the euro. This is in contrast to the ECU which only consisted of intra-regional currencies.

The authors also make the important observation that if the monetary authorities of the East Asian countries intend to implement regional policy coordination, as a premise they need to create a common currency area. It is difficult for them to conduct regional policy coordination unless they have common policy objectives. It is essential that they have common objectives in monetary and exchange rate policies, in order to create a common currency area.

NOTES

1 See, for example, Table 9.1, p. 173 below.

2 ASEAN-6 countries consist of Brunei, Indonesia, Malaysia, the Philippines, Singapore and Thailand.

3 ASEAN-5 countries consist of Indonesia, Malaysia, the Philippines, Singapore and Thailand.

REFERENCES

Dornbusch, R. (1976), "Exchange rate dynamics", *Journal of Political Economy, 84,* pp. 1161-76.

PART TWO

BACKGROUND AND CONTEXT

2. East Asia and the Evolution of Preferential Trading Arrangements in the Asia-Pacific: A Stock-take

Robert Scollay

2.1 INTRODUCTION

In the space of five years the outlook for the configuration of trading arrangements in the Asia-Pacific region[1] has changed dramatically. Upon a previously seemingly stable pattern of existing arrangements there has been superimposed a bewildering kaleidoscope of proposals for new and in some cases overlapping preferential trading arrangements (PTAs) at various stages of negotiation, study or discussion. At least eleven of these new proposals have resulted in concluded agreements,[2] while many others are advancing at varying speeds, and some have stalled. New proposals continue to emerge at frequent intervals. East Asian economies have been at the forefront of these developments. Nine of the eleven newly concluded agreements involve East Asian economies, and the majority of initiatives still under negotiation or study also involve East Asian economies.

Thus East Asia, and with it the wider Asia-Pacific region, has quickly become enmeshed in the proliferation of PTAs that has already been observed over a longer period in other regions of the global trading system. These new developments in the Asia-Pacific region exhibit many of the tendencies and raise all the same issues (summarized, for example, in Panagariya, 1999, Krueger, 1999 and Findlay, 2002) that have been identified in the proliferation of PTAs elsewhere. Which of the tendencies will predominate and how the issues raised will be resolved are crucial questions, the answers to which will largely determine the future evolution of East Asian and, consequentially, Asia-Pacific trading relationships.

This chapter is organized as follows. The next section briefly summarizes the existing situation and how it has arisen. This is followed by an assessment of the economic welfare effects of the various categories of trade arrangement that can be identified among the initiatives at present on the table, as indicated by the results of computable general equilibrium (CGE) simulations. A discussion of the implications of these results then follows, leading into some observations on issues relating to the future evolution of PTAs involving East Asian economies.

2.2 THE STATE OF PLAY: A BRIEF OVERVIEW

In the years immediately prior to 1998 the Asia-Pacific economies had achieved an apparently stable accommodation between regionalism and multilateralism. Three established PTAs were operating in Asia-Pacific sub-regions: NAFTA in North America, AFTA in Southeast Asia, and ANZCERTA (usually known by its shortened acronym, CER) in Australasia. Two new PTAs, Canada-Chile and Mexico-Chile, could be seen as by-products of NAFTA, partially compensating for the failed attempt to bring Chile into NAFTA. While Southeast Asia was fully covered by AFTA, Northeast Asia on the other hand was an "empty-box" in the regional map of PTAs. Japan and Korea maintained their stance of rejecting participation in PTAs in favour of continuing full support for the non-discrimination principle enshrined in GATT Article I, while China was generally viewed as too preoccupied with its transition to a market economy to be seriously interested in participating in new PTAs. There appeared to be a regional consensus that APEC would be the vehicle for further regional trade liberalization outside the confines of the existing PTAs, based on the Bogor Declaration of 1994 in which APEC members committed themselves to the achievement within specified timeframes[3] of free trade and investment in the Asia-Pacific region. APEC's formulation of its "open regionalism" principle suggested that this further liberalization would be non-discriminatory rather than preferential and thus fully consistent with the multilateral approach to trade liberalization based on the WTO's non-discrimination principle. The combination of the apparent consensus around the APEC approach and the continuing rejection of the preferential approach to trade liberalization by Japan and Korea had been sufficient to ensure that an earlier proposal in 1993 for development of an East Asian trade bloc, tentatively known as the East Asian Economic Grouping (EAEG), failed to attract widespread support in East Asia and consequently did not proceed at that time.

A number of events in 1998 and 1999 were decisive in disrupting this apparently stable scenario. The failure of APEC's Early Voluntary Sector Liberalization (EVSL) initiative in 1998, and the collapse of the WTO's Seattle Ministerial meeting in 1999, undoubtedly dented confidence in the ability of APEC members to reach the Bogor goals through the established channels of APEC and the WTO. East Asian perceptions of the US response to the East Asian economic crisis of 1997/98 appeared to give rise to a growing sense among East Asian leaders of the need to establish an independent East Asian economic identity, a development documented, for example, in Bergsten (2000 and 2001). The emergence in 1998 of a proposal for a Japan-Korea free trade agreement (FTA) was a dramatic development not only in the context of relations between those two countries but also in signalling a historic shift by Japan and Korea away from their longstanding aversion to involvement in PTAs – and this historic shift was subsequently underlined when each country moved separately to open negotiations for bilateral FTAs with selected partners.

This change in policy stance by Japan and Korea marked a watershed for the East Asian region as a whole as well as for Japan and Korea. The proposal for a Japan-Korea FTA was followed by suggestions, as yet not fully articulated, of a three-way FTA between Japan, Korea and China, and China subsequently moved to develop its own preferential trading links with Southeast Asia. Northeast Asia, previously the "empty box" in the regional map of RTAs, was thus now moving to become an active player in the preferential trading game. This development radically changed the outlook for regional trade integration in East Asia since Northeast Asia is the dominant centre of economic activity in the western Pacific, accounting for 20.3 per cent of world GNP in 2001, compared to only 1.9 per cent for Southeast Asia and 1.4 per cent for Australia and New Zealand.[4] The prospective engagement of the Northeast Asian economies would thus dramatically increase the significance of preferential trading initiatives in East Asia for East Asia itself, for the Asia-Pacific region as a whole, and for the international trading system.

Since 1998 the number of PTA proposals in the Asia-Pacific region involving East Asian economies has reached well over thirty, ranging along the full spectrum from bilateral PTAs to proposals for a large-scale East Asian trade bloc. Although it can be confidently predicted that not all proposals will lead to completed agreements, it nevertheless seems clear that the involvement of East Asian economies in preferential trading initiatives is accelerating. Obstacles to progress in the WTO's Doha Development Agenda (DDA) negotiations have been widely cited as providing increased incentives and, in some quarters, justifications for a shifting of emphasis to preferential initiatives.

Early East Asian initiatives within this new "wave" of Asia-Pacific RTAs were generally of a bilateral nature, and new bilateral initiatives have continued to emerge at frequent intervals. These have generally involved at least one small or medium-sized East Asian economy in a proposed partnership with one of the three economic giants of the region (for example Singapore-Japan, Singapore-U.S., Korea-Japan, Thailand-China, Thailand-Japan, Hong Kong SAR-China) or with another small or medium-sized economy (for example Singapore-New Zealand, Singapore-Australia,

Singapore-Canada, Korea-Chile, Singapore-Korea, Thailand-Australia, Thailand-New Zealand). There have also been occasional proposals for plurilateral RTAs, such as the "P5" proposal informally floated some years ago for an FTA involving the U.S., Australia, Singapore, Chile and New Zealand, and the current proposal for a trilateral "P3" FTA between Singapore, New Zealand and Chile.

The East Asian bilateral initiatives are thus not restricted to linkages within East Asia itself. Several of the initiatives listed above are trans-Pacific in character, as is the recently concluded Japan-Mexico FTA, while others involve partners in the Oceania sub-region.

At the other end of the spectrum, a proposal emerged within the "ASEAN Plus Three" group[5] – comprising China, Japan, Korean and the ten ASEAN economies – for an FTA based on that group, and an East Asia Vision Group was given the task of developing the concept. An "ASEAN Plus Three" FTA would cover all the East Asian APEC economies except Chinese Taipei,[6] and would thus effectively constitute an "East Asian trade bloc", bringing to fruition the concept originally embodied in the EAEG proposal. A move to establish an East Asian trade bloc would parallel the moves to establish a Free Trade Area of the Americas on the opposite side of the Pacific, and these two developments together would herald the emergence of a "bipolar Pacific" divided between large-scale trade blocs on opposing sides of the ocean. At the global level it would entail the formalization of a "tripolar" world trading system, based on three "mega-blocs" – the EU, the FTAA, and the East Asian bloc – together accounting for approximately 90 per cent of world GDP.[7]

Initially the proposal for an "ASEAN Plus Three" FTA appeared to be gaining considerable traction. More recently, however, attention has been diverted to proposals for FTAs between ASEAN and individual Northeast Asian economies, beginning with China's proposal for a China–ASEAN FTA, to which Japan responded with its own somewhat vaguely defined proposal for an economic partnership agreement with ASEAN which could potentially include an FTA. Rapid initial progress in the China-ASEAN negotiations helped to focus attention on these "ASEAN Plus One" models as alternatives to the "ASEAN Plus Three" concept. The Japanese initiative has been slower to take shape, but it now seems clear that conceptually it includes bilateral FTAs with individual ASEAN economies as well as possibly an overall framework agreement with ASEAN as a group. In November 2002 the U.S. announced an "Enterprise for ASEAN" initiative, which was also envisaged as including an overall framework agreement with ASEAN as a group as well as bilateral FTAs with individual ASEAN countries.

These "ASEAN Plus One" initiatives encouraged ASEAN to think in terms of establishing itself as the "hub" in the East Asian regional trade architecture, in contrast to the traditional expectation that the larger economies in the region would be more natural candidates for "hub" status. In addition to the proposed arrangements with China, Japan and the U.S., an ASEAN-India initiative has also been launched, and 2004 has also seen moves to transform the long-running "AFTA-CER process" into a genuine FTA initiative.[8]

For a group of small economies such as the ASEAN members, together accounting for less than 2 per cent of world GNP in 2002, to set itself up as the "hub" to a group of much larger economies[9] was always going to be a daunting task. Only by establishing and maintaining a high degree of cohesion in their negotiations with the larger economies could the ASEAN economies have any prospect of achieving this goal. In practice, however, the ASEAN economies have found it very difficult to develop and sustain a united negotiating position. Thailand's decision to follow Singapore in negotiating bilateral FTAs with Japan, the U.S., Australia and New Zealand, and to seek a bilateral arrangement also with China, has created further obstacles to a united ASEAN approach. One by one other ASEAN members appear to be responding to the Thai initiative by seeking their own bilateral agreements with their neighbours. Malaysia and the Philippines have opened negotiations with Japan, and Malaysia has also made overtures to the U.S., Australia and New Zealand. Indonesia is also understood to be gearing up for the negotiation of bilateral FTAs.

An important factor driving the spread of these bilateral initiatives by individual ASEAN economies has been the growing awareness of the risk that their position in major markets could be undermined by preferences secured by competitors among their fellow ASEAN members. This "domino effect", reflecting the gravitational "pull" of the larger Asia-Pacific economies in particular, has exacerbated the difficulty ASEAN members have experienced in developing common negotiating positions. As a result it appears increasingly likely that ASEAN's preferential trading arrangements with partners in the Asia-Pacific region and beyond will take the form of a series of bilateral FTAs, rather than the plurilateral "ASEAN Plus One" agreements originally foreshadowed. An element of the latter concept remains in the form of "framework agreements" that continue to be envisaged between the ASEAN members as a group and each major partner, acting in some yet to be fully defined way as an "umbrella" for the bilateral FTAs negotiated by the individual ASEAN members.

An increasing emphasis on bilateralism among the ASEAN economies will reinforce the trend already apparent in the Asia-Pacific region towards the emergence of traditional "hub-and-spoke" configurations of FTAs, involving the establishment by the major economies of the region – the U.S., Japan and China – of networks of bilateral PTAs centred on themselves as "hubs" with the remaining East Asian economies taking their place among the "spokes" within these configurations. Of the three major economies the U.S. leads the way in concluding bilateral FTAs with smaller Asia-Pacific economies, having already concluded agreements with Singapore, Chile and Australia and with negotiations under way with Thailand and Peru.[10] The U.S. has also been particularly forthright in asserting its intention to focus increasingly on bilateral FTAs if its trade aspirations cannot be met through the WTO negotiations. Japan has concluded agreements with Singapore and Mexico, and is in negotiations with Korea, Thailand, Malaysia and the Philippines. China has a bilateral agreement with Thailand and has also foreshadowed negotiations with Australia and New Zealand.

In practice, "hub and spoke" architectures in the region are likely to evolve in increasingly complex ways. In addition to the potential major "hubs" – the U.S., China and Japan – and the ambitions of ASEAN to serve as an alternative "hub", several of the smaller and medium-sized economies in the region could be viewed as setting themselves up as "secondary hubs". Singapore is an obvious example of an East Asian "secondary hub", and Korea also obviously has the potential to take on such a role.

At present, therefore, the two prevalent trends in the development of preferential trading arrangements involving East Asian economies appear to be the incipient emergence of "hub-and-spoke" type configurations, and the continued proliferation of bilateral agreements among the smaller and medium-sized economies of the region. At the same time interest in the concept of East Asia-wide economic integration continues to grow, and the policymaking and research communities in East Asia are now engaged in intensive study and debate on how this objective should best be pursued and achieved. An East Asian FTA based on the "ASEAN Plus Three" group remains as one of the possibilities. The alternative appears likely to be the development of two parallel and overlapping zones of preferential trade centred on China and Japan, in the form either of separate China-ASEAN and Japan-ASEAN FTAs or separate "hub and spoke" configurations of bilateral FTAs centred respectively on China and Japan as the "hubs".

East Asian economies, like other APEC member economies, also remain committed to the APEC objective of non-discriminatory free trade and investment in the Asia-Pacific region by the Bogor target dates. Not surprisingly a debate has developed within APEC as to whether the preferential trading developments now under way in the region will facilitate or undermine the achievement of the APEC goals. Underlying this debate, though rarely explicitly articulated, is the question of whether and to what extent the APEC concept of trans-Pacific integration has been supplanted by the increased focus of East Asian economies on East Asian integration, and to some extent also by the focus of APEC members in the Americas on the western hemisphere integration processes. The debate over the implications of preferential trading developments for APEC also has many parallels with the debate over the implications of the same developments for the multilateral process.[11]

In late 2004 the APEC Business Advisory Council (ABAC) formulated a recommendation to APEC leaders that they should commission a study on the feasibility of establishing a Free Trade Area of the Asia-Pacific (FTAAP). This would effectively involve the conversion of APEC into a preferential trading bloc. The ABAC proposal is analysed in Scollay (2004).

The following section reviews the guidance provided by CGE analyses as to the implications for economic welfare of the different types of trading arrangement currently being pursued or contemplated by the East Asian economies. This review is then used as the basis for a discussion of strategic issues raised for the region and its economies by the trends that appear to be developing.

2.3 ANALYSIS OF ECONOMIC WELFARE EFFECTS

This section draws on the results of CGE simulations of a number of the proposed Asia-Pacific PTAs, reported in a series of papers by Scollay and Gilbert and others (Gilbert, Scollay and Bora, 2004, Scollay and Gilbert, 2001 and 2002, Scollay, Gilbert and Gonzalez Vigil, 2002, Scollay, 2001 and 2004). These simulations were undertaken in order to provide summary comparisons of the potential relative welfare effects of different possible PTA configurations.

The comparative nature of the exercises was facilitated by the fact that the simulations all utilize the same modified version of the standard GTAP (Global Trade Analysis Project) model, a publicly available model the basic structure of which is documented in Hertel (1997). A standard multi-region comparative static formulation of the basic CGE model is used, assuming perfectly competitive markets and constant returns to scale technology. The major departure of the model from those of standard trade theory is the assumption of product differentiation by national origin, controlled by a set of Armington (1969) substitution elasticities. This serves the dual purpose of allowing two-way trade in each product category, and avoiding extreme production and trade responses. All model equations are as in the standard GTAP model and are discussed in detail in Hertel (1997). The model is closed by assuming full employment of all factors of production, and that all returns to these factors accrue to households in the region in which they are employed. Final demand in each region is governed by a single representative household, which allocates regional income across household expenditures, government spending and savings using a Cobb-Douglas function.

The PTAs covered in the simulations are each modelled as a fully comprehensive FTA, that is, involving the removal of all import tariffs on a preferential basis between the assumed members, with each member maintaining their own initial extra-RTA tariffs. In reality, of course, few FTAs have been this "clean". Modelling each FTA on this common basis does however assist the comparative purpose of the exercise, allowing an assessment of the potential gains from each alternative FTA configuration.

The simulations reported in the earlier papers utilized the GTAP4 database, with a base year of 1995, whereas those in the later papers utilize the more recently released GTAP5 database, with a base year of 1997. The database was aggregated in all cases to 20 commodities, and to either 20 regions (in the earlier papers) or 26 regions (in the later papers). Only the results from the later papers, based on the GTAP5 database, will be cited in detail here. The results based on the GTAP4 database will be discussed only in relation to the simulations of bilateral PTAs that were not repeated in the later papers. It is unlikely that the basic conclusions drawn from those simulations would change if they were repeated using the GTAP5 database.

In a number of the papers cited here, detailed results are presented and discussed for production and trade effects at the sectoral level. In this chapter, however, the focus will be on the effects on overall economic welfare, measured by the equivalent variation method, for both members and non-members of the proposed arrangements. This allows for an assessment of the potential overall economic effect of each arrangement, but ignores the adjustments that would occur in production and trade.[12]

The choice of a formulation using comparative statics and assuming perfect competition means that the size of the effects reported from the simulations are likely to represent lower bounds of possible effects. Since in cases where it has been possible to compare the results derived from comparative static simulations with those from dynamic simulations, and the results under the assumption of perfect competition with those derived under assumptions of imperfect competition, it has generally been shown that larger effects are generated by dynamic simulations and by simulations under assumptions of imperfect competition (see for example Scollay and Gilbert, 2000).

As already noted, however, these simulations were undertaken primarily for comparative purposes, and so the main interest is in the relative rather than the absolute size of the reported effects. The use of a common methodology and database is designed to enhance confidence in their reliability for this purpose. Further confidence can be drawn from noting that the reported relative size of the effects of the different arrangements, though not always their absolute size, is broadly consistent with the results of some forty CGE studies surveyed in PECC (2003b).

Bilateral PTAs

Results of the simulations of bilateral PTAs reported in Scollay and Gilbert (2001) demonstrate clearly that the effects on economic welfare of bilateral PTAs between pairs of small Asia-Pacific economies are invariably negligible. This unsurprising finding reflects the fact that the trade flows affected by such PTAs are small, both in absolute terms and relative to the total trade of the countries involved.

On the other hand, bilateral PTAs between small or medium-sized and large Asia-Pacific economies often involve trade flows that represent a substantial share of the trade of the smaller partner. Not surprisingly, therefore, simulations of such PTAs typically indicate substantial welfare gains for the smaller partner, for example for Singapore from its PTAs with Japan and the U.S. At the same time one would expect some negative impact on neighbouring or competitor economies that have significant trade with the same larger partner. This expectation too is borne out by the results which indicate perceptible though generally small negative effects on the excluded neighbours or competitors, for example on New Zealand in the case of a PTA between Australia and the U.S., or on other ASEAN economies in the case of Singapore's PTAs with Japan and the U.S.

Trade Blocs and "Hub-and-Spoke" Configurations

Table 2.1 compares the welfare effects generated by the simulation of an East Asian trade bloc with those from the proposed ASEAN–China and ASEAN-Japan FTAs.

The welfare effects of an East Asian trade bloc on its members are uniformly positive. In several cases, notably Korea, Indonesia, Malaysia, Thailand, Singapore and Vietnam, the welfare gains are very substantial. At the same time there are negative effects on economies excluded from the East Asian bloc. These effects are especially serious for economies that trade intensively with the prospective members of the East Asian bloc, especially East Asian economies excluded from the bloc and Australia and New Zealand. Negative welfare effects are also reported for the United States, Chile and Peru.

When the results for the East Asian bloc are compared with the results for the ASEAN-China and ASEAN-Japan FTAs, it is striking that a less favourable outcome is reported from both the latter two simulations for all three major Northeast Asian economies than in the case of the East Asian trade bloc. Compared to the East Asian bloc scenario, less favourable results for China are reported not only from the Japan-ASEAN FTA, as might be expected, but also from the China-ASEAN FTA. Similarly, the results for Japan are less favourable under the Japan-ASEAN FTA as well as under the China-ASEAN FTA. Korea of course is excluded from both the China-ASEAN and Japan-ASEAN FTAs, so that it is no surprise that its economic welfare should be lower under these scenarios than in the case of the East Asian trade bloc. These results indicate that the three major Northeast Asian economies incur substantial opportunity costs by foregoing the integration of trade among themselves that would occur under an East Asian trade bloc.

The results for the ASEAN economies as a group also indicate substantially lower welfare gains from a China-ASEAN FTA or a Japan-ASEAN FTA than from an East Asian trade bloc. There is, however, some variation in the results for individual East Asian economies. More favourable results are reported for the Philippines under both the China-ASEAN and Japan-ASEAN FTAs, and for Singapore and Malaysia under the China-

ASEAN FTA.

Table 2.1 Welfare Effects of ASEAN Plus Three, ASEAN-China and ASEAN-Japan FTAs

	Effect on Economic Welfare (equivalent variation method) % of GDP		
	ASEAN Plus Three FTA	ASEAN-China FTA	ASEAN-Japan FTA
Australia	-0.2	0.0	-0.1
New Zealand	-0.2	0.0	-0.1
China	0.1	0.0	-0.1
Hong Kong	-0.9	-0.2	-0.2
Japan	0.2	0.0	0.0
Korea	1.1	-0.1	-0.2
Taiwan	-0.7	-0.1	-0.2
Indonesia	1.2	0.2	0.4
Malaysia	0.8	1.1	0.5
Philippines	0.1	0.3	0.2
Singapore	3.1	3.4	2.4
Thailand	1.9	0.4	1.9
Vietnam	5.0	2.0	4.0
ASEAN Total	1.5	0.9	1.1
Canada	0.0	0.0	0.0
United States of America	-0.1	0.0	0.0
Mexico	0.0	0.0	0.0
Peru	-0.1	-0.1	0.0
Chile	-0.2	0.0	-0.1

Source: Scollay and Gilbert (2002).

It is possible, of course, that the ASEAN-China and ASEAN-Japan FTAs could proceed simultaneously but separately, although simulations were not undertaken of this scenario. In this case it may be that the comparison with the results for the East Asian trade bloc would be less unfavourable for the ASEAN economies than the case where these two FTAs are simulated in isolation. A significant improvement in the results for the three Northeast Asian economies is rather less likely, since their trade with each other would remain outside the arrangements.

On the other hand results for excluded economies, particularly those elsewhere in East Asia and the rest of the western Pacific, are unambiguously less unfavourable under the ASEAN-China and ASEAN-Japan FTAs than under the East Asian FTA.

Trade Blocs and APEC

Table 2.2 compares the welfare outcomes from the East Asian trade bloc with those from APEC-wide liberalization, both in the case where APEC members liberalize on a non-discriminatory basis in line with APEC's concept of "open regionalism" and in the case where APEC members liberalize preferentially towards each other. Effectively turning APEC itself into a preferential trade bloc, as is explicitly envisaged in ABAC's proposal for a Free Trade Area of the Asia Pacific. The welfare effects from full multilateral liberalization on a global basis are also shown in order to provide a further benchmark.

As would be expected APEC members excluded from an East Asian bloc register a more favourable welfare impact under APEC-wide liberalization, with the sole exception of Mexico. In particular, the negative effects indicated for western Pacific APEC members when they are excluded from an East Asian trade bloc are replaced by distinctly positive impacts under APEC-wide liberalization.

The welfare effects for all three major Northeast Asian economies are also more favourable under APEC-wide liberalization than under the East Asian trade bloc. Rather more mixed results are indicated for the ASEAN economies. For ASEAN as a group APEC-wide liberalization yields less favourable welfare outcomes than the East Asian trade bloc, though only marginally so in the case of APEC preferential liberalization. Particularly in the latter case significantly more favourable outcomes are also indicated for some individual ASEAN economies, although this is not true of Malaysia, Singapore or Thailand.

Multilateral Liberalization

Comparison of the East Asian and APEC scenarios with full multilateral liberalization bears out the expectation that the latter will yield superior welfare outcomes. For a minority of APEC members (Australia, Japan, Taiwan, the U.S. and Mexico), the welfare outcome from multilateral liberalization is marginally less favourable than from APEC preferential liberalization, and for one member (Thailand) it is less favourable than from the East Asian trade bloc. For other APEC members, however, and for ASEAN as a group, the welfare outcome from multilateral liberalization dominates the outcome from all other scenarios. In Scollay (2004) it is also shown that on an aggregate basis full multilateral liberalization yields superior welfare outcomes not only for the ASEAN group, but also for the Northeast Asian economies taken as a group, for the full APEC membership, for economies outside APEC, and for the world economy as a whole.

These results provide support for the view that an important criterion in any comparative assessment of the East Asia trade bloc and the two APEC alternatives should be the degree to which each alternative might be expected to facilitate eventual full multilateral liberalization.

Table 2.2 Welfare Effects of ASEAN Plus Three FTA and APEC Liberalization

	Effect on Economic Welfare (equivalent variation method) % of GDP		
	ASEAN Plus Three FTA	APEC MFN	APEC Preferential
Australia	-0.2	0.2	0.4
New Zealand	-0.2	0.5	1.0
China	0.1	0.2	0.4
Hong Kong	-0.9	1.7	2.2
Japan	0.2	0.3	0.4
Korea	1.1	1.1	1.3
Taiwan	-0.7	1.0	1.0
Indonesia	1.2	1.0	1.3
Malaysia	0.8	0.5	0.7
Philippines	0.1	-0.3	0.1
Singapore	3.1	2.0	2.4
Thailand	1.9	1.2	1.6
Vietnam	5.0	2.2	5.8
ASEAN Total	1.5	1.0	1.4
Canada	0.0	0.1	0.2
United States of America	-0.1	-0.1	0.0
Mexico	0.0	-0.2	-0.1
Peru	-0.1	-0.1	0.1
Chile	-0.2	0.1	0.4

Source: Calculated from data presented in Scollay (2004)

2.4 IMPLICATIONS OF THE CGE RESULTS

The simulation results accord with the straightforward intuition that larger, more inclusive trade blocs can be expected to produce more favourable outcomes for their members than smaller more limited arrangements. The larger the group the wider the range of products for which internationally competitive producers are likely to be found within the group, resulting in enhanced potential for trade creation and reduced risks of trade diversion. Thus an East Asian trade bloc is likely to yield more favourable welfare outcomes for the majority of its members than the more limited arrangements involving subsets of these economies. In turn, for APEC members as a group as well as for most individual APEC members, the prospective welfare outcomes from implementation of one or other of the possible modes of APEC-wide liberalization are superior to those from an East Asian trading bloc, in some cases by a considerable margin. The logical extension of this line of analysis, that multilateral liberalization on a non-discriminatory basis will produce superior welfare outcomes to those from any regional initiative, including APEC, is also borne out by the results.

The implications for excluded economies follow a contrasting pattern. The larger "ASEAN-plus" configurations, especially an East Asian trade bloc formed by the "ASEAN-Plus-Three" group, are associated with larger economic losses for excluded economies than is the case with more limited PTA arrangements. Furthermore, as would be expected, the losses are heavily concentrated on those excluded economies that trade intensively with the members of each arrangement, and this of course means primarily other APEC economies. The observed pattern is that PTAs based on progressively larger groups of East Asian economies cause progressively larger economic losses for non-members, concentrated on a progressively smaller number of APEC members. The East Asian trade bloc, which of all the "ASEAN-plus" configurations produces the largest welfare gains for its members, also produces the largest welfare losses for Chinese Taipei, Australia and New Zealand. The pattern is broken when the scope of liberalization is broadened to include all APEC members, via one or other of the modes of APEC-wide liberalization. This converts the economic losses of the otherwise excluded western Pacific economies into significant economic gains, while continuing to provide the same or larger benefits for the majority of the "ASEAN Plus Three" economies.

The main conclusions of this analysis are worth emphasizing. PTAs among APEC members are likely to yield economic gains for their members, but are also likely to impose economic losses on non-members. A move to PTAs among larger groups of economies can increase the economic gains of members, but at the same time can impose larger economic losses on non-members. This tension can be resolved by the inclusive APEC-wide approach to liberalization, which delivers greater overall gains to APEC members while eliminating the losses imposed on excluded APEC economies by PTAs among smaller groups of their fellow APEC members.

At first sight the CGE results may suggest less concern over bilateral PTAs since their indicated economic effects on non-members are often rather small, while significant gains may be indicated for at least the smaller partner. However, the proliferation of bilateral PTAs has additional negative effects that are not captured by the CGE simulations. In particular, as economies become involved in multiple PTAs, each with their own specific provisions affecting market access, significant transaction costs are likely to arise for business from the need to comply with the varying requirements of the different PTAs. Inconsistency among the rules of origin in the different agreements may give rise to particularly onerous compliance costs, and additional transaction costs may result from inconsistencies in other provisions as well such as standards and conformance, customs procedures and quarantine procedures.

The spread of intersecting and overlapping PTAs has been called the "spaghetti bowl" phenomenon by Jagdish Bhagwati.[13] The extent of the increased transactions costs associated with "spaghetti bowl" effects is of course an empirical issue. No reliable estimates of these costs are yet available, but useful evidence may soon become available from economies that have recently been rapidly expanding the number of PTAs in which they are involved; Singapore is the obvious case in point in East Asia.

Further potential negative effects arise when the proliferation of PTAs leads to the emergence of "hub and spoke" configurations. The disadvantages for "spoke economies" of "hub and spoke" patterns of PTA development are well known. The inequality in bargaining power between larger and smaller parties is accentuated by the ability of the "hub" to exploit competition among the "spokes", by establishing precedents in the PTAs with individual "spokes" that the "hub" can use to exert pressure for inclusion of similar provisions in agreements with other "spokes". In addition, there is an imbalance in the potential gains from increased market access and any resulting increased investment flows. The "hub" gains access to all the "spoke" markets whereas the "spokes" gain access to the "hub" market alone unless they negotiate separate PTAs with each other. The greater size of market to which access is available from the "hub" also gives the "hub" an advantage over the "spokes" in attracting investment.

While CGE simulations of individual bilateral PTAs between a "hub and a spoke" may suggest substantial gains for the "spoke", a recent study by Gilbert[14] offers persuasive evidence that these gains may prove illusory if the bilateral PTAs become part of a more extensive "hub and spoke" configuration. Gilbert shows that while single PTAs typically yield the expected result of relatively large gains for the "spoke" and small gains for the "hub", the situation is reversed in the case of simultaneous "hub and spoke" PTAs. In this case the gains for the "hub" tend to be more significant while the gains for the "spokes" are much smaller than in the single PTA case. The addition of new "spokes" in a "hub and spoke" configuration thus tends to erode the economic advantages of the existing "spokes". This is analogous to the cases where expansion of existing PTAs to include new members may erode the benefits that the existing members, particularly the smaller members, derived from the PTA.

These arguments may need to be qualified in the cases of some successful "spoke" economies in the APEC region, that appear to be well on the way to securing PTAs with each major "hub" as well as other significant trading partners. Singapore is the obvious example in East Asia. Singapore is in fact unique among East Asian economies in that it has already succeeded in negotiating PTAs covering the majority of its trade. Its PTAs with Australia, Japan, New Zealand and the United States account for just under 60 per cent of its trade.[15] Adding the proportion of its trade covered by AFTA gives a total of 82 per cent of its trade covered by these PTAs. Singapore also has an FTA with the EFTA countries and is in the process of adding Korea, Chile and possibly also Canada and Mexico to its network of FTAs, as well as participating in the China-ASEAN initiative. No other East Asian economy remotely approaches the percentage of trade coverage that Singapore has achieved in its PTAs.

It may be that by negotiating PTAs covering a large proportion of their total trade, successful "spoke" economies can capture virtually all the gains from trade potentially available to them. The outlook is different however for those smaller economies that fail, from whatever reason, to secure PTAs with the major "hubs". These economies face the prospect of significant economic damage as the "hub and spoke" phenomenon spreads.

It is possible also that successful "spokes" may have an incentive to press for the exclusion of potential competitors from "hub and spoke" configurations in which they participate, since this would enhance their expected welfare gains from their own PTAs with the "hubs"-in extreme cases, perhaps, beyond those they could expect from non-discriminatory free trade.

This last point provides one example of the potential for PTAs to lead to increased frictions within the regional and global trading systems. "Hub and spoke" configurations PTAs may give rise to tensions between "hubs" vying for hegemonic influence and between "spokes" jockeying for favoured positions in the markets of the "spokes". Unequal distribution of gains between "hubs" and "spokes" may also be a source of tension or conflict. Even bilateral PTAs may upset excluded economies that find themselves newly discriminated against in the markets of neighbours or close trading partners.

2.5 TOWARDS MORE ECONOMICALLY BENEFICIAL OUTCOMES: IS THERE A FEASIBLE PATH?

When these results and their implications are set against the current trends in the development of preferential trading arrangements in the Asia-Pacific region, a policy conundrum becomes apparent. The configurations that are likely to produce the greatest economic benefits for members are an East

Asian trade bloc, if the analysis is limited to possible arrangements involving only East Asian economies, and APEC-wide liberalization if the scope of possibilities are widened to take in the Asia-Pacific region as a whole. Yet these are not the directions along which the governments of the region have been directing most of their energies. The dominant trends are rather towards the continuing proliferation of bilateral agreements and the development of "hub and spoke" configurations.

Furthermore there are strong economic pressures driving both trends, particularly the trend towards "hub and spoke" configurations. The pressure derives from the "domino effect", whereby economies react to the success of their competitors in securing a PTA with a common trading partner by seeking a PTA of their own with that same partner. The motivation for doing so is to defend their markets in the common trading partner from discrimination arising from PTAs with that partner secured by their competitors. The results of the CGE analyses suggest that this pressure is especially strong where the common partner is a major economic power providing a significant market for smaller economies. The "domino effect" is thus likely to be an especially potent factor behind the development of "hub and spoke" configurations, despite their known disadvantages, but may also contribute to the proliferation of bilateral PTAs among smaller and medium-sized economies.[16]

Thus, while an analysis based solely on the calculus of economic welfare gains and losses would point squarely in the direction of an East Asian trade bloc or some form of APEC-wide liberalization as preferred outcomes for the East Asian economies, it is by no means clear whether or how the current trend towards proliferating bilaterals and development of "hub and spoke" arrangements can be redirected towards one or both of these outcomes. In principle the transition could be made through one or both of the following routes:

- Continued proliferation of bilateral agreements until they cover all bilateral trade flows within East Asia, or within the Asia Pacific region.
- Expansion or amalgamation of existing preferential trading initiatives until they merge into an East Asian trade bloc, or converge toward APEC's trade and investment goals.

It is perhaps easier to envisage this kind of transition occurring in East Asia than in the Asia-Pacific region as a whole, although even in East Asia the obstacles are formidable as will be discussed shortly. For the APEC region as a whole, achievement of such a transition would be a much more challenging task. As Lloyd has pointed out, 210 bilateral PTAs would be required if APEC-wide free trade is to be achieved via bilateral PTAs covering all trade flows among the 21 APEC members.[17] There is also a substantial theoretical literature indicating significant obstacles in the way of expansion or amalgamation of existing initiatives that may need to be faced.[18]

The evolution of "hub and spoke" configurations in the region is also likely to militate against expansion or amalgamation of existing PTAs. One result of this process is likely to be competition between different PTA "models" favoured by the respective "hubs". Each "hub" is likely to have preferences for features in PTAs that are likely to be unacceptable to other "hubs". The U.S. insistence on strong labour and environmental provisions and "TRIPs-plus" provisions, and Japan's insistence on provisions that accommodate its agricultural sensitivities may be cases in point. Different systems of rules of origin are also likely to represent a significant area of difference if not incompatibility between competing "models". As the distinctive features of each of the different "models" become entrenched within the respective "hub-and-spoke" configurations, the eventual amalgamation of the separate configurations is bound to become more difficult.

Political factors are among the most often-cited obstacles to the establishment of an East Asian trade bloc. Such a bloc would have to be based around the three major Northeast Asian economies that constitute the economic core of the East Asian region, and so a fundamental prerequisite for its establishment is a willingness on the part of these three economies to agree to the freeing of trade among themselves. While Japan and Korea are now in the process of negotiating a bilateral FTA, political tensions appear to have inhibited the development of proposals for freeing the bilateral trade flows between these two economies and China, and there is little sign that this situation is likely to change in the near future. The position of Chinese Taipei is another potentially highly contentious issue that would presumably have to be addressed as part of any initiative to create an East Asian trade bloc. If an Asia-Pacific-wide arrangement is being considered, a key question that must be faced is whether it is possible to overcome the political constraints on the freeing of bilateral trade flows between the three major East Asian economies and the United States.

It may not be an exaggeration in fact to say that some of the most economically beneficial PTAs may be the most difficult to achieve in political terms. Less beneficial PTAs may be pursued because they are politically easier to achieve, and this could contribute to the emergence of divisions among economies that may be difficult to bridge.

Agriculture has also loomed large among the obstacles to East Asian economic integration. It is surely no accident that Singapore is the East Asian economy that has enjoyed the greatest success in building up the percentage of trade covered by its PTAs. One characteristic of Singapore that is doubtless significant in explaining this success is that Singapore has no significant agricultural exports, and negotiation of PTAs with Singapore therefore do not encounter problems over agriculture.

On the other hand agriculture is an especially difficult and sensitive sector for a number of East Asian economies, particularly Japan and Korea. Korea managed to include agriculture in its FTA with Chile, but there are many exceptions and deferred items in the coverage of agriculture by that agreement. Even so, agricultural issues caused extensive delays in the negotiation of the agreement, and subsequently a difficult passage through the ratification process in Korea. Strong pressure from Mexico was required to achieve the inclusion of some significant agricultural products in the Japan-Mexico FTA.[19] Agriculture is likely to be one of the most contentious issues in each new PTA negotiated by Japan and Korea, and it will be interesting to observe how agriculture is handled in the proposed Japan-Korea FTA, and in Japan's proposed FTA with Thailand.

Agriculture is not necessarily an easy issue for other East Asian economies either. Although agriculture has been included in the "early harvest" elements of the China-ASEAN initiative, some ASEAN economies, notably the Philippines, have noted that this presents serious difficulty for them. Agriculture would be likely to become even more contentious in any negotiations for an APEC-wide PTA. Agricultural trade features prominently among the contentious trade issues between East Asian economies and some other APEC members, while even two major agricultural exporters such as Australia and the United States were unable to agree on the inclusion of all agricultural products in their recently concluded PTA.

A review of the obstacles to East Asia-wide and Asia-Pacific-wide regional integration must be balanced, however, by reiterating that there continues to be considerable momentum behind the concept of an East Asia-wide economic integration in particular. While it may not be realistic to expect that the East Asian economies could reach agreement in the immediate future on establishment of an East Asian trade bloc, influential thinkers in East Asia continue to emphasize an East Asian PTA as a desirable and even inevitable development in the medium and long term.[20] Political obstacles that appear insuperable in the short term may be dissolved over a longer timeframe. Progress continues to be made in current bilateral PTA negotiations despite difficulties over agriculture, facilitated by a perceptible shift in emphasis from the question of whether agriculture should be included at all to questions of which are the agricultural products that can be included and which are those whose exclusion can be accepted on the grounds of their exceptional sensitivity to one of the parties.[21]

In the meantime a number of regional cooperation initiatives that could be the precursors of more comprehensive economic integration in East Asia have already been implemented or are currently being pursued at the "ASEAN Plus Three" level. To date these initiatives have focused mainly on monetary and financial issues. Notable examples are the Chiang Mai Initiative and the proposals for creation of an East Asian bond market.

The fact that moves towards East Asia-wide free trade are still at an embryonic stage also provides a window of opportunity for East Asian economies to consider whether steps could profitably be taken now to agree on some guiding principles designed to maximize the benefits of any future East Asian FTA. In particular, there may be merit in considering whether at least some common elements of a possible PTA "model" could be agreed. Rules of origin are an example of an area that could repay attention. Restrictive and highly complex rules of origin, such as the "NAFTA type" rules appearing in PTAs negotiated by the U.S., are clearly not conducive to efficient integration of a region's trade. Agreement by East Asian economies on a common approach to rules of origin, based on the premise that these rules should facilitate rather than impede efficient trade, could be a very useful "building block" towards eventual full integration of trade in the East Asian region. Trade facilitating rules of origin should be as straightforward as possible, and should be transparent, clear and consistent, and should not impose unnecessary compliance costs.

Furthermore, if trade facilitating approaches to "model features" such as this can be adopted throughout the East Asian region, it could be hypothesized this will encourage trade among East Asian economies to grow more quickly relative to trade flows governed by PTAs in which the corresponding provisions are more restrictive of trade. This could conceivably create pressure for adaptation of provisions in the latter PTAs towards the more trade-facilitative approach, and thereby encourage at least partial convergence of the "models" employed in the clusters of PTAs that are likely to develop linking East Asian economies to the United States as well as to the major East Asian "hubs".

NOTES

1 The term "Asia-Pacific" here refers to the region geographically bounded by the membership of APEC, embracing the economies of both East Asia and the Pacific seaboard of the Americas, as well as Oceania.

2 Singapore-Japan, Singapore-United States, Singapore-New Zealand, Singapore-Australia, Hong Kong SAR-China, Japan-Mexico, Korea-Chile, United States Chile, United States-Australia, Thailand-China and Thailand-Australia.

3 The target date for achievement of the "Bogor goals" is 2010 for developed APEC economies and 2020 for developing APEC economies.

4 Percentages calculated from data in World Bank, World Development Indicators, 2002.

5 The formation of the "ASEAN Plus Three" group was a reaction to the East Asian crisis of 1997/98. The group's initial focus was on prospects for greater coordination of monetary, financial and exchange rate policies. This resulted eventually in the so-called "Chang-Mai Initiative" (CMI) and proposals for the creation of an Asian Bond Market. Further avenues of cooperation and coordination continue to be explored.

6 It is assumed that Hong Kong China would be included, although this issue has not been clarified.

7 Regardless of the outcome of the FTAA negotiations NAFTA already constitutes a "mega-bloc" in the Americas, accounting for 36 per cent of world GNP in 2002. Thus it is only the formation of an East Asian "mega-bloc" that remains to complete the emergence of the "bipolar Pacific" and "tripolar" world trading system architectures.

8 Proposals for an AFTA-CER FTA have been on the table for several years, but opposition to this concept from some ASEAN members has meant that, at least until very recently, the "AFTA-CER" process has focused on sharing of information and experiences and cooperation on various aspects of trade facilitation.

9 The U.S., Japan and China in 2002 accounted respectively for 32 per cent, 13.5 per cent and 3.8 per cent of world GNP measured at official exchange rates, according to the World Bank's 2002 World Development Report.

10 Peru is negotiating with the U.S. as one of a group of three Andean countries. Colombia and Ecuador are the other two participants in these negotiations. The U.S. also recently concluded an FTA with seven Central American countries, although the latter are not conventionally listed among Asia-Pacific economies, and is also actively pursuing FTAs with a number of partners in other regions.

11 See PECC (2003a) for a review of both debates, and Panagariya (1999) for a more detailed review of the debate on the relationship between regionalism and multilateralism.

12 For a detailed analysis of the production and trade effects indicated by a number of these simulations, see Gilbert, Scollay and Bora (2004).

13 See Bhagwati, Greenaway and Panagariya (1998).

14 See Gilbert (2003).

15 Calculation based on three-year average, 1999-2001, trade data from the IMF's *Direction of Trade* statistics.

16 The "domino effect" is also the basis for the concept of competitive liberalization which seeks to make a virtue out of the negative effects of PTAs on excluded economies, by pressuring the latter to enter similar preferential arrangements and/or to push harder for multilateral liberalization in order to defend their trade interests.

17 See Lloyd (2002). Complete coverage of all 21 trade flows among a group of 21 economies requires [n(n-1)/2] bilateral PTAs.

18 The literature conventionally addresses the question in terms of whether PTAs are "stumbling blocks" or "building blocks" for global free trade, but the analysis can also be applied to the establishment of free trade among a more limited group of economies. The literature is reviewed for example in Panagariya (1999) and the arguments are also

discussed in Scollay (2003).

19 See Watanabe (2004).

20 See for example Kimura (2004).

21 As noted earlier, the recent ABAC proposal for a Free Trade Area of the Asia-Pacific (FTAAP) provides an example of an initiative to revive the thrust towards economic integration across the entire Asia-Pacific region. ABAC recommended that APEC leaders commission a study on the FTAAP concept. The response of APEC leaders to this recommendation was not known at the time of writing.

REFERENCES

Andriamananjara, S., "On the relationship between preferential trading arrangements and the multilateral trading arrangements", presented at PECC Trade Forum meeting, Washington DC, April 2003, available at PECC website; http://www.pecc.net/trade/trade_washington.htm.

Armington, P.S. (1969), "A theory of demand for products distinguished by place of production", *IMF Staff Papers 16,* pp159-76.

Bergsten, C. F. (2000), "Towards a tripartite world", *Economist,* 15 July.

Bergsten, C.F. (2001), "America's two-front economic conflict", *Foreign Affairs,* March/April, pp16-27.

Bhagwati, J., D. Greenaway and A. Panagariya (1998), "Trading preferentially: theory and policy", *Economic Journal, 108,* pp.1128-48.

Findlay, C., (2002), "Old issues in new regionalism", in P. Drysdale and K. Ishigaki, (eds), *East Asian Trade and Financial Integration: New Issues* Australia National University, Canberra, Asia Pacific Press.

Gilbert, J. (2003), "CGE simulation of US bilateral free trade agreements", background paper prepared for conference on Free Trade Agreements and US Trade Policy, Institute for International Economics, Washington DC, 7-8 May.

Gilbert, J., R. Scollay and B. Bora, (2004), "New regional trading developments in the Asia-Pacific" in S. Yusuf, M.A. Talaf and K. Nabeshima (eds) *Global Change and East Asian Policy Initiatives*, Washington DC and New York, World Bank and Oxford University Press, pp. 121-90.

Hertel, T. (1997), *Global Trade Analysis: Modeling and Applications*, New York, Cambridge University Press.

Kimura, F. (2004), "FTAs: The foundation of an East Asian community", *Asia-Pacific Perspectives: Japan +, 2*(7), November.

Krueger, A.O. (1999), "Are preferential trading arrangements trade-liberalizing or protectionist?", *Journal of Economic Perspectives 13*(4), pp.105-24.

Lloyd, P. (2002), "New regionalism and new bilateralism in the Asia Pacific", presented at PECC Trade Forum meeting, Lima, May 2002, available at PECC website: http://www.pecc.net/trade_lima.htm).

Panagariya, A. (1999), "The regionalism debate: an overview", *World Economy 22*, pp.477-51.

PECC (2003a), Asia-Pacific RTAs as avenues for achieving APEC's Bogor goals Singapore, PECC.

PECC (2003b), "Summary of Results of CGE analyses of Asia-Pacific RTAs", appendix to "Asia-Pacific RTAs as avenues for achieving APEC's Bogor goals", paper presented by PECC to the APEC Senior Officials' Trade

Dialogue, Khon Kaen, 27 May 2003 (APEC Document 2003/SOM II/RTAs/FTAs/012).

Scollay, R.(2001), "The Changing outlook for Asia-Pacific regionalism", *World Economy, 24* (9), pp.1135-60.

Scollay, R. (2003), "Issues in the Development of RTAs in the Asia-Pacific region", paper presented at meeting of the PECC Trade Forum, Phuket, Thailand (available at www.pecc.net).

Scollay, R. (2004), "Preliminary assessment of the proposal for a Free Trade Area of the Asia-Pacific (FTAAP): An Issues Paper for the APEC Business Advisory Council (ABAC)", pp1-37.

Scollay, R. and J. Gilbert, (2000), "Measuring the gains from APEC trade liberalization: an overview of CGE assessments", *World Economy 23*(2), pp. 175-97.

Scollay, R. and J. Gilbert (2001), *New Regional Trading Arrangements in the Asia-Pacific?* Washington DC, Institute for International Economics.

Scollay, R. and J. Gilbert (2002), "Impact of East Asian regional or subregional FTAs", report for Australian Department of Foreign Affairs and Trade, pp.1-25.

Scollay, R., J. Gilbert and F. Gonzalez Vigil (2002), Mega-blocs in East Asia: how might they affect each other (and the rest of the world)?, LAEBA Working Paper No. 8, Inter-American Development Bank, Washington DC, pp.1-26.

Watanabe, Y. (2004), "Japan's FTA strategy and the Japan-Mexico FTA", *Gaiko Forum,* Summer, pp.54-63.

3. Global Supply Networks and Multilateral Trade Linkages: A Structural Analysis of East Asia

David Roland-Holst

3.1 INTRODUCTION

Since the middle of the last century the global economy has changed in ways that are transparent and historically intuitive, but also in ways that are subtle and unprecedented. As the global economic regime shifted from post-colonial bilateralism to multilateralism, one of the most dramatic events has been the emergence of private agency. A more open multilateral trading environment appears to be especially congenial to propagation of global supply networks, where private parties diversify their economic ties across complex webs of ownership, contracts, and general factor and product market seeking activities. The result is a remarkably diffuse mosaic of economic activity, coexisting with, and often transcending, official networks of bilateral and multilateral diplomacy and trade negotiation.

In the East Asian region, supply chains have proliferated to an extent, and at a rate, unimagined decades ago. The role of private capital flows in this process has been essential, and we shall see that investment behaviour has exerted a decisive influence on patterns of regional production and trade. An important implication of the resulting supply chain decomposition is that the global network of value creation and income linkages is much more extensive and complex, than would be suggested by bilateral trade statistics alone. For this reason, the significance of existing multilateral ties, as well as the gains from a more liberal trading environment, may be seriously underestimated.

This chapter discusses the phenomena of such global networks and supply chain decomposition generally, and then uses detailed international data to assess their empirical significance with a novel application of multiplier techniques to an international Social Accounting Matrix. Our general results indicate that the complex indirect linkages in these trading systems, largely mediated by intermediate supply and intra-industry trade, can often represent the majority of value creation. For this reason, the multilateral agenda deserves even more attention from policy makers.

The next section provides a general discussion and overview of the issues. This is followed in section 3 by a description of the data resources used for our analysis. In sections 4 and 5, we introduce the multiplier decomposition techniques that we use to estimate the detailed economic impacts of global supply networks. Finally, conclusions are offered in section 6, followed by bibliography.

3.2 AN OVERVIEW OF GLOBAL SUPPLY NETWORKS

Trade patterns in the modern international economy bear only a vague resemblance to their colonial and pre-colonial antecedents. The world trading system, as it evolved from a series of imperial ages down through the post-colonialism of the last century, has steadily expanded both the public and private basis for an international division of labour that is unprecedented in both scope and depth.[1] While trade has always been remarkable in its ability to move resources and resource services over great distances, today's supply chains and systems of overlapping ownership and contracts are beyond the most vivid imaginings of Levantine traders of centuries past.

The changes that have taken place are the result of a combination of public and private forces, working in parallel and often (but not always) in concert to expand and deepen global trade linkages. In this section, we summarize some of the principal mechanisms at work, with particular reference to East Asia.

Public Multilateralism/Globalization: WTO and the Bilateral Contagion

The most visible public agent in today's multilateral trade environment is of course the World Trade Organization, the official embodiment of collective aspirations toward open multilateralism. Certainly, the many rounds of multilateral negotiations sponsored by the WTO and its predecessors have advanced the cause of globalization. Some have argued that membership or even conformity to the WTO is not statistically correlated with trade expansion, but this simple causality test ignores the obvious precedence effect the entire GATT-WTO process has had on all forms of public and private trade dealings.[2] Most observers think it obvious that the spirit of open multilateralism enshrined in WTO rulemaking reflects and facilitates the historic expansion of trade relations.[3] Having said this, however, there are many features of this mechanism that limit the extent and timeliness of what it can accomplish.

While accepting the importance of the WTO, its practical limitations have had both negative and positive effects on trade growth.[4] On the negative side, three areas are of special significance here:

1. The bargaining environment of WTO accession has many imperfections that have been used strategically to limit the scope and pace of liberalization. This occurs primarily in the area of phase-in and exception negotiation, and for this reason might be viewed as temporary. The length of some phase-ins can be quite long, however, leading to persistent distortions.
2. The "water in the tariff" problem: Some incoming members have negotiated phase-in nominal tariff bindings above their existing effective tariff rates, allowing the potential for increased protection upon WTO accession.
3. Some countries have also adapted their protection regimes away from WTO actionable mechanisms. The main culprits here are contingent protection (e.g. anti-dumping clauses) and administrative mechanisms such as Sanitary and Phytosanitary (SPS) Measures.

Despite many strategic attacks on its liberal principals, however, the majority of WTO member trade appears to have been liberalized over the last two decades, and this process may take a dramatic step toward completion if the Doha Round can fulfill its putative goal of phasing out global agricultural protection. This is clearly the biggest residual category of international protectionism and represents a very large distortionary burden on both OECD and non-OECD economies.[5]

Returning to imperfections in the WTO process, this time from the positive side, we note that the bargaining inefficiencies of global trade talks have spawned what might be termed "Bilateral Contagion", a proliferation of Bilateral Trade Agreements (BTAs) and other smaller scale negotiated trade arrangements that are quite self-conscious responses to the WTO process. In particular, bilateral deals have proliferated for several reasons:

1. To lock in early gains from liberalization with proximate trading partners, accepting the principles of the WTO on a smaller scale rather than waiting for a Round to deliver such gains at a later date.
2. To gain "first mover advantage" by establishing presence in a partner's market before WTO entrants flock in.
3. As a blueprint for WTO accession. China, Vietnam, and perhaps other new and aspiring WTO members have used a BTA with the US as a blueprint or template for their WTO accession. This was done for

> many reasons, among them the desire to establish negotiating capacity, learn standards, phase in liberalization, signal intent multilaterally and finally, to obtain strategic support from an influential WTO member.

All these factors are attributable to imperfections in the global negotiating mechanism, yet they have facilitated trade liberalization. Some authors have argued that agendas of bilateralism, regionalism, and globalism are not necessarily compatible and may indeed inhibit one another.[6] It is obvious, however, that the general trend in international trade has been toward a lowering of average distortionary burdens on the price system and facilitation of the flow of goods and services. Each of these agreements, on whatever scale, has played a role in this process. Eventually, a global WTO-type agreement may have to tie up many loose ends and reconcile partially conflicting regional or bilateral standards, but the trend toward proliferation of trade linkages has been greatly advanced by the WTO and hundreds of smaller scale trade deals.[7]

In the East Asian theatre, the dominant issue is of course China's emergent economy. By using the WTO as a platform for projecting itself into the global economy, China lent decisive impetus to multilateralism generally. As this author has argued elsewhere in a detailed study of China's WTO accession, East Asia now finds itself in a unique position *vis-à-vis* globalization. China can apparently go it alone with WTO accession, in the sense that other regional or bilateral agreements offer it only small benefits in addition to those it gets in the long run from WTO accession. The rest of East Asia, however, could gain very substantially, and in two ways, by drawing China into a regional arrangement.

First, China's internal market will grow to become a great prize for regional exporters, and those with early and established market access are likely to gain the most. Second, joining with China in early and rapid bilateral or multilateral trade liberalization would permit East Asian exporters to get on the China-WTO "bandwagon", leveraging Chinese burgeoning exports to the OECD as intermediate suppliers. This phenomenon, which I have termed the Asian Trade Triangle, calls for rapidly growing Chinese exports to the western OECD. This in turn induces rapid growth of Chinese absorption from its own region to meet the needs for supply expansion. This in turn leads to rapidly expanding exports from the rest of East Asia to satisfy Chinese absorption.[8]

Thus, China sets the pace for rapid progress toward East Asian multilateralism, at once directly and indirectly tied to the WTO process. Regardless of the WTO policies of individual East Asian economies, the need to respond strategically to China's WTO initiative will impel them toward more liberal trade regimes and expand the scope and depth of official regional trade ties.

Private Multilateralism/Globalization: The Invisible Handshake

While policy makers can certainly exert influence on global trade, through a combination of rule making, negotiating initiatives, and their many ways of influencing expectations, trade linkages are ultimately animated by private agency. This is especially so in today's world, where state trading is probably smaller in relative terms than ever. Indeed, one of the most arresting features of modern globalization is the unprecedented initiative and pervasive influence of private sector forces. Nowhere is this more apparent than in the East Asian region.

Over the last generation the Pacific Basin has yielded a new paradigm of market-directed economic coordination and the kind of synergistic multilateral growth envisioned by classical trade theorists, significantly improved upon by modern private enterprise. While elements of traditional comparative advantage exert a strong influence on resource allocation in individual countries, specialization is much less extreme than that would be extrapolated from historic trade patterns. Multinational business exerts a pervasive influence on growth and resource allocation patterns in these economies, replicating abroad to exploit not only natural resources but also internal markets in each country. By infusing each FDI destination with new capital, technology, and expertise, thousands of foreign private interests contribute simultaneously to greater economic diversity within each economy and greater uniformity across economies. For the poorer countries the result is a broader basis for employment and opportunity in their own economy, leading to greater diversification, stability, and generally higher rates of productivity and wage growth.

Two of the most compelling aspects of this new, private multilateralism are its spontaneity and (*de facto*) collaborative nature. Historically, economic policy in general, and trade policy in particular, was closely circumscribed by official institutions representing abstract notions of national interest. Like many forms of regulation, the relatively simplistic agendas of national trade policy do not mesh well with complex and often conflicting incentives/signals that permeate today's international commerce. But the risks of commerce always carry the prospect of reward and, for every reticent trade negotiator, there may be hundreds of firms eager to establish a lucrative foreign partnership or open a new market. The resulting "Invisible Handshakes" ultimately serve national interest by transcending it, reaching beyond the short-term perspective of (for example) domestic protection to broaden the basis for economic activity globally and take a (national) material interest in the resulting economic growth.

Capital mobility is the primary mechanism for this kind of private globalization, but it has many attendant features that warrant closer inspection. First, it should be emphasized that much FDI is really doubly targeted, at both an internal and external market.[9] Every investor in export capacity knows that there is, or may someday be, a local market for the same product. Foreign investors in Chinese export industries are well aware of the dynamism of this country's domestic market, and are likely seeking another first mover advantage in terms of local market presence even when their first beachhead is in an export zone. Indeed, the implicit opportunity presented by its emergent internal economy has given China an edge in the global FDI "beauty contest" over many smaller or more slowly growing developing countries.

Second, by converse logic, investors in the local market are often mindful of the existence, or emergence, of neighbouring markets that can provide later opportunities or simply a marketing hedge for excess local supply. Just as Mexico used the NAFTA to enhance its attractiveness as an FDI destination for US export capacity, so might low income ASEAN attract FDI to produce exports for Japan, China, and the Asian Tiger economies.

These kind of inter-country comparisons lead to relatively complex and strategic portfolio decisions for foreign investors, and we have seen a kind of resource cost arbitrage across regions with varying economic structures and stages of progress. What this looks like to the causal observer is a continuing process of supply chain decomposition, distributing intermediate linkages across many economies. Obviously, the incentive to do this is economic, reflecting a complex mix of cost advantages and market access motives. The ability to do it, however, is largely dependent upon the local, national, and multilateral regulatory environment, which exerts many influences on this behaviour via both administrative constraints and costs.

In East Asia, direct costs of supply chain decomposition are relatively low, except where there are very tight administrative constraints. The latter can be formal, like regional trade restrictions (e.g. North Korea, some bilateral relations with China), or informal, like corruption or civil insecurity. Otherwise, supply chains are spreading rapidly in the region and, as we shall see in the empirical results below, there are already significant multilateral income-expenditure linkages across East Asia. Clearly, additional commitments by regional governments to facilitate this, by a combination of rulemaking and infrastructural investments, will only accelerate the process.

Accompanying the direct allocation of capital along these supply chains are two elements that can have an essential influence on local economic development, value added and accumulation of intermediates, including in particular capital goods and technology. Consider an example of one multinational firm, although in most cases the process being described applies to a mosaic of independent or partially cross-controlled firms. Allocating capital across a distributed supply chain confers different components of the cumulative production process upon different locations. With this allocation come two hierarchies, one of pecuniary value added (i.e. the margin between cost of components and value of deliverables) and one of capital/technology. Each of these represents an important local benefit of FDI, one direct and the other indirect. The former is easier to measure, but the latter can make a more decisive impact on long-term development.

In the past, developing countries have often been content to attract any form of FDI that stimulates employment, seeking in the first instance to capture value added. What some have learned from frustrating experience, however, is that the quality of FDI can be as important as its quantity. Many Latin American countries have seen inbound FDI pour into resource-intensive sectors, often simply displacing expatriated domestic interests (capital flight). In these cases the predominate form of employment remains unskilled labour, and low wage traps that have been in place since colonial times are simply perpetuated. Even worse, such FDI is often simply displacing real or implicit (devaluation driven) domestic capital flight, leading to a zero sum outcome for the domestic economy.

More sustained FDI benefits, on the other hand, can arise from inbound capital flows associated with production activities that upgrade domestic technology and, especially, promote local skill development and intermediate linkages. Many of the most successful Asian FDI stories include all these components. Technology transfer has been an essential primer for growth in the dynamic Asian economies. Rapid and relatively egalitarian increases in living standards have resulted in steady, technology induced appreciation of the skill base in the same economies.

The success of individual FDI experiences can in significant part be measured by the recipient's progress from simply accumulation of foreign capital and technology to its assimilation.[10] The distinction is an essential one, because it measures the extent to which the benefits of modernization can be internalized and put to the task of promoting autonomous domestic growth and innovation.

Bamboo Capitalism

The process of regional supply chain decomposition represents much more than capital allocation. For a recipient country, inbound FDI represents employment, value added capture, and a place in the regional and global hierarchy of technology and growth. Moreover, localization of a node in an international supply chain stimulates intermediate linkages that would not arise from the internal market. These spillovers not only promise longer-term endogenous growth benefits, but they help to articulate local markets and commercial networks that can serve a variety of purposes and, eventually, contribute to the development of autonomous local markets. Each big green field FDI development in the NIEs spawned a community of small intermediate and appurtenant suppliers who have since achieved maturity as independent suppliers for the domestic and/or export market.[11]

In East Asia, this phenomenon is already well established and might be referred to as Bamboo Capitalism. In these situations, because of network externalities in local production and finance, complete markets are sprouting from nodes in the international root system of intermediate supply. This culminating feature of FDI-driven supply chain decomposition has created a diverse and vibrant population of independent local industries around the East Asian region. Many of these emergent enterprises are still bound to their original roots via ownership or contracts, but, increasingly, they arise as independent enterprises who contribute to the dynamics of regional and global competitiveness and innovation.

The further supply chains (the root system) are decomposed and extended geographically, the faster and more profuse will be the proliferation of new enterprises. This phenomenon is already part of history for Japan, Korea, and the Asian Tigers, and now we see these countries joining Western investors to propagate bamboo across China and lower income ASEAN. Even within China this phenomenon has entered a secondary phase, where local enterprises are decomposing supply chains across the country's 28 provincial economies.

Increasingly, the issue for localities is not whether or not they are in a network, but where they lie in the network's implicit hierarchy. The sophistication, extent, and especially the capital intensity of their component task will ultimately determine what kind of long-term benefits network membership confers upon them. In this implied (and very real) competition for value added allocation, localities and nations must compete with a combination of local human and nonhuman resources, facilitating infrastructure, a congenial regulatory environment, and lastly, inviting domestic market conditions. The latter recalls our earlier discussion, where we identified the scale of the internal market as an important strategic asset for countries trying to attract FDI. Finally, there is no absolute standard for all these competitive elements, since foreign investors make their choices by comparing alternative venues.[12]

3.3 GLOBAL TRADE DATABASE

While the phenomena discussed above are remarkable and fascinating, it is reasonable to ask how we might assess their importance empirically. Given the microeconomic nature of the process of supply chain decomposition and the dynamic role of private agency in building these networks, data on constituent linkages would be nearly impossible to obtain and of doubtful reliability in any case. Indeed, one could make a liberal argument that the benefits of this activity are manifest in the simple fact of its existence, and the private sector needs no quantitative guidance from economists. For policy makers, however, it would still be useful to elucidate the geographic composition of gains from these economic linkages, as it might justify more concerted and focused efforts to facilitate trade and other economically beneficial activities.

In this chapter, we use trade data as a proxy for the more complex web of global financial linkages that underlie the processes we have been talking about. In particular, we use a global trade database to construct an international Social Accounting Matrix (SAM) that captures expenditure and income linkages between countries and domestic institutions.[13] Basically, we set up an international table with ten countries/regions and detailed bilateral trade flow data. Trade data may not capture the initial allocation of foreign capital across countries, nor the repatriated profit flows. Despite this, it accurately details the supply chain linkages that are responsible for the majority of direct and indirect international income creation.

The basic information set used for our estimation is the Global Trade Analysis Project (GTAP) Version 5.0 database.[14] The original data set, calibrated to 1997, is defined across 66 country/region groupings and 57 economic sectors. For this chapter, we aggregate the regions to those of primary interest and consolidate agricultural, energy, and food processing sectors. The regions and sectors used in the present application are listed below in Tables 3.1 and 3.2.

Table 3.1 Regional aggregation

Region	Label	Name
1	chn	China
2	jpn	Japan
3	kor	Korea
4	twn	Taipei, China
5	asn	ASEAN
6	usa	United States
7	eur	Western Europe
8	row	Rest of the World

3.4 BLOCK MULTIPLIER DECOMPOSITION

As indicated above, we want to use international trade data to elucidate the expenditure-income linkages arising from global supply networks. While direct trade flow data are revealing, they only capture, however, direct bilateral effects. In the real economy, a myriad of interactions delineate the path from initial expenditure to ultimate incomes. This is particularly the case with trade in an era of globalization, where international supply chains are ever more elaborate and indirect linkages often represent the majority of value creation.

To more fully capture these complex, trade mediated interactions, we develop an international multiplier model based on the multilateral SAM estimated from the GTAP database. Detailed decomposition analysis with this model will reveal regional trade interactions at unprecedented levels of detail. To further analyse this issue we apply two separate methods, block decomposition and path decomposition. The former was popularized by Sir Richard Stone (1981) and applied by Pyatt and Round (1985), Roland-Holst and Tarp (2003) and others, and we shall discuss it first.[15]

Table 3.2 Sectoral aggregation

Number	Label	Name
1	agr	Agriculture
2	enr	Energy and Minerals
3	pfd	Processed food
4	txa	Textiles and apparel
5	lum	Wood products
6	ppp	Paper products publishing
7	pyc	Petroleum coal products
8	crp	Chemical rubber plastic products
9	nmm	Mineral products n.e.s
10	met	Metals
11	mvh	Motor vehicles and parts
12	otn	Transport equipment n.e.s
13	ele	Electronic equipment
14	ome	Machinery and equipment n.e.s
15	omf	Manufactures n.e.s
16	ely	Electricity
17	gdt	Gas manufacture distribution
18	wtr	Water
19	cns	Construction
20	trd	Trade
21	tps	Transport services
22	cmn	Communication
23	fin	Financial services
24	obs	Business services n.e.s
25	ros	Recreation and other services
26	osg	Public administration
27	dwe	Dwellings
28	cgd	Investment goods

For simplicity, consider the case of three countries/regions. Schematically, the individual country (k) SAM looks like

$$T_k = \begin{bmatrix} T_{kk} & F_k \\ V_k & X_k \end{bmatrix}$$

where the component matrices denote commodity flows (T), final demand (F), value added (V), and other domestic accounts (X). Note that the commodity flow table T_{kk} is intended to include domestic supply for domestic use, exports by destination, and imports by origin.

Now consider a consolidated SAM for all three countries, partitioned as follows

$$S = \begin{bmatrix} T_{11} & T_{12} & T_{13} & X_{1x} \\ T_{21} & T_{22} & T_{23} & X_{2x} \\ T_{31} & T_{32} & T_{33} & X_{3x} \\ X_{x1} & X_{x2} & X_{x3} & X_{xx} \end{bmatrix} \quad (3.1)$$

where the subscripts denote the three countries and the X matrices now include domestic demand $X_{kx} = [F_k]$ and $X_{xk} = [V_k]$.

To evaluate economy-wide multiplier effects and linkages to external trade, first consider the expenditure shares[16]

$$A = \begin{bmatrix} A_{11} & A_{12} & A_{13} & A_{1x} \\ A_{21} & A_{22} & A_{23} & A_{2x} \\ A_{31} & A_{32} & A_{33} & A_{3x} \\ A_{x1} & A_{x2} & A_{x3} & A_{xx} \end{bmatrix} \quad (3.2)$$

and define the additive decomposition

$$A_{-X} = B + C \quad (3.3)$$

A_{-X} denotes the sub-matrix of A, with only inter-country transactions and

$$B = \begin{bmatrix} A_{11} & 0 & 0 \\ 0 & A_{22} & 0 \\ 0 & 0 & A_{33} \end{bmatrix} \quad (3.4)$$

$$C = \begin{bmatrix} 0 & A_{12} & A_{13} \\ A_{21} & 0 & A_{23} \\ A_{31} & A_{32} & 0 \end{bmatrix} \quad (3.5)$$

From standard accounting identities one then obtains

$$
\begin{aligned}
y &= Ay + x \\
&= By + Cy + x \\
&= (I - B)^{-1}Cy + (I - B)^{-1}x \\
&= [I - (I - B)^{-1}C]^{-1}(I - B)^{-1}x \\
&= (I - D)^{-1}(I - B)^{-1}x \\
&= (I - D^2)^{-1}(I + D)(I - B)^{-1}x \\
&= M_3M_2M_1x \\
&= Mx
\end{aligned}
\tag{3.6}
$$

where $D = (I - B)^{-1}C$, and

$$
M_1 = (I - B)^{-1} = \begin{bmatrix} (I\text{-}A_{11})^{-1} & 0 & 0 \\ 0 & (I\text{-}A_{22})^{-1} & 0 \\ 0 & 0 & (I\text{-}A_{33})^{-1} \end{bmatrix} \tag{3.7}
$$

is a matrix of domestic economy-wide multiplier effects. These are the standard multipliers from domestic production-factor-consumption linkages and could be further decomposed with methods proposed by Stone (1981) or Pyatt and Round (1979). The activity block in the upper left corner corresponds to the standard Leontief inverse. The second factor matrix details the so called direct or open loop linkages between domestic institutions, i.e.,

$$
M_2 = (I + D) = \begin{bmatrix} I & D_{12} & D_{13} \\ D_{21} & I & D_{23} \\ D_{31} & D_{32} & I \end{bmatrix} \tag{3.8}
$$

where, for example $D_{12} = (I\text{-}A_{11})^{-1}A_{12}$ defines cumulative unrequited outflows from country 1 to 2, taking account of the combined effects of cumulative domestic output effects (the Leontief inverse) and direct export linkages (A_{12}). Finally, closed loop effects are detailed in the third factor matrix

$$M_3 = (I - D^2)^{-1} = \begin{bmatrix} E_{11} & E_{21} & E_{31} \\ E_{21} & E_{22} & E_{32} \\ E_{31} & E_{23} & E_{33} \end{bmatrix}$$

$$= \begin{bmatrix} I - D_{12}D_{21} - D_{13}D_{31} & D_{13}D_{32} & D_{12}D_{23} \\ D_{23}D_{31} & I - D_{21}D_{12} - D_{13}D_{31} & D_{21}D_{13} \\ D_{32}D_{21} & D_{31}D_{12} & I - D_{31}D_{13} - D_{32}D_{23} \end{bmatrix}^{-1} \quad (3.9)$$

This last factor matrix represents the income effects originating in one (column) country, passing through trade linkages, and returning to the recipient row country. The E_{ij} multipliers aggregate all the indirect income gains accruing between i and j from the existing pattern of international trade linkages.

The M_i matrices enter the decomposition multiplicatively and the contribution of each to economy-wide income generation is difficult to interpret directly. It is more transparent to use the additive component matrices

$$N_1 = M_1 \quad (3.10)$$

$$N_2 = (M_2 - I)M_1 \quad (3.11)$$

$$N_3 = (M_3 - I)M_2M_1 \quad (3.12)$$

which together satisfy $M = N_1 + N_2 + N_3$.

For the international SAM we defined as endogenous the five East Asian countries/regions of China, Japan, Korea, Taipei, China, and ASEAN. With the Rest of the World defined as exogenous, we then calculated the multiplier decomposition as in the above derivations, producing a series of 165x165 tableaux detailing trade induced global network linkages for East Asia.[17]

To give a general indication about patterns of long-term income generation, we focus in this section on households. Table 3.3 shows total multiplier effects on household income, for each of the five East Asian economic areas, as these would result from a one (currency) unit increase in demand for exports from each of the five. More specifically, results are grouped by national household (five rows each), then by exporting country (each row), for each export (column). For example, in the first column, and row, Chinese households gain 4.26 Yuan in the long run from each additional Yuan of Chinese agricultural (agr) exports. The first entry in the second row indicates that, because of linkage effects, Chinese households would in the long run see their incomes rise by 0.41 Yuan for each Yuan increase in demand for Japanese agricultural exports, and so on.

Before discussing these results, we refer to Table 3.4, which will aid interpretation. This table has the same layout in terms of bilateral correspondences, but it measures something different. Table 3.4 lists percentages of total multiplier effects attributable to the feedback component (N3) of global supply networks. The remainder of the multiplier (N1+N2) is due to direct domestic and direct bilateral transfer effects. Generally speaking, these shares are small for domestic sectoral stimulus, but vary considerably when capturing linkages to trading partners. Cross country multipliers seem to embody between 20 and 60 per cent network feedback effects, depending mainly on the trade dependence of the sector under consideration. For example, agriculture is generally relatively low in terms of N3 or network linkage, while electronic goods are quite high.

Returning to the total effects in Table 3.3, we see that the global network linkages in part explain differences in these effects. Own-sector, or domestic effects, are generally much larger than cross country ones, because the multiplier chains are much more internalized for own-sector export demand stimulus. Note also that the multipliers vary across countries, with Japan's being generally larger because of its absolute size in regional expenditure accounts. Countries that are more trade dependent, like Taipei and China, will have larger N3 components, but in cases where trade may be constrained (like that with China) these values fall off.

Generally speaking, then, we find that indirect (closed loop) global network effects can account for anywhere from about 20 per cent to two thirds of total income effects in trade, often outweighing the direct effect of bilateral demand and supply linkages. In these cases, at least, it is clear that the regional basis of trade is more important to livelihoods than direct import and export flows would suggest. For this reason, while bilateralism can accelerate trade and domestic market expansion, it should not be pursued at the expense of more highly articulated, multilateral trade and investment linkages. For example, trade diversion arising from a BTA could be detrimental if, as our results indicate, the more complex web of distributed supply chains account for more than half the domestic income arising from trade.

3.5 PATH DECOMPOSITION

The previous section showed that block decomposition of the SAM can elucidate the linkages between distinct national economies. Income-expenditure linkages can be computed and decomposed according to three different categories of interdependence, providing us with a detailed view of the extent and magnitude of the forces responsible for income generation as they work their way through the main linkages. To obtain a more comprehensive description of these linkage effects, however, we need to go one step further and identify the specific paths or channels by which expenditure propagates income effects across the global economy.

The structural path analysis put forth by Lantner (1974) and Gazon (1979) to study abstract linear systems of equations has been used by several authors to examine input-output systems. Recognizing the applicability of this technique to extended linear models, Defourny and Thorbecke (1984) showed the rich information structure that could be derived by applying this approach in a SAM framework. Following the ideas in the contributions by these authors, we now examine international trade with this technique for the first time, shedding new light on the complex interactions that carry income effects across supply networks.

To summarize the methodology, each pair $<i,j>$ of indices in the underlying SAM accounts is called an arc. A path is a sequence s of indices $s=<i,k,l,...,m,j>$ which can be decomposed into consecutive arcs $<i,k>$, $<k,l>,...,<m,j>$. A path with non-repeating indices is termed an elementary path. A circuit of influence is a path s such that the first and last index coincide. The influence of account i on account j through a path s will be represented by $(i\text{->}j)_s$. To estimate the income effect of account i on account j along $<i,j>$, note from the basic expenditure relationship, before economy-wide linkages are taken into account, we have:

$$\frac{\partial y_j}{\partial y_i} = a_{ji} \tag{3.13}$$

Thus any exogenous income increase affecting i gives rise to a direct income increase in j measured by entry (j,i) of the transpose of the column normalized (expenditure share) matrix A. Due to the linear structure of the model, the *direct* income influence along an elementary path $s=<i,k,...,m,j>$ is a composite effect of the direct influences along the constituent arcs, i.e.

$$D^P_{(i\to j)s} = a_{ki} ... a_{jm} \tag{3.14}$$

Table 3.3 Long term household income multipliers

China	agr	enr	pfd	txa	lum	ppp	pyc	crp	nmm	met	mvh	otn	ele	ome	omf	ely	gdt	wtr	cns	trd	tps	cmn	fin	obs	ros	osg	dwe	cgd
China	4.26	3.82	3.91	3.69	3.77	3.43	3.35	3.22	3.86	3.29	3.13	3.00	2.18	3.05	3.73	4.03	3.93	4.32	3.94	4.07	3.89	4.06	4.12	4.00	3.68	4.09	4.57	4.80
Japan	.41	.24	.42	.84	.44	.41	.29	.40	.43	.41	.39	.37	.42	.44	.49	.40	.31	.42	.42	.42	.39	.41	.41	.42	.41	.42	.42	.42
Korea	.35	.24	.35	.54	.42	.29	.23	.31	.35	.34	.32	.26	.31	.31	.41	.30	.03	.31	.33	.32	.27	.31	.32	.29	.32	.32	.32	.33
Taipei,China	.31	.23	.30	.47	.47	.31	.25	.31	.35	.34	.30	.22	.33	.34	.44	.30	.21	.32	.33	.32	.29	.31	.31	.31	.31	.32	.32	.32
ASEAN	.36	.27	.36	.54	.36	.33	.29	.33	.40	.38	.33	.21	.34	.35	.45	.33	.33	.34	.35	.40	.32	.33	.31	.25	.32	.34	.35	.35

Japan	agr	enr	pfd	txa	lum	ppp	pyc	crp	nmm	met	mvh	otn	ele	ome	omf	ely	gdt	wtr	cns	trd	tps	cmn	fin	obs	ros	osg	dwe	cgd
China	2.34	2.25	2.27	2.43	2.33	2.31	2.12	2.45	2.42	2.47	2.93	2.22	3.06	2.70	2.39	2.36	2.33	2.43	2.44	2.36	2.31	2.46	2.37	2.32	2.44	2.42	2.44	2.44
Japan	9.03	2.36	9.32	8.19	7.28	10.21	5.65	9.31	9.27	9.56	9.72	8.74	9.52	9.31	9.01	10.01	7.49	10.75	10.22	10.73	9.49	10.68	10.60	10.64	10.37	10.64	11.11	11.22
Korea	1.57	.57	1.59	1.77	1.59	1.64	.78	1.94	1.82	1.76	1.85	1.48	2.35	2.30	1.82	1.48	.09	1.68	1.77	1.69	1.50	1.69	1.71	1.55	1.64	1.73	1.76	1.78
Taipei,China	2.11	1.04	2.21	2.53	2.20	2.46	1.29	2.84	2.86	2.80	3.17	1.81	3.09	3.26	2.72	2.28	1.35	2.62	2.65	2.61	2.33	2.59	2.59	2.56	2.60	2.61	2.64	2.65
ASEAN	2.13	1.64	2.04	2.19	2.14	2.04	1.51	2.31	2.44	2.67	3.64	1.66	2.82	3.02	2.17	2.04	2.09	2.21	2.31	2.11	1.98	2.26	2.06	1.60	2.10	2.17	2.29	2.28

Korea	agr	enr	pfd	txa	lum	ppp	pyc	crp	nmm	met	mvh	otn	ele	ome	omf	ely	gdt	wtr	cns	trd	tps	cmn	fin	obs	ros	osg	dwe	cgd
China	.29	.27	.28	.39	.30	.35	.30	.34	.30	.32	.27	.26	.33	.29	.30	.29	.29	.30	.30	.29	.28	.29	.29	.28	.29	.30	.30	.30
Japan	.15	.06	.16	.23	.14	.15	.12	.16	.15	.17	.15	.14	.18	.16	.16	.15	.12	.15	.15	.15	.14	.15	.15	.15	.15	.15	.16	.16
Korea	3.44	.74	3.29	3.00	2.44	3.33	1.29	2.65	2.79	2.36	3.18	2.52	2.36	2.59	2.87	3.25	.12	3.72	3.46	3.89	2.96	3.82	4.04	3.48	3.47	3.85	4.11	4.33
Taipei,China	.14	.08	.15	.23	.16	.18	.09	.20	.17	.20	.19	.17	.22	.18	.18	.15	.09	.17	.17	.17	.15	.17	.17	.17	.17	.17	.17	.17
ASEAN	.19	.15	.19	.32	.20	.20	.15	.23	.20	.27	.24	.15	.26	.20	.21	.19	.19	.20	.21	.20	.18	.21	.19	.18	.19	.20	.20	.21

Taipei,China	agr	enr	pfd	txa	lum	ppp	pyc	crp	nmm	met	mvh	otn	ele	ome	omf	ely	gdt	wtr	cns	trd	tps	cmn	fin	obs	ros	osg	dwe	cgd
China	.27	.25	.25	.35	.28	.28	.23	.32	.28	.29	.25	.25	.30	.27	.29	.26	.26	.27	.28	.26	.25	.27	.26	.26	.26	.27	.27	.27
Japan	.11	.04	.12	.16	.14	.12	.07	.12	.11	.12	.11	.11	.14	.12	.14	.11	.09	.12	.12	.12	.11	.12	.12	.12	.11	.12	.12	.12
Korea	.07	.03	.07	.11	.09	.07	.04	.08	.08	.07	.07	.06	.11	.07	.10	.07	.01	.07	.07	.07	.06	.07	.08	.07	.07	.07	.08	.08
Taipei,China	2.93	.97	2.88	2.81	2.32	3.03	1.29	2.39	2.65	2.62	2.21	1.90	2.10	1.98	2.83	3.29	1.76	3.79	3.21	3.89	3.08	3.84	3.91	3.74	3.67	3.85	4.07	4.19
ASEAN	.14	.10	.13	.26	.14	.15	.10	.17	.16	.18	.13	.08	.17	.14	.17	.13	.13	.14	.14	.13	.12	.14	.13	.10	.13	.14	.14	.14

ASEAN	agr	enr	pfd	txa	lum	ppp	pyc	crp	nmm	met	mvh	otn	ele	ome	omf	ely	gdt	wtr	cns	trd	tps	cmn	fin	obs	ros	osg	dwe	cgd
China	.33	.33	.35	.33	.43	.33	.44	.34	.32	.30	.29	.26	.39	.30	.33	.34	.34	.32	.32	.33	.32	.32	.31	.31	.32	.32	.33	.33
Japan	.28	.34	.30	.32	.51	.29	.30	.29	.29	.28	.28	.25	.33	.28	.30	.30	.25	.29	.30	.29	.28	.29	.28	.29	.28	.29	.29	.29
Korea	.23	.30	.25	.25	.64	.24	.27	.24	.25	.20	.22	.17	.27	.21	.28	.25	.05	.24	.24	.24	.23	.23	.24	.24	.24	.23	.24	.24
Taipei,China	.28	.53	.28	.33	.77	.29	.46	.31	.32	.26	.26	.18	.41	.24	.32	.34	.32	.29	.30	.28	.27	.28	.28	.27	.27	.28	.28	.28
ASEAN	3.01	2.30	2.76	2.30	2.86	2.33	2.01	1.95	2.28	1.44	1.85	.69	1.47	1.21	2.03	2.76	2.93	2.98	2.55	2.86	2.54	2.77	2.76	2.05	2.55	2.89	2.99	3.43

Table 3.4 Per cent of household income arising indirect (N3) from global network linkages

China	agr	enr	pfd	txa	lum	ppp	pyc	crp	nmm	met	mvh	otn	ele	ome	omf	ely	gdt	wtr	cns	trd	tps	cmn	fin	obs	ros	osg	dwe	cgd
China	4.2	4.5	4.5	5.9	5.1	5.2	5.4	5.9	4.8	5.6	6.0	5.4	10.0	6.3	5.1	4.5	4.6	4.3	4.7	4.4	4.5	4.5	4.3	4.4	4.9	4.5	4.0	3.9
Japan	18.5	22.3	19.1	13.7	23.8	19.3	22.6	19.7	18.3	19.8	19.5	18.8	22.3	19.0	17.9	19.4	19.9	19.2	19.3	19.1	19.4	19.1	19.1	19.2	19.1	19.1	19.1	19.1
Korea	27.3	23.1	28.4	23.2	32.8	33.8	26.4	36.4	31.6	29.6	33.2	33.7	44.0	40.7	28.9	31.2	24.1	32.5	32.7	32.2	33.6	33.0	32.7	33.6	31.3	32.9	32.7	32.7
Taipei,China	40.8	41.8	44.0	37.9	37.9	46.8	41.8	52.8	47.2	46.7	55.8	48.6	58.9	52.0	37.6	46.8	44.6	48.1	47.3	48.0	46.1	47.9	47.8	47.5	48.5	47.9	48.1	48.2
ASEAN	33.6	34.0	32.3	31.3	34.1	35.1	30.6	39.4	34.3	39.9	53.9	41.1	46.9	46.9	29.7	35.5	36.2	36.8	36.9	30.2	35.5	38.3	37.1	37.6	36.5	36.6	37.4	36.5

Japan	agr	enr	pfd	txa	lum	ppp	pyc	crp	nmm	met	mvh	otn	ele	ome	omf	ely	gdt	wtr	cns	trd	tps	cmn	fin	obs	ros	osg	dwe	cgd
China	34.5	34.4	34.7	37.4	37.3	35.2	38.5	36.3	34.0	33.1	25.9	32.1	35.8	31.0	34.4	34.3	34.6	33.8	33.5	33.9	33.6	33.4	33.5	33.7	33.5	33.9	33.8	33.9
Japan	6.7	16.5	6.7	11.1	10.3	6.2	8.5	6.8	6.9	6.8	6.4	6.5	8.2	7.4	7.7	6.2	6.5	5.9	6.3	6.0	6.3	5.9	5.9	6.0	6.0	6.0	5.8	5.8
Korea	28.5	59.3	29.0	33.6	46.4	26.1	43.9	23.6	25.6	25.2	24.3	24.3	26.0	19.6	29.6	28.9	57.6	26.4	26.0	26.7	26.3	25.9	26.3	27.6	27.0	26.0	26.0	26.0
Taipei,China	25.1	51.0	23.8	28.0	41.6	23.1	40.5	21.8	21.3	21.4	18.6	23.9	30.1	19.0	25.3	25.5	31.9	22.6	22.7	22.5	22.6	22.5	22.5	22.4	22.1	22.7	22.6	22.6
ASEAN	23.8	23.7	24.3	33.7	24.0	24.3	25.6	23.8	22.7	23.1	14.9	19.0	24.2	19.1	26.5	23.5	23.1	22.9	22.9	24.8	23.1	23.0	22.7	23.6	22.7	23.0	22.7	23.0

Korea	agr	enr	pfd	txa	lum	ppp	pyc	crp	nmm	met	mvh	otn	ele	ome	omf	ely	gdt	wtr	cns	trd	tps	cmn	fin	obs	ros	osg	dwe	cgd
China	26.6	27.2	26.9	22.8	27.6	22.0	25.6	24.5	26.4	24.8	29.7	27.0	32.4	28.5	26.1	26.7	26.6	26.6	26.5	26.6	27.0	27.0	26.6	26.6	27.0	26.4	26.6	26.7
Japan	41.1	68.4	40.3	49.6	52.9	42.2	38.2	40.4	42.3	38.5	41.2	42.1	42.3	41.2	43.6	42.6	42.3	42.0	42.1	41.9	42.0	41.6	41.6	42.1	41.7	41.8	42.0	42.0
Korea	1.7	5.0	1.9	2.9	3.4	1.7	3.1	2.4	2.3	2.6	1.9	2.0	3.4	2.5	2.5	1.7	4.7	1.6	1.8	1.6	1.8	1.5	1.5	1.6	1.7	1.6	1.5	1.5
Taipei,China	46.5	70.1	45.6	42.2	63.5	41.0	62.8	40.1	47.5	40.9	41.2	31.3	48.4	47.0	48.4	47.9	54.1	45.3	45.5	44.8	45.2	44.9	44.7	44.7	44.7	44.7	45.0	45.0
ASEAN	32.1	32.1	32.2	28.0	32.2	29.8	31.3	29.4	35.0	28.3	32.9	28.5	30.5	37.9	34.1	31.6	31.5	31.6	31.5	32.2	31.2	31.0	30.1	25.9	30.9	31.2	31.7	31.6

Taipei,China	agr	enr	pfd	txa	lum	ppp	pyc	crp	nmm	met	mvh	otn	ele	ome	omf	ely	gdt	wtr	cns	trd	tps	cmn	fin	obs	ros	osg	dwe	cgd
China	19.7	20.1	20.3	16.8	20.3	18.6	23.0	17.3	18.8	18.4	22.2	18.9	23.9	20.7	18.7	20.3	20.4	19.7	19.5	20.1	20.2	20.1	19.9	19.4	20.4	19.6	19.7	19.7
Japan	43.6	69.7	43.6	58.4	43.3	44.1	52.2	43.5	45.9	42.5	43.6	42.6	43.0	44.8	41.9	45.2	46.4	44.3	44.1	44.1	43.3	43.9	43.8	43.4	44.2	44.0	44.3	44.4
Korea	65.5	85.5	65.7	61.0	73.1	63.9	77.7	64.7	64.3	67.7	66.0	62.7	54.1	68.4	58.9	66.7	84.6	64.7	64.8	63.9	62.9	63.2	63.0	62.9	64.1	63.5	63.9	63.8
Taipei,China	1.8	4.3	1.8	2.8	3.5	1.9	3.4	2.7	2.4	2.4	2.7	2.2	3.9	3.3	2.5	1.7	2.2	1.6	1.9	1.5	1.7	1.5	1.5	1.6	1.6	1.6	1.5	1.5
ASEAN	36.6	37.1	36.1	27.3	35.7	30.3	38.2	30.5	34.5	32.7	46.2	41.3	35.9	40.2	34.6	36.7	36.4	36.2	35.6	38.7	36.5	36.1	36.2	36.1	36.3	35.9	36.3	36.3

ASEAN	agr	enr	pfd	txa	lum	ppp	pyc	crp	nmm	met	mvh	otn	ele	ome	omf	ely	gdt	wtr	cns	trd	tps	cmn	fin	obs	ros	osg	dwe	cgd
China	34.1	32.9	31.5	39.3	27.8	34.6	25.7	37.0	36.0	39.5	42.7	39.3	39.1	40.5	36.2	33.7	33.0	35.9	36.5	34.5	34.3	36.7	35.9	35.6	36.4	35.9	36.0	35.9
Japan	21.3	9.7	20.8	31.5	15.4	21.6	16.5	22.0	21.6	22.6	22.2	23.0	23.0	23.8	23.5	20.7	19.5	21.9	21.6	22.0	21.0	22.1	22.1	22.2	22.0	22.1	22.1	22.2
Korea	31.5	11.8	29.0	37.4	13.7	29.7	15.6	33.0	31.7	38.0	35.4	35.5	38.2	42.6	30.4	26.6	11.5	30.7	31.5	30.8	28.6	32.1	31.6	27.7	30.5	31.9	32.2	32.5
Taipei,China	31.1	9.4	32.4	34.7	14.5	34.1	13.5	35.7	35.2	41.5	43.8	39.5	31.2	49.0	36.7	27.2	17.6	35.8	34.4	36.4	34.6	36.4	36.5	36.6	36.9	36.2	36.3	36.5
ASEAN	3.3	3.4	3.6	5.7	3.7	4.2	4.0	5.6	5.0	8.3	7.3	9.8	9.2	9.9	5.4	3.5	3.3	3.4	4.2	3.6	3.6	3.8	3.4	3.7	3.8	3.5	3.5	3.1

In any given path s there may exist feedback effects among its indices. Account i influences k but k in turn may influence i, either directly or through other intermediary indices. Accounts influence themselves through loops as well. All of these feedback effects taking place along circuits in the path work to amplify the magnitude of the direct influence being transmitted over the path. The expanded influence will be called *total* influence, the ratio of total to direct influence being the income path-multiplier

$$T^{P}_{(i\to j)s} = D^{P}_{(i\to j)s}\mu^{P}_{s} \tag{3.15}$$

Notice, on the other hand, that more than one elementary path, each one with its respective feedback circuits, may span two indices i,j. Therefore the total income influence along a path does not capture the full or global influence in the network of channels linking i and j. Let $S=\{s/i,j\}$ be the set of all elementary paths joining i and j. By additivity, the *global* price influence is defined as:

$$G^{P}_{(i\to j)s} = \sum_{s\in S} T^{P}_{(i\to j)s} = \sum_{s\in S} D^{P}_{(i\to j)s}\mu^{P}_{s} \tag{3.16}$$

The last equality, where μ_{ji} is the (j,i) entry in the multiplier matrix M, follows from the fact that S includes all connecting paths between accounts i and j. Direct, total and global influence are three distinct components that make up the transmission mechanism underlying income determination.

Applying these techniques to the international SAM for 1997 we can examine in detail the process by which diverse economic activities are tied together by downstream supply chain linkages, and how these chains transmit income effects within economies and across the global marketplace. For policy makers, this can elucidate many otherwise unanticipated consequences of policies targeted elsewhere in the economy.

Given that the underlying multiplier matrix is 165x165, the number of possible paths for even a single bilateral linkage numbers in the tens of thousands. To keep things manageable, we shall focus the present discussion on an instructive set of examples, revealing only those network chains that contribute more than a reasonable minimum to income-expenditure linkages. Returning to the block decomposition of the previous section, consider linkages between, for example, Japanese households and the Japanese electronics sector. In Table 3.3 above, we see that the total multiplier effect on Japanese households, induced by a unitary increase in export demand for Japanese electronics, is 9.515. We also note from the block decomposition information in Table 3.4 that only 8.21 per cent of this effect is due to feedback from global supply networks.

Using the path technique, we can completely decompose this bilateral expenditure-income chain and examine the contribution of each constituent multilateral linkage. Table 3.5 provides the details, explicating components of this multiplier effect up to direct effects of 0.001 or more. The result is a list of 38 paths, with up to four bilateral components, accounting for 76.5 per cent of the total multiplier effect. Note first of all that international linkages play no role in these components, which is consistent with the block decomposition estimate indicating weak feedback. Second, we see that 45.8 per cent of the total effect (last column) is captured in direct factor payments (to Unskilled and Skilled Labour and Capital) within the sector, remitted to domestic households. These effects are supplemented by fiscal linkages (row 4) and downstream links to a variety of other domestic sectors (ppp, crp, nmm).

The first example reveals the complexity of income determination, but sheds little or no light on international linkages. To better understand the role of global supply chains, however, it is more revealing to examine international bilateral linkages. Table 3.6 shows the results of path analysis for the bilateral link between the Chinese electronics sector and Japanese households. Here we see a very diffuse pattern of linkages, with the stronger ones (direct effect > 0.001) accounting for only 32.5 per cent of the total income effect under consideration. Not surprisingly, the strongest paths between China's electronics sector and Japanese households are through the Japanese electronics sector, which accounts for about two-thirds of the effects under consideration or 21.8 per cent of the total. This channel suggests the essential role of intra-industry trade and the global supply chain in contributing to domestic income growth.

To better see the role of these supply chain effects consider now the results in Table 3.7, showing the paths of income linkage from Chinese electronics to Japanese electronics. Note, first of all, that this is in fact a component path of the previous example, since chn-ele->jpn-ele was the primary channel from Chinese electronics to Japanese household income. In this more detailed example, however, we see that intra-industry trade propagates income effects from China to Japan through all three of the other East Asian countries/regions considered. This is the essential characteristic of modern global supply networks, that indirect and feedback effects along intermediate delivery channels tie income-expenditure effects across geographically dispersed economies.

A final example generalizes these results by examining another path emanating from Chinese electronics, this time to the ASEAN electronics sector (see Table 3.8). As would be expected the total effect is smaller because ties are weaker than to Japanese electronics, but the complexity of the underlying pattern of network linkages is comparable. A total of seven paths, traversing every economy in the region, accounts for 87.7 per cent of the total linkage. It is noteworthy in this case, however, that ASEAN's direct

Table 3.5 Income linkages from Japanese electronics to Japanese households

Path		Global Effect	Direct Effect	Path Mult	Total Effect	% of Global	Total %
1	jpn-ele -> jpn-Usk -> jpn-hhs	9.515	0.141	11.396	1.603	16.8	16.8
2	jpn-ele -> jpn-Skl -> jpn-hhs		0.087	11.396	0.991	10.4	27.3
3	jpn-ele -> jpn-Cap -> jpn-hhs		0.155	11.396	1.768	18.6	45.8
4	jpn-ele -> jpn-gov -> jpn-hhs		0.013	16.134	0.208	2.2	48.0
5	jpn-ele -> jpn-ppp -> jpn-Usk -> jpn-hhs		0.003	11.547	0.030	0.3	48.3
6	jpn-ele -> jpn-ppp -> jpn-Skl -> jpn-hhs		0.002	11.547	0.021	0.2	48.6
7	jpn-ele -> jpn-ppp -> jpn-Cap -> jpn-hhs		0.003	11.547	0.031	0.3	48.9
8	jpn-ele -> jpn-crp -> jpn-Usk -> jpn-hhs		0.006	11.652	0.074	0.8	49.7
9	jpn-ele -> jpn-crp -> jpn-Skl -> jpn-hhs		0.004	11.652	0.043	0.5	50.1
10	jpn-ele -> jpn-crp -> jpn-Cap -> jpn-hhs		0.009	11.652	0.103	1.1	51.2
11	jpn-ele -> jpn-crp -> jpn-gov -> jpn-hhs		0.001	16.388	0.023	0.2	51.4
12	jpn-ele -> jpn-nmm -> jpn-Usk -> jpn-hhs		0.002	11.437	0.021	0.2	51.7
13	jpn-ele -> jpn-nmm -> jpn-Skl -> jpn-hhs		0.001	11.437	0.013	0.1	51.8
14	jpn-ele -> jpn-nmm -> jpn-Cap -> jpn-hhs		0.002	11.437	0.023	0.2	52.0
15	jpn-ele -> jpn-met -> jpn-Usk -> jpn-hhs		0.011	13.078	0.144	1.5	53.5
16	jpn-ele -> jpn-met -> jpn-Skl -> jpn-hhs		0.006	13.078	0.083	0.9	54.4
17	jpn-ele -> jpn-met -> jpn-Cap -> jpn-hhs		0.011	13.078	0.139	1.5	55.9

Table 3.5 (continued)

18	jpn-ele -> jpn-met -> jpn-gov -> jpn-hhs	0.001	18.503	0.021	0.2	56.1
19	jpn-ele -> jpn-ome -> jpn-Usk -> jpn-hhs	0.002	11.529	0.020	0.2	56.3
20	jpn-ele -> jpn-ome -> jpn-Skl -> jpn-hhs	0.001	11.529	0.012	0.1	56.4
21	jpn-ele -> jpn-ome -> jpn-Cap -> jpn-hhs	0.002	11.529	0.018	0.2	56.6
22	jpn-ele -> jpn-ely -> jpn-Cap -> jpn-hhs	0.004	11.516	0.050	0.5	57.1
23	jpn-ele -> jpn-trd -> jpn-Usk -> jpn-hhs	0.020	11.607	0.228	2.4	59.5
24	jpn-ele -> jpn-trd -> jpn-Skl -> jpn-hhs	0.012	11.607	0.144	1.5	61.0
25	jpn-ele -> jpn-trd -> jpn-Cap -> jpn-hhs	0.010	11.607	0.120	1.3	62.3
26	jpn-ele -> jpn-tps -> jpn-Usk -> jpn-hhs	0.005	12.083	0.056	0.6	62.9
27	jpn-ele -> jpn-tps -> jpn-Skl -> jpn-hhs	0.003	12.083	0.035	0.4	63.3
28	jpn-ele -> jpn-tps -> jpn-Cap -> jpn-hhs	0.003	12.083	0.032	0.3	63.6
29	jpn-ele -> jpn-fin -> jpn-Usk -> jpn-hhs	0.003	11.572	0.031	0.3	63.9
30	jpn-ele -> jpn-fin -> jpn-Skl -> jpn-hhs	0.002	11.572	0.021	0.2	64.2
31	jpn-ele -> jpn-fin -> jpn-Cap -> jpn-hhs	0.003	11.572	0.034	0.4	64.5
32	jpn-ele -> jpn-obs -> jpn-Usk -> jpn-hhs	0.0121	1.875	0.143	1.5	66.0
33	jpn-ele -> jpn-obs -> jpn-Skl -> jpn-hhs	0.008	11.875	0.098	1.0	67.0
34	jpn-ele -> jpn-obs -> jpn-Cap -> jpn-hhs	0.019	11.875	0.223	2.3	69.4
35	jpn-ele -> jpn-obs -> jpn-gov -> jpn-hhs	0.001	16.707	0.018	0.2	69.6

Table 3.5 (continued)

36	jpn-ele -> jpn-osg -> jpn-Usk -> jpn-hhs	0.031	11.950	0.365	3.8	73.4
37	jpn-ele -> jpn-osg -> jpn-Skl -> jpn-hhs	0.018	11.950	0.210	2.2	75.6
38	jpn-ele -> jpn-osg -> jpn-Cap -> jpn-hhs	0.007	11.950	0.082	0.9	76.5

Table 3.6 Income linkages from Chinese electronics to Japanese households

Path		Global Effect	Direct Effect	Path Mult	Total Effect	% of Global	Total %
1	chn-ele -> jpn-ele -> jpn-Usk -> jpn-hhs	3.059	0.018	13.242	0.234	7.6	7.6
2	chn-ele -> jpn-ele -> jpn-Skl -> jpn-hhs		0.011	13.242	0.144	4.7	12.4
3	chn-ele -> jpn-ele -> jpn-Cap -> jpn-hhs		0.019	13.242	0.258	8.4	20.8
4	chn-ele -> jpn-ele -> jpn-gov -> jpn-hhs		0.002	18.748	0.030	1.0	21.8
5	chn-ele -> jpn-ele -> jpn-crp -> jpn-Cap -> jpn-hhs		0.001	13.538	0.015	0.5	22.3
6	chn-ele -> jpn-ele -> jpn-met -> jpn-Usk -> jpn-hhs		0.001	15.195	0.021	0.7	23.0
7	chn-ele -> jpn-ele -> jpn-met -> jpn-Cap -> jpn-hhs		0.001	15.195	0.020	0.7	23.6
8	chn-ele -> jpn-ele -> jpn-trd -> jpn-Usk -> jpn-hhs		0.002	13.488	0.033	1.1	24.7
9	chn-ele -> jpn-ele -> jpn-trd -> jpn-Skl -> jpn-hhs		0.002	13.488	0.021	0.7	25.4
10	chn-ele -> jpn-ele -> jpn-trd -> jpn-Cap -> jpn-hhs		0.001	13.488	0.017	0.6	26.0
11	chn-ele -> jpn-ele -> jpn-obs -> jpn-Usk -> jpn-hhs		0.002	13.799	0.021	0.7	26.6
12	chn-ele -> jpn-ele -> jpn-obs -> jpn-Skl -> jpn-hhs		0.001	13.799	0.014	0.5	27.1
13	chn-ele -> jpn-ele -> jpn-obs -> jpn-Cap -> jpn-hhs		0.002	13.799	0.032	1.1	28.2
14	chn-ele -> jpn-ele -> jpn-osg -> jpn-Usk -> jpn-hhs		0.004	13.886	0.053	1.7	29.9
15	chn-ele -> jpn-ele -> jpn-osg -> jpn-Skl -> jpn-hhs		0.002	13.886	0.031	1.0	30.9
16	chn-ele -> asn-ele -> jpn-ele -> jpn-Usk -> jpn-hhs		0.001	17.867	0.023	0.8	31.7
17	chn-ele -> asn-ele -> jpn-ele -> jpn-Cap -> jpn-hhs		0.001	17.867	0.025	0.8	32.5

Table 3.7 Income linkages from Chinese electronics to Japanese electronics

Path		Global Effect	Direct Effect	Path Mult	Total Effect	% of Global	Total %
1	chn-ele -> jpn-ele	0.379	0.125	1.883	0.236	62.3	62.3
2	chn-ele -> kor-ele -> jpn-ele		0.003	2.142	0.007	2.0	64.3
3	chn-ele -> twn-ele -> jpn-ele		0.006	2.128	0.013	3.4	67.7
4	chn-ele -> asn-ele -> jpn-ele		0.009	2.545	0.023	6.2	73.9
5	chn-ele -> chn-ome -> jpn-ome -> jpn-ele		0.000	3.640	0.001	0.2	74.1
6	chn-ele -> kor-ele -> asn-ele -> jpn-ele		0.000	2.884	0.001	0.2	74.3
7	chn-ele -> twn-ele -> kor-ele -> jpn-ele		0.000	2.418	0.000	0.1	74.3
8	chn-ele -> twn-ele -> asn-ele -> jpn-ele		0.001	2.859	0.002	0.5	74.9
9	chn-ele -> asn-ele -> kor-ele -> jpn-ele		0.000	2.884	0.001	0.2	75.1
10	chn-ele -> asn-ele -> twn-ele -> jpn-ele		0.000	2.859	0.001	0.2	75.3
11	chn-ele -> asn-ele -> asn-ome -> jpn-ome -> jpn-ele		0.000	3.876	0.000	0.1	75.4

Table 3.8 Income linkages from Chinese electronics to ASEAN electronics

Path		Global	Direct Effect	Path Effect	Total Mult	% of Effect	Total Global %
1	chn-ele -> asn-ele	0.216	0.097	1.617	0.157	72.8	72.8
2	chn-ele -> jpn-ele -> asn-ele		0.005	2.546	0.013	5.9	78.7
3	chn-ele -> kor-ele -> asn-ele		0.002	1.839	0.004	1.8	80.6
4	chn-ele -> twn-ele -> asn-ele		0.008	1.824	0.014	6.4	87.0
5	chn-ele -> jpn-ele -> twn-ele -> asn-ele		0.000	2.860	0.000	0.2	87.2
6	chn-ele -> kor-ele -> jpn-ele -> asn-ele		0.000	2.885	0.000	0.2	87.4
7	chn-ele -> twn-ele -> jpn-ele -> asn-ele		0.000	2.860	0.001	0.3	87.7

links to China and Japan account for 78.7 per cent of the total. This implies that ASEAN's third party supply links are relatively undiversified, and that its links to Korea and other regional economies are indirect. While the individual ASEAN economies may have complex internal supply chains, these results suggest that more regional diversification could increase both the level and reliability of ASEAN electronics revenues arising from trade.

3.6 CONCLUSIONS AND EXTENSIONS

Beneath the official veneer of open multilateralism and WTO sponsored globalization, there is a remarkably diverse and dynamic mosaic of private commercial linkages that link the world's economies. These linkages are generally incorporated in global networks or supply chains, where tens, hundreds, even thousands of intermediate product linkages are realized through bilateral deliveries within and across boundaries. This system has grown in scope and complexity well beyond the administrative capacity of individual enterprises and nation states, and relies for its existence on price mediated market interactions. With better understanding of this complex web of linkages, policy makers can see both the rewards of multilateralism and the importance of policies that facilitate it.

In this chapter we discussed the evolution of these global supply networks, particularly in the context of East Asia and in recognition of the catalytic role played by international capital allocation or FDI. What we see in today's global economy is a process of supply chain decomposition, where FDI is distributing production tasks across an international matrix of intermediate producers. Individual components of this production matrix are chosen for a variety of reasons, only one of which is the traditional Ricardian or Heckscher-Ohlin criteria of relative resource cost. At least as important for many firms is market access, domestically or in a neighbouring country. Transport costs, infrastructure, network externalities, and administrative climate are also important. Finally, it makes sense for firms to diversify their supply chains simply as a hedging strategy, where the components of risk can be local, national, or global.

In East Asia, this process has advanced very quickly and pervasively, facilitated by both western FDI and a "stepladder effect" where more advanced Asian economies re-allocate production to less advanced ones. In the process of distributing supply chains, foreign investors in the region create new nodes of production in different localities, and another indirect phenomenon emerges. Bamboo Capitalism describes a process where fully autonomous enterprises and markets sprout from these nodes in the "root system" of global intermediate supply. This process is long established in the Tiger economies and can be seen to emerge now in China (even across

China) and other emerging Asian economies. The result is replication of industries and markets at an exponential rate.

To better understand the empirical significance of these phenomena, we developed an international Social Accounting Matrix with detailed bilateral trade statistics. This international SAM was then used for multiplier decomposition analysis, and the results of this were reported on with a few generic examples and more exhaustive tables for motivated readers. The general inference that emerges from these results is that multilateralism is indeed a much more pervasive phenomenon than simple bilateral trade statistics would suggest. Indeed, we find that anywhere between 20 and 70 percent of total income realized in bilateral linkages arises from very long and complex multilateral chains of income-expenditure linkages. These network effects reach across geographic boundaries and sectors in ways that would be quite impossible for policy makers or trade negotiators to anticipate by intuition alones. These "general equilibrium" trade linkages are at once responsible for the majority of international value creation and trade itself. For this reason, the conventional view of gains from trade seriously understates the value of more open multilateralism.

Global supply networks have leveraged the world's resource base and a more liberal trading environment to increase incomes in ways more pervasive than most of us can imagine, and broadening the basis for these activities can only amplify these benefits, distribute them ever more widely and reduce the risks of economic concentration and instability.

NOTES

1 There are many historical overviews of this issue. More recently see Coates (1997) and, in the East Asian regional context, Lee and Roland-Holst (1998).

2 See e.g. Rose (2002).

3 See e.g. Anderson et al. (2000), Brown et al. (2001), Hoekman and Kosteki (1995), Kahler (1995), and UNCTAD (1999).

4 See for example Hoekman and Leidy (1993), Schiff and Winters (1998), and World Bank (2000).

5 Recent global estimates (Beghin et al. 2002) indicate that abolishing OECD farm protection would raise rural incomes in developing countries by more than US$60 billion per year, a figure larger than even the most ambitious goals for expanded development assistance.

6 See in particular Bhagwati et al. (1998) and Panagariya (1999).

7 There are many able surveys of regionalism, especially recent initiatives that appear impelled by globalization. See e.g. World Bank (2000), Martin and Winters (1996), and Frankel (1998).

8 Roland-Holst and Van Der Mensbrugghe (2002).

9 Local market FDI targeting has long been practiced and recognized, but it takes on added significance in Asia because of rapid domestic growth experiences. For example, Toshiba arrived in China about a decade ago as an investor in export capacity. By the end of 2002, Toshiba had 32 production facilities in China, and was selling two-thirds of its output in the domestic market for a total value of over US$2 billion. For more on such FDI

spillovers and strategies, see e.g. Singh and Jun (1995), Smarsynska (2002), and Aizenmann and Marion (2001).

10 See, for example, Yoshitomi et al. (2003).

11 An intermediate supplier, as the name implies, provides intermediate goods directly to the primary (in this case foreign financed) firm. An appurtenant supplier supplies to the local market created by the principal's presence. The latter includes everything from makers of intermediate goods to beauty salons, but the multiplier effects represented by these enterprises can easily outweigh direct income generated from the principal firm. These insights were suggested as long ago as Kindleberger (1969), and are implicit in much of the FDI case study material (see Razin (2002) for a survey).

12 Recognition of this fact reveals much about the profound influence China's emergence has had on the East Asian region.

13 The SAM approach is more thoroughly explicated in a variety of sources, including Reinert and Roland-Holst (1997), Pyatt and Round (1985), and Stone (1981).

14 This dataset is extensively documented on the www.gtap.org website.

15 The reader should be reminded that multiplier estimation is based on an assumption of local excess capacity that permits us to ignore local variations in prices. While this assumption may be open to empirical question in some Western domestic economies, the East Asian region has exhibited remarkable supply elasticity in recent years. Indeed, price deflation with rising supply is a greater preoccupation in the region than capacity constraints. To the extent that supply might be constrained, our multipliers will overestimate induced income effects. In any case, however, the point of the present exercise is not to precisely calibrate income effects precisely, but to reveal their extent.

16 These are given in the following tables.

17 More detailed results, including the complete multiplier matrix and factor matrices used to produce these results, may be obtained from the author.

BIBLIOGRAPHY

Aizenman, Joshua and Nancy Marion (2001), "The merits of horizontal versus vertical FDI in the presence of uncertainty", NBER Working Paper w8631, December.

Anderson, Kym, Joe Francois, Tom Hertel, Bernard Hoekman and Will Martin (2000), "Potential gains from trade reform in the new millennium", Paper presented at the *Third Annual Conference on Global Economic Analysis*, held at Monash University, 27-30 June.

Asia-Pacific Economic Cooperation (APEC) (1997), "The impact of trade liberalization in APEC", Singapore: APEC Secretariat.

Beghin, J., D. Roland-Holst and D. van der Mensbrugghe (2002), "Global agriculture trade and the Doha Round: what are the implications for North and South?", *Staff General Research Papers* 4080, Iowa State University, Department of Economics.

Bergsten, C. Fred (2000), "East Asian regionalism: toward a tripartite world", *The Economist*, July 15, pp. 20-22.

Bhagwati, Jagdish and Arvind Panagariya (eds) (1996), *The Economics of Preferential Trade Agreements*, Washington, DC: AEI Press.

Bhagwati, Jagdish, David Greenaway and Arvind Panagarya (1998), "Trading preferentially: theory and policy", *Economic Journal*, *108* 1128-48.

Brown, Drusilla K., Alan V. Deardorff and Robert M. Stern (1992), "A North American Free Trade Agreement: analytical issues and a computational assessment", *The World Economy*, *15*, pp. 15-29.

Brown, Drusilla K., Alan V. Deardorff and Robert M. Stern (2001), "CGE modeling and analysis of multilateral and regional negotiating options", *Research Seminar in International Economics Discussion Paper*, No. 468, School of Public Policy, The University of Michigan, Ann Arbor.

Coates, A.W. (1997), *The Post-1945 Internationalization of Economics*, Durham, N.C. and London: Duke University Press.

Defourny, J and E. Thorbecke (1984), "Structural path analysis and multiplier decomposition within a social accounting matrix framework", *Economic Journal 94,* pp.111-36.

Drysdale, Peter and David Vines (eds) (1998), *Europe, East Asia and APEC: A Shared Global Agenda?* Cambridge: Cambridge University Press.

Francois, Joseph and Kenneth Reinert (1997), *Applied Methods for Trade Policy Analysis : A Handbook*, New York, NY: Cambridge University Press.

Frankel, Jeffrey A. (ed) (1998), *The Regionalization of the World Economy*, Chicago: University of Chicago Press.

Fung, K.C. (1998), "Accounting for Chinese trade: some national and regional considerations", in R.E. Baldwin, R.E. Lipsey, and J.D. Richardson (eds) *Geography and Ownership As A Basis for Economic Accounting,* Chicago: University of Chicago Press.

Gazon, J (1979), "Une nouvelle methodologie:l'approche structurale du pouvoir ab sein des structures fortement connexes", *Economie Applique XXXIV(4)* pp.749-784.

Goto, Junichi (1990*), Labor in International Trade Theory: A New Perspective on Japanese-American Issues*, Baltimore: Johns Hopkins University Press.

Goto, Junichi and Koichi Hamada (1994), "Economic preconditions for Asian regional integration", in T. Ito and A.O. Krueger (eds), *Macroeconomic Linkage: Savings, Exchange Rates, and Capital Flows*, Chicago: University of Chicago Press.

Hertel, Thomas W. (ed). (1997), *Global Trade Analysis: Modeling and Applications*, New York, NY: Cambridge University Press.

Hoekman, B and M. Kostecki (1995), *The Political Economy of the World Trading System: From GATT to WTO*, New York/Oxford: Oxford University Press.

Hoekman, B. and M. Leidy (1993), "Holes and loopholes in regional integration agreements", in K. Anderson and R. Blackhurst (eds), *Regional Integration.* London: Harvester-Wheatsheaf.

Kahler, Miles (1995), *International Institutions and the Political Economy of Integration.* Washington, DC: Brookings.

Kawai, Masahiro and Shujiro Urata (1996), "Trade imbalances and Japanese foreign direct investment: bilateral and triangular issues", in K.H. Jung and J.H. Yoo, (eds*), Asia-Pacific Economic Cooperation: Current Issues and Agenda for the Future*, Seoul: Korea Institute for International Economic Policy.

Kindelberger, C.P. (1969), *American Business Abroad: Six Lectures on Direct Investment*, New Haven: Yale University Press.

Kohsaka, Akira (1996), "Interdependence through capital flows in the Pacific Asia and the role of Japan", in T. Ito and A.O. Krueger (eds), *Financial Deregulation and Integration in East Asia,* Chicago: University of Chicago Press.

Kohsaka, Akira (ed) (1995), *Capital Flows in the Pacific Region: Past Trends and Future Prospects,* Osaka: Japan Committee for Pacific Economic Outlook.

Kohsaka, Akira (ed) (1997), *Exchange Rate Fluctuations and Macroeconomic Management*, Osaka: Japan Committee for Pacific Economic Outlook.

Lantner, R. (1974), *Theorie de la Dominance Économique*, Paris:Dunod.

Lee, Hiro and Brian Woodall (1998), "Political feasibility and empirical assessments of a Pacific Free Trade Area", in H. Lee and D. Roland-Holst, (eds), *Economic Development and Cooperation in the Pacific Basin: Trade, Investment, and Environmental Issues*, Cambridge: Cambridge University Press.

Lee, Hiro and David Roland-Holst (1995), "Trade liberalization and employment linkages in the Pacific Basin," *The Developing Economies*, *33* 155-84.

Lee, Hiro and David Roland-Holst (1999), "Cooperation or confrontation in U.S.-Japan trade? Some general equilibrium estimates", *Journal of the Japanese and International Economies, 13* 119-39.

Lee, Hiro and David Roland-Holst (eds) (1998), *Economic Development and Cooperation in the Pacific Basin: Trade, Investment, and Environmental Issues*, Cambridge: Cambridge University Press.

Lee, Hiro, and David Roland-Holst (1994), "Shifting comparative advantage and the employment effects of US-Japan trade", *The World Economy, 17* 323-45.

Lee, Hiro, David Roland-Holst and Dominique van der Mensbrugghe (1999), "APEC trade liberalization and structural adjustment: policy assumptions," *APEC Discussion Paper Series,* APEC Study Center, Graduate School of International Development, Nagoya University, March.

Martin, Will, and L. Alan Winters, (eds) (1996), *The Uruguay Round and the developing countries*, Cambridge, UK: Cambridge University Press.

OECD (1999), "Open markets matter: the benefits of trade and investment liberalization", Policy Brief, Paris, October.

Panagariya, Arvind (1999), *Regionalism in Trade Policy: Essays on Preferential Trading,* London: World Scientific.

Pyatt, G and Round, J.I.(eds), (1985), *Social Accounting Matrices: A Basis for Planning",* Washington: World Bank.

Razin, Assaf (2002), "FDI Flows: a critical look," NBER Reporter, Spring.

Reinert, Kenneth A. and David Roland Holst (1997), "Social accounting matrices", in J.F. Francois and K.A. Reinert (eds), *Applied Methods for Trade Policy Analysis*, Cambridge: Cambridge University Press.

Roland-Holst, David (2002), *" An Overview of PRC's Emergence and East Asian Trade Patterns to 2020",* ADB Institute Research Paper No 44, Tokyo: Asian Development Bank.

Roland-Holst, David and Finn Tarp (2003), "Economic reform and structural price transmission: lessons from an emerging Asian economy", Discussion Paper 0301, Central Institute for Economic Management, Hanoi, January.

Roland-Holst, David and Dominique van der Mensbrugghe (2002), "Regionalism versus globalization in the Americas: empirical evidence on opportunities and challenges", published jointly in *Integration and Trade* and *Économie Internationale*, Institute for the Integration of Latin America and the Caribbean/Inter-American Development Bank and Centre d'Études Perspectives et d'Informations Internationales, Washington and Paris, forthcoming.

Rose, A.K. (2002), "Do We Really Know that the WTO Increases Trade?", Centre for Economic Policy Research, Discussion Paper, No.3538.

Schiff, Maurice and L. Alan Winters (1998), "Regional integration as diplomacy", *World Bank Economic Review 12(2)* 271-96.

Singh, Harinder and Kwang W. Jun (1995), "Some new evidence on determinants of foreign direct investment in developing countries." Working Paper 1531, World Bank, Washington.

Smarsynska, Beata (2002), "Does Foreign Direct Investment Increase the Productivity of Domestic Firms? In Search of Spillovers through Backward Linkages," Working Paper 2920, Washington: World Bank.

Stone, Richard (1981), *Aspects of Economic and Social Modelling",* Geneva: Librairie Droze.

Tan, Hung (2002), "Foreign Direct Investment Spillovers in Developing Countries," mimeo, Washington: World Bank.

Tan, Kong Yam (1998), "Regionalism in the Pacific Basin: strategic interest of ASEAN in APEC," in H. Lee and D. Roland-Holst (eds), *Economic Development and Cooperation in the Pacific Basin: Trade, Investment, and Environmental Issues*, Cambridge: Cambridge University Press.

United Nations Conference on Trade and Development (UNCTAD) (1999), *A Positive Agenda for Developing Countries: Issues for Future Trade Negotiations*, Geneva: United Nationsi

Urata, Shujiro (1993a), "Changing patterns of direct Investment and the implications for trade and development", in C.F. Bergsten and M. Noland (eds), *Pacific Dynamism and the International Economic System, Washington*, DC: Institute for International Economics.

Urata, Shujiro (1993b), "Japanese Foreign Direct Investment and its impact on foreign trade in Asia", in T. Ito and A.O. Krueger (eds), *Trade and Protectionism*, Chicago: University of Chicago Press.

Urata, Shujiro (1994), "Trade liberalization and productivity growth in Asia: introduction and major findings", *The Developing Economies, 32* 363-72.

Urata, Shujiro (1997), "Deepening the economic linkages in trade, Foreign Direct Investment and labor", in O.H. Cheong (ed), *East Asian Economies: Sustaining Growth and Stability*, Kuala Lumpur: Institute of Strategic and International Studies.

Urata, Shujiro (1998a), "Regionalization and the formation of regional institutions in East Asia", in K. Fukasaku, F. Kimura, and S. Urata (eds), *Asia and Europe: Beyond Competing Regionalism*, Sussex: Academic Press.

Urata, Shujiro (1998b), "Foreign Direct Investment and APEC" in V.K. Aggarwal and C.E. Morrison (eds), *Asia-Pacific Crossroads: Regime Creation in Asia and the Pacific*, New York: St. Martin's Press.

Urata, Shujiro (1999), "Japanese Foreign Direct Investment in Asia: its impact on export expansion and technology acquisition of the host countries", in N. Kumar (ed), *Globalization, Foreign Direct Investment and Technology Transfer: Impact on and Prospects for Developing Countries*, London and New York: Routledge and UNU Press.

Urata, Shujiro (2000), "Intra-firm technology transfer by Japanese manufacturing firms in Asia," in T. Ito and A.O. Krueger (eds), *The Role of Foreign Direct Investment in East Asian Economic Development*, Chicago: University of Chicago Press.

World Bank, (2000), *Trade Blocs* Policy Research Report, World Bank/Oxford University Press.

Yoshimoti, M and ADB Institute Staff (2003), *Post-Crisis Development Paradigms in Asia"*, May, ADB Institute.

PART THREE

ISSUES IN TRADE AND INVESTMENT COOPERATION IN EAST ASIA

4. International Production/Distribution Networks and FTAs[1]

Fukunari Kimura and Mitsuyo Ando

4.1 INTRODUCTION

In East Asia, movements toward the formation of FTAs (free trade agreements) have been increasingly activated. One of the interesting phenomena in this process is that countries in the region, including Japan, Korea, China, and the ASEAN countries, implicitly share a common view that the integration effort must ultimately head for the economic integration of the whole East Asian region, even though each country's current efforts to conclude FTAs are largely uncoordinated. It was not an old story that the concept of "East Asia" as a natural entity heading economic integration was accepted by a majority of people in the region. One of the important elements supporting the concept of an integrated East Asia is the formation of international production/distribution networks during the past decade. Although Australia and New Zealand as well as India, Russia, and others are of course important for East Asian countries, they are not regarded as part of East Asia because they are not fully participating in international production/distribution networks.

Indeed, we can observe an important qualitative change in the East Asian economy during the last decade. Ten years ago the World Bank (1993) characterized *the East Asian Miracle* by well-managed macroeconomic fundamentals and market-friendly microeconomic government policies. However, the role of foreign direct investment (FDI) was not fully analysed in the report. It was actually the timing of changes in FDI hosting policies that started transforming the major characteristics of developing East Asia. We can then observe an unprecedented formation of international production/distribution networks in East Asia during the following decade.

The formation of these networks in East Asia is "unique" at this moment in time in the following aspects: first, these networks have already become a substantial component of each country's economy in the region so that each country's manufacturing sector and international trade cannot be discussed without considering their existence. Second, these networks involve a large number of countries at different income levels in the region. Cross-country differences in factor prices and other location advantages are effectively utilized in the formation of vertical production chains. Third, these networks include both intra-firm and arm's-length relationships, partially across different firm nationalities. Multinational enterprises (MNEs) as well as indigenous firms in each country are forming sophisticated inter-firm relationships. Similar networking is being developed in the U.S.-Mexico nexus and the Germany-Czech/Hungary/Poland connection, but they have not reached the level of maturity observed in East Asia.

Although the political effort of concluding FTAs has intensified with a sense of emergency, the required contents of FTAs have not been fully discussed. We argue that FTAs should be designed so as to further activate the international production/distribution networks in East Asia. In the background to the formation of the networks, the ASEAN forerunners and China made a drastic change in development strategies in the mid-1980s or in the early 1990s. In the process of policy reform, though, the old system of fostering import-substituting industries has partially been preserved. This negative heritage has become an unbearable burden for further development, and restoring the overall policy consistency must thus be incorporated within the scheme of FTAs. On the other hand international production/distribution networks have grown with the flavour of the new economic logic of fragmentation theory, in addition to the traditional comparative advantage theory. The new role of government requires a set of policies that was not traditionally emphasized. Further activating the networks calls for new policy packages within the scheme of FTAs. If a region-wide political integration is aimed for at all the contents of FTAs must be designed so as to be consistent with the new characteristics of the East Asian economy.

FTAs are flexible and convenient political tools for pursuing the regional policy agenda. More than 140 FTAs/customs unions have been concluded in the world, and the contents of these agreements are of wide variety. A common and essential component of these agreements is the bilateral/regional liberalization of trade in goods, which is disciplined by GATT Article XXIV. Other elements, including commitments dictated by GATS Article V, vary across agreements; i.e., various forms of FTAs/customs unions are allowed even while keeping GATT/WTO consistency. In designing the region-wide economic integration, the characteristics and the required policy reform of the East Asian economy must certainly be taken into account.

This chapter reviews the nature and characteristics of international production/distribution networks in East Asia in the following section. Section 3 then discusses in detail the role of FTAs in rationalizing import-substituting industries. Section 4 proposes new elements of FTAs for further activating international production/distribution networks. The last section concludes.

4.2 INTERNATIONAL PRODUCTION/DISTRIBUTION NETWORKS[2]

The international production/distribution networks consist of vertical production chains extended across countries in the region and distribution networks throughout the world. Firms belonging to the machinery industries including general machinery, electrical machinery, transport equipment, and precision machinery, are major players though some firms in other industries such as textiles and garments also develop networks.

When discussing the current international division of labour in East Asia, the theory of comparative advantage, based on the relative production costs in autarky, is still valid to some extent. Technological gap and factor price differences explain location patterns of industries to some extent. However, in interpreting the mechanics of international production/distribution networks, we must at least incorporate a new line of thought into our analytical framework.

The fragmentation theory is a powerful tool when we analyse patterns of FDI going to LDCs to formulate cross-border production sharing systems.[3] Traditional international trade theory primarily explains industry-wide location patterns. In East Asia, however, production-process-wide location patterns were often observed. Fragmentation theory neatly presents the logic behind such a location pattern.

The original idea of fragmentation theory is presented as Figure 4.1. Imagine that before fragmentation, a big factory in the electronic machinery industry taking care of the entire production process from upstream to downstream is initially located in Japan. It is located in Japan because the industry is capital or human capital intensive. However, if we look at detailed production processes in the factory, various kinds of production blocks may be identified. Some are surely human capital intensive, requiring the employment of highly skilled technicians. Some, however, could be unskilled and labour intensive, suitable for mass production with massive labour inputs. There would be a production process that is extremely capital intensive so that 24-hour operation is a must to accelerate capital depreciation. If we can separate these production blocks and locate them in different places (called "fragmentation"), we may reduce the total production cost. The key to successful fragmentation is how far the production cost of each fragmented production block can be reduced and how small is the cost of service links connecting the separated production blocks.

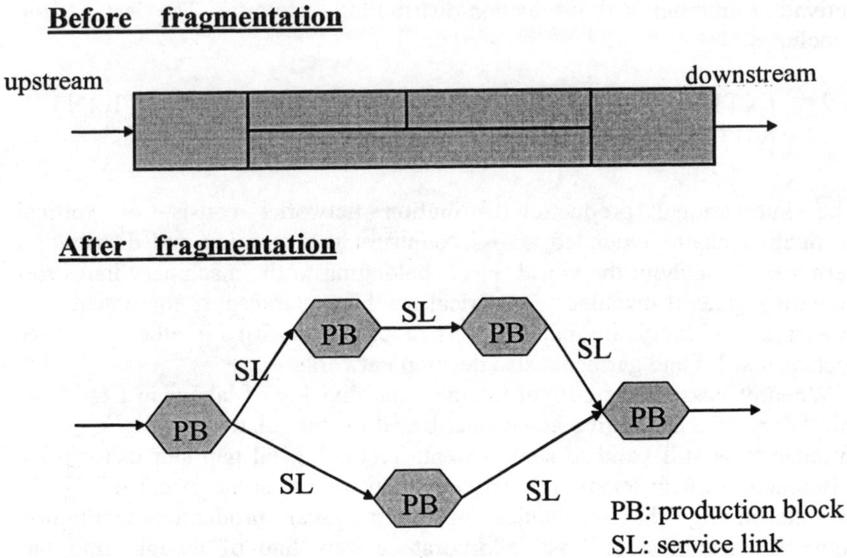

Figure 4.1 Fragmentation: an illustration

Source: The authors.

To apply the fragmentation theory, we believe that the expansion of the model into two-dimensional space is effective.[4] The horizontal axis of Figure 4.2 represents geographical distance between the original position and the new location of a fragmented production block. In this horizontal direction, the saving of production cost *per se* in the production block arises from location advantages in the new location. The source of the service link cost, on the other hand, is due to geographical distance. The dotted line denotes the national border, which generates large differences in both production cost per se and service link cost.

The vertical axis represents uncontrollability; i.e., it denotes how far the firm concerned controls fragmented production blocks. The dotted line is the boundary of the firm, setting distinctive differences between intra-firm fragmentation and arm's-length fragmentation. Fragmentation in the vertical direction generates the saving of production cost *per se* by exploiting the benefit of "de-internalization" advantages or ownership advantages of business partners. Fragmentation along the uncontrollability axis is particularly important in interpreting the international production/distribution networks in East Asia where various forms of arm's-length transactions are notably active.

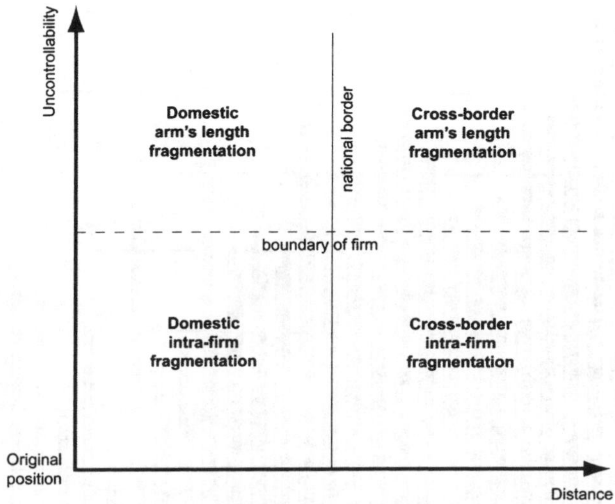

Figure 4.2 Two dimensions of fragmentation

In East Asia, fragmentation and agglomeration obviously go together. The forces of fragmentation and agglomeration sometimes work in the opposite direction. However, there are a few logical reasons that support both at the same time, particularly in the context of East Asia. First, service links themselves typically have strong economies of scale, and, therefore, fragmented production blocks tend to locate with concentration. Second, it is difficult for developing countries to improve both the infrastructure and policy environment throughout their territories; rather, location advantages are improved in particular spots or places. This fact again causes fragmented production blocks in limited locations. Third, arm's-length transactions often require geographical proximity in order to guarantee closer monitoring, efficient technology exchanges, and precise delivery timing. Typical agglomeration in East Asia consists of vertical production chains.

The formation of international production/distribution networks in East Asia is a very recent phenomenon. Figure 4.3 presents shares of machinery and machinery parts and components in total exports and imports in major East Asian countries and selected countries in the rest of the world.[5] The figure reveals that the shares of machinery in total exports and imports are indeed large in East Asia. Except for Japan's imports and Indonesia's exports

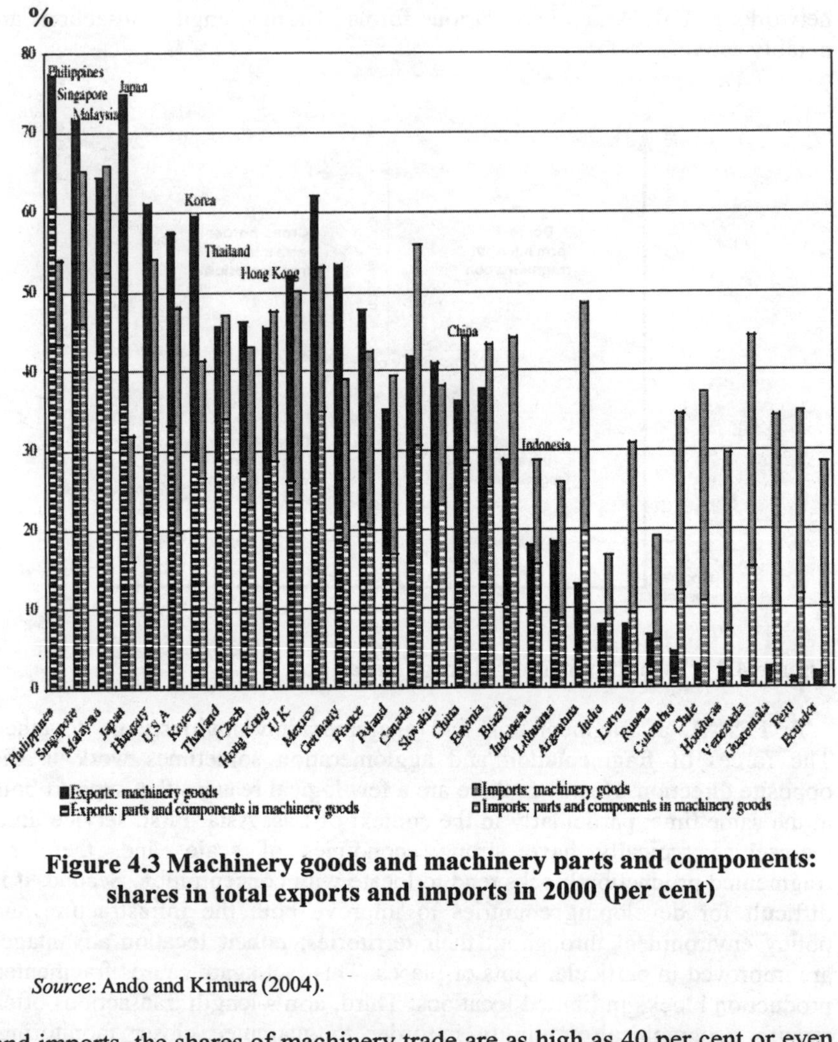

Figure 4.3 Machinery goods and machinery parts and components: shares in total exports and imports in 2000 (per cent)

Source: Ando and Kimura (2004).

and imports, the shares of machinery trade are as high as 40 per cent or even higher up to 70 per cent. The figure also confirms that the shares of parts and components in machinery trade are notably large; they are 40 per cent to 50 per cent or even reach 80 per cent in some cases for the Southeast Asian countries. These facts vividly indicate that the international production/distribution networks, particularly in machinery industries, have become a substantial component of the East Asian economies. We observe similar patterns in the connection between the U.S. and Mexico and between Western Europe and Central/Eastern Europe. For other countries, however, we must conclude that international production/distribution networks are immature relative to the ones in East Asia.

Table 4.1 decomposes trade of machinery and its parts and components by major East Asian economy at the HS 6-digit level into one-way trade, vertical intra-industry trade, and horizontal intra-industry trade in 1990, 1996, and 2000.[6] Trade in East Asia was, in the past, dominated by inter-industry, one-way trade, but we observe a drastic increase in intra-industry trade, particularly vertical intra-industry trade in the machinery sectors. One important observation here is that countries with lower income often export more expensive products, compared to countries with higher income. This is an indication that vertical intra-industry trade is caused by process-wide division of labour rather than vertical product differentiation.

It is extremely difficult to statistically capture the proportion of intra-firm and arm's-length transactions. The micro data of affiliates of Japanese firms, however, provide some hints. Table 4.2 presents (a) the destination of sales and (b) origin of purchases by Japanese affiliates in East Asia and China with decomposition into intra-firm and arm's-length transactions. Although the data shows changes only in the three years from 1995 to 1998, arm's-length transactions are expanding their share over intra-firm transactions.

4.3 RE-ORGANIZING IMPORT-SUBSTITUTING INDUSTRIES

In the background to network formation, there was an important policy change in the forerunners of the Southeast Asian countries and China. East Asian countries have traditionally applied a "dual track approach"; i.e., trying to foster both import-substituting industries and export-oriented industries at the same time. Furthermore, in contrast with Japan, Korea, and Taiwan, the Southeast Asian countries and China actively utilized incoming FDI not only in export-oriented industries but also in some major import-substituting industries.

The weights between import-substituting industries and export-oriented industries were, however, changed over time. From the 1970s to the mid-1980s, these countries introduced selective FDI primarily in import-substituting industries. Although FDI for export promotion was also invited, potentially competing domestic industries were insulated by policies that limited the activities of foreign companies, for example, to geographically segregated export-processing zones at that time. In the mid-1980s for Malaysia and Thailand and in the early 1990s for the Philippines, Indonesia, and China, these countries began to switch their FDI hosting policy from selective acceptance to basically "accept everybody" policy. While keeping trade protection for import-substituting industries, they started trying to host as many foreign companies as possible and formulate industrial clusters.

Table 4.1 Development of the pattern of machinery trade in East Asia: the cases of China, Indonesia and Japan

	Machinery goods			Machinery parts and components		
	1990	1996	2000	1990	1996	2000
(a) China						
One-way	**51.6**	**43.3**	**27.1**	**25.5**	**12.0**	**8.8**
One-way, exports>imports	13.7	16.3	15.5	2.3	3.3	2.6
Intra-industry trade	48.4	56.7	72.9	74.5	88.0	91.2
Horizontal IIT	3.2	11.0	7.9	3.7	20.4	8.3
Vertical IIT	**20.1**	**43.5**	**63.6**	**18.2**	**64.8**	**81.1**
Vertical IIT: price of exports> price of imports	5.0	8.0	5.8	8.7	8.9	9.5
Not classified IIT	25.2	2.2	1.4	52.6	2.7	1.8
(b) Indonesia						
One-way	**93.3**	**73.5**	**65.6**	**89.5**	**66.4**	**57.8**
One-way, exports>imports	1.8	11.8	38.4	0.3	6.1	32.2
Intra-industry trade	6.7	26.5	34.4	10.5	33.6	42.2
Horizontal IIT	1.6	4.9	4.4	3.7	7.2	5.7
Vertical IIT	**5.0**	**21.6**	**29.9**	**6.8**	**26.4**	**36.5**
Vertical IIT: price of exports> price of imports	2.8	11.5	18.2	2.3	13.0	19.9
Not classified IIT	0.0	0.0	0.0	0.0	0.0	0.0
(i) Japan						
One-way	**45.6**	**32.6**	**26.2**	**38.9**	**30.3**	**21.3**
One-way, exports>imports	43.1	31.6	25.6	38.4	29.8	20.8
Intra-industry trade	54.4	67.4	73.8	61.1	69.7	78.7
Horizontal IIT	10.3	11.9	8.4	21.1	13.6	9.6
Vertical IIT	**40.8**	**53.2**	**63.8**	**37.7**	**55.5**	**68.5**
Vertical IIT: price of exports> price of imports	6.9	19.3	25.4	9.5	22.2	29.7
Not classified IIT	3.4	2.2	1.6	2.4	0.6	0.6

Data source: Ando (2004).
Note: see Ando (2004) for the details as well as the results of other East Asian countries.

Such policy changes may not have been a deliberate, well-planned reform; rather, the reform was accomplished as a result of a piecemeal improvement of the policy environment to maintain FDI inflows when confronted with the economic depression of the mid 1980s and with the emergence of China as a major attractor of FDI in the early 1990s.

Table 4.2 ***Arm's length/intra firm sales and purchases by Japanese manufacturing affiliates in East Asia (million, JPY, %)***

		Affiliates in East Asia				Affiliates in China			
		1995		1998		1995		1998	
(a) Sales									
Value	Manufacturing sectors	12,299,770		12,324,572		732,434		1,756,528	
	Electric machinery sector	5,107,148		5,191,673		311,034		749,951	
Share									
(1)	Japan	**18.8**	**(28.7)**	**25.4**	**(32.9)**	**29.0**	**(29.7)**	**23.6**	**(22.5)**
	Arm's length: Japan	3.1	(3.2)	6.8	(8.7)	4.5	(1.4)	7.0	(6.7)
	Intra-firm: Japan	15.7	(25.5)	18.6	(24.2)	24.5	(28.3)	16.6	(15.8)
(ii)	Local	**58.4**	**(38.0)**	**49.2**	**(32.3)**	**44.7**	**(34.1)**	**53.5**	**(40.8)**
	Arm's length: local	49.2	(34.6)	45.4	(27.6)	42.6	(31.6)	50.4	(36.3)
	Intra-firm: local	9.2	(3.4)	3.8	(4.7)	2.1	(2.5)	3.1	(4.5)
(iii)	Intra-region (other than Japan and local)	**13.3**	**(19.6)**	**16.9**	**(24.9)**	**21.0**	**(30.8)**	**17.6**	**(31.7)**
	Arm's length: intra-region	6.8	(7.9)	8.9	(11.1)	3.4	(2.9)	3.4	(4.5)
	Intra-firm: intra-region	6.5	(11.6)	8.0	(13.8)	17.6	(27.9)	14.2	(27.2)
(i+ii+iii)	East Asia (total)	**90.5**	**(86.3)**	**91.5**	**(90.1)**	**94.7**	**(94.6)**	**94.7**	**(95.0)**
	Arm's length: East Asia (total)	59.1	(45.7)	61.1	(47.4)	50.5	(35.9)	60.8	(47.5)
	Intra-firm: East Asia (total)	31.4	(40.6)	30.4	(42.7)	44.2	(58.7)	33.9	(47.5)
(b) Purchases									
Value	Manufacturing	6,913,965		7,501,823		430,484		1,062,301	
	Electric machninery	2,834,205		3,711,079		209,214		532,101	
Share	Manufacturing								
(i)	Japan	**40.3**	**(38.9)**	**35.1**	**(37.0)**	**49.1**	**(53.3)**	**36.1**	**(33.3)**
	Arm's length: Japan	9.5	(5.4)	14.5	(13.3)	10.1	(8.2)	17.6	(13.9)
	Intra-firm: Japan	30.8	(33.5)	20.6	(23.7)	39.0	(45.1)	18.5	(19.4)
(ii)	Local	**40.3**	**(33.8)**	**43.3**	**(35.8)**	**29.2**	**(18.7)**	**44.3**	**(33.7)**
	Arm's length: local	34.2	(29.0)	40.2	(33.5)	22.7	(16.9)	41.8	(31.1)
	Intra-firm: local	6.1	(4.8)	3.1	(2.3)	6.5	(1.8)	2.5	(2.6)
(iii)	Intra-region (other than Japan and local)	**14.4**	**(24.8)**	**18.6**	**(26.3)**	**20.3**	**(27.0)**	**18.3**	**(32.1)**
	Arm's length: intra-region	7.9	(13.4)	9.8	(12.9)	4.5	(4.6)	3.6	(5.0)
	Intra-firm: intra-region	6.5	(11.4)	8.8	(13.4)	15.8	(22.4)	14.7	(27.1)
(i+ii+iii)	East Asia (total)	**95.0**	**(97.5)**	**97.0**	**(99.1)**	**98.6**	**(99.0)**	**98.7**	**(99.1)**
	Arm's length: East Asia (total)	51.6	(47.9)	64.5	(59.8)	37.3	(29.7)	63.0	(50.0)
	Intra-firm: East Asia (total)	43.4	(49.6)	32.5	(39.4)	61.3	(69.3)	35.7	(49.1)

Data source: Kimura and Ando (2004).

Notes: Figures in parenthesis are of the electric machinery sector.
See original data source for the cases of affiliates in other countries.

The dual trade approach requires a complicated policy package. To invite export-oriented foreign companies, what a country has to do is simple but difficult; it must provide the world's best or second best location advantages for incoming investors. Trade protection of course negatively affects location advantages. In order to at least partially neutralize the negative effects of import-substituting industry protection, the Southeast Asian countries extensively introduced a duty drawback system, i.e., the system of refunds of duties and indirect taxes on imported inputs in export production. Combined with a unilateral tariff reduction for semiconductor-related products under the initiative of APEC, ratios of customs revenues to c.i.f. import values in these countries substantially declined throughout the 1990s (see Figure 4.4).

Such minor policy adjustments have gradually used up their effectiveness, and more substantial policy reform has become unavoidable. Particularly in the Southeast Asian countries the Asian currency/financial crisis, as well as competition with China over location advantages, has slowed down their economies. Keeping inefficient import-substituting industries has become a serious burden for these economies.

For developing countries heading towards higher national income through industrialization, fostering import-substituting industries has been a natural choice for a long time. When the technological level is not high enough to export its products, it is natural to start production for its domestic market. Development strategies with extensive import substitution were once applied by almost all developing countries from the 1950s or 1960s. In the case of the Southeast Asian countries, they attempted to promote import substitution in some specified industries by introducing foreign companies. Such industries included automobiles, domestic electric appliances, and food processing, as well as petrochemicals and iron and steel in some countries.

A serious problem of such development strategies is their enormous cost and the low probability of success. When local indigenous firms are promoted production can be started with strong policy incentives to fill a gap in productivity between domestic and foreign markets. In many countries, trade protection is applied to provide such incentives because it brings about relatively low politico-economic costs to implement compared with other policy measures. When foreign companies are invited to substitute imports firm-level technological gaps can be neglected, and thus the necessary level of incentives may be lower. However, location disadvantages must still be compensated up to the level where foreign companies can break even. Policy packages necessarily become complicated combinations of regulations and incentives.

Unfortunately for small developing countries the smaller the domestic market the higher is the required protection cost. When the size of the potential market is as large as that of China and India, foreign companies may try to establish subsidiaries earlier to preempt the market even if they cannot gain profits in the short run. In contrast, countries with small markets are cursed in a multitude of ways. The smaller the market the more difficult it is for foreign companies to reach the minimal level of production efficiency. To make things worse the protection cost in upstream production is necessarily borne by downstream industries, and the lack of agglomeration also enhances the production cost. In the end, countries with a small market and lack of agglomeration must pay enormous and long-lasting costs for protection.

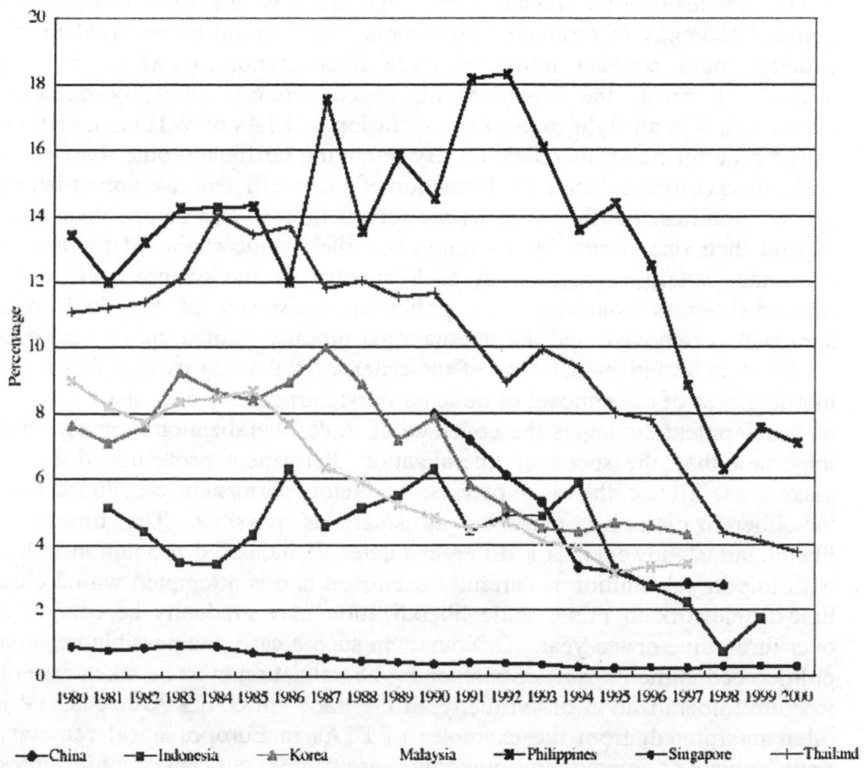

Figure 4.4 Custom duties import ratios in the East Asian countries
Source: Ando and Estevadeordal (2003).

Since the 1980s, the so-called neo-classical school and the advocates of the Washington consensus have harshly attacked import substitution development strategies. These advocates are somewhat compassionate towards developing countries trying to implement import-substituting-type industrial promotion at least in the short run, and would like to emphasize that some successful examples do exist. However, it must be admitted that such development strategies have often been implemented without careful cost-benefit analysis and appropriate time discount rates. Once trade protection is in place strong inertia of politico-economic forces to maintain the protection starts to develop. Unless a strong commitment is made in the dynamic design of policies, the cost of protection would be borne eternally. When the immediate removal of protection becomes optimal, this should be done. Even when some temporary protection is justified, we must design industrial promotion policies with protection removal in five to 15 years.

The conclusion of FTAs are one of the effective measures to break the political economy of prolonged protection. There would be no problem if a country could conduct unilateral trade liberalization. However, if it is difficult to break the argument of vested interests only by domestic discussion, it is all right to use the conclusion of FTAs or WTO negotiations as leverage for trade liberalization. By removing tariffs and other barriers to trade, market forces dictate the formation of a new efficient division of labour across countries. Inefficient firms are forced to exit, and competitive firms expand their operations. MNEs reorganize their value chains of production from the pattern segregated in each country to the pattern with wider networks across countries. The policy inconsistency of the dual track approach is removed, and the international production/distribution networks are likely to be activated. One of the criteria for the quality of FTAs is the thoroughness of the removal of trade barriers. Particularly from the viewpoint of development strategies the coverage of trade liberalization is much more important than the speed of liberalization. Permanent protection does not make sense. Hence, the range of sensitive sectors permanently excluded from the liberalization list must be as small as possible. The timing of liberalization, however, is a different matter. If industrial promotion policy with import substitution is carefully examined and is attempted with a clear time framework in mind, trade liberalization may gradually be conducted over three, five or ten years. Of course, in such a case, the possible negative politico-economic impacts of postponing liberalization must be taken care of. Required liberalization of "virtually all the trade" in GATT Article XXIV is often interpreted, from the examples of FTAs in Europe, as (a) removing trade barriers of commodities covering more than 90 per cent of trade values, and (b) not allowing a specific sector as a whole to be excluded from the liberalization list. This policy discipline is not consistent with standard economic arguments in a number of senses, but allowing incomplete coverage of liberalization must be particularly criticized. Loose discipline under "the enabling clause" should also be warned against in this context.

4.4 FURTHER ACTIVATING INTERNATIONAL PRODUCTION/DISTRIBUTION NETWORKS

Another important element of an East Asian FTA must be policy measures to further activate international production/distribution networks. The restriction of import-substituting industries, discussed in the last section, is a common policy agenda to FTAs in other parts of the world. On the other hand, elements that affect export-oriented industries are special for an East Asian FTA at this moment in time.

Although the sophisticated international production/distribution networks in East Asia have steadily developed, there is considerable room for improving the policy environment in order to further activate them. The current business environment in East Asia is far from borderless. In the Southeast Asian countries, in particular, cross-border transactions are accompanied with substantial frictions, and markets are segmented. How to reduce two kinds of service link costs as well as how to enhance location advantages and "de-internalization" advantages are urgent issues in the policy agenda for the East Asian countries.

There are four tiers of contents that should be included in an East Asian FTA in order to stimulate these networks. The first tier is of course trade/FDI liberalization. However, it is not enough to liberalize trade and FDI. Because of tariff reductions for electronic products and the duty drawback system, export-oriented firms are not paying large tariffs anymore. Trade protection is not a prime problem for them. That is why we need other tiers of contents.

The second tier is trade/FDI facilitation. The Japan Business Council for Trade and Investment Facilitation annually conducts a questionnaire survey of Japanese firms and compiles an extensive list of issues and requests relating to foreign trade and investment.[7] From this a considerable number of complaints and requests related to trade/FDI facilitation can be found. APEC has vigorously studied trade facilitation, and a lot can certainly be learned from their efforts. The establishment of an issue-solving ombudsman system would also be included in the agenda.

The third tier is institution building to improve the business environment. This includes (a) the harmonization/convergence of standards related to sanitary and phytosanitary measures (SPS), technical barriers to trade (TBT), and the environment, (b) the construction of a legal framework as well as the mechanics for the implementation of intellectual property rights, (c) the establishment of investment rules, and (d) the improvement of the dispute settlement mechanism. Some of them require substantial capacity building on the side of developing countries and may thus take time. However, the conclusion of FTAs could be a good starting point, involving explicit commitments.

The fourth tier is economic cooperation. Because East Asia includes countries at various income levels and at different development stages, economic cooperation, though it should be on the basis of equal-footing cooperation in a way, can be a good catalyst for deeper integration. Financial and technical support for constructing economic infrastructure is still needed, particularly for the ASEAN latecomers. Cooperation in various kinds of human resource development and capacity building is effective in most of the countries in the region. These elements can be incorporated in FTAs.

Most of the measures listed in the second, third, and fourth tiers cannot easily be handled by the WTO-based negotiations, but FTAs have an advantage in being able to take care of them due to a more certain strength of commitment. In addition, these measures mostly benefit everybody on a nondiscriminatory basis, rather than generating a new dimension of discrimination. By incorporating these elements in the scheme of FTAs, East Asia can present a new model of economic integration.

4.5 CONCLUDING REMARKS: CAN JAPAN WORK?

There are various views and evaluations on the current situation of Japan in relation to FTAs. Although some stress the fortress of vested interest, particularly in agriculture, we believe that the multi-layered approach in external economic policies has steadily gained support by the public. The experience of concluding FTAs with Singapore and Mexico has yielded a precious learning effect. The framework of a Japan-ASEAN Economic Partnership was addressed in the AEM-METI meeting, and serious official negotiations on bilateral FTAs has started with Korea, Thailand, the Philippines, and Malaysia since early 2004. Among these the FTA with the Philippines was announced to have been almost completed in November 2004.

The protection of agriculture and its related products is a big problem. However, in the opinion of the authors, concluding FTAs cannot be an icebreaker because FTAs require the trade liberalization of just a small subset of agriculture-related products. Opening to trade for these products may certainly provide some stimulus but is not likely to trigger the overall reform of agricultural policy. Substantial reform must wait for the WTO's agricultural negotiation where Japan has to make a serious commitment. On the other hand, agriculture may not become a crucial stumbling block to concluding FTAs with most countries. The Ministry of Agriculture, Forestry, and Fishery (MAFF) is at least ready for preparing some decent liberalization of agriculture-related products in order to at least clear the 90 per cent rule.

Agriculture now generates just 1 per cent plus of Japanese GDP and thus is in a sense a small problem. On the other hand, further activating international production/distribution networks will yield a substantial impact on the Japanese economy. Global commitment of corporate firms has been, and will be, an essential boost for economic reform in Japan. Not only for the sake of development of the East Asian economy but also on behalf of the Japanese economy itself, the energy of Asian economic dynamism is important. The authors hope that Japan and other East Asian countries will take the opportunity to further upgrade their economic integration.

NOTES

1 The original version of this chapter was presented at the third APEF International Conference on "New East Asian Regionalism: Perspectives from Individual Countries" held at Keio University, Tokyo, Japan on 18-20 September, 2003. We would like to thank constructive discussion.

2 The contents of this section are drawn from a series of the authors' recent research including Ando and Kimura (2004) and Kimura and Ando (2003, 2004).

3 As for the fragmentation theory, see Jones and Kierzkowski (1990), Arndt and Kierzkowski (2001), Deardorff (2001a, 2001b), and Cheng and Kierzkowski (2001).

4 See Kimura and Ando (2004) in detail.

5 Machinery is defined here as HS 84-92; i.e., general machinery, electric machinery, transport equipment, and precision machinery.

6 We present here the cases of China, Indonesia, and Japan as examples. Please see Ando (2004) for the full version of the table.

7 See http://www.jmcti.org/mondai/top_e.html.

REFERENCES

Ando, Mitsuyo and Antoni Estevadeordal (2003), "Trade policy formation in Latin America and Asia-Pacific: a comparative analysis". presented at the LAEBA Panel at the FIEALC Meeting "Globalization in Asia and Latin America: trade, investment and finance", held in Osaka, Japan on 24 September, 2003.

Ando, Mitsuyo and Fukunari Kimura (2004), The formation of international production and distribution networks in East Asia in T. Ito and A. Rose (eds), *International Trade (NBER-East Asia Seminar on Economics, Volume 14)*, Chicago: The University of Chicago Press.

Ando, Mitsuyo (2004), "Fragmentation and vertical intra-industry trade in East Asia". The former version was presented at the Western Economic Association International, 79th Annual Conference.

Arndt, S. W. and H. Kierzkowski (2001), *Fragmentation: New Production Patterns in the World Economy*, Oxford: Oxford University Press.

Cheng, Leonard K. and Henryk Kierzkowski (2001), *Global Production and Trade in East Asia* Boston: Kluwer Academic Publishers.

Deardorff, A. V. (2001a), "Fragmentation in simple trade models". *North American Journal of Economics and Finance*, 12 121-37.

Deardorff, Alan V. (2001b), "Fragmentation across Cones." in Sven W. Arndt and Henryk Kierzkowski, (eds), *Fragmentation: New Production Patterns in the World Economy*, Oxford: Oxford University Press.

Fujita, Masahisa, Paul Krugman and Anthony J. Venables (1999), *The Spatial Economy: Cities, Regions, and International Trade*. Cambridge: The MIT Press.

Jones, R. W. and Henryk Kierzkowski (1990), "The role of services in production and international trade: a theoretical framework", in Ronald W. Jones and Anne O. Krueger (eds), *The Political Economy of International Trade: Essays in Honor of Robert E. Baldwin*, Oxford, Basil Blackwell.

Kimura, Fukunari. (1998), "Japanese multinationals and regional integration in Asia". in Kiichiro Fukasaku, Fukunari Kimura and Shujiro Urata, (eds), *Asia and Europe: Beyond Competing Regionalism*. Brighton: Sussex Academic Press.

Kimura, Fukunari and Mitsuyo Ando (2003), "Fragmentation and agglomeration matter: Japanese multinationals in Latin America and East Asia". *North American Journal of Economics and Finance*, 14(3), 287-317.

Kimura, Fukunari and Mitsuyo Ando (2004), "Two-dimensional fragmentation in East Asia: conceptual framework and empirics". Forthcoming in the special issue of *International Review of Economics and Finance*.

Krugman, Paul. (1991) "Increasing Returns and Economic Geography." *Journal of Political Economy 99*, 183-99.

Krugman, Paul (1995), *Development, Geography, and Economic Theory*. Cambridge: The MIT Press.

World Bank (1993), *The East Asia Economic Miracle: Economic Growth and Public Policy,* Oxford: Oxford University Press.

5. Regional Trade Agreements and their Effect on Non Member Exports and Production[1]

Ryuhei Wakasugi and Kazuhiko Itoh

5.1 INTRODUCTION

The rapid expansion of regional trade agreements (RTAs) has been a major trend in international trade over the past ten years. In 2001, 239 RTAs were notified to the secretariat of the WTO. Several RTAs that had been reported before the establishment of the WTO were, in fact, inactive. Over 100 of these were reported after the establishment of the WTO. Thus, RTAs were actually formed only over the past ten years. The total trade volume of RTA member countries is more than 60 per cent of the volume of international trade. For example, the following are the percentage shares of world exports for the year 2000 of various RTAs: the EU, 35 per cent; NAFTA, 19 per cent; and AFTA, 7 per cent. While the percentages of world imports for the year 2000 of the same RTAs are: the EU, 36 per cent; NAFTA, 25 per cent; and AFTA, 6 per cent. The formation of RTAs is certainly becoming a worldwide trend. The countries that did not participate in RTAs in the year 2000 were China, Taiwan, the Republic of Korea, Japan, and a few other countries. The increase in RTAs is promoted by countries that realize the inadequate functioning of the existing GATT/WTO framework despite the growth of borderless economic activities in the global market. They demand further liberalization of trade and investment in the international market and form RTAs to supplement the inadequate functioning of the GATT/WTO.

In spite of this worldwide trend, to this day Japan has not participated in RTAs. Several reasons are cited for Japan's policy. There were only a few trade partners in the neighbourhood that wanted to form RTAs with Japan. Japan took a policy stance to give greater priority to the multilateral trading system based on the GATT/WTO than to bilateral trade liberalization. The participation in RTAs needs the liberalization of trade in not only the manufactured sector but also the agricultural sector, which is the most politically difficult issue in Japan. The Japanese government has not taken a positive attitude to participation in RTAs, since the liberalization of the agricultural sector has not been undertaken so far. Instead of an RTA Japan has participated in APEC, which is based on the concept of "open regionalism". Although APEC appears similar to an RTA, it is completely different from an RTA which imposes liberalization onto its participants. The possibility of executing the liberalization plan included in the Bogor Declaration of the APEC summit meeting in 1994, seems to be very low. Recently, confidence on the liberalization plan in APEC has been rapidly diminishing in Japan. The formation of RTAs are more binding than APEC in reaching a consensus.

Economic and political interests are both important factors in the formation of an RTA. For example, the EU has its roots in the European Coal and Steel Community (ECSC), which was founded for the reconstruction of the European economy after World War II. It went on to become the EEC, and has finally developed into the current group of 25 member countries. It has recently expanded its scope to include Central and Eastern European countries. Its development is supported by the political will to build a unified Europe. MERCOSUR had a political intention to make South America both economically and politically independent. The purpose of the East Asian Economic Community (EAEC) was also to demonstrate political collaboration in East Asia.

The discussion of RTAs in Japan, however, is conducted more on the basis of economic interests than political intent. Such a lack of political intent in the formation of RTAs in Japan makes it remarkably different from other countries. In Japan, forming regional economic zones based on political intention was even regarded as a taboo at one time. This is a legacy from the experiences of World War II.

The Japanese business community strongly supports the formation of RTAs with countries in East Asia and Mexico. For example, in Mexico, a NAFTA member country, several Japanese affiliate firms operate their plants for production of commodities to be exported to NAFTA member countries. If Japan does not form an RTA with Mexico while Mexico forms an RTA with other countries, these countries will have an advantage over Japanese exporters to Mexico. This will serve as a motivating factor for Japan to form an RTA with Mexico. The Chinese initiative to form an RTA with ASEAN has compounded the need for Japan to do the same. The formation of an RTA between China and ASEAN is easier than that between ASEAN and Japan, since both ASEAN member countries and China are developing countries and can form an RTA under the conditions of GATT articles that are less stringent than Article XXIV. Consequently, the Japanese business community is seriously concerned that Japan's exclusion from RTAs in East Asia will undermine its opportunity to export to new RTA member countries in East Asia.

GATT Article XXIV does not prohibit the formation of a customs union and a free-trade area if it neither raises barriers to trade between countries within such territories, nor makes the duties and other regulations on trade between countries within the territories and other countries higher or more restrictive than the corresponding duties and other regulations existing in the same territories prior to the formation of the customs union and the free-trade area. Article XXIV provides only the legal procedure and does not present welfare implications so clearly. Kemp and Wan (1976) presented the conditions of a customs union that are consistent with Article XXIV if it raises the economic welfare of the member countries of the customs union, without undermining the welfare of non-member countries. This proposition is called the Kemp-Wan Theorem which states that "there exists a common tariff vector and a system of lump-sum compensatory payments, involving only members of the union, such that there is an associated tariff-ridden competitive equilibrium in which each individual, whether a member of the union or not, is not worse off than before the formation of the union". As a condition to satisfy welfare improvement after the formation of a customs union, Kemp and Wan (1976) point to whether the trade volume of the member countries in the customs union with other countries remains at the same level prior to the establishment of the customs union once having properly adjusted for a common tariff on imports from other countries.

Ohyama (1999, 2002, 2003) extends the welfare comparison criterion of the customs union to the partial free-trade area, within which the tariff on some industries is abolished but the tariff on other industries still remains. Ohyama (1999, 2002, 2003) presents, as a proposition, the conditions for forming a partial free-trade area so as to raise the welfare of member countries without undermining the welfare of non-member countries. His proposition preserves the condition that the trade volume of every commodity of the member countries in the free-trade area with other countries remains at the same level prior to the establishment of the free-trade area by properly adjusting the tariff of each member country on imports from other countries, and that the trade volume of the tariff-imposed commodities of the member countries in the free-trade area with other member countries remains at the same level prior to the establishment of the free-trade area by properly adjusting the tariff of each member country in the free-trade area. If an RTA always causes negative effects on the trade volume of non-member countries, and if the conditions presented by the Kemp-Wan Theorem and Ohyama's Proposition are not satisfied, the RTA will be thought to be inconsistent with GATT Article XXIV. We must be cautious in forming inconsistent RTAs even though it may bring a positive effect to the economies and trade of member countries. In this sense, Ohyama's Proposition provides empirical studies with an analytical foundation to judge those RTAs that will be permissible.

The main purpose of this chapter is to empirically investigate whether currently established RTAs are inconsistent with the conditions presented by Ohyama's Proposition. In the next section we introduce a methodology for estimation. The third section presents the data used for the estimation and the results. The fourth section shows the effects of RTAs on the foreign production of Japanese firms. Finally, in section 5, we present some concluding remarks.

5.2 RTAs AND THE TRADE FLOW OF NON MEMBER COUNTRIES

Analytical Framework

A simple partial economic analysis of an RTA reveals its positive effects on member countries and negative effects on countries excluded from the RTA. We can also currently observe a considerable number of economic estimations based on computable general equilibrium analysis, concluding that an RTA has positive effects on the economies of member countries but negative effects on those of non-member countries.[2] These discussions do not provide evidence on how an RTA actually affects the trade of non-member countries.

It is not easy to estimate numerically whether the formation of an RTA will actually be disadvantageous to the trade volume of non-RTA member countries in a consistent way based on the Kemp-Wan Theorem and Ohyama's Proposition, because an RTA would have caused the dynamic development of their economies through market expansion, technological innovation and so on. The expansion of trade and the economy, the realization of economies of scale in production, and the encouragement of competition in the markets of member countries caused by the establishment of an RTA, will have both direct and indirect effects on international trade. The expansionary effect on the market of member countries will increase exports from non-member countries to member countries. Consequently, the indirect trade expansion effect on non-member countries may balance out the direct negative effects of an RTA on them, and may ultimately result in net positive effects.

Even if, including such dynamic effects, the trade volume of non-member countries is reduced after the formation of the RTA, such an RTA will be inconsistent with GATT Article XXIV and harmful to world welfare. In other words an increase or equivalence of trade volume of non-member countries with member countries after the formation of an RTA is a necessary condition for approving its formation, although it is not a sufficient condition. The purpose of this analysis is to empirically examine how the trade flow and foreign production of Japan, as a non-RTA member country, are affected by the participation of its trade partners in an RTA.

In order to identify the effect of an RTA, we must normalize the trade volume between the two countries. The effect of an RTA is estimated by how much the trade volume of the non-member countries with the member countries deviates from the normalized trade volume between non-member and member countries. To identify the effect of an RTA after normalizing the trade volume between two countries, we use the gravity equation to determine the trade volume between the two countries. The analytical framework for statistical investigation is as follows.

We examine the bilateral flow of trade between two countries: country i and country j. Country i is a non-RTA member country and country j is an RTA member country. It is assumed that the volume of bilateral trade flow across the two countries is determined by the gravity model equation, shown by Equation (5.1):

$$EX_{ij} = \alpha_0 Y_i^{\alpha_1} PY_i^{\alpha_2} Y_j^{\alpha_3} PY_j^{\alpha_4} D_{ij}^{\alpha_5} A_{ij}^{\alpha_6} \varepsilon_{ij} \qquad (5.1)$$

where EX_{ij} is the volume of exports from country i to country j; Y_i and Y_j are the real GDPs of country i and country j, respectively; PY_i and PY_j are the real per capita GDPs of country i and country j, respectively; D_{ij} is the geographical distance between the capitals of country i and country j; and A_{ij} refers to other factors that either aid or restrict trade between country i and country j. The theoretical foundations of the gravity equation have been provided in Anderson (1979), Bergstrand (1985, 1989), and Helpman and Krugman (1985). The gravity equation is a reduced form of a partial equilibrium subsystem of a general equilibrium trade model with nationally differentiated products.

Equation (5.1) shows that the volume of trade between two countries is determined by Y_i, PY_i, Y_j, PY_j, and D_{ij}, provided no country-specific factors are operating. If there are pairs of country-specific factors after controlling the trade flow by Y_i, PY_i, Y_j, PY_j, and D_{ij}, they are included in A_{ij}. For example, the variable A_{ij} varies according to whether country j, as a trade partner of country i, is an RTA member country. If membership of an RTA has a significant effect on the trade flow between two countries, the estimated coefficient of A_{ij}, that is α_6, is not zero.

Effects of Participation in an RTA on Japanese Trade

A simple way to examine the effects of RTAs on the exports of a non-member country, such as Japan, is to estimate how the trade flow has been distorted by the participation of its trade partners in RTAs. In estimating the coefficient of the explanatory variable, A_{ij}, we use a dummy variable that yields a value of one in the case where country j participates in RTAs and yields the value of zero in other cases. In this study, we adapt the specification by indexing Japan as the source country i so as to examine the bilateral trade flow from the perspective of Japan. The equation for estimation is specified as follows:

$$\begin{aligned} \ln EX_{ijt} &= \alpha_0 + \alpha_1 \ln Y_{jt} + \alpha_2 \ln PY_{jt} + \alpha_3 D_{ij} \\ &+ \alpha_{4,1} DUM1_{jt} + \alpha_{4,2} DUM2_{jt} + \alpha_{4,3} DUM3_{jt} + \alpha_{4,4} DUM4_{jt} + \varepsilon_{ijt} \end{aligned} \tag{5.2}$$

where j represents the indices of country i's trade partners, and t represents the year. We will assume the following dummy variables:

$$DUM1_{jt} = \begin{cases} 1: \text{if country } j \text{ is a member of NAFTA at } t \text{ year} \\ 0: \text{otherwise} \end{cases}$$

$$DUM2_{jt} = \begin{cases} 1: \text{if country } j \text{ is a member of EU at } t \text{ year} \\ 0: \text{otherwise} \end{cases}$$

$$DUM3_{jt} = \begin{cases} 1: \text{if country } j \text{ is a member of AFTA at } t \text{ year} \\ 0: \text{otherwise} \end{cases}$$

$$DUM4_{jt} = \begin{cases} 1: \text{if country } j \text{ is a member of MERCOSUR at } t \text{ year} \\ 0: \text{otherwise} \end{cases}$$

In Equation (5.2), with regard to the values of the coefficients, we expect:

(i) The sign of the coefficients, $\alpha_{4,1}, \alpha_{4,2}, \alpha_{4,3}, \alpha_{4,4}$, will be positive if the RTA causes trade expansionary effects on the trade flow from country i to member countries. The sign of the coefficients will be negative if the RTA has negative effects on country i's trade with the member countries.

(ii) The estimated values of coefficients $\alpha_{4,1}, \alpha_{4,2}, \alpha_{4,3}, \alpha_{4,4}$ represent the magnitude of the trade expansionary or reduction effects. For example, $\alpha_{4,1} > \alpha_{4,2} > \alpha_{4,3} > \alpha_{4,4}$ means that NAFTA has the largest expansionary effects on the trade of country i. The EU is ranked second, AFTA third, and MERCOSUR has the lowest expansionary effects, or may have negative effects on the trade of country i.

Effects on Trade Volume

In this section, we investigate the different changes in the trade flow among RTA member countries, such as the member countries of NAFTA, EU, AFTA, and MERCOSUR, and the trade flow between RTA member and non-member countries. In particular the export effect on a non-member, country i, that is the volume of Japanese exports, to country j. We adapt the specification by indexing Japan in the same way as Equation (5.2). Equation (5.3) is used for this estimation:

$$\begin{aligned} \ln EX_{ijt} &= \alpha_0 + \alpha_1 \ln Y_{jt} + \alpha_2 \ln PY_{jt} + \alpha_3 D_{ij} \\ &+ \alpha_{4,1} DUM1_{jt} * \ln EXP_{jt,NAFTA} + \alpha_{4,2} DUM2_{jt} * \ln EXP_{jt,EU} \qquad (5.3) \\ &+ \alpha_{4,3} DUM3_{jt} * \ln EXP_{jt,AFTA} + \alpha_{4,4} DUM4_{jt} * \ln EXP_{jt,MERCOSUR} \\ &+ \alpha_5 EXROW_{jt} + \varepsilon_{ijt} \end{aligned}$$

where $EXP_{jt,NAFTA}$ is the export flow from country j to all the NAFTA member countries at t year, $EXP_{jt,EU}$ is the export flow from country j to all the EU member countries at t year, $EXP_{jt,AFTA}$ is the export flow from country j to all the AFTA member countries at t year, and $EXP_{jt,MERCOSUR}$ is the export flow from country j to all the MERCOSUR member countries at t year. $EXROW_{jt}$ is the export flow from country j to all the non-member countries except country i at t year. From Equation (5.3), we can obtain the following:

$$\alpha_{4,m} = \frac{\partial \ln EX_{ijt}}{\partial \ln EXP_{jt,m}}, \; m = NAFTA, EU, AFTA, MERCOSUR$$

$$\alpha_5 = \frac{\partial \ln EX_{ijt}}{\partial \ln EXROW_{jt}}$$

In the above equations the estimated value of elasticity $\alpha_{4,m}$ represents the percentage change in export flow from country i to country j induced by a one per cent change in exports from country j to other RTA member countries, in which country j participates. The estimated value of elasticity α_5 represents the percentage change in export flow from country i to country j induced by a one per cent change in exports from country j to non-RTA member countries. With regard to the values of elasticity, $\alpha_{4,m}$ and α_5, we expect the following:

(i) If $\alpha_{4,m}$ is positive the RTA has dynamic and expansionary effects on the trade flow of country i.

(ii) If α_5 is greater than $\alpha_{4,m}$ the trade flow from country i to country j is induced by more from the development of trade of country j with non-RTA member countries, than by the development of trade of country j with RTA member countries.

5.3 DATA AND ESTIMATION RESULTS

We estimate the coefficients of Equations (5.2) and (5.3) by specifying country i to be Japan. Then, the dependent variable, EX_{ijt}, represents the trade flow from Japan to foreign countries. The data on Japanese exports is based on the customs clearance statistics of the Japanese Ministry of Finance. Y_j is the real GDP of country j. YP_j is the real per capita GDP of country j. The GDP data source is the World Bank's "World Development Indicators". D_{ij} represents the geographical distance between Tokyo and the capital of country j. EXP_j is the export flow from country j to RTA member countries. $EXROW_j$ is the export flow from country j to all non-RTA member countries except Japan. Both these statistics are obtained from the "Direction of Trade Statistics" produced by the IMF.

The estimation is conducted using trade statistics between Japan and its major trade partners, consisting of 59 countries, from 1989 to 2000, by two methods: the ordinary least-squares method and by panel data analysis.[3] The results of the estimations are shown in Table 5.1.

The results are summarized as follows:

(1) The trade flow volume is positively correlated with the size and level of per capita income of the importing country, but is negatively correlated with the geographical distance between the two countries. The estimated coefficients of three explanatory variables all have a high level of statistical significance. This result is, apparently, consistent with the theoretical foundation of the gravity equation.

(2) With regard to the coefficients of the dummy variables of the RTAs, NAFTA and AFTA, these are positive and have a high level of statistical significance. This shows that, after being controlled by the fundamental variables of the gravity equation, Japanese exports to NAFTA and AFTA member countries are larger than its exports to other countries. Therefore, with regard to Japanese trade with NAFTA and AFTA member countries, these RTAs did not negatively affect Japanese exports to these countries; instead, their effect was positive.

(3) The coefficients of the dummy variables for the EU and MERCOSUR are negative. The former shows a high level of statistical significance although the latter shows statistical insignificance after being controlled by the fundamental variables of the gravity equation.

(4) The effect of trade flow of RTA member countries on Japanese exports indicates the elasticity representing the percentage change in export flow from Japan to foreign countries induced by a one percent change in exports of an RTA member country j, to other RTA member countries. The values of the export flow of NAFTA and AFTA are positive and statistically significant. The elasticity of exports among AFTA member countries, in particular, is larger than the elasticity of exports among NAFTA member countries.

(5) The elasticity of exports to EU and MERCOSUR member countries is not statistically significant.

(6) The elasticity representing the percentage change in export flow from Japan to a trade partner that is induced by a one per cent change in exports from the trade partner to non-RTA member countries, is computed to be about 0.5 and is statistically significant. The figure is larger than any other effect of exports to RTA member countries.

Table 5.1 Estimation of the effects of RTAs on Japanese exports

	Estimation 1 (1989-2000)			Estimation 2 (1989-2000)		
	OLS	Fixed Effects	Random Effects	OLS	Fixed Effects	Random Effects
GDP of trade	0.7735**	0.7722**	0.7731**	0.3498**	0.3090**	0.3345**
partners	(27.6029)	(27.4492)	(27.8693)	(6.6870)	(5.8113)	(6.3778)
Per capita	0.2922**	0.2933**	0.2926**	0.1860**	0.1787**	0.1833**
GDP of trade partner	(9.2486)	(9.2506)	(9.3565)	(6.0277)	(5.8120)	(5.9704)
Distance	-0.9480**	-0.9449**	-0.9435	-0.8122**	-0.8130**	-0.8125**
from Japan	(-12.1980)	(-12.1733)	-(12.3298)	(-11.168)	(-11.2407)	(-11.2378)
NAFTA	0.4903*	0.5594*	0.5131*			
Dummy	(1.9879)	(2.2226)	(2.0902)			
EU Dummy	-0.4387**	-0.4175	-0.4318			
	(-3.7690)	(-3.5444)	(-3.7373)			
AFTA	1.0161**	1.0797**	1.0372**			
Dummy	(6.7079)	(6.8762)	(6.8426)			
MERCOSUR	-0.3668	-0.2961	-0.3464			
Dummy	(-1.6186)	(-1.2693)	(-1.5191)			
Exports to				0.0951**	0.1144**	0.1024**
NAFTA Countries				(4.7469)	(5.5770)	(5.0841)
Exports to				0.0019	0.0105	0.0051
EU Countries				(0.1734)	(0.9696)	(0.4783)
Exports to				0.1268**	0.1414**	0.1323**
AFTA Countries				(7.6540)	(8.3823)	(7.9630)
Exports to				0.0058	0.0339	0.0164
MERCOSUR Countries				(0.2134)	(1.2091)	(0.5982)
Exports to				0.4701**	0.5103**	0.4852**
Other Countries than RTAs				(9.2915)	(9.9038)	(9.5980)
Constant	4.2930**		4.2962**	4.2981**		4.3405
	(5.4437)		(5.4985)	(5.8564)		(5.9408)
Adjusted R^2	0.7374	0.7360	0.7376	0.7732	0.7759	0.7731
Sample Size (N=59, T=12)	708	708	708	708	708	708
Hausman test of HO:RE vs FE CHISQ			1.2741			11.2300
P value			0.9891			0.1890

Notes: Figures in parentheses are t values; * and ** indicate 5 per cent and 1 per cent statistical significance, respectively.

These results can be interpreted as follows: the formation of these RTAs did not necessarily affect trade between Japan and these member countries negatively. The formation of NAFTA and AFTA affected exports from Japan to these member countries positively. Furthermore, it must be noted that the growth in Japanese exports is caused more substantially by trade expansion between member and non-RTA member countries than by trade expansion among member countries. Japan has benefited more from worldwide trade expansion than from the regional trade expansion among member countries of RTAs. Thus, global, rather than regional, trade liberalization is indispensable to the export growth of non-RTA member countries like Japan.

5.4 EFFECT OF RTAs ON FOREIGN PRODUCTION OF JAPANESE FIRMS

Model for Estimation

It can be assumed that the foreign production of country i 's firms in country j, the host country, is a result of vertical fragmentation of the production process and is a substitute for the exports from country i to country j.[4] Thus, the production in country j by the subsidiaries of country i is regarded as a substitute for their exports. This assumption enables us to use the gravity equation to determine the volume of foreign production in the same way as the trade flow. The production in the host country j by country i's firms is expressed by equation (5.4) as follows:

$$LP_{ij} = \alpha_0 Y_i^{\beta_1} PY_i^{\beta_2} Y_j^{\beta_3} PY_j^{\beta_4} D_{ij}^{\beta_5} A_{ij}^{\beta_6} \varepsilon_{ij} \qquad (5.4)$$

where LP_{ij} is the volume of the production in country j by country i's firms.

The effects of RTAs on foreign production will be estimated, based on Equation (5.5), in the same way as its effects on trade. Here, we adapt the specification by indexing Japan as the source country i so as to examine the effects on the foreign production of Japanese affiliates.

$$\begin{aligned} \ln LP_{ijt} &= \beta_0 + \beta_1 \ln Y_{jt} + \beta_2 \ln PY_{jt} + \beta_3 D_{ij} \\ &+ \beta_{4,1} DUM1_{jt} + \beta_{4,2} DUM2_{jt} + \beta_{4,3} DUM3_{jt} + \beta_{4,4} DUM4_{jt} + \varepsilon_{ijt} \end{aligned} \qquad (5.5)$$

Where, j represents the indices of country i' s trade partners, and t represents the year. We will define the dummy variables as follows:

$$DUM1_{jt} = \begin{cases} 1: \textit{if country } j \textit{ is a member of NAFTA at } t \textit{ year} \\ 0: \textit{otherwise} \end{cases}$$

$$DUM2_{jt} = \begin{cases} 1: \textit{if country } j \textit{ is a member of EU at } t \textit{ year} \\ 0: \textit{otherwise} \end{cases}$$

$$DUM3_{jt} = \begin{cases} 1: \textit{if country } j \textit{ is a member of AFTA at } t \textit{ year} \\ 0: \textit{otherwise} \end{cases}$$

$$DUM4_{jt} = \begin{cases} 1: \textit{if country } j \textit{ is a member of MERCOSUR at } t \textit{ year} \\ 0: \textit{otherwise} \end{cases}$$

We can expect the value of the estimated coefficients to be as follows:

(i) The estimated value of the coefficients, $\beta_{4,1}, \beta_{4,2}, \beta_{4,3}, \beta_{4,4}$, will be positive if RTAs have expansionary effects on the foreign production of country i. The value will be negative if RTAs have negative effects on the foreign production of country i.

(ii) The estimated values of the coefficients represent the magnitude of the expansionary or contractionary effects on foreign production. For example, $\beta_{4,1} > \beta_{4,2} > \beta_{4,3} > \beta_{4,4}$ implies that NAFTA has the highest expansionary effect on the foreign production of country i's firms. The EU is ranked second, AFTA is third, and MERCOSUR has the lowest, in fact a negative, effect on foreign production of country i's firms.

Further, we will now examine differences in the trade flow among RTA member countries and that between RTA member and non-member countries excluding country i, and the effect on the production of non-member country i's firms in country j. We compare how the RTAs affect the production in country j differently among NAFTA, EU, AFTA and MERCOSUR. Equation (5.6) is used for the estimation:

$$\begin{aligned} \ln LP_{ijt} = {} & \beta_0 + \beta_1 \ln Y_{jt} + \beta_2 \ln PY_{jt} + \beta_3 D_{ij} \\ & + \beta_{4,1} DUM1_{jt} * \ln EXP_{jt,NAFTA} + \beta_{4,2} DUM2_{jt} * \ln EXP_{jt,EU} \\ & + \beta_{4,3} DUM3_{jt} * \ln EXP_{jt,AFTA} + \beta_{4,4} DUM4_{jt} * \ln EXP_{jt,MERCOSUR} \\ & + \beta_5 EXROW_{jt} + \varepsilon_{ijt} \end{aligned} \tag{5.6}$$

where $EXP_{jt,NAFTA}$ is the export flow from country j to all the NAFTA member countries at t year, $EXP_{jt,EU}$ is the export flow from country j to all the EU member countries at t year, $EXP_{jt,AFTA}$ is the export flow from country j to all the AFTA member countries at t year, and $EXP_{jt,MERCOSUR}$ is the export flow from country j to all the MERCOSUR member countries at t year. $EXROW_{jt}$ is the export flow from country j to all non-member countries except country i at t year. From Equation (5.6), we can obtain the following:

$$\beta_{4,m} = \frac{\partial \ln LP_{ijt}}{\partial \ln EXP_{jt,m}}, \; m = NAFTA, EU, AFTA, MERCOSUR$$

$$\beta_5 = \frac{\partial \ln LP_{ijt}}{\partial \ln EXROW_{jt}}$$

From the above equations we can see that the estimated value of elasticity β_4, represents how much of the percentage change of foreign production by country i's firms in country j is induced by a one per cent change in exports from country j to other member countries of the RTA in which country j participates. The estimated value of elasticity β_5, represents how much of the percentage change of foreign production by country i's firms in country j is induced by a one per cent change of exports from country j to non-RTA member countries. With regard to the values of elasticities β_4 and β_5 we expect the following:

(i) If the value of β_4 is positive, it can be inferred that RTAs affect foreign production positively.

(ii) If β_5 is greater than $\beta_{4,m}$, it can be inferred that the production in country j by country i's firms is affected more by the development of trade between country j and non-member countries than by the development of trade between country j and other RTA member countries.

Data and Estimation

Exports from country i and foreign production by its firms are simultaneously determined. Therefore, Equations (5.5) and (5.6) must not be estimated independently, without considering the estimations of Equations (5.2) and (5.3). It is necessary that the effects of RTAs on both trade and foreign production are simultaneously estimated. Here, Seemingly Unrelated Regression (SUR) techniques are used to estimate Equations (5.2) and (5.5), and Equations (5.3) and (5.6), jointly. This method accounts for the simultaneous nature of the two equations.

The dependent variable LX_{ijt} is the volume of production in country j by country i's firms. In this estimation the volume of production of Japanese foreign affiliates is used. The source of this data is from "The Survey of Overseas Business Activities of Japanese Firms", by the Japanese Ministry of Economy, Trade, and Industry. These statistics provide data on the overseas production of Japanese affiliates in 26 countries.[5] The explanatory variables are the same as the variables that appear in the previous section. The estimated results are presented in Table 5.2.

The results are summarized as follows:

(1) The volume of production by Japanese foreign affiliates is positively correlated with the size of the economy and the level of per capita income of the host country. This correlation is highly statistically significant.

(2) Although the geographical distance between the investing and host countries affects negatively the size of foreign production, the degree of its effect is lower than that of the case of bilateral exports.

(3) With regard to the estimation of dummy variables of the RTAs, the coefficients of NAFTA, AFTA and the EU are positive. The coefficient of AFTA only shows a high level of statistical significance. This result shows that, after being controlled by the fundamental variables of the gravity equation, Japanese foreign production in the RTA member countries is not negatively affected by Japan's lack of participation in RTAs.

(4) The effects of the trade flow of RTA member countries on Japanese foreign production in the RTA member country j is shown by the elasticity representing the percentage change in foreign production of Japanese firms in country j induced by a one per cent change in exports from RTA member country j to other RTA member countries. The values are positive in the case of NAFTA and AFTA and statistically significant. The elasticity of exports among AFTA member countries, in particular, is larger than the elasticity of

exports among NAFTA member countries. Trade expansion within AFTA resulted in more foreign production by Japanese firms than did trade expansion within NAFTA.

(5) The estimated values of the elasticity of exports among EU member countries and MERCOSUR are of low statistical significance.

(6) With regard to the elasticity value representing the percentage change in the production of Japanese foreign affiliates induced by a one per cent change in exports of its trade partner to non-RTA member countries, its value is over 0.6. This figure is not only statistically more significant but also larger than any other coefficient presenting the effects of RTAs.

It can be observed that the formation of RTAs positively affected foreign production of Japanese firms in their member countries, and RTAs did not negatively affect their foreign production. The growth in the production of Japanese foreign affiliates, however, is caused more importantly by trade expansion between member and non-RTA member countries than by that amongst member countries. Thus, global trade expansion, rather than regional trade expansion between RTA member countries, is indispensable to the creation of Japanese foreign production.

5.5 CONCLUDING REMARKS

One of the major characteristics of international trade during the 1990s and early 2000s is the expansion of regional trade agreements. To this day Japan has not participated in RTAs except the Japan-Singapore Economic Partnership Agreement. There are several reasons for the low level of development of RTAs between Japan and other countries. There were only a few trade partners in the neighbourhood that wanted to form RTAs with Japan. Japan took a policy stance to give greater priority to the multilateral free trading system based on the GATT/WTO rather than to bilateral trade liberalization. Japan has been giving its policy priority to accomplishing the multilateral free trading system based on the GATT/WTO. On this pretext the trade liberalization based on the bilateral trade agreement has been avoided. This negative attitude toward RTAs in Japan, however, has been disappearing in the 2000s. The Japanese business community is strongly pushing the government of Japan to form RTAs with East Asia, Mexico and other countries.

GATT Article XXIV does not prohibit the formation of a customs union and a free-trade area if it neither raises barriers to trade between countries within such territories, nor makes the duties and other regulations on the trade between countries within the territories and other countries higher or more restrictive than the corresponding duties and other regulations existing in the same territories prior to the formation of the customs union and the free-trade area. As a condition to satisfy welfare improvement after the

Table 5.2 Multivariate regression estimation of the effects of RTAs on Japanese exports and foreign production

	Regression 1	(1992-2000)	Regression 2	(1992-2000)
	EX	LP	EX	LP
GDP of trade partners	0.7109** (18.3056)	0.9833** (13.7705)	0.3160** (4.7316)	0.4086** (3.2087)
Per capita GDP of trade partner	0.2996** (11.7749)	0.5156** (11.0229)	0.1619** (5.6143)	0.3118** (5.6735)
Distance from Japan	-1.1620** (-16.8936)	-0.6347** -(5.0183)	-0.8400** (-10.6070)	-0.1371 (-0.9084)
NAFTA Dummy	0.5194** (3.4128)	0.3858 (1.3788)		
EU Dummy	-0.1881 (-1.7030)	0.2141 (1.0539)		
AFTA Dummy	1.2495** (11.7210)	2.0213** (10.3124)		
MERCOSUR Dummy	-0.4381* (-2.3148)	-0.2982 (-0.8571)		
Exports to NAFTA Countries			0.0759** (6.2258)	0.0762** (5.5770)
Exports to EU Countries			-0.0028 (-0.3232)	0.0318 (1.9548)
Exports to AFTA Countries			0.1063** (9.4087)	0.1770** (8.2162)
Exports to MERCOSUR Countries			-0.0434* (-2.2985)	-0.0307 (-0.8525)
Exports to Other Countries than RTAs			0.4711** (6.7660)	0.6992** (5.2682)
Constant	7.1047** (9.2573)	-2.5072 (-1.7767)	5.4770** (7.3565)	-5.2210** (-3.6787)
R^2	0.7953	0.6586	0.8367	0.7071
Sample Size (N=26, T=9)	234	234	234	234

Notes: Figures in parentheses are t values; * and ** indicate 5 per cent and 1 per cent statistical significance, respectively.

formation of a customs union the Kemp and Wan Theorem points to whether the trade volume of the member countries in the customs union with other countries remains at the same level prior to the establishment of the customs union by properly adjusting the common tariff on imports from other countries. Ohyama's Proposition, as an extension of the Kemp-Wan Theorem, presents the conditions for forming a partial free-trade area that will raise the welfare of member countries without undermining the welfare of non-member countries. They are expressed by the trade volume of the member countries in the free-trade area with other countries remaining at the same level prior to the establishment of the free-trade area, by properly adjusting the tariff of each member country on imports from other countries. If the conditions presented by the Kemp-Wan Theorem and Ohyama's Proposition are not satisfied the RTA will be thought to be inconsistent with GATT Article XXIV. In this sense, Ohyama's Proposition provides empirical studies with an analytical foundation to judge whether an RTA will be permissible.

This study aimed at empirically examining how the bilateral trade flow and the foreign production of a non-RTA member country are affected by the establishment of an RTA, by taking Japan as an example of a non-member country. From the results of the estimation based on the gravity equation, it was observed that the formation of NAFTA and AFTA did not necessarily negatively affect Japan's trade with those member countries. However, the growth in Japanese exports is largely caused by trade expansion between member and non-member countries rather than by trade expansion within member countries. Japan has benefited more from worldwide trade expansion than from regional trade expansion with RTA member countries.

With regard to the production of Japanese affiliates in foreign countries, the estimation results reveal that the formation of NAFTA and AFTA did not negatively affect foreign production of Japanese firms in their member countries. However, the empirical examination shows that growth in the foreign production of Japanese affiliates is largely caused by trade expansion between member and non-RTA member countries rather than by trade expansion within member countries. This means that Japanese foreign production can be attributed mainly to global trade expansion rather than to regional trade expansion within RTA member countries.

These findings reveal that the expansion of trade and the foreign production of Japan have been caused by worldwide trade expansion rather than by regional trade expansion, although RTAs did not necessarily affect Japanese trade and production in foreign countries negatively. Thus, global, rather than regional, trade liberalization is indispensable to the growth of Japanese exports to, and production of, Japanese affiliates in RTA member countries.

These results provide Japanese trade policy with a suggestive conclusion: the pursuit of a multilateral free trading system based on the GATT/WTO is still very important for Japan, although the importance of RTAs is increasing. Japanese trade policy must be formulated on the basis of liberalizing the world trade system within the GATT/WTO framework, as well as deepening the regional free trade system through the introduction of RTAs.

APPENDIX 1: THE LIST OF 59 COUNTRIES AND REGIONS

Argentina, Australia, Austria, Bangladesh, Belgium, Bolivia, Brazil, Bulgaria, Cambodia, Canada, Chile, China, Colombia, Cyprus, Denmark, Finland, France, Germany, Greece, Hong Kong, Hungary, India, Indonesia, Iran, Ireland, Italy, Korea, Laos, Malaysia, Malta, Mexico, Myanmar, Netherlands, New Zealand, Nigeria, Pakistan, Panama, Papua New Guinea, Paraguay, Peru, Philippines, Poland, Portugal, Romania, Saudi Arabia, Singapore, Spain, Sri Lanka, Sweden, Switzerland, Taiwan, Thailand, Turkey, United Kingdom, United States, Uruguay, Venezuela, Vietnam, and Zambia.

APPENDIX 2: THE LIST OF 26 COUNTRIES AND REGIONS

Argentina, Australia, Belgium, Brazil, Canada, China, France, Germany, Hong Kong, India, Indonesia, Italy, Korea, Malaysia, Mexico, Netherlands, New Zealand, Philippines, Singapore, Spain, Switzerland, Thailand, United Kingdom, United States, Vietnam, and Taiwan.

NOTES

1 The authors are grateful for insightful comments on the earlier version of this chapter from the participants of the Third APEF International Conference on "New East Asian Regionalism: Perspectives from Individual Countries" held at Keio University, 19-20 September, 2003. They are also grateful for valuable comments from participants of the Korea International Economic Association Convention held at Yonsei University on 5 December, 2003 and the Odawara Conference of the Keio Economic Association held on 25-27 December, 2003.

2 Tustsumi and Kiyota (2002) provide an analysis of the effects of an RTA on Japan and the world economy. They conducted several types of numerical simulations based on the standard CGE model provided by the Global Trade Analysis Project (GTAP) in order to analyse the changes in economic growth, exports and economic welfare, according to options available for Japanese participation in RTAs. In particular, they focused on three cases; an RTA by ASEAN+3 countries (China, Korea and Japan), an RTA by ASEAN+2 countries (China and Korea, excluding Japan), and an RTA by the United States and Japan. They estimated the difference in the rate of economic growth, the volume of exports, and the level of economic welfare in comparison with the current economy as of the year 2000 as a standard case. The results revealed that the formation of an RTA between ASEAN+3, and the formation of an RTA between the United States and Japan, will result in trade and welfare expansion to the global economy as well as to the economy of Japan. However, the formation of an RTA between ASEAN+2, excluding Japan, will have positive effects on both the global economy and member countries, but negative effects on the rate of economic growth of Japan. Based on these findings, it is suggested that RTAs will expand trade and raise the rate of economic growth of member countries but will have adverse effects on the trade

and economy of non-member countries.

3 A list of these countries is contained in Appendix 1.

4 Smith (2001) also regards the sales of foreign subsidiaries as exports from the foreign country.

5 The sample size is limited to 26 countries by the number of countries covered by the data of the positive production of Japanese affiliates in foreign countries. See the list of countries of Appendix 2.

REFERENCES

Anderson, James E. (1979), "A theoretical foundation for the gravity equation", *American Economic Review, 69*, 106-16.

Bergstrand, Jeffrey H. (1985), "The gravity equation in international trade: some microeconomic foundations and empirical evidence", *The Review of Economics and Statistics, 67*, 474-81.

Bergstrand, Jeffrey H. (1989), "The generalized gravity equation, monopolistic competition, and the factor-proportions theory in international trade", *The Review of Economics and Statistics, 71*, 143-53.

Helpman, Elhanan and Paul R. Krugman (1985), *Market Structure and Foreign Trade: Increasing Returns, Imperfect Competition, and the International Economy*, Cambridge, MA: The MIT Press.

Kemp, Murray C. and Henry Y. Wan (1976), "An elementary proposition concerning the formation of customs union", *Journal of International Economics,* 6, 95-7.

Ohyama, Michihiro (1999), "Economic significance of GATT/WTO rules (in Japanese)", *Keizai-kenkyu, 50,* 1-10.

Ohyama, Michihiro (2002), "Economic significance of GATT/WTO rules", in *Economic Theory and International Trade*, edited by Alan D. Woodland, Cheltenham: Edward Elgar.

Ohyama, Michihiro (2003), "Partial Free Trade Area and Economic Welfare (in Japanese)", a paper presented at the Odawara Conference of the Keio Economic Association.

Smith, Pamela J. (2001), "How do foreign patent rights affect U.S. exports, affiliate sales, and licenses?" *Journal of International Economics, 55*, 411-39.

Tsutsumi Masahiko and Kozo Kiyota (2002), "Effects of Free Trade Agreement on Japanese economy: an analysis based on CGE model (nihon wo meguru jiyuu-boueki-kyoutei no kouka: CGE moderu niyoru bunseki, in Japanese)", *JCER Discussion Paper,* No. 74.

6. Trade Integration in ASEAN: An Application of the Panel Gravity Model

Seyed Komail Tayyebi

6.1 INTRODUCTION

The past few years have seen an improvement in interest and activity in the formation of regional trade blocs (RTBs) in the Asia-Pacific region, mostly in the form of preferential trading arrangements (PTAs). For example, Japan and Singapore signed an Economic Partnership Agreement in February 2002. Japanese policymakers have also proposed a Japan-ASEAN Comprehensive Economic Partnership, and an ASEAN-Peoples Republic of China Free Trade Area was proposed by the Peoples Republic of China (PRC) and endorsed by ASEAN's ten leaders in the organization's ministerial meeting in Brunei in October 2001. These recent events follow more than a decade of increasing numbers of PTAs in the Asia-Pacific region. At present, about 97 per cent of total global trade involves countries that are members of at least one PTA. These developments have resulted in an increased concentration on the role of RTBs, and their important new role in today's global economy.

This chapter aims at developing an empirical investigation of the determinants of export flows, accounting for the presence of effective determinants. We concentrate on ASEAN as an example of an East Asian region, and we test an econometric model with the purpose of disentangling the features that affect the intensity of regional trading flows. In this sense our econometric applications rely on some of the main features belonging to gravity models. A type of "Gravity Model" is specified in this regard, theoretically and empirically, to test the hypothesis of the extent to which trade integration affects the intra-trade flows of ASEAN members and their own volumes of imports and exports. At the same time, we try to improve the technique by extending the range of topics these models may concern. We proceed by taking a first glance at gravity models; we then go beyond the gravity approach.

This chapter is organized as follows. Section 6.2 provides a theoretical discussion on the relationship between globalization and economic integration, while section 6.3 presents some data on economic and social indicators from which the current conditions of ASEAN members can be recognized. To specify an empirical model in accordance with integrating trade in ASEAN, the position of the gravity model in the economic integration literature is first explained in section 6.4, and then the final forms of the model in two different classified trade integrating blocks for ASEAN members are specified in section 6.5. Section 6.6 analyses the results obtained by using Panel Data in the estimation process. Finally, section 6.7 will present some concluding remarks.

6.2 GLOBALIZATION AND ECONOMIC INTEGRATION

Rapid progress in globalization has pushed mostly developing countries to improve their legal systems, currency exchange and convertibility, accounting systems, educational exchanges and other necessary policies, in order to be fully accepted and integrated into the implementation of an RTB (Bryant and Massey 1999). More importantly, as these countries develop infrastructure to deal across borders with their regional trading partners, in many cases they are also putting into place economic and regulatory policies that set the stage for global integration. In addition, multinational corporations, technology and capital flows, will accelerate national liberalization of trade and trans-border labour and capital exchanges. This permits nations to develop global strategies through RTBs.

Accordingly, as globalization touches more and more countries, international institutions and organizations will be required to expand their abilities to handle public policy, regulatory, audit, human welfare and conflict obstacles. Their ability to manage and assist, especially developing countries, in these areas will mean assurance of the countries' long-term participation in the global economy. For these countries to survive and catch up, further economic and humanitarian assistance will be required as a well-executed strategy.

Regionalization: An Introduction to Globalization

The theory of economic integration expresses that countries make efforts to combine trade liberalization strategies with protective policies, to minimize trade restrictions amongst themselves and to collaborate in financial activities. After integration, trade transactions, followed by a decrease in costs and resource reallocation, will result in an increase in products, trade and then economic welfare for members. Economic integration relies upon economic transaction promotion and unification of resources of two or several isolated systems that leads to a rise in the capability of the larger integration system.

Integration moves gradually towards a global reality, so that all countries around the world are trying to omit or reduce trade obstacles in order to finally reach a global regionalization. GATT, and now the WTO, is involved in conjunction with such activities. In fact, regionalization stands for liberalizing economic activities in such areas as trade, investment and financial flows among partners in a region. Therefore, it can be claimed that "regional integration" is an introduction to global integration, or so-called "sub-globalization".

Economic integration comprises various stages so that each stage is more complete than the previous ones, and where more obstacles are removed with respect to the former stages to enable more trade and economic cooperation amongst countries (Gurler, 2000). A "Preferential Trade Arrangement" (PTA) is the most primary sort of economic integration, while an "economic union" is the most complete version in that members coordinate the conduct of monetary and fiscal policies. More specifically, RTBs start at the lowest level of affiliation with the preferential trade arrangement, to a free trade area, a customs union, a common market and economic union, and to complete economic and monetary union. The tighter the union, the more dependent the member countries are ultimately on one another (Nafziger 1997).

As the expansion of integrated RTBs will play a crucial role in the world economy, the future evolution of the WTO and globalization will be closely linked to their development. It is, therefore, important to formulate both private and public policy initiatives that stimulate continued global economic networking and interdependence. In these circumstances, developing countries can be better positioned to ensure regional autonomy and success through smaller regional trading collectives, or sub-blocs.

There are many studies in the literature that have focused, particularly, on the impact of trade regionalization. Soloaga and Winters (1999), for instance, examine "the second wave of regionalism" that began in the early 1990s and led to new PTAs in different blocs. Accordingly, they are concerned with nine PTAs that have been crucially expanded during the last decade. Specifically, in their research, Soloaga and Winters (1999) investigate the effect on trade flows in these trade blocs during the period 1980-86, through estimating and comparing results derived from various trade models before and after this regionalization.

Martinez-Zarzoso and Nowak-Lehmann (2001) conduct an investigation of the main determinants of trade flows between the European Union (EU) and Mercosur members. They use a trade gravity model to explore how specified factors play a role in trade flows during the 1988-96 period. Their results indicate that potential exports for Mercosur would be predicted to increase relatively more than their actual real exports in 1996.

6.3 ASEAN AS AN INTEGRATED BLOC

To recognize the current conditions of ASEAN members, the following subsections explain their economic and social indicators for 2001.

Economic Indicators

Table 6.1 introduces six macroeconomic variables, indicating the different economic situations for the ten members of the block. According to data represented by the table, Indonesia has the highest value for GDP, whereas Laos and Cambodia possess the lowest GDP, respectively. In addition, Myanmar, Singapore and Malaysia have benefited from a high rate of GDP growth, exceeding 8 per cent. In contrast, Brunei and Thailand achieved the lowest GDP growth rate (1 and 1.9 per cent, respectively). All five founding members of ASEAN captured the highest values of trade flows, while most new members, with poorer economic conditions, are in the lowest extreme. Singapore, Malaysia, Indonesia and the Philippines experienced a distinct increase in their imports from the world during the period of the 1970s. For all four, world imports surged in the mid-1980s. They have also increased their imports from regional partners, but at a much slower pace and well before the revival of the ASEAN group in 1991 (World Economic Outlook and World Development Indicators, 1998).

This revival seems to have impacted the various countries differently. Indonesia's ratio of regional to world imports has not changed over a 25-year period, hovering at 8 per cent. At the other extreme the Philippines has increased its ratio of regional to world imports from close to zero to 14 per cent during the same quarter century. Both Malaysia and Singapore's ratios of regional to world imports have also increased dramatically from 10 per cent to 22 and 35 per cent, respectively. The revival of the ASEAN pact seems to coincide closely with this noticeable increase for the Philippines and Singapore. For other members such as Vietnam, Cambodia and Brunei, they share a high rate of trade flows with respect to their GDP, on average 55.5, 54.2 and 51 per cent, respectively. This shows the important role of outward orientation for these countries, enabling them to play an active role in the bloc.

The Philippines has a high share of "*Hi-Technology Exports*" with respect to total exports (70.2 percent), while Malaysia and Singapore are in comparable positions in terms of such exports. Foreign direct investment (FDI) plays an important role in driving the process of globalization, and in this context ASEAN members have had varying experiences. Singapore, Malaysia and Thailand are quite active in FDI, capturing values of about US$8.6, US$3.8 and US$3.8 billion in 2001, respectively. It is evident that Singapore's recent growth has been dependent substantially on the attraction of FDI (Tayyebi and Tavakoli 2000).

Table 6.1 Economic indicators of ASEAN members in 2001

Country	GDP (Billion US$)	GDP (Growth (%))	Exports (Billion US$)	Imports (Billion US$)	Hi-tech. (Exports, % of Manufactured Exports)	FDI (Million US$)
Brunei	4.8	1*	3.73	1.03	9	-
Cambodia	3.4	6.3	1.81	2.08	-	113.1
Indonesia	141.3	3.4	59.8	49.3	13.4	3278
Laos	1.7	5.7	0.41	0.70	-	23.9
Malaysia	88	8.3	98.2	109.8	56.9	3800*
Myanmar	Na	9.7	Na	Na	Na	208.3
Philippines	71.4	3.2	39.2	37.9	70.2	1800
Singapore	91.5**	9.4**	121.73	115.96	59.7	8600
Thailand	115.3	1.9	76.2	68.7	31.1	3800
Vietnam	32.9	6.8	18	18.7	-	1300

Source: World Development Indicators Database, April 2003.
Notes: * This value belongs to 1997.
** These values belong to 2000.

Social Indicators

There are five non-economic variables indicated in Table 6.2, representing a sample of some key social indicators for ASEAN members. This indicates that Indonesia has the largest population among ASEAN members amounting to about 209 million people, while Vietnam is in the second position with about 79.5 million people. In the lowest extreme, about 4.1 and 3.5 million people respectively crowd Singapore and Brunei. The population growth rate in the region ranges between 0.7 and 2.3 percent, with the highest and lowest rates belonging to Thailand and Laos, respectively. One important conclusion is that this bloc of countries, with a total population of about 526 million people, and GDP of about US$1.7 billion, can benefit potentially from a larger regional market for goods and services based upon integrating trade relations.

The tremendous infrastructural progress through telecommunications, information technology (IT) and free-trade practices undoubtedly assist rich and poor countries in the region to link together into an integrated trading bloc. According to Table 6.2, data for personal computers and Internet users indicate adequate instruments of IT, which are available in the region. Thus, the numbers of about 79 personal computers per 1000 people on average and about 18 million Internet users in 2001, points out that the poor ASEAN members can benefit from collaboration with the rich members.

Table 6.2 Social indicators of ASEAN members in 2001

Country	Population (Million)	Population Growth Annual (%)	Personal Computers Per 1000 people	Internet Users Million
Brunei	3.5	1.6	74.6	0.035
Cambodia	12.3	1.8	1.5	0.01
Indonesia	209	1.3	11	4.0
Laos	5.4	2.3	3	0.01
Malaysia	23.8	2.1	126.1	6.5
Myanmar	48.3	1.2	1.1	0.01
Philippines	78.3	2.1	21.7	2.0
Singapore	4.1	0.8	508.3	1.5
Thailand	61.2	0.7	27.8	3.5
Vietnam	79.5	1.2	11.7	1.0

Source: World Development Indicators Database, April 2003.

6.4 THE GRAVITY MODEL IN THE ECONOMIC INTEGRATION LITERATURE

The gravity equation has been derived theoretically through the properties of the Cobb-Douglas function. The assumption of monopolistic competition ensures this condition. In this sense, Anderson (1979) argues that a sufficient condition for obtaining a gravity equation is the assumption of perfect product specialization, which implies that each commodity is produced in just one country.

Tinbergen (1962) and Pöyhönen (1963) were the first authors to apply the gravity equation to analyse international trade flows. Since then the gravity model has become a popular instrument in empirical foreign trade analysis. The model has been successfully applied to flows of varying types such as migration, foreign direct investment, and more specifically to international trade flows. According to this model, exports from country i to country j are explained by their economic sizes (GDP or GNP), their populations, direct geographical distances and a set of dummies incorporating some kind of institutional characteristics common to specific flows.

The traditional basic specification of the gravity model includes supply factors of the export country (population and GDP), demand factors of the import country (population and GDP), and trade supporting and impeding determinants (mostly transport costs or proxies thereof, geographical and cultural measures of bilateral proximity, etc.). Fixed exporter (importer) effects capture the general propensity to export (import) of a country. Fixed time effects account for the business cycle and changes in openness across either all countries or members of a region.

From an analysis of variance (ANOVA) point of view the three orthogonal factors – time, exporter and importer effects – do not span the whole vector space of possible treatments explaining changes in bilateral exports. Possible interactions between the exporter and importer dimensions are removed. It is noted that these effects could either be treated as random or as fixed (Baldwin 1994). The proper treatment of the effects may depend on the data sample and underlying interests. From an econometric point of view it would be unwise to ignore this possible source of interaction if interactions have a significant impact that can be tested (Christensen, 1987).

Moreover, while the exporter (importer) effect measures the general openness of a country with respect to its partner countries included in the sample, the bilateral effect accounts for any time invariant geographical, historical, political, cultural, different language, and other bilateral influences which lead to differences from a country pair's tendency to trade. Since the major part of these effects usually remains unobserved, including bilateral interaction effects is the natural way to control for them.

Theoretical support of the research in this field was originally very poor, but, since the second half of the 1970s, several theoretical developments have appeared in support of the gravity model. Anderson (1979) made the first formal attempt to derive the gravity equation from a model that assumed product differentiation. Bergstrand (1989) has also explored the theoretical determination of bilateral trade in a series of papers, in which gravity equations were associated with simple monopolistic competition models. Helpman and Krugman (1985) used a differentiated product framework with increasing returns to scale to justify the gravity model. More recently, Deardorff (1995) has proven that the gravity equation characterizes many models and can be justified from standard trade theories. The differences in these theories help to explain the various specifications and some diversity in the results of the empirical applications.

There are a large number of empirical applications in the literature of international trade, which have contributed to the improvement of the performance of the gravity equation. Some of them are closely related to our work. First, in recent papers, Mátyás (1997), Cheng and Wall (1999) and Egger (2000) improved the econometric specification of the gravity equation. Second, Bergstrand (1989), Wei, (1996), Soloaga and Winters (1999), Limao and Venables (1999) and Bougheas *et al*. (1999) among others, contributed to the refinement of the explanatory variables considered in the analysis and to the addition of new variables.

According to the generalized gravity model of trade the volume of exports between pairs of countries, Xij, is a function of their incomes (GDPs), their populations, their geographical distance and a set of dummies,

$$X_{ij} = \beta_0 Y^{\beta 1}i\, Y^{\beta 2}j\, N^{\beta 3}i\, Y^{\beta 4}j\, D^{\beta 5}ij\, A^{\beta 6}ij\, uij \qquad (6.1)$$

where Yi (Yj) indicates the GDP of the exporter (importer), Ni (Nj) are populations of the exporter (importer), Dij measures the distance between the two countries' capitals (or economic centres) and Aij represents any other factors aiding or preventing trade between pairs of countries. uij is the error term. An alternative formulation of Equation 6.1 uses per capita income instead of population,

$$X_{ij} = \gamma_0\, Y^{\gamma 1}i\, Y^{\gamma 2}j\, YH^{\gamma 3}i\, YH^{\gamma 4}j\, D^{\gamma 5}ij\, A^{\gamma 6}ij Uij \qquad (6.2)$$

where YHi (YHj) are the exporter (importer) GDPs per capita. The two models above are equivalent and the coefficients are expressed as: $\beta_3 = -\gamma_3$; $\beta_4 = -\gamma_4$; $\beta_1 = \gamma_1 + \gamma_3$; $\beta_2 = \gamma_2 + \gamma_4$. The second specification (Equation 6.2) is usually chosen when the gravity model is applied to estimate bilateral exports for specific products, whereas the specification given by Equation 6.1 is often used to estimate aggregated exports.

For estimation purposes the model given by Equation 6.1, in log-linear form for a single year, is expressed as,

$$Ln\, X_{ij} = \beta 0 + \beta 1\, Ln\, Y_i + \beta 2\, Ln\, Y_j + \beta 3\, Ln\, N_i + \beta 4\, Ln\, N_j + \beta 5\, Ln\, D_{ij} + \textstyle\sum_h \delta h\, Pijh + U_{ij} \qquad (6.3)$$

where *Ln* denotes variables in natural logs. *Pijh* is the sum of preferential trade dummy variables. *Pijh* takes the value one when a certain condition is satisfied (e.g. belonging to a trade bloc), zero otherwise. Generally speaking the gravity model can include dummy variables for trading partners sharing a common language and common border, as well as trading bloc dummy variables evaluating the effects of preferential trading agreements. The coefficients of all these trade variables (δh) are expected to be positive.

A high level of income in the exporting country indicates a high level of production, which increases the availability of goods for export. Therefore, it is expected that β_1 will be positive. The coefficient of Y_j, β_2, is also expected to be positive since a high level of income in the importing country suggests higher imports. The coefficient estimate for population of the exporters, β_3, may be positive or negative depending on whether the country exports less when it is big (absorption effect) or whether a big country exports more than a small country (economies of scale). The coefficient of the importer population, β_4, also has an ambiguous sign for similar reasons. The distance coefficient is expected to be negative since it is a proxy of all possible trade cost sources. Traditionally, the gravity model uses distance to model transport costs. However, Bougheas *et al.* (1999) showed that transport costs are a function not only of distance but also of public infrastructure. They augmented the gravity model by introducing additional infrastructure variables (stock of public capital and length of motorway network). Their model predicts a positive relationship between the level of infrastructure and the volume of trade, which is supported using data from European countries.

6.5 EMPIRICAL MODEL AND ESTIMATION RESULTS

In this section we use an empirical specification of the gravity model denoted by Equation 6.3 to estimate the effects of integration among ASEAN members on the volume of trade flows. Any attempt at estimating this equation, which assumes the intercept ($\beta 0$) is homogeneous for trading-partner pairs, yields biased results. In the following we will demonstrate the fact that the crucial source of the mentioned bias is as a result of failure to apply the Ordinary Least Squares (OLS) method to deal with the heterogeneity among bilateral trade relationships. We will implement this through the F- Leamer test.

Accordingly, one of the solutions to control for heterogeneity is the use of the Panel Data procedure, which allows the intercepts of the gravity equation to be specific to each trading pairs (Cheng and Wall, 1999).

Generally formed the gravity model using Panel Data is as follows:

$$\text{Ln } X_{ijt} = \alpha_0 + \alpha_t + \alpha_{ij} + \beta' W_{ijt} + U_{ijt} \qquad (6.4)$$

$$t=1, 2, 3, \ldots, T \text{ and } W'_{ijt} = [\, W_{it},\, W_{jt}, \ldots]$$

where, X_{ijt} is trade flows between country i and country j in year t, and W'_{ijt} is the 1* k row vector of gravity variables (GDP, population, etc. for both countries i and j). In this model the intercept contains three parts; the first is the same for all years and individuals including country pairs, α_0, the other becomes specific to year t and the same to all individuals, α_t, while the third refers to specific individuals, but the same to all years, α_{ij}. α_{ij}, is the so-called individual effect which is allowed to be different across trading-partner pairs, namely $\alpha_{ij} \neq \alpha_{ji}$.

The estimation results obtained by OLS, therefore, show serious problems of biasness due to the restriction that the country pair intercept terms equal zero (or $\alpha_{ij} = \alpha$). Furthermore, if α_t is used in the model, Panel Data will convert to "Two Way Panel Data", otherwise we will have "One Way Panel Data" (Baltagi, 1995).[1]

The Panel Data procedure consists of three estimation sets; first, Between

Estimates that capture differences between individuals, but ignores any information within them. It is usually used to estimate long-run coefficients (Martinez-Zarzoso and Nowak-Lehmann, 2001). Second, Fixed Effects (FE) estimates in which it is assumed that the slope of the gravity equation is the same for all trading partner pairs, but there are specific intercepts for each of them that would be correlated or uncorrelated with explanatory variables. This procedure is also well known as the Least Squares Dummy Variables (LSDV) method (Hsiao, 1986). The third relies on Random Effects (RE) estimates or the Variance Components method in which there exist intercepts (α_{ij}s), affiliating the same distribution function with average α and variance $\sigma^2\alpha$, that are uncorrelated with the explanatory variables. Since individual effects (α_{ij}) are included in the regressions, we have to decide whether they are treated effectively as fixed or random effects. In order to distinguish between the FE and RE method we investigate through the Hausman Test for the null hypothesis that the explanatory variables and individual effects are uncorrelated. The fixed effects estimates are consistent with both the null and alternative hypotheses, whereas the random effects estimates are only compatible with the null hypothesis. Therefore, the RE method is preferred if the null hypothesis holds, otherwise the FE method will be applicable.

Trade Integration in all ASEAN Members (Case I)

In order to investigate the effects of trade integration on all ASEAN members' trade flows, we use data available for members for the years 1994-2000 to estimate the gravity model specified below. The equation to be estimated explains trade flows between a country i as the exporter and a specific trading partner j , as the importer. It is thus specified as follows in Equation 6.5;

$$\text{Ln } X_{ijt} = \alpha_{ij} + \beta_1 \text{ Ln } Y_{it} + \beta_2 \text{ Ln } Y_{jt} + \beta_3 \text{ Ln } N_{it} + \beta_4 \text{ Ln} N_{jt} + \beta_5\, ASEIntr + \beta_6\, ASEExp + \beta_7\, ASEImp + \beta_8\, Dummy97 + U_{ijt} \qquad (6.5)$$

Where, Ln denotes variables in natural logs, X_{ijt} is the value of trade flows from country i to country j and vice-versa. Y_{it} and Y_{jt} denote exporter and importer's GDP, while N_{it} and N_{jt} show their population volumes, respectively. In principle, a high level of income in the exporting country indicates a high level of production that increases the availability of exportable goods. Therefore, we expect β_1, indicating the income elasticity of the exporter, to be positive. The coefficient of LnY_j, β_2, is also expected to be positive, since a high level of income in the importing country suggests more imports. The estimated coefficient for the exporter's population, β_3, can be negative or positive, which depends somehow on the export policy of a country. The coefficient will be negative in the country if production of exporting goods is under pressure from an internal absorption effect, whereas it is positive for another country that is faced with the conditions of dominant economies of scale, particularly in its production process of exporting goods (Martinez-Zarzoso and Nowak-Lehmann, 2001). For similar reasons the coefficient of the importer's population, β_4, also has an ambiguous sign. *ASEIntra* is a dummy variable, which is an indicator of the extent of trade integration in ASEAN. It takes the value of one as both the exporter and importer are members of ASEAN. The variables *ASEExp* and *ASEImp* represent the degree of openness in the bloc due to exports and imports, respectively. The *ASEExp* dummy variable has a value of one when the exporter is an ASEAN member, but the importer is not. Furthermore, the dummy variable *ASEImp* has a value of one if the importer and exporter are respectively a member and non-member of the bloc. Dummy97 refers to the effects of the Southeast Asia Crisis that happened in mid-1997 and continued to the end of 1998. Therefore, the variable takes a value of one for the years 1997 and 1998, and zero otherwise. It is expected that the crisis may have affected ASEAN's trade flows inversely. U_{ijt} is a normally distributed error term with $E(U_{ijt}) = 0$.

It should be noted that we do not estimate directly the coefficients of the relevant constants of each individual trading partner pair such as geographical distance, contiguity and common languages, which do not change over time. Otherwise they would be collinear with individual effects. Therefore, in order to investigate such determinants on trade flows, we run another regression of individual effects on geographical distance and some dummies in which the respective equation is defined as in Equation 6.6:

$$IE_{ij} = \alpha_o + \alpha_1 D_{ij} + \alpha_2 A_{ij} + \alpha_3 Lang_{ij} + e_i \tag{6.6}$$

where, IE_{ij} stands for individual effects, D_{ij} denotes geographical distance and A_{ij} is a dummy variable taking the value one when two countries share the same border (even water border), and zero otherwise. *Lang* is a dummy variable taking the value of unity as two countries (as a trading partner pair) have a similar language, and zero otherwise.

Trade Integration in the Major Founding ASEAN Members (Case II)

The five major founding ASEAN members, Singapore, Malaysia, Indonesia and the Philippines, have played the major role in conducting economic integration in the bloc. Thus, a new functional form of the gravity model is again specified as follows in Equation 6.7:

$$\begin{aligned} \text{Ln}\, X_{ijt} = {} & \alpha_{ij} + \beta_1 \text{Ln}\, Y_{it} + \beta_2 \text{Ln}\, Y_{jt} + \beta_3 L_{ijt} + \beta_4 \text{Ln}\, Rer_{it} \\ & + \beta_5 \, ASEIntr + U_{ijt} \end{aligned} \tag{6.7}$$

where L_{ijt} depicts the Linder variable implying that the availability of structural dissimilarities of an economy can affect trade relations between countries. As dissimilarities between countries fall, trade flows should go up. In principle the Linder variable is calculated by the following Equation 6.8:

$$L_{ijt} = \text{Ln}\left((Yp_{it} - Yp_{jt})^2\right) \quad (6.8)$$

where, Yp_{it} (Yp_{jt}) is the GDP per-capita of the exporter (importer). The closer the GDP per capita to each other, the larger the value of bilateral trade is likely to be implemented. The coefficient of L_{ijt} is thus expected to be negative. Rer_{it} denotes the real effective exchange rate of an exporter in terms of US dollars, explaining the price effect in the external sectors of countries.

Ultimately, the variable *ASEIntra* is defined here to indicate the integration effect of the five major members on the trade flows of ASEAN. Since *ASEIntra* (from Equation 6.7) does not change over time, its modified version is given by Equation 6.9:

$$\text{ASEIntr} = \text{ASEIntra} * L_{ijt} \quad (6.9)$$

More clearly, the effects of the integration variable on trade flows can be considered as the slope of the Linder variable.

Similarly, as described before, we will estimate Equation 6.10 to examine the effects of geographical distance, contiguity and common language on trade flows:

$$IE_{ij} = \alpha_o + \alpha_1 D_{ij} + \alpha_2 A_{ij} + \alpha_3 Lang_{ij} + e_i \quad (6.10)$$

6.6 ESTIMATION RESULTS

To estimate the models we have collected annual data on bilateral trade flows between the ASEAN members and all other non-members (as major ASEAN members' partnerships) from the IMF's *Direction of Trade Statistics Yearbook* (various years). Furthermore, the World Bank Data Base (Global Development Finance and World Development Indicators, 2003) has been used to provide statistics on GDP, GDP per capita, real effective exchange rate and population by country. Finally, data for geographical distance, contiguity and common market have been collected from Haveman's website, available at:http://www.eiit.org/Trade Resources/ Data/Gravity. Thus, the data collected are used for the estimation process in accordance with both cases discussed in the previous section.

Case I

The gravity model, as specified in Equation 6.5, is estimated by use of Panel Data, containing 1991 observations on both 304 cross-section individuals of ASEAN members and their major trade partners for the period 1994-2000. The estimation results are summarized in Table 6.3 and are based upon methods of pooling data (OLS), mean estimates of Between Group (BG), Fixed Effects (FE) and Random Effects (RE). According to the results obtained by the first two methods (pooling and between groups), all coefficients are roughly the same in their signs, values and significance, while income elasticity coefficients, particularly those of exporters, captured by both FE and RE have decreased relatively and get closer to unity.

As the values of the F-test show the null hypothesis of the same individual effects cannot be accepted, this implies that the OLS results are biased and, more specifically, there exists heterogeneity for each pair of trade partners. This means that the problem of heterogeneity should be controlled through concentrating on different individuals effects.

A comparison of the estimation results reveal that FE and RE are more reliable than the pooling data (OLS) and mean methods. The main reason is that the former methods detect the existence of heterogeneity in individuals (countries). The estimation results arising from the FE and RE procedures are shown in the third and fourth columns of Table 6.3. In addition, the Hausman statistic indicates that the FE results are more reliable than those obtained by RE.

The estimation results obtained by FE (within group) indicates that the GDP coefficients of both exporters and importers have positive signs, and, as expected, are statistically significant at the 95 per cent confidence level. Estimates for these GDP coefficients are about 0.91 per cent and 1.4 per cent, respectively. Although positive the coefficients of exporters' population are not significant. This implies that a change in the exporters' population does not affect its trade relations with the other countries, suggesting that ASEAN members export mostly non-labour-intensive goods. In contrast, the coefficient of importers' population has a negative sign and is significantly different from zero at the 5 per cent significance level. According to this estimated value a one per cent increase in population of the importer leads to a decrease of 1.21 per cent in the volume of trade flows between the two partners. Based upon this result the importer's economy would be more inward-oriented as its population grows, that is its demand for imports tends to decline.

Table 6.3 Estimation results for Case I

Explanatory Variables	Pooling Data	Between Estimates	FE Estimates	RE Estimates
Constant	-6.5 (-13.7)	-7.63 (-7.42)	-	-6.66 (-6.71)
Y_{it}	1.4 (23.44)	1.21 (10.13)	0.91 (3.82)	1.30 (16.13)
Y_{jt}	1.30 (21.9)	1.08 (8.8)	1.40 (7.31)	1.21 (15.7)
N_{it}	-0.85 (-16.72)	-0.65 (-5.48)	0.015 (0.033)	-0.54 (-7.68)
N_{jt}	-0.55 (-12.25)	-0.62 (-6.42)	-1.21 (-1.93)	-0.63 (-8.67)
ASEIntra	2.81 (17.64)	2.87 (7.32)	1.03 (4.58)	1.22 (11.34)
ASEExp	1.34 (9.13)	1.52 (3.86)	0.78 (4.47)	0.78 (10.09)
ASEImp	1.38 (7.64)	1.63 (3.95)	0.74 (4.78)	0.79 (10.34)
Dummy97	-0.22 (-2.90)	6.31 (5.88)	-0.078 (-1.91)	-0.13 (-4.46)
$\overline{R^2}$	0.63	0.69	0.94	0.92
Number of Observations	1991	304	1991	1991
F-statistic	42.57 (p = 0)			
Hausman-statistic	24.65 (p = 0)			

Note: Values of the t-ratio are represented in parentheses. Also, the probability of null hypothesis acceptance for the F-statistic and Hausman statistic is available in parentheses.

Being statistically significant the dummy variables explain the impact of trade integration on ASEAN's trade flows. The coefficient for *ASEIntra* explores the positive effect of integration on members' trade relations. The value of 1.03 for the dummy variable coefficient (*ASEIntra*) reveals the fact that trade between the bloc members is 1.8 times more than that expected from the gravity variables.[2] More specifically, trade integration can increase trade between the members by 180 per cent. Similarly, the coefficient of *ASEExp* indicates that the exports of ASEAN members to non-members is about 1.2 times more than the anticipated level that the gravity model may predict. Thus, integration in ASEAN can lead to members' total exports rising by 120 per cent. In addition, the positive coefficient of *ASEImp* also shows that integration in the bloc causes a simultaneous increase in members' exports and imports (from non-members), implying that the conduct of trade liberalization works efficiently in the South East Asian region. Accordingly, ASEAN members' imports from non-members are about 110 per cent more than the expected level that the main gravity variables (e.g. GDP) are able to predict it to be. It is thus concluded that trade liberalization, as well as openness, are the pertinent determinants of trade integration and economic cooperation in the bloc.

Dummy97 stands for the episodes of financial crisis that occurred for most South East Asian countries in 1997. According to the results obtained this episode negatively affected ASEAN trade flows, and was statistically significant at the 10 per cent level. The value of reduction is measured at about 7.8 per cent.

Overall, the estimations related to FE and RE, and represented in Table 6.4, are relatively close to each other, particularly in terms of the signs and coefficient values (except for exporter's population). A slightly higher explanatory power, as measured by the $\overline{R}^2$ indicates that FE should be preferred with respect to RE.

We turn now to estimate the effects of geographical distance (D_{ij}), contiguity (A_{ij}) and common language ($Lang_{ij}$) on the volume of trade transactions between the ASEAN members and their major trade partners, and in doing so we regress the estimated individual effects (IE_{ij}) obtained from Equation 6.4 on such variables. The new estimated equation is as follows:

$$IE_{ij} = \underset{(4.86)}{1.16} - \underset{(-3.32)}{1{*}10^{-5}\,Dij} + \underset{(1.29)}{1.05\,A_{ij}} + \underset{(0.927)}{0.39\,Lng_{ij}} \quad \overline{R}^2 = 0.051 \qquad (6.11)$$

The estimation results obtained indicate that only the coefficient for the distance variable is statistically significant and has the expected sign, even though its value is quite low. Due to the very low value of $\overline{R}^2$, this implies that a number of cultural-social determinants are required to explain individual effects. Moreover, the results are consistent with the existence of heterogeneity between each of the trading partner pair, involved in α_{ij}, rather than common language, contiguity etc.

Case II[3]

As Equation 6.8 specified in the previous section a new version of the trade gravity model also employs the "Similarity Linder" variable (L_{ijt}) and the exporter effective real exchange rate variable (Rer_{it}), to explore how structural similarities and price competition can affect ASEAN trade flows.

Regarding the poor results obtained by OLS and cross-section mean (Between Group) methods and the existence of bias for those results, as shown in the second and third columns of Table 6.4, Panel Data is again applied to enable us to consider heterogeneous individual effects.[4]

Table 6.4 Estimation results for Case II

Explanatory Variables	Pooling Data	Between Estimates	FE Estimates	RE Estimates
Constant	4.22 (2.46)	16.73 (1.84)	-	-15.15 (-17.43)
Y_{it}	0.23 (6.27)	0.22 (2.37)	0.49 (4.64)	0.76 (13.83)
Y_{jt}	0.13 (2.45)	0.098 (10.82)	1.38 (11.38)	0.89 (15.18)
L_{ijt}	0.078 (3.77)	0.078 (1.67)	0.0047 (0.35)	0.02 (1.81)
Rer_{it}	-0.65 (-1.91)	-3.34 (-1.67)	0.32 (2.87)	0.21 (2.49)
ASEIntr	0.027 (3.86)	0.022 (1.26)	0.39 (4.01)	0.13 (6.15)
$\bar{R}^2$	0.05	0.041	0.951	0.939
Number of Observations	1074	154	1074	1074
F-statistic	142.87 (p = 0)			
Hausman-statistic	71.648 (p = 0)			

Note: Values of the t-ratio are represented in parentheses. Also, the probability of null hypothesis acceptance for the F-statistic and Hausman statistic is available in parentheses.

Columns 4 and 5 of the table indicate estimation results obtained by both FE and RE methods. The Hausman test assists us to find out if the results obtained by FE and RE are again acceptable and more reliable, while the null hypothesis of consistency for RE estimates can be rejected. Thus, statistically significant income elasticity coefficients explain positive changes in ASEAN members' trade flows by about 0.48 and 1.39 per cent. Because of the incorrect sign plus the insignificance for the coefficient of the Linder variable, this implies that current structural similarities/dissimilarities in ASEAN countries have not affected significantly the trade relations with trade members of the bloc. In addition, a statistically significant coefficient of the exchange rate reveals the fact that an increase in this variable leads members to show a positive export reaction.

The significant coefficient of the bloc integration variable denoted by *ASEIntr* indicates trade flows between the five major members of ASEAN of about 48 per cent more than the level that might be predicted by a quantitative gravity variable.

Finally, a regression of individual effects on geographical distance, contiguity and language variables (shown by Equation 6.10) indicates a positive role of the distance between countries in individual effects, while its unexpected value is very low and thus unimportant. The poor results for the determination coefficient ($\bar{R}^2 = 0.091$) indicates that the explanatory power of the equation is also very low, implying that it is necessary to consider other factors affecting integration.

$$IE_{ij} = \underset{(50.191)}{-20.5} + \underset{(3.34)}{17*10^{-5}}\, D_{ij} - \underset{(-0.95)}{1.12}\, A_{ij} - \underset{(-1.23)}{0.92}\, Lang_{ij} \quad \bar{R}^2 = 0.091 \qquad (6.12)$$

6.7 CONCLUDING REMARKS

To examine the effect of integration on ASEAN's trade flows this chapter has investigated its impact upon bloc members through an application of the trade gravity model. After conducting a theoretical discussion of the gravity model, an empirical framework has been specified so that it considers all ASEAN members that can be involved in integrated economic relations. Trade integration was modelled for five of the founding major members consisting of Singapore, Malaysia, Indonesia, Thailand and the Philippines. Because of the presence of various individual effects and heterogeneity in trading-partners pairs (as individuals), the Panel Data method was appropriately applied for the estimation process.

Overall, the estimation results obtained indicate that trade integration between ASEAN members and their partners, on the one hand, and among themselves, on the other hand, would increase the amount of ASEAN's trade flows. The results reveal that as a larger number of countries take part in amalgamating trade relations, the effectiveness of cooperation among members can be more pronounced.

Consequently, the implications of the current study is that most nations which exist in the bloc are able to benefit from integrating economic activities, even though they are heterogeneous in their economic and social conditions. In principle, to secure their relations more strongly, they should understand and accomplish the advantages of bilateral trade relations and economies of scale.

NOTES

1 Under the method of Two Way Panel Data, α_t is present in the regression model that stands for the time effect, whereas it is not included in a regression estimated by the One Way Panel Data method (Baltagi, 1995).

2 Since the model is specified in log-log form and dummy variables are measured by binary numbers, the actual coefficients of these variables can be computed as: [e*(dummy variable coefficient) – 1] = [e((1.03) – 1]=1.8, where e is the Neper number.

3 The five major countries of ASEAN being: Singapore, Malaysia, Indonesia, Thailand and the Philippines.

4 The F-test also confirms the hypothesis of no pooling of time series and cross-section data.

REFERENCES

Anderson, J. E. (1979), "A theoretical foundation for the gravity equation", *American Economic Review*, *69*, pp.106-16.

ASEAN Secretariat (2001), available at: http://www.aseansec.org.

Baldwin, R. (1994), *Towards an Integrated Europe*, London: CEPR.

Baltagi, B. H. (1995), "Econometric Analysis of Panel Data", New York: John Wiley & Sons Ltd.

Bergstrand, J. H. (1989), "The generalized gravity equation, monopolistic competition, and the factor-proportions theory in international trade", *Review of Economics and Statistics*, *67*, pp. 474-81.

Bougheas et al. (1999), "Infrastructure, transport costs and trade" *Journal of International Economics, 47*, pp. 169-89.

Bryant, S. K. and K. Massey (1999), "The effects of regional trading blocks on globalization", in K. Fatemi and. E. W. Nichols (eds), Globalization in the 21st Century, Vol. I, Calexico, CA: International Trade and Finance Association, pp.143-51.

Christensen, R. (1987), *Plain Answer to Complex Questions, the Theory of Linear Models*, New York: Springer Texts in Statistics.

Cheng, I. H. and H. J. Wall (1999), "Controlling for heterogeneity in gravity models of trade", Federal Reserve Bank of St. Louis, pp.1-29.

Deardorff, A. V. (1995), "Determinants of bilateral trade: does gravity work in a neoclassic world?", NBER Working Paper 5377.

Egger, P. (2000), "A note on the proper econometric specification of the gravity equation", *Economics Letters*, *66*, pp. 21-40.

Evenett, J. and W. Keller (1998), "On theories explaining the success of the gravity equation", Rutgers University.

Gurler, D. (2000), "Role and function of regional blocks and arrangement in the formation of the Islamic common market", *Preliminary Proceeding of the International Seminar on Ways and Means to Establish an Islamic Common Market*, Tehran, The Institution for Trade Studies and Research, pp.1-16.

Haveman's website, available at http://www.eiit.org/Trade Resources/ Data/Gravity

Helpman, E. and P. Krugman (1985), *Market Structure and Foreign Trade, Increasing Returns, Imperfect Competition, and the International Economy*, Cambridge, MA / London: MIT Press.

Hsiao, C. (1986), *Analysis of Panel Data*, New York: Cambridge University Press.

IMF (1998), *Direction of Trade Statistics Yearbook*, New York: International Monetary Fund.

International Financial Statistics (1997 and 2001), International Monetary Fund.

Limao, N. and A. J. Venables (1999), "Infrastructure, geographical disadvantage and transport costs' policy", Research Working Paper 2257, World Bank.

Martinez-Zarzoso, I. and F. Nowak-Lehmann (2001), at: http://www.gwdg.De/~uwia/ pdf /iai-bb77.pdf, pp.1-23.

Mátyás, L. (1997), "Proper econometric specification of the gravity model", *The World Economy*, *20,* (3), pp. 363-68.

Nafziger, W. E. (1997), *The Economics of Developing Countries*, 3rd Edition, New Jersey: Prentice Hall.

Poon, J. P. and K. Pandit (1996), "Pacific trade and regionalization, 1965-1990", *The International Trade Journal, 10,* (2), pp.199-221.

Pöyhönen, P. (1963), "A tentative model for the volume of trade between countries", *Weltwirtschaftliches Archiv, 90,* pp.93-9.

Salvatore, D. (1996), "Globalization and international competitiveness', in D. Dimon et al. (eds) *Competitiveness in International Business and Trade,* Vol. II, Laredo, TX: Texas A&M International University, USA, pp. 341-55.

Soloaga, I. and L.A., Winters (1999), "Regionalism in 1990s: what effects on trade?", Development Research Group of World Bank, pp.1-32.

Tanzi, V. (2000), "Globalization, Technological Developments, and the Work of Fiscal Termites", IMF Working Paper.

Tayyebi, S. K and A., Tavakoli (2000), "Globalization of economy, international competition and the status of the OIC member countries", Selected Paper Presented at the Seminar on Expansion of Economic and Trade Co-operation between Islamic Countries, The Institution for Trade Studies and Research, Tehran, pp. 2-36.

Tinbergen, J. (1962), *Shaping the World Economy, Suggestions for an International Economic Policy*, New York.

Wall, H. J. (2000), "Gravity model specification and the effects of the Canada-U.S. border", Working Paper No 2000-024A, Federal Reserve Bank of St. Louis.

Wei, S.-J. (1996), "Intra-national versus international trade: how stubborn are nations in global integration?" NBER, Working Paper 5531.

World Development Indicators, (1998), Reports of the World Bank.

World Bank (April 2003), *World Development Indicators Database.*

World Bank (1999), *Global Development Finance and World Development Indicators.*

World Bank (1998), *World Economic Outlook and World Development Indicators.*

World Bank (2002), *Global Development Finance and World Development Indicators.*

7. Key Factors in Foreign Direct Investment Utilization in ASEAN+3

Yanyun Zhao and Zhao Lei

7.1 INTRODUCTION

Globalization and regional economic integration are the two major trends in global economic development. In order to improve their international competitiveness and to become stronger in the context of economic globalization, many countries are actively participating in the process of regional economic integration or regionalism. The global leader of regional economic integration, the European Union, expanded its membership to 25 countries in May 2004 by adding ten additional members from Central and Eastern Europe. In North America NAFTA, consisting of the United States, Canada and Mexico, was established in 1994, and there are ongoing efforts by 34 countries in the Americas to establish a free trade area, under the Free Trade Area of the Americas, by 2005.

As the region with the fastest rate of economic development in the second half of the last century, East Asia has, more recently, also made attempts at closer economic integration. ASEAN (Association of Southeast Asian Nations), which was founded in 1967, and ASEAN+3 (China, Japan and Korea) have become very active in recent years in expanding the process of regionalism in East Asia. Over the past three to four decades the ASEAN+3 countries have made considerable economic advances. In the new economy era characterized by more intense competition, how can the countries in ASEAN+3 maintain their rapid development and competitiveness? We think, no matter the individual country or group of countries, competence in the utilization of Foreign Direct Investment is one of the most important factors.

This chapter will statistically analyse the topic - "What factors are influential to one country or country group in the utilization of FDI, and what is the relative importance of these different factors?" We aim to reflect economic trends by means of statistical models. In the following section we will first introduce the system of dependent and independent variables for use in our analysis; then, in section 3, we will conduct a comparative analysis between ASEAN+3 and the EU on the influential factors affecting the utilization of FDI by using a Panel Data model. In doing so we attempt to find the common and different factors affecting the utilization of FDI and discussing where the ASEAN+3 countries may be lagging. Finally, in section 4, we will conduct a rigorous analysis for each country of ASEAN+3 on their utilization of FDI by using a Partial Least Squares (PLS) model, with the objective of identifying the key differences among these countries. The data base for this study is the *The World Competitiveness Yearbook (1994-2003)* issued by IMD (International Institute for Management Development, Lausanne, Switzerland). Due to data limitations we can only focus upon data for Indonesia, Malaysia, the Philippines, Thailand, Singapore, China, Japan and Korea to reflect the situation for ASEAN+3 as a whole. In addition, we can only obtain data for 14 countries to represent the situation in the EU, because Luxembourg's data is incomplete.

7.2 THE VARIABLES FOR ANALYSIS

There has been considerable economic research on the factors affecting FDI utilization, including political risk, macro economic policy, market size, labour cost, trade freedom, infrastructure, culture differences, etc. Dunning (1980) and Green and Cunningham (1975) found that GDP had a close positive correlation with the utilization of FDI; Jun and Singh (1996) conducted research on the effect of tariff walls, export direction policy and political risk on FDI utilization, and they concluded that these factors have a positive impact; Torrisi (1985) found that a favourable balance of trade has a negative effect on FDI utilization. However, because of different sample sizes and analytical method adopted the effect of each factor on FDI utilization has been found to vary, and hence considerable debate over the importance of each of these factors remains.

Based on economic theory and the results derived from previous studies, we now outline the analytical framework to be adopted in this study. We use total FDI, FDI per capita and real growth in FDI as separate dependent variables; and select 13 variables as potential influential factors from seven aspects, namely economic strength, market demand, internationalization, finance, labour force and cost, government management and infrastructure. The variables selected are, more specifically, as follows:

1. Dependent variables

   Y1: Total FDI

   Y2: FDI per capita

   Y3: Real growth in FDI

2. Independent variables
   2.1 Economic strength
      X1: GDP per capita
   2.2 Market demand
      X2: Private final consumption expenditure per capita
      X3: Real growth in private final consumption expenditure per capita
   2.3 Internationalization
      X4: Imports of goods and commercial services
      X5: Exports of goods and commercial services
   2.4 Finance
      X6: Restrictions on the degree to which foreign companies can access local Capital Markets
      X7: Difficulty in the degree to which credit flows from banks to business
   2.5 Labour force and cost
      X8: Total hourly compensation for manufacturing workers
      X9: Labour force
   2.6 Government management
      X10: Efficiency in the degree to which it can adapt its policies to new economic realities
      X11: Number of murders, violent crimes or armed robberies per 100,000 inhabitants
   2.7 Infrastructure
      X12: Computers per capita
      X13: Efficiency degree of the distribution infrastructure of goods and services.

7.3 AN INFLUENTIAL FACTORS ANALYSIS OF THE UTILIZATION OF FDI USING A PANEL DATA MODEL

In this section, based on the above variables, we will use a Panel Data model to compare FDI utilization among members of the EU, ASEAN+3, and ASEAN+1 (viz. ASEAN+China). However, Japan and Korea are countries who mainly invest abroad, and, consequently, their influential factors on FDI utilization are likely to be different from the other countries in ASEAN+3. It will be of interest to identify how their FDI influencing factors differ from other countries in ASEAN+3.

Introduction of the Panel Data Model

The Panel Data model is a kind of combined data model, and is mainly used for cross sections of individuals observed over time. It can reflect the object's changing trends in two different directions: time series and cross section. It can also analyse the object's characteristics in different time and units, at the same time studying the correlation among the different variables and predicting their variation. It can use the sample's information comprehensively and reduce the influence brought by multi-collinearity, making the research more rigorous.

There are many basic types of Panel Data model. In the analysis conducted here we choose the variable-intercept model, which is used most widely nowadays. Its basic form is as follows:

$$y_{it} = \alpha_i + \beta' x_{it} + u_{it} \qquad i = 1,\ldots,N \ ; \ t = 1,\ldots,T$$

In the above formula individual time-invariant α_i represents the influence brought by different individuals omitted by the model, and individual time-varying variable u_{it} represents the influence brought by the factor which varies synchronously with cross section and time series and also is omitted by the model. There are two kinds of variable-intercept models: fixed-effects model and random-effects model. Since we only use the sample to infer, we select the fixed-effects model.

Panel Data Modelling Results

The nine equations contained in Tables 7.1-7.3 all pass the F test and the weighted R^2 of the six equations corresponding to Y1 and Y2 are all higher than 0.7, indicating a good fit. However, the weighted R^2 of the equations corresponding to Y3 are all lower than 0.5, so we need to be more cautious and conservative about the influencing variables in this case. In view of this, we select out the remarkable variables for Y1 and Y2 with the standard α =0.2, and α =0.05 for Y3. These remarkable variables have been highlighted in italics in the following tables. Furthermore, because the variables have already been standardized the coefficients reflect the relative importance of each variable. Since we care about the variable structure of an economic region as a whole, we have not list the individual time-invariant α_i for each country.

First, let us see for the three regions the key factors influencing the structure of total FDI. We find the following main characteristics:

Table 7.1 Dependent variable Y1

EU

Variable	Coefficient	Std. Error	t-Statistic	Prob.
X1	*0.299808*	0.176758	1.696149	0.0926
X2	*-0.224719*	0.141413	-1.589101	0.1148
X3	0.032280	0.033154	0.973628	0.3323
X4	-0.350427	0.947613	-0.369799	0.7122
X5	-0.554276	0.770000	-0.719838	0.4731
X6	0.018212	0.056064	0.324843	0.7459
X7	*-0.190856*	0.067278	-2.836832	0.0054
X8	0.155224	0.146063	1.062715	0.2902
X9	*-3.318754*	2.090471	-1.587562	0.1152
X10	-0.012040	0.048762	-0.246922	0.8054
X11	-0.057975	0.060980	-0.950730	0.3438
X12	0.064565	0.063422	1.018020	0.3108
X13	0.089887	0.083982	1.070313	0.2868

ASEAN+3

Variable	Coefficient	Std. Error	t-Statistic	Prob.
X1	*3.244645*	0.572783	5.664698	0.0000
X2	*-2.078424*	0.572058	-3.633242	0.0006
X3	0.055728	0.057570	0.967994	0.3370
X4	*0.925734*	0.268909	3.442550	0.0011
X5	*-0.616091*	0.395363	-1.558291	0.1245
X6	-0.006783	0.097136	-0.069830	0.9446
X7	*0.172142*	0.085304	2.017974	0.0481
X8	0.058465	0.224036	0.260963	0.7950
X9	-1.811705	1.586022	-1.142295	0.2579
X10	0.031649	0.090113	0.351220	0.7267
X11	*-0.207502*	0.051894	-3.998593	0.0002
X12	*-0.240000*	0.085989	-2.791057	0.0071
X13	0.134745	0.161270	0.835528	0.4068

ASEAN+1

Variable	Coefficient	Std. Error	t-Statistic	Prob.
X1	*1.798308*	0.546153	3.292682	0.0020
X2	-0.095153	0.591908	-0.160756	0.8731
X3	0.081693	0.070358	1.161097	0.2523
X4	*0.619320*	0.376053	1.646895	0.1072
X5	*-0.779327*	0.421715	-1.847994	0.0718
X6	0.030084	0.168344	0.178704	0.8591
X7	*0.185044*	0.116626	1.586636	0.1203
X8	-0.152368	0.303347	-0.502289	0.6182
X9	-0.687361	2.108192	-0.326043	0.7461
X10	0.004850	0.129161	0.037552	0.9702
X11	*-0.299266*	0.052537	-5.696241	0.0000
X12	*-0.193130*	0.109171	-1.769068	0.0843
X13	0.223921	0.242640	0.922854	0.3615

Table 7.2 Dependent variable Y2

EU

Variable	Coefficient	Std. Error	t-Statistic	Prob.
X1	*0.949488*	0.263876	3.598231	0.0005
X2	*-0.604234*	0.194274	-3.110222	0.0024
X3	*0.058462*	0.042403	1.378715	0.1707
X4	0.485162	0.874755	0.554626	0.5802
X5	-0.354294	0.706327	-0.501600	0.6169
X6	0.004743	0.072122	0.065766	0.9477
X7	*-0.273819*	0.081778	-3.348303	0.0011
X8	0.169242	0.201752	0.838863	0.4033
X9	*-2.526039*	1.840917	-1.372163	0.1727
X10	-0.000203	0.056469	-0.003589	0.9971
X11	*-0.280922*	0.121576	-2.310665	0.0227
X12	-0.009705	0.094950	-0.102216	0.9188
X13	0.126282	0.111112	1.136531	0.2581

ASEAN+3

Variable	Coefficient	Std. Error	t-Statistic	Prob.
X1	*4.239653*	0.908414	4.667095	0.0000
X2	*-3.059791*	0.867869	-3.525636	0.0008
X3	-0.001052	0.027154	-0.038729	0.9692
X4	*0.395877*	0.241596	1.638591	0.1066
X5	*-0.524361*	0.282457	-1.856430	0.0684
X6	0.051740	0.057038	0.907115	0.3680
X7	-0.043461	0.036952	-1.176143	0.2443
X8	*0.150485*	0.090414	1.664397	0.1013
X9	0.306019	0.486547	0.628960	0.5318
X10	0.018448	0.036628	0.503654	0.6164
X11	*-0.177643*	0.065952	-2.693544	0.0092
X12	*-0.172009*	0.100746	-1.707349	0.0930
X13	0.019849	0.063040	0.314870	0.7540

ASEAN+1

Variable	Coefficient	Std. Error	t-Statistic	Prob.
X1	*3.679541*	0.679676	5.413668	0.0000
X2	-0.775164	0.642816	-1.205889	0.2348
X3	-0.025455	0.031373	-0.811368	0.4218
X4	-0.098271	0.148728	-0.660739	0.5125
X5	0.074867	0.188154	0.397903	0.6928
X6	0.045925	0.066897	0.686509	0.4963
X7	*-0.074453*	0.046725	-1.593448	0.1187
X8	0.124937	0.111097	1.124578	0.2673
X9	-0.456105	0.688246	-0.662707	0.5112
X10	*0.059583*	0.045099	1.321143	0.1938
X11	*-0.404094*	0.078335	-5.158566	0.0000
X12	*-0.416209*	0.122015	-3.411121	0.0015
X13	0.059877	0.098961	0.605061	0.5485

Table 7.3 Dependent variable Y3

EU

Variable	Coefficient	Std. Error	t-Statistic	Prob.
X1	*0.273393*	0.098109	2.786630	0.0062
X2	*-0.229397*	0.070441	-3.256575	0.0015
X3	0.035269	0.026010	1.355975	0.1778
X4	0.446135	0.354691	1.257814	0.2111
X5	-0.533137	0.309216	-1.724157	0.0874
X6	0.061794	0.031938	1.934818	0.0555
X7	0.017180	0.039206	0.438213	0.6621
X8	-0.004748	0.099685	-0.047630	0.9621
X9	0.071477	0.810721	0.088165	0.9299
X10	-0.005688	0.027892	-0.203918	0.8388
X11	0.002007	0.026182	0.076659	0.9390
X12	-0.043353	0.043269	-1.001932	0.3185
X13	-0.050920	0.042375	-1.201667	0.2320

ASEAN+3

Variable	Coefficient	Std. Error	t-Statistic	Prob.
X1	0.197232	0.934150	0.211136	0.8335
X2	-0.831698	1.179740	-0.704984	0.4836
X3	0.035454	0.053934	0.657357	0.5135
X4	0.775677	0.492794	1.574039	0.1208
X5	-0.475299	0.575732	-0.825556	0.4124
X6	-0.209463	0.139217	-1.504581	0.1378
X7	*0.181505*	0.082960	2.187852	0.0327
X8	0.432326	0.216966	1.992602	0.0509
X9	-0.629029	1.127685	-0.557805	0.5791
X10	-0.044120	0.090741	-0.486218	0.6286
X11	-0.037431	0.071661	-0.522335	0.6034
X12	-0.037566	0.110403	-0.340260	0.7349
X13	-0.234791	0.175022	-1.341490	0.1849

ASEAN+1

Variable	Coefficient	Std. Error	t-Statistic	Prob.
X1	0.183319	0.746104	0.245702	0.8071
X2	-0.455524	0.800124	-0.569317	0.5722
X3	0.079747	0.089881	0.887253	0.3801
X4	0.519696	0.442741	1.173813	0.2472
X5	-0.382388	0.521367	-0.733433	0.4675
X6	-0.150776	0.259415	-0.581215	0.5643
X7	*0.527452*	0.214173	2.462735	0.0181
X8	0.540508	0.386034	1.400155	0.1690
X9	-0.121376	2.411350	-0.050335	0.9601
X10	-0.075889	0.165369	-0.458907	0.6487
X11	-0.057334	0.071537	-0.801459	0.4275
X12	-0.001442	0.131657	-0.010949	0.9913
X13	-0.485649	0.425302	-1.141891	0.2601

1. Macro economic variable X1 (GDP per capita) has a remarkably positive effect for all three regions, and is almost the most influential of all the variables. This conclusion accords with Dunning (1980), and reflects that the degree of economic development is a fundamental factor for a country in FDI utilization.
2. X7 (difficulty in the degree of credit flowing from banks to business) also has a notable effect on the three regions. For the EU its effect is negative but for the other two it is positive. A country's degree of maturity in the finance market and its financial efficiency can be identified from this variable. For the EU, after a long period of economic development and financial accumulation, its domestic financial organizations already have strong competence and unhindered financing channels. This results in a situation where, to some extent, their domestic investment and foreign investment are substitutable. That is "If I can borrow money from the domestic banks easily, why should I trouble to use foreign money?" So, the more easily that loans flow to business, the larger is domestic investment and the more restrained is FDI. But for ASEAN+3, and especially for ASEAN+1, the situation is completely different. The countries in this area are mostly developing countries and their financial organizations are not strong enough to supply all the necessary finance for development. The big gap in funding needs to be filled by foreign investment. So, not only is there no replacement effect between domestic investment and FDI, but it is also more attractive for foreign investment if the recipient country has a more mature financial market and higher financial efficiency because this is a more beneficial situation in which foreign investment can operate and develop.
3. Some variables are distinct in two regions: first, X2 (Private final consumption expenditures per capita) acts negatively in all three regions, and this is particularly marked in the EU and ASEAN+3. This is mainly due to the influence of some countries, such as the UK, Sweden, China, Korea, Indonesia, that have a particularly negative relationship between X2 and Y1. A reason for this is that the reduction of consumption expenditures per capita results in a lack of aggregate domestic consumption, so in order to stimulate the growth of the economy each country needs to encourage investment. Various kinds of measures will then be used to attract foreign investment, and this, consequently, results in the growth of utilization of FDI. Second, we find that X4 (Imports of goods and commercial services), X5 (Exports of goods and commercial services), X11 (Number of murders, violent crimes or armed robberies per 100,000 inhabitants), X12 (Computers per capita) all have a prominent effect with the same direction of effect in ASEAN+3 and ASEAN+1. Of the four variables the effect of X11 is most intuitive. The crime rate reflects one country's public security environment and further reflects government management and political stability. From a safety of

life and money perspective, not many people would invest in an unsafe and unstable country. This result is supported by Jun and Singh (1996).

We can try to understand the positive correlation between X4 (Imports of goods and commercial services) and total FDI from a macro perspective. Most countries in ASEAN+3 are not standing at the upper end of the technology spectrum. To maintain their competitiveness they not only need to import considerable amounts of advanced machinery and technology, but they also need the support of foreign funds. From this sense we can say that it is more a kind of correlation between X4 and total FDI, instead of causality. That X5 (Exports of goods and commercial services) acts negatively on total FDI is because the expansion of exports will bring in a large amount of foreign exchange, and this income will become one part of domestic capital. So, to some degree, it can replace FDI. This conclusion is consistent with Torrisi (1985). We will find in the following analysis that this kind of negative effect stands out in Japan and Korea. X12 (Computers per capita) reflects one country's information infrastructure. The negative relationship between X12 and total FDI seems, at first sight, to be contradictory, but this need not be so. In the wake of rapid developments in information and communications technology, most countries in ASEAN+3 have made great efforts to develop their information industry and intensify the construction of information infrastructure. During this process they need considerable foreign investment. But with the maturity of the information infrastructure, on the one hand, the space for investment is becoming more and more cramped. On the other hand information infrastructure has begun to make profits and this has produced a substitutable effect for FDI to a certain extent. So the negative relationship is not difficult to understand. What is more, as seen from the driving influence of the information technology industry globally, there exists an over-advanced development in the investment in the information technology industry. Many companies have closed down due to an inability to generate sufficient expected profits. This seriously affects the utilization of FDI, and, as will be found in the following analysis, this kind of negative effect stands out in Japan and Korea.

4. X9 (labour force) has a remarkable negative effect for the EU. This reflects that most countries in the EU have advanced into a knowledge-focused economy. In this economic system, once surpassing the market demand, the larger is the labour force the lower will be business efficiency. This will further aggravate the country's burden and lose its attraction to foreign investors.

From the influencing structure of Y2 (FDI per capita), we find that there is no substantive change for the EU. However, because the countries in ASEAN+3 all have a large population density and most of them are labour-focused, X8 (Total hourly compensation for manufacturing workers) becomes distinct, while X7 (Difficulty in the degree of credit flowing from banks to business) becomes unimportant. From the micro company viewpoint the higher the worker's salary the less attractive is FDI. But the above positive effect is possibly because a country's salary level is directly related to its level of economic development. So that a higher salary level means a higher economic development level, and, furthermore, a higher amount of utilization of FDI.

The influencing structure of Y3 (Real growth in FDI) differs noticeably from that of Y1 and Y2, with most variables of little significance. For the EU, GDP per capita and private final consumption expenditures per capita are comparatively important. The reason for which is the same as that explained before. For ASEAN+3 and ASEAN+1, only X7 (Difficulty in the degree of credit flowing from banks to business) is a marked variable.

To reflect the relative importance of different variables in the same region, we use the following Figures 7.1-7.3 to indicate their importance to Y1 in the three regions. Generally speaking, the following main conclusions, based on the above analysis and charts, can be identified:

1. Compared with the EU more factors have an effect on the utilization of FDI in ASEAN+3, and among them GDP per capita has the biggest influence.
2. Economic strength and finance both have an important effect on the utilization of FDI in all regions. But, because the financial development level is different, finance's effect on the utilization of FDI is positive for ASEAN+3 while it is negative for the EU.
3. International trade has a prominent effect on the utilization of FDI in ASEAN+3. Exports have a negative effect while imports have a positive effect. International trade is not important for the utilization of FDI in the EU.
4. A safe social environment and stable political situation are attractive to FDI, especially for ASEAN+3.
5. The influential factors on the utilization of FDI of ASEAN+3 are almost the same as those of ASEAN+1. But Japan and Korea are the type of countries who mainly invest abroad, so the relative importance of some of these variables changes noticeably because of them.

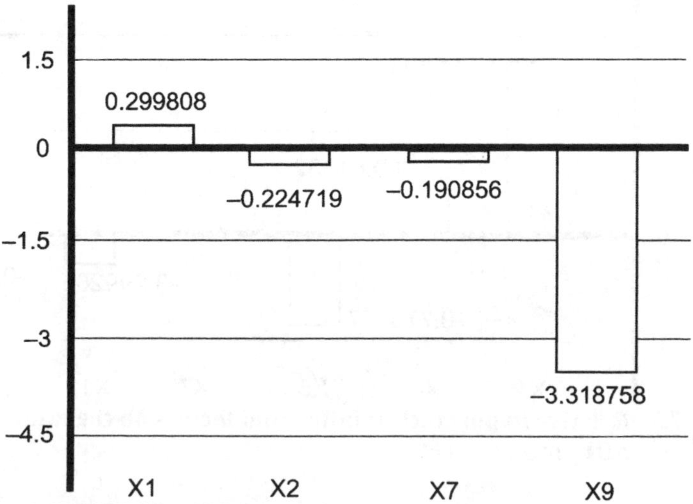

Figure 7.1 Relative importance of influential factors on the utilization of FDI for the EU

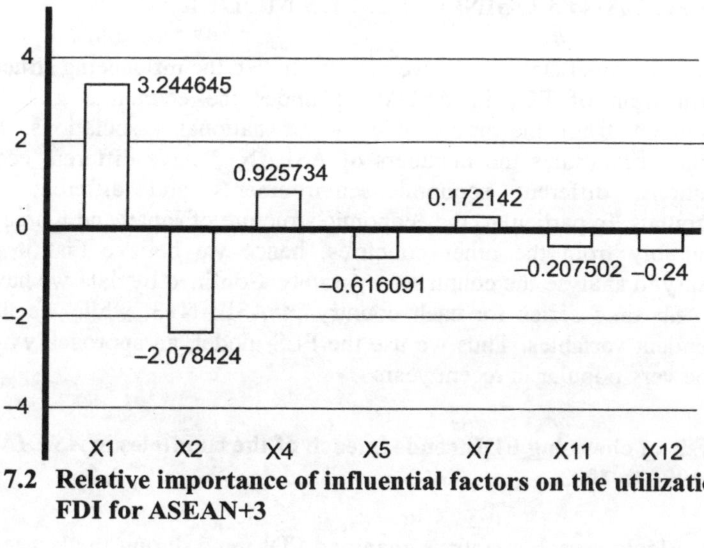

Figure 7.2 Relative importance of influential factors on the utilization of FDI for ASEAN+3

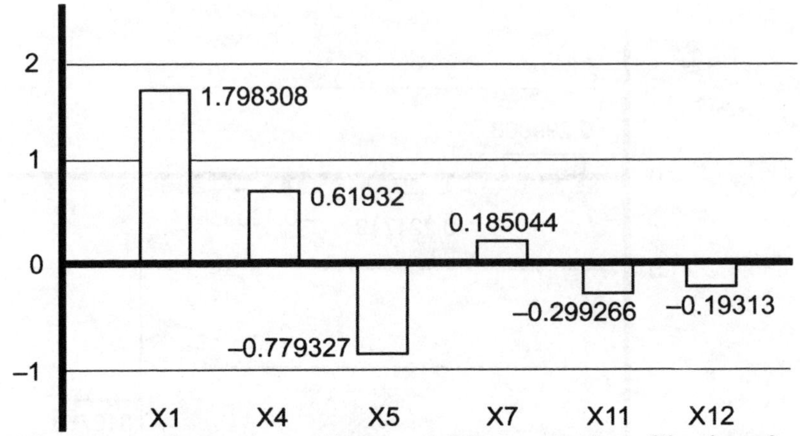

Figure 7.3 Relative importance of influential factors on the utilization of FDI for ASEAN+1

7.4 AN INFLUENTIAL FACTOR ANALYSIS ON THE UTILIZATION OF FDI FOR EACH COUNTRY IN ASEAN+3 USING THE PLS MODEL

In the above Panel Data model we mainly studied the influencing structure on the utilization of FDI in ASEAN+3 under the economic globalization environment from the point of view of national associations. But as individual economies the members of ASEAN+3 have different economic foundations, different economic environments and different cultural backgrounds. In particular, the economic structure of Japan and Korea differs considerably from the other countries, hence we believe that it is also necessary to analyse the countries separately. Confined by data we have only a ten-year time series for each country in ASEAN+3, while we have 13 independent variables. Thus we use the PLS model, an approach which has become very popular in recent years.

Analysis of changing FDI trends in each of the countries in *ASEAN+3* from 1994 to 2003

First we look at each country's changing FDI trend during the last ten years (only trends in total FDI are used).

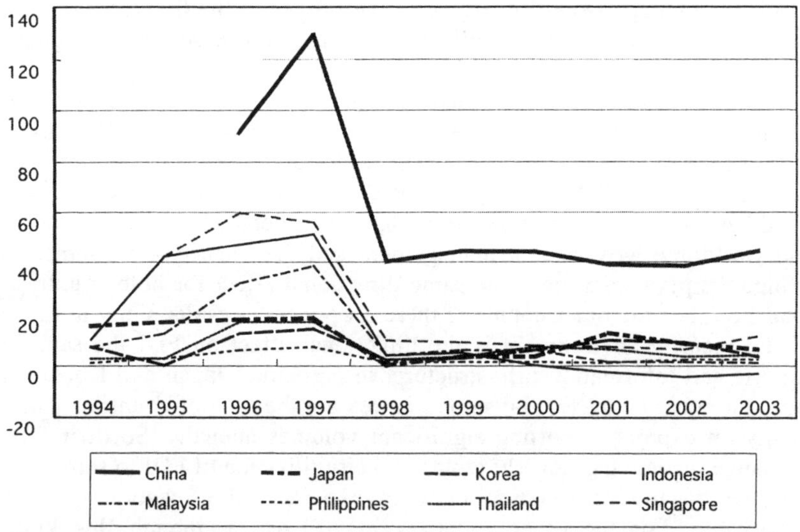

Source: Asian Development Bank

Figure 7.4 Changing FDI trends in each country in ASEAN+3 from 1994 to 2003 (US$, billions)

From Figure 7.4 we can clearly see that: first, the amount of utilization of FDI varied considerably from 1994-1998, with most countries peaking in 1997. With the onset of the Asian financial crisis, however, all countries experienced a sharp reduction in the amount of utilization of FDI in 1998, and thereafter coming to stability at a noticeably lower level. Second, the amount of utilization of FDI by China is much higher than that for the other seven countries, although China experienced the largest absolute decline during the period of the crisis. Third, comparatively speaking, the fluctuation of Japanese and Korean FDI during the past ten years has been smaller than that for the other countries. After bottoming out in 1998, 1999 and 2000, their amount of FDI utilization has since improved. Finally, Indonesia's FDI utilization has been the most adversely affected since 1997, with negative FDI for the past three years.

PLS Modelling Results

The results from using the PLS model are contained in Tables 7.4-7.6. In the Panel Data analysis we generalized the common traits of ASEAN+3. We focus upon the different characteristics of 8 ASEAN+3 countries in this section. Since the variables have been standardized before the analysis, the coefficients in the model reflect the relative importance of each variable.

Based on a comparison of coefficients we select out the five most important variables for each country's utilization of FDI, and these are highlighted in italics in each of the tables below.

First, the main factors identified in Tables 7.4-7.6 affecting the utilization of FDI for each of these countries is summarized in Table 7.7. The direction of influence of these factors can also be seen from Tables 7.4-7.6. Second, we find that for total FDI utilization in the cases of Japan and Korea, but not for the other countries - economic strength, market demand, exports, labour cost and workforce, government management and the security environment and computers per capita, have the same directional effect for both countries on total FDI. For the other countries there are variable results. Only in the case of the security environment is the directional effect on FDI the same. For exports and information infrastructure, in particular, Japan and Korea differ from the other countries. Japan and Korea are the type of countries that rely highly on exports, exporting significant volumes annually. So their foreign exchange income has notably replaced their utilization of FDI to some extent, and the negative correlation between exports and utilization of FDI is remarkable. For the other countries in ASEAN+3, though this kind of substitution effect also exists, it is not salient because of their relatively small exports. However, we can predict that with the development of these countries' economies the export effect will be more distinct. In terms of the information infrastructure Japan and Korea have a relatively more advanced basis, and their available investment space has narrowed. The other countries, because of their late starting date for development, can attract large amounts of investment into the construction field of information infrastructure.

As to the influencing structure of FDI per capita, because the data has been standardized and the population did not change much during this ten year period, the results obtained suggest that Y2 is very similar to that of Y1. As for Y3, the PLS modelling results are only experimental and many of its coefficients cannot be directly explained.

In today's world no matter the individual country or the kind of national association, all aim at improving their own international competitiveness. This study has asserted that competence in the utilization of FDI is one of the most important factors in attaining this. This study has attempted to find the most influential factors on FDI utilization for the ASEAN+3 countries, and provide a solid foundation for future research on this topic.

Table 7.4 Dependent variable Y1

	China	Japan	Korea	Indonesia	Malaysia	Philippines	Thailand	Singapore
X1	0.3636	0.0780	*6.2413*	-0.0162	0.1596	0.2068	0.1551	*0.5443*
X2	-0.7615	-0.1878	*-3.9023*	*-0.5463*	-0.2076	0.1366	0.2307	*0.3424*
X3	0.2989	-0.1238	-0.6882	0.0113	0.1360	-0.2514	*0.2892*	0.0042
X4	*-1.1696*	*0.2474*	-0.3978	*0.8504*	0.0509	0.1773	-0.0804	-0.0895
X5	*1.6187*	-0.0880	-0.8499	*0.4337*	0.1389	-0.1042	0.0702	0.0152
X6	*0.9347*	0.1871	-0.3116	0.0762	*-0.2858*	-0.2520	-0.1294	-0.0913
X7	-0.0542	*0.4074*	*-1.7044*	0.4144	*0.3524*	*0.8648*	*0.3675*	0.1393
X8	0.4363	*0.4120*	0.9125	0.3340	0.0633	0.1210	*0.4634*	-0.2849
X9	-0.5568	*-0.4367*	*-1.1232*	*0.4415*	-0.0374	*0.3149*	*0.3651*	*-0.5804*
X10	-0.5500	-0.1210	-0.3585	-0.0028	*0.7734*	*0.5706*	-0.1955	-0.2166
X11	*-1.5611*	-0.1194	-0.4484	*-1.1781*	*-0.3790*	*-0.3897*	*-0.3582*	*-0.9545*
X12	0.2888	-0.1201	-0.2269	0.2644	-0.2003	0.2292	0.1994	*0.4190*
X13	*-1.1635*	*-0.3160*	*2.4662*	0.2476	*-0.2646*	*0.2826*	-0.0146	-0.1300

Table 7.5 Dependent variable Y2

	China	Japan	Korea	Indonesia	Malaysia	Philippines	Thailand	Singapore
X1	0.3612	0.0584	*6.7522*	-0.0193	0.1614	0.2220	0.1589	*0.5387*
X2	-0.7523	-0.1732	*-4.2590*	*-0.5456*	-0.2132	0.1489	0.2458	*0.3171*
X3	0.2803	-0.1209	-0.7555	0.0116	0.1391	*-0.2759*	*0.2942*	-0.0072
X4	*-1.1529*	*0.2421*	-0.5090	*0.8441*	0.0533	0.1990	-0.0767	-0.0615
X5	*1.5894*	-0.0819	-1.0017	*0.4297*	0.1432	-0.0682	0.0672	0.0100
X6	*0.9329*	0.1902	-0.3428	0.0794	*-0.2657*	*-0.2653*	-0.1335	-0.0571
X7	-0.0363	*0.4076*	*-1.7860*	0.4170	*0.3537*	*0.8714*	*0.3745*	0.1545
X8	0.4220	*0.4076*	0.9873	0.3387	0.0541	0.1182	*0.4664*	-0.2533
X9	-0.5562	*-0.4337*	*-1.3272*	*0.4359*	-0.0455	0.2644	*0.3608*	*-0.5654*
X10	-0.5484	-0.1219	-0.4231	-0.0095	*0.7547*	*0.5378*	-0.1971	-0.2123
X11	*-1.5568*	-0.1210	-0.4476	*-1.1727*	*-0.4093*	*-0.3520*	*-0.3525*	*-0.8947*
X12	0.2670	-0.1317	-0.2024	0.2636	-0.1703	0.1965	0.1983	*0.3751*
X13	*-1.1511*	*-0.3135*	*2.6416*	0.2482	*-0.2697*	0.2577	-0.0049	-0.1620

Table 7.6 Dependent variable Y3

	China	Japan	Korea	Indonesia	Malaysia	Philippines	Thailand	Singapore
X1	0.2868	*-2.9136*	*2.6139*	-0.1861	-0.0670	0.3001	-0.5008	0.3424
X2	-0.2471	*2.0602*	-0.5024	*-0.2473*	*-1.1477*	-0.7608	*-1.1854*	-0.1263
X3	*1.3462*	*-1.1106*	-0.3101	*0.8326*	-0.1193	-0.3449	-0.4193	0.0410
X4	*-1.3895*	-0.7118	-0.5681	*0.2472*	0.1794	0.9421	0.1065	*-0.3506*
X5	*2.3444*	*1.2103*	*-0.6761*	*-0.2362*	-0.1266	0.1650	*-1.4329*	-0.2042
X6	0.6188	1.0978	-0.0436	0.2361	-0.1381	*-2.3275*	-0.2335	*-0.6943*
X7	-0.4699	0.0544	0.3711	0.1800	*1.0005*	0.6998	*-0.6964*	0.0045
X8	*1.5340*	-0.3068	-0.5682	*0.3316*	*-0.9609*	1.0616	-0.0552	-0.1161
X9	0.3236	-0.2447	*-0.6930*	-0.0725	*0.6787*	*-1.1332*	-0.0617	*-0.4684*
X10	-0.1539	-0.5588	*-0.5832*	-0.2355	0.1012	*2.5372*	0.2875	-0.3150
X11	-0.0348	-0.5075	*-1.0065*	0.0129	*-0.6252*	*-2.7336*	*-1.4214*	*-1.3814*
X12	0.6909	*-1.3126*	0.3700	0.0914	0.0229	*-1.1619*	-0.2624	*1.4489*
X13	*-1.5649*	0.1086	-0.1225	0.1022	0.2199	-0.2800	*-0.6908*	-0.2341

Table 7.7 Main influential factors on the utilization of FDI for each country in ASEAN+3

Country	Main influential factors
China	Imports and exports, Financial walls, Infrastructure, Security environment
Japan	Imports, Financial market and efficiency, Labour cost, Infrastructure
Korea	Economic strength, Market demand, Financial market and efficiency, Labour supply, Infrastructure
Indonesia	Market demand, Imports and exports, Labour supply, Security environment
Malaysia	Financial walls, Financial market and efficiency, Government management of economy, Security environment, Infrastructure
Philippines	Financial market and efficiency, Labour supply, Government management of economy, Security environment, Infrastructure
Thailand	Real growth in market demand, Financial market and efficiency, Labour cost, Security environment
Singapore	Economic strength, Market demand, Labour supply, Security environment, Information infrastructure

REFERENCES

Centre for Research on Competitiveness and Assessment (2001), "The Development Report on China's International Competitiveness (2001)", 21st Century Development Topic Research, China Renmin University Press, Beijing, China.

Changchun, Zhang (2002), "Factor analysis on investment environment of FDI", *Management World (11).*

Dunning, J.H. (1980), " Toward an eclectic theory of international production: some empirical tests", *Journal of International Business Studies 11(1) (Spring/Summer),* pp 9-31.

Danhui, Yi (2002), "Data analysis and the application of Eviews", China Statistics Press.

Green, R and W. Cunningham (1975), "The determinants of US foreign investment: an empirical explanation", *Management International Review 15 (2/3),*pp113-20.

Hsiao, Cheng (1986), "Analysis of panel data", Cambridge, UK: University of Cambridge.

IMD, *The World Competitiveness Yearbook*(1994-2003), Lausanne, Switzerland.

Jun, K.W. and H Singh (1996), "The determinants of foreign direct investment: new empirical evidence", *Transnational Corporations, 5(2),* pp. 67-106.

Torrisi, C.R. (1985), "The determinants of direct foreign investment in a small LDC", *Journal of Economic Development 10,* pp 27-45.

Xiaoqun, He (1997), *Regression Analysis and Economic Data Modelling*, Beijing, China: China Renmin University Press.

PART FOUR

COUNTRY PERSPECTIVES ON ASIAN REGIONALISM

8. The ASEAN Perspective on East Asian-wide Regionalism

Suthiphand Chirathivat[1]

8.1 INTRODUCTION

The East Asian region has long viewed and practiced welfare gains from trade through unilateral liberalization or non-discriminatory treatment within the multilateral process, now known as the World Trade Organization (WTO). This same approach was echoed by the region and embodied as an integral part of the principles of the Asia Pacific Economic Cooperation Forum (APEC), with its emphasis on open regionalism. Even ASEAN, with its formal trading arrangements in Southeast Asia, has always strongly advocated an outward orientation of its regionalism approach by fostering more trade and investment, both inside and outside the bloc.

Thus, before the recent widespread adoption of new bilateral and sub-regional preferential trade arrangements (PTAs), East Asia, as a whole, could be proudly said to practice fully market-driven as opposed to institution-led integration, a practice that forms part of regional arrangements in Europe and the Americas. Indeed, the commitment to such a policy framework contributes to growth, development and greater integration with the global economy. Even with the end of the Cold War and up to before the recent financial crisis of the late 1990s in East Asia, the region seems to have been content with this route to trade liberalization no matter what had happened in other regions of the world.

The financial crisis of 1997-98, however, blunted growth and set new challenges for the afflicted nations to think more about the increased vulnerability of the region in a globalized world. By the turn of the century, up to the present, the whole East Asian region is suddenly awakening to the need to promote closer economic cooperation within the region. Bilateral, sub-regional and even East Asia-wide PTAs have been widely discussed with some starting to be implemented, while many others are still in the pipeline awaiting to be further implemented. This outcome has caused concern about the rationale for such initiatives and the implications that would follow from such a strategy.

This chapter sets a less ambitious goal, which is to discuss some of the key issues that appear to the author. As the formation of RTAs in East Asia will encompass quite a wide range of issues, it is interesting to focus on some that might appear to be meaningful to the region. In what ways and why is a new regionalism emerging in East Asia? These are important questions raised in section 8.2. Section 8.3 will discuss the appropriate conceptual framework that might be adopted for the implementation of RTAs in East Asia. Implications for countries and the region will be assessed in section 8.4. The final section will shed light on policy direction for the future.

8.2 EMERGENCE OF NEW REGIONALISM IN EAST ASIA

East Asia was slow to start its own regionalism. With the exception of ASEAN, there were no formal regional PTAs up to the late 1990s. The region was still divided by the Cold War and adhered to multilateralism in trade negotiations. The outward orientation of regional economies with the rest of world has been successful, as shown by trade patterns, investment orientation, technology transfer and further development. There are welfare implications of continental trading blocs which could lower welfare for each continent (Stein and Frankel (1994)) and this was widely discussed in East Asia.

The emergence of the East Asian economies, the collapse of the mid-term review of multilateralism and the formation of trade blocs in Europe (the EU) and the Americas (NAFTA) provoked an idea of East Asian regionalism. The initiative in favour of this regional arrangement was proposed by former Malaysian Prime Minister Mahathir Mohamed. However, the proposal for an East Asian Economic Grouping (EAEG)[2] or the actual East Asian Free Trade Area (EFTA) was heavily criticized by the US, and Japan threatened not to join such a grouping thereby causing a reappraisal of such a proposal by other East Asian countries. China was viewed as too preoccupied with its own transition to a market economy to give serious thought to such an initiative. APEC then advanced very quickly in the late 1980s to promote mutilateralism encompassing the Asia-Pacific region. Since then, APEC has been used as a vehicle for further regional trade liberalization à la WTO-plus.

The region's only preferential trade grouping was ASEAN, which was upgraded to the ASEAN Free Trade Area (or AFTA) in response to increasing regionalism at the beginning of the 1990s. The grouping was joined by Vietnam in 1995, Laos and Myanmar in 1997, and, lastly, Cambodia in 1999. This resulted in ASEAN having a membership of ten Southeast Asian countries. ASEAN governments aim to push regional trade liberalization as a step towards global free trade. In this sense regional integration through ASEAN appears to be consistent with global free trade, thus making it an interesting regional integration framework among developing countries (Chirathivat (1996), Ariff (2001)).

ASEAN looks at AFTA not as inward-looking trade liberalization, but rather as an investment–driven integration that would serve as a "training ground" for global competition. Precisely speaking, ASEAN extra-regional trade linkages are much stronger and more meaningful than intra-regional trade patterns. AFTA is meant to expose and enhance the potential of the ten member countries as a group to greater investment-driven growth. Hence, the main objective of AFTA is not to increase intra-ASEAN trade *per se*, but rather to provoke attention to the ASEAN region as an area in which to invest, produce and compete efficiently within the global economy. As an outward-looking regionalism, ASEAN sets clear objectives to establish linkages with other countries and regional groupings that would create more opportunities and new challenges for the region.

As for the Asia-Europe Meeting (or ASEM), this inter-regional grouping was formed in response to completing the linkages between East Asia and the European Union. Because East Asia is strongly involved with the Asia Pacific region through APEC, the EU felt the need not to miss opportunities with the emergence of the region. In the mid 1990s Europe and Asia set about completing this inter-bloc formation with the creation of ASEM in 1996. The ASEM dialogue has had to somewhat rethink its future orientation after the financial and economic crisis of 1997-98. For the moment, the two-yearly Leaders Meeting seems to serve both sides, East Asia and the EU, to share their concerns with respect to recent changes and to offer thoughtful direction for policy and future partnerships.

With the financial crisis of 1997-98 the East Asian region felt the need to promote closer economic cooperation. Although regionalism is regarded as a second best policy, many countries have started to explore these paths. It is gaining acceptance because policymakers see advantages in regionalism itself. These advantages are interpreted as "competitive liberalization" which means an opening up of markets and an easing of regulations within the group that would possibly treat an outsider country unfavourably. The effects of competitive liberalization contributed in a way to a rise in regionalism worldwide and also in East Asia.

To date, most Northeast and Southeast Asian countries have been included in one or more bilateral or sub-regional PTAs. In just a few years various types of trade arrangements have been proposed or are under negotiation, and some have been agreed upon and are being implemented (see Table 8.1). Indeed, Japan and China, for the first time, have either signed or are negotiating PTAs.There is also a proposal to create the East Asian Free Trade

Table 8.1 Preferential Trade Agreement participation in East Asia

Country/ Grouping	Partners	Status of Agreement, 2003	Country/ Grouping	Partners	Status of Agreement, 2003
ASEAN	China	Agreement Signed	Malaysia	China	Under Negotiation
	India	Agreement Signed		Japan	Under Negotiation
	Japan	Agreement Signed		USA	Proposed
	USA (TIFA)	Under Negotiation			
	CER	Under Study	Philip-pines	China	Under Negotiation
	ASEAN+3	Under Study		Japan	Under Negotiation
	EU (Treaty)	Proposed		USA	Proposed
China	ASEAN	Agreement Signed	Singapore	Australia	Agreement Signed
	Australia	Proposed		Canada	Under Negotiation
	Hong Kong	Agreement Signed		EFTA	Agreement Signed
	Macau	Proposed		EU	Proposed (rejected by EU)
	Malaysia	Under Negotiation			
	N.Zealand	Proposed		India	Under Negotiation
	Philippines	Under Negotiation		Japan	Agreement Signed
	Thailand	Agreement Signed		Korea	Under Study
				Mexico	Under Negotiation
Hong Kong	China	Agreement Signed		N.Zealand	Agreement Signed
	Macau	Agreement Signed		Taiwan	Proposed
	N.Zealand	Under Negotiation		USA	Agreement Signed
Japan	ASEAN	Agreement Signed	Taiwan	Costa Rica	Proposed
	Canada	Proposed		Japan	Proposed
	Chile	Under Study		N.Zealand	NZ withdrew from Negotiations
	Korea	Under Study			
	Malaysia	Under Negotiation		Panama	Under Negotiation
	Mexico	Under Negotiation		Singapore	Proposed
	Philippines	Under Negotiation		USA	Proposed
	Singapore	Agreement Signed			
	Thailand	Under Negotiation			
			Thailand	Australia	Under Negotiation
Korea	Australia	Under Study		Bahrain	Agreement Signed
	China	Under Study		China	Agreement Signed
	Chile	Agreement Signed		India	Agreement Signed
	Japan	Under Study		Japan	Under Negotiation
	Mexico	Under Negotiation		Korea	Under Study
	N.Zealand	Under Study		Mexico	Under Study
	Peru	Proposed		N.Zealand	Under Study
	Singapore	Under Study		Peru	Under Negotiation
	Thailand	Under Study		S.Africa	Under Study
	USA	Under Negotiation		USA	Under Study
				BIMSTEC	Under Study

Note: "Proposed" refers to agreements that have been officially proposed with varying degrees of formality by one government to another. Numerous other proposals have been made, primarily by business groups. Most proposals are then referred for study to either national think tanks or consultants and/or joint working parties established by the partners. Negotiations usually do not begin until governments have received the results from these studies.
Source: Adapted from Ravenhill, John (2003), *Asia Pacific Issues*, East West Centre, No.6, June, p.3.

Area (EAFTA) or ASEAN+3 grouping that covers the whole of East Asia. Much of these new initiatives pose strong challenges to participants, outsiders of the region, and even the multilateral trading system.

With these trends, bilateral agreements represent the new dynamics towards regional and global free trade. Although it is difficult to know its short-term effects the long-run effects seem to be positive (see Lloyd (2002)). Japan, Korea and Singapore have started, or signed, several bilateral agreements and some are being implemented. China and several Southeast Asian countries like Thailand, Malaysia and the Philippines, have also quickly followed with similar agreements. To date the whole East Asian region now seems busy dealing with these bilateral FTAs in one way or another.

Among the ASEAN members, Singapore embraced these bilateral FTAs early. Singapore's aim is that these will be "WTO-plus" rather than a "WTO-substitute" (Rajan et al. (2001)). Dissatisfied with the ASEAN and APEC process, and progress, in regional and unilateral liberalization, recent initiatives by Singapore reflect such a spirit.[3] Singapore's interest in free trade with Japan and the US reflects its *de facto* close trade and investment linkages with, and dependence on, these two markets. Thailand is the second ASEAN country to go in this direction and is catching up very quickly in a "competitive liberalization" policy. Although the country has still to conclude a number of bilateral arrangements, in time to come it also needs to pay increasing attention to overlapping areas arising from this involvement.

8.3 CHALLENGES FOR THE CONCEPTUAL FRAMEWORK

Regional trade liberalization is an important and complex issue in an increasingly globalized economy, and no less so for East Asia. It requires providing difficult answers to questions as to whether, and if so how best, it should be pursued (Bhagwati and Panagariya (1999), Dutta (1999), and Winters (2001)). To make such an assessment requires focus on some of the important questions that need to be answered. The issue of costs and benefits will first come to mind and whether the formation of these PTAs will help to raise or to lower economic welfare. Then, there is also the debate on the virtues and dangers of PTAs, and whether these arrangements can reinforce or hinder multilateral trade liberalization. In the case of East Asia, this renewed regionalism in the form of bilateral and regional arrangements is really complex. Answers to these questions are not easy.

These new significant features in East Asia, however, require closer analysis. Understanding the reasons behind this formation are also the key to focus, rightly or wrongly, on further policy thought. Market access issues or the "fear of exclusion from major markets" (Lloyd (2002), p. 7) has been advanced as one of the major factors that lead to the formation of new bilateral RTAs.[4] This argument can explain in large part the pattern of bilaterals as much as the move towards bilaterals in the region. The effect of this new regionalism in East Asia is now regarded as a big issue in terms of its multi-level PTAs; bilateral, sub-regional and region-wide.

There are, however, causes for concern from this new regionalism in East Asia. First, there is discrimination against non-members, and there are trade diversion effects. If competitive suppliers are unable to participate, as they are not part of the bilateral PTAs, then global welfare could suffer. For instance, the lowest income ASEAN countries are often excluded from this new regionalism. Second, the coverage of existing and proposed PTAs in East Asia is far from uniform. There will also be overlapping systems of bilateral and sub-regional trade liberalization. For example, the ASEAN-China FTA means China has to deal with ten different liberalization schemes. Third, the outcome from liberalization schemes depends largely on negotiations and political decisions. Negotiations in the presence of a limited number of countries could facilitate more powerful countries to dictate the terms of this agreement (Ravenhill (2003), p.4). In its negotiations with Singapore and Thailand, for example, the Japanese government seems to be able to exclude trade liberalization in sectors that it considers politically sensitive. Fourth, multiple PTAs could lead to hubs and spokes (Wonnacott (1996)). Over the longer run, new regionalism in East Asia would lead to a new trading environment of "give and take" where the spokes have to run to the hubs in order to get something out of it. Japan and China, for instance, could potentially be further hubs for these new RTAs. ASEAN is also driving fast with its new concluded arrangements aspiring to be one of the future hubs of the region as well. Finally, negotiating and applying multiple bilateral arrangements consumes considerable negotiating resources at the national level. For smaller countries, in particular, this can represent a major resource burden, having a number of skilled people tied up in trade negotiations. At the practical level strict rules of origin, intended to prevent the transhipment of products, will represent cumbersome routine work for custom officials, and could result in a limited expansion of trade between trade arrangement partners.

Some of the causes for concern should be included into the scope and framework for future collaboration. At the moment, efforts to pursue these bilateral and sub-regional PTAs are often expressed as part of FTAs. If that is the case, these countries need to look carefully at the economic effects of these arrangements. This chapter offers some thoughts on the key issues relating to the formation of multiple FTAs in East Asia as follows.

First, trade creation and trade diversion often represent the costs and benefits arising from any efforts at bilateral or regional trade liberalization. With an FTA, tariff and non-tariff barriers among the member states are supposed to be eliminated while maintaining them against outsiders. East Asian nations' efforts towards bilateral FTAs are being pursued as a comprehensive FTA that would also mutually recognize member countries' systems and rules like intellectual property rights protection, competition policy and FDI liberalization. The Japan-Singapore economic partnership could be cited as a good example of this type of comprehensive FTA.

Second, if transaction costs among prospective members of a bloc are low, trade creation is likely to be large and trade diversion small. Transaction costs are introduced into the cost function of the regional trading partners. In this sense, transaction costs involved in the process of exchange would include items such as transportation, communications, bureaucratic red tape and transhipping because of customs and border regulations, all of which are significant for the East Asian region.[5]

Third, the impact of transaction costs can foster market widening. Through increased access for regional partners, there is the opportunity for increasing returns to scale. East Asia is well placed to gain "external economies of scale". Under favourable conditions with increasing returns, an RTA can be trade creating since they may push down relative labour costs and improve prices to internationally competitive levels (Bhagwati and Panagariya (1996).

Fourth, there are also issues in which strict FTAs, in many ways, might differ from a customs union. Rules of origin can serve as an additional trade barrier in an FTA, in ways that cannot occur under a customs union (Krueger (1997a)). Thus, an understanding of the differences between an FTA and a customs union becomes important, especially for issues like overlapping FTAs in which several East Asian countries are now becoming involved. From a welfare point of view "an FTA cannot lead to any more trade creation than a customs union and when rules of origin export any protection, an FTA leads to more trade diversion than does a customs union" (Krueger (1997b), (1999)).

Overall, efforts toward bilateral and sub-regional or even region-wide arrangements are being pursued, not as FTAs *per se* but rather by means of comprehensive economic partnerships (CEPs) based on preferential trade arrangements (PTAs), some sub-regional, and mostly bilateral. This new type of FTA looks like a new comprehensive framework to foster East Asian integration, thus requiring the need to address these challenges properly. Indeed, the CEPs that have been concluded more recently, as well as those under negotiation among the East Asian countries, deal with a number of issues beyond a traditional FTA at the same time (Elek (2003)).[6] It is more likely that CEPs will become important principles towards wider cooperation in East Asia. CEPs could represent a significant policy option available to the East Asian region in pursuit of trade liberalization more fully at the regional and multilateral level. Thus, it is possible for the East Asian economies to proceed with border liberalization alongside with non-border barriers to trade and investment facilitation. In addition, these CEPs could help East Asia to implement region-wide cooperation arrangements to reduce risks and vulnerabilities related to an unstable international economic environment.[7]

In essence CEPs "contain a PTA for liberalizing border barriers together with a set of cooperative arrangements for reducing various costs and risks of trade and investment among the partners" (Elek (2003)). Many CEPs in prospect in East Asia are likely to pursue innovative arrangements to deal with these new aspects of trade liberalization and facilitation. The EU has applied such an all-or-nothing concept known as "acquis communautaire".[8] Such an approach looks inappropriate for East Asia, as the region consists of a more diverse group of economies. It is likely, therefore, that the region should seek its own approach with regard to these cooperative arrangements with the objective of liberalizing and facilitating trade and investment.

The key issue for East Asia is whether, and how, bilateral and sub-regional CEPs can play a constructive part in promoting closer economic arrangements, ranging from unilateral to multilateral, alongside the APEC process and the WTO. The answer to this lies in the construction of CEPs based on principles that best fit possible linkages for wider mutual partnerships. Elek (2003) provides an interesting thought on how CEPs should further expose its principles, orientation and policy implications. For the ASEAN region the recent conclusion of bilateral FTAs with China, India and Japan, all using CEPs as the policy framework, has provoked debate on how the grouping would advance its trade liberalization with CEPs.

8.4 IMPLICATIONS OF EAST ASIA-WIDE REGIONALISM

The analysis of the previous sections suggests that multiplying RTAs in East Asia should reflect market forces, and promote greater regional integration with the global economy. At present, various bilateral and sub-regional FTAs are rapidly increasing in number, making it difficult to assess if they are being developed to their fullest potential. However, policy makers and academics can discuss their principles, orientation and policy implications. This section proposes to analyse, first, the implications of East Asia-wide regionalism through reductions in trade barriers in order to evaluate their implications for regional partners.

If a regional trading bloc is to be formed, there are costs and benefits that need to be assessed thoroughly. As a regional preferential treatment involves directly the reduction of trade barriers in each regional partner, it requires careful consideration of all major aspects of the direct effects of the FTA and the changes in economic policy that might follow. To do so this study applies the Global Trade Analysis Project (GTAP) model (see Appendix 1). For the ASEAN countries, they already have had such experience for a number of years in the form of AFTA. But, should ASEAN+3 eventuate, with a population moving up to almost two billion, this FTA will be the largest in the world.

For the former ASEAN-6 the average tariff rates collected from Japan,

China and Korea are quite different. The level is high for Japan (19.9 per cent) and low for Korea (4.6 per cent) and China (2.3 per cent) (see Table 8.2). This is mainly due to the products - motor vehicles and parts, and some other manufactured products, in which ASEAN countries tax heavily on imports. On the other hand average tariff rates collected from ASEAN products is also different in the three countries. Japan has the lowest level (2.2 per cent) among the three while China has the highest (9.4 per cent). From Table 8.2, China obviously imposes a high tariff barrier on ASEAN products for most agricultural exports including processed rice, vegetable oils and fats, sugar, beverages and tobacco products, and on various manufactured exports like wearing apparel, motor vehicles and parts, and electronic equipment.

Table 8.2 Average tariff rates of ASEAN, China, Japan and Korea

	ASEAN collected from				ASEAN subject to collection from		
	China	Japan	Korea		China	Japan	Korea
Grain nec	0.76	41.94	45.00	Meat products	23.92	24.45	28.05
Gas	13.90	13.90	0.00	Dairy products	12.59	18.23	21.63
Textiles	11.34	11.28	14.21	Food products nec	27.69	12.71	26.08
Wearing apparel	4.52	6.63	14.44	Beverage, tobacco products.	49.72	16.63	10.47
Wood products	14.68	5.53	7.64	Wearing apparel	31.50	11.73	12.07
Motor vehicles and parts	10.71	59.17	39.36	Leather products	10.18	11.51	9.56
Average	2.34	19.88	4.56	Average	9.37	2.16	6.22

Source: CAMGEM Development Project, Faculty of Economics, Chulalongkorn University.

As for trade barriers among the three Northeast Asian countries, China represents the most protected country in terms of its average tariff rates collected from Korea and Japan (see Table 8.3). Korea stands in the middle, with Japan the least protected in terms of tariff collection. In terms of product categories, China collects a high tariff from Japan for products like vegetables and oils, food products, textiles, wearing apparels and motor vehicles and parts. In the case of Korea, they are subject to high tariff collection for products like vegetables and fruit, fishery, animal products, vegetable oil and fats, beverages and tobacco products, textiles, wearing apparels and motor vehicles and parts. As for Korea and Japan, they are also quite protective of their agricultural and some manufactured products. These are animal products, milk, sugar, food products, fruit, vegetables, textiles and wearing apparels.

With an FTA, if the principle is fully implemented, the regional framework, by abolishing trade barriers, allows trade expansion among the regional partners to be realized through trade creation and trade diversion effects as mentioned in section 2. The removal of trade barriers should lower costs, increase intra-regional trade and increase economic efficiency. This will help to boost real income in the regional economies as resources flow to sectors where they can be more efficiently and productively utilized. In order to look at changes resulting from such an FTA, it requires the application of analytical tools enabling further analysis and interpretation of its effects.

To simulate the effects of an East Asian Free Trade Area (EAFTA), one could apply a general model application known as the Global Trade Analysis Project (GTAP). In such an application it is assumed that rates of trade protection are reduced to zero, the ultimate goal of eliminating all tariff and non-tariff measures. Based on the average level of protection in ASEAN, China, Japan and Korea, one could assess the macroeconomic impact of tariff elimination as follows (see Tables 8.4 and 8.5).

Essentially, ASEAN seems to gain the most with an increase in real GDP at market prices of 3.36 per cent, mainly from its own internal effects. Japan stands to gain the least with an increase of only 0.08 per cent in real GDP at market prices. China and Korea, meanwhile, achieve an increase in real GDP at market prices of 1.66 per cent and 1.86 per cent respectively. These gains are mainly derived, for both countries, from the regional effects of the FTA.

Table 8.3 Average tariff rates of China, Japan and Korea

		China collected from		Japan collected from		Korea collected from	
		Japan	Korea	China	Korea	Japan	China
1	Vegs, fruit and nuts	19.58	25.93	6.44	5.45	55.92	35.59
2	Crops nec	7.70	14.21	5.98	7.08	11.87	8.73
3	Fishing	14.97	26.20	5.04	5.08	10.15	15.01
4	Meat products	26.11	24.82	16.56	1.15	27.53	29.83
5	Poultry, seafoods	21.59	28.72	7.51	6.38	16.41	18.11
6	Veg. oil and fats	36.66	39.73	0.30	2.62	16.22	6.56
7	Food products nec	36.52	32.09	13.23	14.21	44.65	29.78
8	Beverages, tobacco products	59.42	48.83	11.31	10.01	1.31	21.87
9	Textiles	26.21	25.88	10.06	10.15	8.65	11.03
10	Wearing apparel	33.21	32.91	12.06	11.74	12.53	12.90
11	Motor vehicles and parts	66.27	64.14	0.04	0.07	7.57	7.81
12	Manufactures nec	19.24	19.58	2.36	1.75	7.59	7.69
	Average	13.72	9.71	6.99	1.73	6.44	7.37

Source: Same as Table 8.2.

In terms of net welfare, ASEAN also stands to gain the most. However, this gain is also shared among the other three countries. ASEAN, similar to

China, looks to be a net gainer as the cost of the rise in the price of land, wage rate and reduction in the price of capital are taken into consideration.

Also, most countries seem to gain from a much greater expansion of trade with the tariff elimination (see Table 8.6). China stands to gain the most in all other markets although the country also sees other regional partners gaining better access into its own market.

The results also show a low degree of trade diversion for both ASEAN and China. On the other hand it indicates that Japan's and Korea's exports to third markets could be slowed down by the FTA, especially to the EU and the USA. Overall, trade diversion from the FTA is equal to 6.5 per cent for the US and 4.7 per cent for the EU.

Table 8.4 Macroeconomic impact of tariff liberalization on ASEAN-6 and China

Variable	ASEAN-6				China			
	Overall	Internal	External	Regional	Overall	Internal	External	Regional
Rental price of capital (%)	-2.43	-3.06	0.61	0.08	-1.61	-0.27	0.18	-1.58
Rental price of land (%)	9.94	4.21	6.39	-0.84	11.37	-0.76	0.21	12.12
Labour wage rate (%)	2.39	1.47	1.95	-0.75	3.27	0.03	0.06	3.18
Terms of trade (%)	-0.81	-1.39	0.80	-0.14	-1.50	-0.49	0.12	-1.19
Real GDP (factor cost) (%)	3.13	3.04	0.80	-0.56	1.47	0.17	-0.06	1.34
Real GDP (market prices) (%)	3.36	3.37	0.76	-0.59	1.66	0.22	-0.07	1.49
Real investment (%)	5.52	5.44	1.39	-1.00	4.01	0.46	-0.12	3.71
Export volumes (%)	6.90	6.88	0.95	-0.68	16.13	1.75	0.06	14.58
Import volumes (%)	6.49	6.06	1.66	-0.90	20.38	2.34	0.12	18.35
Trade balance (US$millions)	-2398.65	-3189.42	212.16	442.23	-3185.47	-1188.02	181.72	-2332.65
Welfare (US$millions)	13248.79	10921.06	6840.15	-3480.63	6343.16	308.53	-106.79	5936.18

Source: Same as Table 8.2.

China would, most likely, profit from the cost advantage of imported inputs from regional partners like ASEAN, which would enable China to be more competitive and export even more to third markets. ASEAN would also gain from decreased input prices for intermediate and capital goods imports, which would encourage most ASEAN countries to invest and export more to the East Asian region and the world.

The implications of tariff liberalization are clear to a certain extent. The assessment of non-tariff liberalization, on the other hand, is not an easy exercise, since it involves various measures that are not easily captured. As the tariff equivalent of a non-tariff measure is not easily estimated, this study applied the non-tariff measures incidence to measure non-tariff protection.[9]

Table 8.5 Macroeconomic impact of tariff liberalization on Japan and Korea

	Japan				Korea			
Variable	Overall	Internal	External	Regional	Overall	Internal	External	Regional
Rental price of capital (%)	1.53	-0.07	0.74	0.87	1.32	-0.09	0.41	1.01
Rental price of land (%)	-0.67	-0.62	0.18	-0.21	5.09	-0.69	0.79	5.09
Labour wage rate (%)	1.54	-0.16	0.81	0.89	4.88	0.00	0.60	4.30
Terms of trade (%)	1.77	-0.23	0.94	1.05	0.87	-0.20	0.33	0.75
Real GDP (factor cost) (%)	0.09	-0.04	0.06	0.06	1.72	0.03	0.13	1.55
Real GDP (market prices) (%)	0.08	-0.04	0.06	0.06	1.86	0.05	0.13	1.69
Real investment (%)	0.11	-0.10	0.10	0.09	4.03	0.14	0.25	3.67
Export volumes (%)	4.66	0.51	0.93	3.31	7.22	0.53	0.36	6.44
Import volumes (%)	7.10	0.33	1.91	4.90	9.18	0.44	0.66	8.18
Trade balance (US$millions)	1480.26	18.33	985.52	517.38	-2147.61	-214.01	13.70	-1961.59
Welfare (US$ millions)	11399.89	-2539.16	6556.24	6968.56	7939.04	-152.21	1013.16	7083.51

Source: Same as Table 8.2.

The average level of non-tariff rates is generally higher than tariff rates (see Table 8.7). For instance, China's average non-tariff protection against ASEAN imports is exceptionally higher than for most bilateral trading partners. China alone imposes such a high protection for Japan and Korea as well. Korea, on the other hand, seems to be the least protected country among all regional partners, then followed by Japan and ASEAN.

Average non-tariff rates of ASEAN collected from the three countries are high for products like poultry and seafoods, vegetable oil and fats, food products, petroleum and coal products and motor vehicles and parts. On the other hand, average non-tariff rates of China collected from ASEAN are high for most of the products. For Japan, these rates are high for processed rice, forestry and beverages and tobacco products. For Korea, these rates are important for processed rice and dairy products.

Table 8.6 Impact on trade flows as a result of tariff liberalization

Imports											
Exports	**Thailand**	**ASEAN**	**China**	**Japan**	**Korea**	**Australia**	**India**	**USA**	**EU**	**Others**	**Total**
Thailand	0.00	3.28	54.89	13.96	12.69	4.35	1.42	6.50	4.66	3.32	8.38
ASEAN	-7.07	0.05	43.95	9.19	16.20	2.30	1.02	3.95	2.68	2.47	5.18
China	45.01	21.22	0.00	30.84	60.84	4.41	0.86	4.74	4.43	3.96	12.67
Japan	25.15	15.95	56.78	0.00	14.09	-7.34	-7.85	-8.38	-8.82	-8.49	2.46
Korea	31.20	10.73	59.23	7.49	0.00	-4.92	-6.09	-5.66	-6.80	-6.60	4.97
Australia	-7.43	-0.54	-6.32	0.33	2.09	0.00	-0.87	-1.11	-1.71	-1.48	-0.68
India	-5.18	0.28	-12.57	-2.89	-3.25	-0.94	0.00	-0.60	-0.71	-0.18	-0.89
USA	-6.38	-1.78	-12.92	0.91	-7.53	0.31	-0.85	0.00	-0.69	-0.50	-1.07
EU	-9.61	-5.88	-24.48	-0.23	-4.76	0.64	-0.44	0.19	-0.51	-0.30	-0.92
Others	-4.21	-0.82	-14.39	0.78	-1.16	0.18	-0.65	-0.13	-0.77	-0.55	-1.08
Total	4.83	3.41	8.70	5.05	5.31	-0.62	-1.16	-0.91	-0.75	-0.90	0.38

Source: Same as Table 8.2.

Table 8.7 Average non-tariff rates of ASEAN, China, Japan and Korea

	ASEAN subjected to				ASEAN collected from		
	China	Japan	Korea		China	Japan	Korea
Forestry	96.78	76.65	0.05	Poultry, seafoods	23.77	53.14	43.88
Dairy products	24.98	0.00	38.93	Veg. oil and fats	25.03	8.01	66.69
Processed rice	100.00	100.00	100.00	Food products nec	12.40	24.97	51.65
Beverages, tobacco prods	52.18	37.15	6.55	Petroleum, coal products	14.30	14.72	18.09
Paper prods, publishing	85.08	5.07	0.00	Motor Vehicles and parts	6.06	21.04	18.14
Average	69.08	4.21	1.17	Average	9.99	8.68	12.54

Source: Same as Table 8.2.

Table 8.8 Average non-tariff rates of China, Japan and Korea

	China collected from		Japan collected from		Korea collected from	
	Japan	Korea	China	Korea	China	Japan
1 Vegs, fruit and nuts	0.46	0.00	14.27	2.00	66.32	56.49
2 Plant-based fibres	92.95	89.48	20.98	0.00	0.00	0.00
3 Livestock	92.09	99.06	10.42	13.98	27.47	82.91
4 Wool, silkworm cocoons	100.00	0.00	0.00	0.00	59.47	57.10
5 Forestry	3.23	2.97	54.13	88.92	2.92	12.95
6 Meat products	0.00	0.00	21.90	0.12	0.00	7.43
7 Veg. oil and fats	67.82	95.06	1.04	0.00	2.84	0.96
8 Dairy products	4.42	12.33	0.00	0.00	33.30	7.31
9 Processed rice	0.00	0.00	100.00	0.00	99.91	0.00
10 Food products nec	10.98	18.32	23.57	38.53	12.71	7.86
11 Beverages, tobacco prods	78.60	45.17	47.49	81.92	3.47	0.03
12 Leather products	70.96	52.96	0.00	0.00	0.00	0.00
13 Motor vehicles and parts	68.45	75.78	0.00	0.00	0.00	0.00
Average	45.38	37.78	22.60	17.34	23.72	17.93

Source: Same as Table 8.2.

As for the average non-tariff rates of China collected from Japan and Korea, these are high for products like plant-based fibres, livestock, vegetable oil and fats, beverage and tobacco products, and motor vehicles and parts (see Table 8.8). Meanwhile, Japan concentrates its protection on products from China and Korea mostly on products like livestock, forestry, meat products, processed rice and food products. Finally, Korea opts to protect its products from import competition from China and Japan on most agricultural products like vegetables, fruit and nuts, livestock, wool and silkworm cocoons, dairy products and processed rice.

The non-tariff measures' macroeconomic impact, as shown in Tables 8.9 and 8.10, is most significant for China, as its overall GDP could rise by up to 6.3 per cent and its overall welfare could also rise substantially if they were to be eliminated. ASEAN and Korea could also gain quite remarkably in terms of a rise in GDP, welfare and the price of land. Japan is at the bottom in terms of benefits to GDP. However, there are still meaningful gains to be made for Japan in terms of welfare from its rise in the rental price of capital.

China gains in terms of GDP but at the expense of a worsening trade balance, which deteriorates even more than that for ASEAN. Japan's trade balance, on the other hand, improves, while Korea's trade balance with the region is not much affected. China seems to be a net gainer in terms of exports to third markets as its products become more price competitive, with increased supply to most major countries like the USA and the EU (see Table 8.11). ASEAN experiences an expansion in exports to the Chinese market. This concentration towards the Chinese market could occur at the expense of a reduction of trade flows to ASEAN's major markets like the USA, EU and others. Japan and Korea appear to experience a similar fate.

The overall result points to the fact that there would certainly be trade gains for the regional partners from such an FTA. China seems to gain the most in terms of its rise in GDP and trade with regional partners and the world. As for the other regional partners, like ASEAN, Japan and Korea, they could also gain from such efforts at trade liberalization. ASEAN could gain from a rise in GDP, which would be relatively more than Japan and Korea. However, it seems that all ASEAN, Japan and Korea need to do is to export their inputs, like intermediate products and capital goods, to supply China's need to produce and trade with the rest of the world.

It looks like China could come out as a net trade gainer as trade creation will easily offset trade diversion with the rest of its regional partners. On the other hand, the attention of the other trade partners on China would result in slight trade diversion, as other regional partners will look to the new opportunities to trade with China as long as China's economy and its demand continue to grow. It remains to be analysed how these countries could use these opportunities to strengthen their economic partnerships. With strong growth of China, ASEAN and Korea, this could be an interesting picture in terms of future regional growth and development.

8.5 CONCLUSION

Long before new regionalism in East Asia the region strongly advocated the multilateral framework known as GATT. Even ASEAN, its own version of a free trade area starting in 1993, was targeted to be consistent with open regionalism, and conducive for inside and outside investors and traders to make their presence felt in the region. After the financial crisis of 1997-98, however, a proliferation of overlapping FTAs in East Asia has occurred. The crisis also gave rise to a strong impetus for the renewal of region-wide initiatives for further economic integration.

Table 8.9 Macroeconomic impact of non-tariff liberalization on ASEAN and China

Variables	ASEAN				China			
	Overall	Internal	External	Regional	Overall	Internal	External	Regional
Rental price of capital (%)	-0.40	-1.53	1.37	0.00	-4.96	-0.98	0.20	-4.43
Rental price of land (%)	14.46	0.41	15.87	-1.50	17.21	-1.65	1.30	18.41
Labour wage rate (%)	2.97	0.75	4.08	-0.96	6.39	1.90	0.12	4.46
Terms of trade (%)	0.51	-0.92	1.92	-0.21	-4.90	-1.68	0.21	-3.96
Real GDP (factor cost) (%)	2.29	1.39	2.05	-0.64	5.68	1.81	-0.04	3.85
Real GDP (market prices) (%)	2.34	1.60	1.91	-0.67	6.29	1.99	-0.06	4.22
Real investment (%)	4.09	2.85	3.28	-1.17	10.59	3.04	-0.19	7.84
Export volumes (%)	4.13	3.90	1.63	-0.77	31.01	7.50	0.21	24.64
Import volumes (%)	4.82	3.48	3.33	-1.06	35.21	9.22	0.21	27.89
Trade balance (US$millions)	-1131.86	-2417.74	556.67	448.16	-6163.30	-3143.66	544.86	-4409.21
Welfare (US$millions)	13074.22	3876.04	16603.16	-4059.93	29034.24	9365.09	98.62	18100.69

Source: Same as Table 8.2.

The challenges arising from FTA formation could be tremendous for East Asia. The removal of trade barriers is supposed to lower costs, increase intra-regional trade and increase economic efficiency. This will help to change the calculus of resource allocation and market sharing among the regional partners. For the moment, a new bilateralism has caused concerns for its future orientation. As these FTAs are varied and different from country to country their ultimate approach is often expressed in terms of comprehensive economic partnerships (CEPs). The discussion is how this competitive liberalization will support a region-wide regionalism in the long run.

Table 8.10 *Macroeconomic impact of non-tariff liberalization on Japan and Korea*

Variables	Japan				Korea			
	Overall	Internal	External	Regional	Overall	Internal	External	Regional
Rental price of capital (%)	1.69	-0.09	0.49	1.34	3.36	-0.04	0.36	3.22
Rental price of land (%)	-4.09	-3.76	0.32	-0.79	13.36	-2.06	1.38	15.05
Labour wage rate (%)	1.95	-0.15	0.53	1.55	6.40	-0.33	0.58	6.41
Terms of trade (%)	2.08	-0.35	0.63	1.78	3.05	-0.26	0.32	3.14
Real GDP (factor cost) (%)	0.23	0.01	0.04	0.16	2.03	-0.12	0.18	2.03
Real GDP (market prices) (%)	0.23	0.01	0.04	0.16	1.91	-0.11	0.17	1.90
Real investment (%)	0.43	-0.04	0.07	0.34	3.47	-0.26	0.29	3.51
Export volumes (%)	3.70	0.61	0.58	2.62	4.37	-0.01	0.44	4.14
Import volumes (%)	6.39	0.31	1.23	4.88	7.34	-0.22	0.70	7.13
Trade balance (US$millions)	1165.23	77.35	628.78	684.90	-168.00	-64.64	35.84	-58.44
Welfare (US$ millions)	17572.68	-1058.34	4414.33	13331.45	11398.28	-777.87	1123.82	11453.45

Source: Same as Table 8.2.

The implications of East Asia-wide regionalism, or ASEAN+3, have been discussed in this study. This suggests that the costs and benefits of reducing trade barriers for regional partners need to be assessed properly. China, evidently, represents the most protected country compared to ASEAN-6, Korea and Japan. With trade liberalization China seems to gain the most in terms of GDP and trade gains. ASEAN could also make GDP gains, and relatively more so than Japan and Korea. ASEAN, Japan and Korea emphasize exporting their products to supply China's vast market, which could encourage a slight trade diversion especially with those developed countries outside the region.

Table 8.11 Impact on trade flows as a result of non-tariff liberalization

Exports \ Imports	Thailand	ASEAN	China	Japan	Korea	Australia	India	USA	EU	Others	Total
Thailand	0.00	-1.09	146.73	12.37	36.30	-3.32	-5.54	-2.84	-3.55	-5.96	6.31
ASEAN	-9.07	-4.10	130.10	8.46	6.28	-4.30	-3.85	-2.93	-4.19	-4.61	3.01
China	81.90	45.13	0.00	33.38	31.86	17.97	10.15	21.44	19.99	19.01	24.59
Japan	13.83	9.16	87.53	0.00	-0.59	-8.45	-8.67	-9.66	-10.28	-9.92	1.99
Korea	35.42	2.47	99.69	2.36	0.00	-13.90	-13.33	-14.84	-15.69	-15.52	2.46
Australia	-2.18	1.90	-19.27	-4.19	8.10	0.00	2.90	-0.46	0.50	-0.14	-1.20
India	-7.87	1.95	-32.22	-2.85	3.06	-3.68	0.00	-1.12	-1.31	-0.53	-1.39
USA	-3.68	-0.67	-25.43	-0.52	7.96	0.00	-0.86	0.00	-0.97	-0.87	-1.00
EU	-4.70	-2.89	-35.36	2.06	8.68	0.27	-0.45	-0.10	-0.74	-0.72	-1.08
Others	-0.98	1.50	-29.60	0.30	7.07	0.29	-0.38	0.12	-0.73	-0.63	-1.59
Total	4.89	2.86	14.96	4.52	6.90	-1.08	-1.55	-0.98	-0.87	-1.30	0.41

Source: Same as Table 8.2.

With a more integrated Asia-wide region current developments and future challenges are multiple. On the one hand it must be hoped that the current proliferation of bilateral deals will turn out to support, and not to substitute, efforts towards Asia-wide regionalism. The policy framework to assist this initiative must be market-driven and carried out with a view to increasing economic efficiency, better resource allocation and openness for more competition. On the other hand there is a need to develop in parallel a long-term end goal of an Asia-wide regionalism that fits the present economic development needs of the East Asian economies, and leads to their further integration with the global economy.

APPENDIX 8.1

Summary of the Global Trade Analysis Project (GTAP) model applied in this study

This chapter has made use of the GTAP model, well known to international trade economists. The Chulalongkorn CAMGEM Project is based on this model and has been applied to a number of important global trade analyses. The GTAP model in its latest version contains 45 countries and 50 production sectors.

The model is structured on the following elements: (a) a regional household whose Cobb-Douglas preferences are defined over composite private expenditures, composite public sector expenditures and savings; (b) demand arising from private expenditures governed by a constant difference of elasticity (CDE) function; (c) production described by a multi-level Leontief-type production function defined over value added and intermediate inputs generated from the Social Accounting Matrix (SAM) constructed for each region, with value added produced through a constant elasticity of substitution (CES) function; and (d) macro closure of a CGE model with balances in each region composed of government deficits or surpluses, aggregate saving and investment, and balance of trade.

Finally, equilibrium of the model is defined as a set of prices and quantities for goods and factors in all regions such that (a) demand equals supply for all goods and factors; (b) each industry earns zero profit; and (c) gross investment equals aggregate savings in each region. The model is neoclassical in nature as prices in each region's product and factor markets are assumed to be flexible, and arable land for agriculture in each region is assumed to be fixed.

NOTES

1 The author would like to thank Dr. Sothitorn Mallikamas for providing useful comments on this chapter.
2 Later to become known as an East Asian Economic Caucus (EAEC).
3 Indeed there is also the argument of "those who run faster should run faster and ought not to be held back by those who choose not to run or do so at a snail's pace" (Rajan et al. (2001), p.8).
4 In this context, exclusion does not mean a total denial of market access, that is total exclusion, but rather it means market access on less favourable terms relative to some other country or countries.
5 These may represent ten or more percentage points of total value added (Reynolds

(1995), p.11).

6 CEPs usually consist of a PTA to liberalize border barriers to trade complemented by a number of arrangements to address new issues in order to facilitate trade and investment among the participants of the CEP. So, these partnerships are more than traditional trading arrangements.

7 As the implementation of East Asia-wide liberalization such as ASEAN+3 could be more difficult to realize.

8 With several hundred arrangements, known as directives, issued from the EU Commission in Brussels.

9 Based on TRAINS developed by UNCTAD, Core Non-tariff measures (NTMs) are classified into three categories: quantitative controls, price controls and financing. This does not include measures like automatic licensing, monopolistic controls, technical barriers, and others.

BIBLIOGRAPHY

Abe, S. (1996), "Prospects for Asian economic integration". in S. Nishijima and P.H. Smith (eds), *Cooperation or rivalry? Regional Integration in the Americas and the Pacific Rim*. Boulder, Colorado: Westview Press.

Ariff, M. (2001), "Regional integration and global free trade: working at cross-purposes?" in Akio Hosono. *Regional integration and development policy: a comparative study of East Asia and the Americas* (mimeo).

Bhagwati, J. and A. Panagariya (eds) (1996), *The economics of preferential trade agreements*. Washington D.C.: The American Enterprise Institute.

Bhagwati, J., P. Krisna and A. Panagariya (eds)(1999), *Trading Blocs: Alternative Approaches to Analysing Preferential Trade Agreements*. Cambridge MA: MIT Press.

Chirathivat, S. (1996), "ASEAN economic integration with the world through AFTA". in J. Tan, (ed) *AFTA in the Changing International Economy*. Singapore: Institute of Southeast Asian Studies, pp. 21-41.

Chirathivat, S. (2001a), Interdependence between China and Southeast Asian economies on the eve of the accession of China into the WTO in I. Yamazawa and K. Imai (eds) (2001) *China Enters WTO: Pursuing the Symbiosis with the Global Economy*, Tokyo: The Institute of Developing Economies, pp. 132-51.

Chirathivat, S. (2001b), "Emerging integration trends in post-crisis Asia and implications for the Asia-Europe relationship". (mimeo).

Dutta, M. (1999), *Economic regionalization in the Asia-Pacific: Challenges to Economic Cooperation*. Cheltenham, UK: Edward Elgar.

Dutta, M. (2002), "Asian economic community: intra-community macro and micro-economic parameters" A paper presented at the conference on "Asian economic cooperation in the new millennium: China's economic presence", jointly organized by ACAES and Peking University, 27-29 May (mimeo).

East Asia Vision Group Report (2001), "Towards an East Asian community: region of peace, prosperity and progress", 16 July (mimeograph).

Elek, A. (2003), "East Asian economic integration: critical policy choices", APEC Study Center Consortium Conference, Phuket, Thailand, 25-28 May.

Krueger, A.O. (1997a), "Free trade agreement versus customs unions". *Journal of Development Economics 54*, pp. 169-87.

Krueger, A. O. (1997b), "Problems in overlapping free trade areas". in T. Ito and A.

Krueger. *Regionalism and Multilateral Trade Arrangements*. Chicago: The University of Chicago Press.

Krueger, A.O. (1999), "Are preferential trading arrangement trade-liberating or protectionist?" *Journal of Economics Perspectives, 4*, pp.105-24.

Lamghammer, R. (1995), "Regional integration in East Asia: institutionalised regionalism?" *Welwirtschaftliches Archiv 13*. Heflt. pp. 167-201.

Lloyd, P.J. (2002), "New bilateralism in the Asia-Pacific", *The World Economy,.25*, (9), September, pp. 1279-96.

Mallikamas, S. (2002), *A Study of Thailand's Readiness to Establish Free Trade Areas*, CAMGEM Development project, Faculty of Economics, Chulalongkorn University.

Okamoto, J. (ed) (2003), *Whither Free Trade Agreements? Proliferation, Evaluation and Multilateralization*, Tokyo: IDE.

Rajan, R.S., R. Sen and R. Siregar (2001), *Singapore and Free Trade Agreements*, Singapore: Institute of Southeast Asian Studies.

Ravenhill, J. (2003), "The move to preferential trade in the Western Pacific Rim", *Asia-Pacific Issues*, East-West Center, Hawaii, 69, June.

Reynolds, C.W. (1995), "Open regionalism: lessons from Latin America for East Asia". A paper presented at the workshop on The political economy of regional development and cooperation in the Pacific Basin, with special reference to APEC University of Notre Dame, 12-14 October (mimeo).

Scollay, R. (2003), "The proliferation of RTAs and the future of Asia-Pacific economic integration", APEC Study Consortium Conference, Phuket, Thailand, 25-28 May.

Stein, E. and J Frankel (1994), "The welfare implications of continental trading blocs in a model with transport costs", Pacific Basin Working Paper Series, 94-03, Federal Reserve Bank of San Francisco.

Urata, S. (2003), "A shift from market-led to institution-led Regional economic integration in East Asia", A paper presented at the JSPS-NRCT Workshop on "Perspectives on flows, middle class, state and market for Asia", Bangkok, 14-15 January.

Viner, J. (1950), *The Customs Union Issue*, Carnegie Endowment for International Peace, New York.

Winters, L. Alan (2001), "Regionalism for developing countries: assessing costs and benefits". in Sajal Lahiri (ed) *Regionalism and Globalization: Theory and Practice*. London and New York: Routledge, pp. 113-43.

Wonnacott, R.(1996), "Trade and investment in a hub-and-spoke system versus a free trade area", *The World Economy, 19(3)*, pp. 237-52.

Yamazawa, I. (1992), "On Pacific economic cooperation", *Economic Journal, 102*. November, pp. 1519-29.

9. Korea's Perspectives on East Asian Regionalism

Chan-Hyun Sohn and Hyun-Hoon Lee

9.1 INTRODUCTION

In recent years, there has been a new tide of regionalism in East Asia. Korea is not an exception. Korea concluded a free trade agreement (FTA) with Chile in October 2002 and has pursued/considered a similar agreement with some countries in the East Asia and Pacific region, including Japan, Singapore, China, Mexico and Thailand. This movement represents a clear break from Korea's strong history of multilateralism.

East Asia's recent regionalism is, in large part, due to the enlargement of the EU and growing Pan-American moves to increase free trade arrangements, such as expanding the North American Free Trade Agreement (NAFTA) into the proposed Free Trade Area of the Americas (FTAA) (which includes the entire American continent except Cuba). In particular, the United States, the major export market for most East Asian countries and long-time proponent of multilateralism under the framework of the GATT/WTO, has recently pursued bilateral and regional FTAs as a new reality of the global multilateral trading system.[1]

The second factor is the slow process of liberalization under the WTO. The failure of the WTO to begin a new round of multilateral negotiations in Seattle in 1999 illustrated the difficulty of pushing through comprehensive multilateral liberalization. Even at present the world trading system is caught in a log-jam due to unresolved issues in the current Doha Round of negotiations. Therefore, countries in East Asia that are largely dependent on world trade do not want to be left to the mercy of multilateral trade talks, and have pursued FTAs with like-minded economies. In addition, economies such as the US and the EU have stronger negotiating power than the developing countries in the WTO. Accordingly, negotiations within the WTO have, increasingly, seen a movement of agendas toward issues other than tariffs, such as the environment, intellectual property rights, labour standards and competition policy, which are of more interest to the US and the EU but are of less interest to the East Asian countries.

The third factor is the East Asian financial crisis of 1997-98, which demonstrated the risk of contagion and investors' perception of the region as a "single market". This factor may have operated as a trigger, which explains the timing of the recent movement towards regionalism in East Asia. The impotence of the Asia Pacific Economic Cooperation Forum (APEC) and ASEAN in the wake of the financial crisis added to the grievances of crisis-hit East Asian countries (Lloyd and Lee, 2001).

The purpose of this chapter is to review recent movements toward regionalism in East Asia and discuss how Korea (and other countries of East Asia) should respond to these movements. Section 2 summarizes recent developments in RTAs in East Asia. Section 3 then summarizes responses from Korea that were made in the last few years. Section 4 discusses how Korea should respond in the future in both plurilateral and bilateral contexts. In particular, we present six important selection criteria that could be useful in determining eligible FTA partners for Korea. Some concluding remarks are given in section 5.

9.2 RECENT DEVELOPMENTS OF RTAs IN EAST ASIA

Until the Asian crisis erupted in 1997, East Asian economies had pursued a multilateral approach to trade. In particular, Japan, China and Korea were the world's only major economies that had yet to conclude an FTA. The sole exception was ASEAN, which had been planning an FTA for several years with the target date of 2002. However, a new tide of regionalism is emerging in East Asia. A number of bilateral FTAs have been concluded and are being negotiated or studied. Table 9.1 summarizes the regional trade arrangements involving East Asian countries.

Singapore, the most trade-reliant ASEAN member, started the ball rolling by signing FTAs with 17 countries including New Zealand (2000), Japan (2002), Australia (2003), the United States (2003) and Jordan (2004). Singapore is currently negotiating/laying the groundwork for similar bilateral FTAs with Canada, India, Korea, Mexico, Sri Lanka, Bahrain, Egypt and Taiwan.

Thailand is also one of the leading proponents of the creation of bilateral FTAs, signing an FTA with China in 2003, a Closer Economic Relations (CER) Framework Agreement with India in 2003 and a Closer Economic Relations and free-trade agreement (CER-FTA) with Australia in 2004. It has also negotiated similar FTA deals with the USA, Japan, Chile, New Zealand, Papua New Guinea, Peru and Bahrain, and aims to reach bilateral FTAs with

Table 9.1 Regional Trade Agreements Involving East Asian Countries

Country	Concluded			Under negotiation		Joint Study		Proposal
		Signed	Enforced		Initiated		Initiated	
Singapore	AFTA	Jan 1992	Jan 2003	P3(Singapore, NZ, Chile)	Sep 2003	Taiwan	Sep 2002	Bahrain
	New Zealand	Nov 2000	Jan 2001	Canada	Oct 2001			China
	Australia	Nov 2002	Jul 2003	India	May 2003			Egypt
	EFTA	Jun 2002	Jan 2003	Korea	Nov 2000			Kuwait
	Japan	Jan 2002	Nov 2002	Mexico	Jul 2000			Pakistan
	US	Jan 2003	Jan 2004	Sri Lanka	Aug 2003			
	Jordan	May 2004	--	Panama	Feb 2004			
				Bahrain	Oct 2003			
				Egypt	Feb 2004			
				Peru	Nov 2004			
				Qatar	Dec 2004			
Thailand	AFTA	Jan 1992	Jan 2003	US	Jun 2004	Korea	Nov 1999	Bangladesh
	China PTA	Oct 2003	--	Japan	-		- Mar 2001	Kuwait
	India	Oct 2003	--	Chile	-			Malaysia
	Macao	Oct 2003	--	New Zealand	Jun 2004			Oman
	Australia	2004		Papua New Guinea	-			Qatar
				Peru	Oct 2003			Saudi Arabia
				Bahrain	Dec 2002			Taiwan
								UAE
Philippines	AFTA	Jan 1992	Jan 2003	Japan	Feb 2004			Taiwan

Table 9.1 continued

Country	Concluded			Under negotiation		Joint Study		Proposal
		Signed	Enforced		Initiated		Initiated	
Taiwan	Panama	Aug 2003	--			Singapore	Sept 2002	Philippines
						US	Dec 2002	Thailand
						Japan	Dec 2003	
India	Sri Lanka	Dec 1998	--	Singapore	May 2003			China
	Bangladesh	Mar 2003	--	ASEAN	Jan 2004			Japan
	Afghanistan	Mar 2003	--					Korea
	MERCOSUR	Jan 2004	--					
	Thailand	Oct 2003	--					
ASEAN	AFTA	Jan 1992	Jan 2003	Japan	Sept 2003	Korea	Mar 2004	Australia/New Zealand
	China	Nov 2004		CER	Sept 2001			US
				Singapore-China	Nov 2002			EU
				India	Jan 2004			+3 (China, Japan, Korea)
								+5(China, Japan, Korea, CER)
								+5 (China, Japan, Korea, HK, Taiwan)

Table 9.1 continued

Country	Concluded	Signed	Enforced	Under negotiation	Initiated	Joint Study	Initiated	Proposal
China	Hong Kong	Jun 2003	--	New Zealand	Apr 2004	Australia	Oct 2003	Chile
	Macao	Oct 2003	--	GCC	Sept 2004	Japan-Korea	Feb 2003	India
	ASEAN	Nov 2004	--	Chile	Jan 2005			Singapore
								SACU
Japan	Singapore	Jan 2002	Nov 2002	Korea	Dec 2003	Australia	Jun 2003	Brazil (MERCOSUR)
	Mexico	Sep 2004	Jan 2005	Philippines	Feb 2004	Chile	May 2000	Canada
				Malaysia	Jan 2004	Taiwan	Dec 2003	India
				Thailand	Jan 2004	China-Korea	Feb 2003	New Zealand
				Indonesia	Spring 2005 (planned)			
				ASEAN	Apr 2005 (planned)			
Korea	Chile	Oct 2002	Apr 2004	Japan	Dec 2003	Australia	Nov 2002	Canada
				Singapore	Apr 2004	New Zealand	Mar 2000 - Aug 2001	India
				EFTA	Jan 2005	Thailand	Nov 1999 - Mar 2001	US
				ASEAN	Spring 2005 (planned)	China-Japan	Feb 2003	EU
						Mexico	Oct 2004	
						India	Dec 2004	

Sources: Various newspaper websites. For Singapore, http://www.mti.gov.sg. For ASEAN, http://www.aseansec.org. For Japan, http://www.meti.go.jp. For Korea, http://www.mofat.go.kr.

countries like Korea, Bangladesh, Qatar, Oman, Kuwait, the United Arab Emirates, Saudi Arabia, Malaysia and Taiwan.

The Philippines is also exploring the possibility of signing FTAs with countries outside ASEAN. It is currently negotiating an FTA deal with Japan. Taiwan also signed its first FTA with Panama in August 2003, and is exploring similar FTAs with a number of countries such as Japan, Singapore and the United States.

China has also been very active in pursuing FTA deals with countries in East Asia. In November 2004, it reached an FTA with ASEAN for trade in goods. It is now negotiating/studying FTAs with countries such as New Zealand, Chile, Australia, Japan and Korea. Japan signed an FTA in January 2002 with Singapore and another in September 2004 with Mexico. Japan is currently under official negotiation for concluding FTAs with Korea, Thailand, Malaysia and the Philippines, among which a basic agreement was reached in November 2004 with the Philippines. The negotiations with Indonesia and ASEAN as a whole will be initiated in the first half of 2005.

Multi-country agreements are also being negotiated, proposed or studied in East Asia. During an ASEAN+3 summit in 1999, South Korea proposed establishing an expert panel, the East Asia Vision Group, as the first step in exploring the possibility of forging a regional cooperation mechanism. This group discussed ways to develop the ASEAN+3 grouping into a regional cooperation forum. At the ASEAN+3 summit in November 2001, Korea also called for the formation of an East Asian economic community equivalent to the East Asian Free Trade Area (EAFTA), that could serve as an East Asian economic arrangement to counterbalance other major regional economic blocs such as NAFTA and the EU.

The Philippines has also proposed the EAFTA. A Northeast Asian Free Trade Area consisting of China, Japan and Korea is also being studied. At the ASEAN+3 summit in November 1999, Japan, Korea and China agreed to launch a joint research project involving institutes from the three countries to discuss the possibility of forming an FTA among themselves in Northeast Asia. Since then the three countries have held a summit every year at the ASEAN+3 meetings, and have held regular meetings between their finance ministers.[2]

Thus, in the East Asian region, each one of the major economies is involved in negotiations with more than one other country or a group of countries on the formation of bilateral/plurilateral agreements. This trend toward regionalism is likely to spread to other East Asian countries.

The recent regionalism of East Asia is not altogether new, as Mahathir Mohamed, the former Prime Minister of Malaysia, proposed an East Asian Economic Group (EAEG) a decade ago. However, the EAEG proposal was not pursued, largely because the United States strongly objected and the proposed member countries, Japan and Korea in particular, were reluctant in the face of this objection.

Regionalism in East Asia has also been proceeding on financial issues. For example, the Manila Framework drawn up in November 1997 was aimed at achieving financial stability in the region through cooperation between East Asian countries. Fourteen countries from the Asia-Pacific region have participated in the Framework, which covers many issues including intra-regional financial cooperation, mutual cooperation to strengthen financial architecture and surveillance, and cooperation in monitoring intra-regional capital movements.

In May 2000, ASEAN+3 members announced the Chiang Mai Initiative and agreed to build a network of currency swap arrangements. A currency swap agreement was signed at their annual summit meeting in Singapore in November 2000, and there has been much discussion about creating an Asian Monetary Fund (AMF) and common currency baskets. The idea of an AMF was proposed by Japan in September 1997, and Japan expressed its willingness to contribute more than half of the funds needed (US$100 billion). Hong Kong, Taiwan and Singapore have also indicated their intention of participating in the AMF, and Korea and most other East Asian countries agreed to the idea. Even China, which was against the idea at first, has changed its attitude.[3] The East Asia Vision Group also studied a joint surveillance of short-term capital movements and an early warning system in East Asia. The group later proposed the establishment of an East Asian Monetary Fund and a regional exchange rate coordination mechanism, with the long-term goal of creating a common currency area.

Hong Kong and the Philippines have proposed the creation of the Asian Currency Unit (ACU). An Asian Bank for Reconstruction and Development, an Asian BIS (Bank for International Settlement) and a Northeast Asian Development Bank have also been proposed.

9.3 KOREA'S RESPONSE

Until the mid 1990s Korea's trade policy had long been based on multilateral trade liberalization, with regional trading arrangements largely ignored. However, in recent years, Korea has become actively engaged in looking at establishing FTAs with its trading partners, as regionalism emerges as a new axis of the global trade system.

As a first step, Korea started an FTA negotiation with Chile in 1998 that reached a conclusion in October 2002. The Korea-Chile FTA became effective as of April 2004. Korea has also been negotiating/examining FTAs with a number of economies. Korea started formal government level talks with Japan for an FTA in December 2003, aiming to sign the FTA by the end of 2005. There is strong apprehension in Korea that an FTA with Japan may lead to even larger trade deficits with Japan. Korea, however, expects that a Korea-Japan FTA can be a stepping-stone toward a greater China-Korea-Japan FTA or Northeast Asian FTA, and the ultimate creation of an East

Asian Economic Community.

In February 2004, Korea began talks with Singapore on an FTA, with the aim of concluding the negotiation by the end of 2004. Korea expects that a Korea-Singapore FTA would lay the foundation for trade expansion in Southeast Asia. Korea picked Singapore as its first FTA partner among ASEAN nations because the city-state's lack of an agricultural sector would make negotiations easier, with farm products being a sensitive issue in Korea.

As both China and Japan have begun actively seeking FTAs with ASEAN, Korea also held the first meeting of a joint study with ASEAN in March 2004 for the feasibility of a Korea-ASEAN FTA. Korea has also participated in informal talks on the need for the formation of an ASEAN+3.

In May 2004, Korea agreed to launch joint studies on the creation of FTAs with Mexico and a group of European countries (Switzerland, Norway, Iceland, Leichtenstein). Korea has also finished a joint feasibility study of FTAs with New Zealand and Thailand, respectively, and has considered concluding FTAs with Canada, India, New Zealand, Australia, the EU and the US.

In short, although its basic trade policy is still focused on strengthening the multilateral system, Korea now believes that FTA promotion is essential for maintaining its regional competitiveness in consideration of the rising FTA deals between Asian countries. With this background the following sections discuss the current status of Korea's major FTA initiatives.

Korea-Chile FTA

Background and current status

The initiative for a Korea-Chile Free Trade Agreement began in November 1998 from the Inter-Ministerial Committee on International Economic Coordination. The main objective of the FTA was to overcome the structural weakness of the Korean economy, which was heightened after the financial crisis, and to maximize the economic benefits of market expansion and foreign investment.

Before establishing FTAs with larger trade partners such as the US and Japan, however, Korea needed to pursue strategic FTAs with smaller partners in order to minimize risk and possible losses and to gain negotiating and operational experience. In this respect, Chile was chosen as Korea's first partner because it showed a strong interest in concluding an FTA. Also, Korea believed that Chile's open trade policy, and its accumulated experience in concluding FTAs with other countries, would certainly serve as a guide to conducting successful negotiations.

In December 1998 the Korean government formed a special task force on a Korea-Chile FTA that consisted of five specific technical groups covering:

market access, trade rules, services, intellectual property and legal procedures. A Korea-Chile FTA Joint Committee Meeting was held in Chile in order to discuss specific negotiation procedures.

In April 1999 the Korean and Chilean governments initiated the first meeting of the high-level working group for FTA negotiations. The main goal of this meeting was to discuss in depth the current economic situation of the two countries and major issues related to an FTA based on previously exchanged questionnaires. The second meeting was held in June 1999 in Santiago, Chile. This meeting was particularly important because the two countries, after extensive exchanges of information, decided to design the Framework Agreement in a general meeting. Based on the draft of the Framework Agreement proposed by the Korean delegation, they agreed on three basic principles of a Korea-Chile FTA: a comprehensive FTA, liberalization in all areas and transparency. The comprehensive FTA implies their commitment to abide by the basic terms and conditions of GATT/WTO, which emphasizes wider sectoral coverage while avoiding the misuse of the agreement for narrow and discriminatory arrangements. The scope of the coverage includes seven specific areas: goods, services, investment, intellectual property rights (IPR), government procurement, competition policy, and dispute settlement and other legal matters.

After two successful high-level negotiation meetings, the two heads of state officially launched the Korea-Chile FTA negotiations at the APEC summit meeting in September 1999. After the official declaration, a high-level negotiating group conducted six rounds of negotiations during the 1999-2002 period.

During the six negotiations the two sides elaborated and reviewed the draft text of the agreement, and exchanged their preliminary tariff concession schedules. However, some disagreements arose over the tariff concessions for politically sensitive sectors. Korea had proposed that some sensitive sectors such as agriculture should be exempted, but Chile insisted on making no exceptions and, if they were to be made, wanted to exclude some manufacturing products from the tariff concession. Finally, in October 2002, the Korea-Chile FTA negotiation reached a conclusion with special treatment of those sensitive sectors. However, the Korea-Chile FTA faced strong resistance from farmers in Korea, and it took a while for the National Assembly to ratify the FTA. The Korea-Chile FTA became effective as of April 2004.

Analysis of economic effects

An assessment of the economic effects of a Korea-Chile FTA using a CGE model for three basic scenarios was conducted by KIEP in 1998.[4] The first scenario was based on complete tariff elimination across all sectors in both countries. The second scenario was based on complete tariff elimination in general sectors and partial tariff reduction for agricultural products and livestock. The final scenario assumes zero tariffs in all sectors except for agriculture and livestock.

According to Table 9.2 the three scenarios would bring almost the same positive results for Korea's welfare level, with an increase of about US$950-960 million per year. On the other hand, Korea would see its GDP increase by 0.01 per cent in all three scenarios. Growth of Korea's exports to Chile (US$660 million) would exceed that of imports (US$240-260 million), thereby resulting in an additional trade surplus of $US400-420 million in all three cases.

Table 9.2 Expected economic effects of a Korea-Chile FTA

Unit: US$ million

	Overall Tariff Liberalization	50% Tariff Reduction in Agriculture	With Agriculture Excluded
Welfare	960	960	950
GDP (%)	0.01	0.01	0.01
Exports	660	660	660
Imports	260	250	240
Trade Balance	400	410	420

Source: Cheong and Yi (2000).

Future challenges

The successful completion of an FTA with Chile will be of special importance for Korea's future FTA policy because other potential agreements will heavily depend on the first model. In particular, it will bear an important symbolic meaning for other potential FTAs under consideration with large economies.

Korea considers Chile an appropriate FTA partner due to not only economic but also strategic considerations. As the two countries share complementary trade and production structures, the conclusion of a Korea-Chile FTA, in general, will bring mutual benefits in the short term. Moreover, in the long term, the strategic location of Chile will serve as a gateway for Korea to gain access to the huge Latin American market, and expand to other free trade areas previously established by Chile. However, some obstacles and challenges still lie ahead for the successful conclusion of a Korea-Chile FTA.

Geographical distance

Frankel (1997), in his work, *Regional Trading Blocs,* emphasized the importance of distance, using the concept of a gravity model. Based on this model, it is assumed that trade between countries depends positively on their size and inversely on distance. The effect of distance on trade is directly associated with three categories of costs: shipping costs, time-related costs and cultural unfamiliarity costs. In order to reduce these costs, and maximize the benefits of trade liberalization, it is desirable to form regional trade agreements between neighbouring countries, i.e. within a natural trading bloc.[5]

From this perspective a Korea-Chile FTA can be regarded as an unnatural trading bloc, where a country forms a bloc with a country on a different continent with which it has a relatively small volume of trade. The formation of such unnatural trading blocs may have smaller effects on welfare and trade expansion as intercontinental transport costs are very high. Therefore, the main challenge will be how to develop efficient infrastructures in three cost-related areas (shipping costs, time-related costs and cultural unfamiliarity) between the two countries so that the disadvantages of such long distance trading may be alleviated.

Response from politically sensitive sectors

One of the main obstacles in pursuing a Korea-Chile FTA will be the response from politically sensitive sectors. Due to the complementary structure of Korean and Chilean industry, trade liberalization will certainly bring benefits to Korea's competitive export sectors, including electronics, automobiles and chemicals. However, an import surge is expected in politically sensitive sectors in which Chile has a comparative advantage, including agriculture, forestry and fisheries.

While the manufacturing sector has generally shown a positive attitude toward a Korea-Chile FTA, the primary sector, in particular agricultural groups, has expressed deep concern. The fiercest opposition has come from producers of fruit such as grapes, kiwis and apples, in which Chilean exports, both natural and processed, are highly competitive and maintain a dominant position in the world market. Korean farmers and agricultural organizations fear that imports of grapes, kiwi fruit and apples from Chile will dramatically increase as a result of tariff elimination, resulting in decreased sales and prices of domestic products and reduced income for farmers.

The need for support and active participation of the private sector

For the successful ratification of a Korea-Chile FTA it is important that business and industrial groups, that will be the main beneficiaries of the FTA, take an active role in the process. They can provide technical assistance and useful advice that reflect the practical needs and problems they come across in their daily business transactions and will facilitate the implementation of an FTA through technical cooperation, strategic alliances and private investment.

On the other hand, public promotional efforts regarding the ongoing process and its possible benefits and challenges are needed so that the general public does not fear that such economic opening will lead to a surge of foreign imports and massive unemployment. In fact, public concern is unavoidable as this is Korea's first FTA. Therefore, policymakers need to work in a consistent and responsible manner to gain public confidence and support for its FTA policy.

Compatibility with multilateral initiatives

Regional integration agreements, by their preferential and discriminatory nature, seem to contradict the basic principles of the multilateral trading system based on Most-Favoured-Nation (MFN) rules. However, accepting them as a reality, the designers of GATT/WTO tried to make such agreements compatible with a rule-based multilateral approach and a more open world trading system.

However, some economists still argue that the current spread of regional trading blocs is undermining the principle of MFN treatment under GATT/WTO, as such agreements have many loopholes and the GATT/WTO does not effectively enforce its requirements for such regional agreements. As a Korea-Chile FTA also corresponds to such preferential and discriminatory trade agreements, the central concern is how to make the rules and procedures consistent with the multilateral rules of GATT/WTO.

Korea and Chile have traditionally favoured a multilateral approach as their basic policy option for fostering trade and investment liberalization; therefore both countries committed themselves to faithfully abiding by the rule-based requirements of GATT/WTO on forming an FTA in order to not undermine the basic principle of non-discrimination and bringing harm to third countries. This position is reflected in the three basic principles of the Korea-Chile Framework Agreement: a comprehensive FTA, liberalization in all areas and transparency in implementation. This very spirit should be respected throughout the whole process of FTA negotiation and implementation.

Korea-Japan FTA

Background and current status

From the viewpoint of geographic proximity and cultural similarity Korea and Japan could have maintained a much more cooperative relationship, yet, for almost 30 years since the normalization of diplomatic ties, bilateral relations have fallen short of expectations due to various issues. These include the import sources diversification programme, disputes over the Dokdo Island, past affairs, the prohibition of importing cultural products from Japan, and Korea's huge trade deficit with Japan due to the high degree of its economic dependency.

Recently, however, Korea and Japan have been actively seeking to pursue a bilateral FTA. Talks on a Korea-Japan FTA started in 1998 when President Kim Dae-Jung and then Japanese Prime Minister Keizo Obuchi proposed the Action Plan for a New Korea-Japan Partnership for the 21st Century. The Action Plan suggested the promotion of trade, investment and cultural exchanges as the main targets of cooperation. As the first concrete step the two governments agreed to conduct joint studies on the economic effects of a Korea-Japan FTA at the private-sector level in October 1998. For that purpose Korea and Japan established a 21st Century Korea–Japan Economic Relations Study Committee, and a joint study was simultaneously conducted by KIEP (Korea Institute for International Economic Policy) and IDE/JETRO (Institute of Developing Economies/Japan External Trade Organization) on the feasibility of a Korea-Japan FTA.

In May 2000, a joint symposium, "Toward a Korea-Japan FTA: Assessments and Prospects", was held in Seoul where the two sides presented the results of their respective studies and shared their views on ways to pursue an FTA. Although no official negotiations have yet been launched the private sector took the lead in early 2001 in the form of a "Business Forum", which featured extensive exchanges of views on pursuing a mutually beneficial FTA. The first joint meeting of the Business Forum was held in Seoul in September 2001, co-hosted by the Korea Chamber of Commerce (KCC) and the Japan-Korea Industrial Technology Foundation (JKITCF). Responding to the Business Forum's recommendation that both governments hasten to conclude a bilateral FTA, a tripartite joint study group consisting of government officials, industry representatives and scholars was established and held its first meeting in July 2002.

In December 2003 the two nations started formal government level talks for an FTA, aiming to sign the FTA by the end of 2005.

Economic effects of a Korea-Japan FTA[6]

Effects of Tariff Elimination

Here we compare three different CGE analyses conducted by KIEP, Korea Institute for Industrial Economics and Trade (KIET) and IDE. The effects of a Korea-Japan FTA on the macroeconomic sector are summarized in Table 9.3. As for real GDP the KIEP and KIET studies give the same result: a 0.07 per cent fall in Korea's real GDP. This decrease in domestic production would be due to the lower demand for investment and increased net imports from Japan, as well as the shift of domestic resources to inefficient sectors with lower factor productivity such as agriculture and light industries. On the other hand the effects of a Korea-Japan FTA on welfare are somewhat different. According to the KIEP analysis the subsequent deterioration of real income would bring a 0.19 per cent reduction of welfare. In contrast, the KIET report estimates that the welfare level will increase by 0.48 per cent, which is attributed to the expansion of private consumption stimulated by the reduction of prices of Japanese imports after tariff elimination.

Although KIEP's estimates of export and import growth rates (2.32 per cent and 3.40 per cent respectively) are higher than KIET's (0.43 per cent and 1.0 per cent), both studies equally expect that the growth rate of Korea's total imports will exceed that of total exports, thus aggravating the overall trade balance. In contrast, IDE estimated that the growth in Korea's total exports (2.80 per cent) would surpass total imports (2.47 per cent).

Korea's trade balance with Japan is expected to record an additional trade deficit of US$6.1 billion and US$3.4 billion, respectively, according to KIEP and KIET. IDE's analysis also expects that Korea's trade deficit will grow additionally by US$3.88 billion. The increased trade deficit with Japan comes from the expansion of bilateral trade. This is due to Korea's inelastic structure of trade with Japan and trade diversion resulting in an additional shift to Japanese imports, as well as Korea's worsening terms of trade resulting from the elimination of its relatively higher tariff rates.[7] However, both the KIEP and KIET studies estimate that trade balances with third countries will improve, recording a trade surplus of US$2.8–US$4.6 billion. Therefore, Korea's total trade balance will post a deficit increase of only US$590 million-US$1.5 billion.

On the other hand the IDE study expects that Korea's trade surplus with third countries will be greater than the trade deficit with Japan, thereby resulting in a US$290 million improvement in Korea's overall trade balance.

Table 9.3 Economic effects of a Korea-Japan FTA

Unit: US$ billion

Economic Indicators (Korea)		KIEP	KIET	IDE
Welfare (%)		-0.19	0.48	-
Real GDP (%)		-0.07	-0.07	-
Changes in Total Exports (%)		2.32	0.43	2.80
Changes in Total Imports (%)		3.40	1.00	2.47
Trade Balance	Changes in Trade Balance with Japan	-6.09	-3.36	-3.88
	Changes in Trade Balance with Other Regions	4.56	2.77	4.17
	Changes in Total Trade Balance	-1.54	-0.59	0.29

Sources: KIEP (2000), IDE (2000) and KIET (1999).

Overall economic effects (tariff elimination + productivity enhancement)

The KIEP report extends its analysis by assuming that a Korea-Japan FTA will attract a yearly average of US$3 billion of FDI, mainly from Japan. If this is invested mainly in Korea's heavy and chemical industries, it is expected to increase Korea's factor productivity by 1 percentage point annually through the cross-sectoral reallocation of production resources. Based on this assumption the KIEP study estimates the combined effects of tariff elimination and productivity enhancement under a Korea-Japan FTA (Table 9.4).[8]

According to the KIEP analysis, with the combination of the effects of tariff elimination and productivity enhancement, Korea's total trade balance with the world is expected to improve by US$1.48 billion. Korea can expect real GDP growth of 2.81 percentage points and an annual welfare level improvement of 11.24 percentage points. It expects that the trade deficit with Japan will expand further by US$6.53 billion. However, with the more than US$7 billion improvement of the trade surplus with the rest of the world, Korea's total trade balance is expected to improve slightly by US$1.48 billion.

Future challenges

The peculiarities of the Korea-Japan economic relations identified below may act as real barriers to realizing a successful Korea-Japan FTA. The key question is how to design a Korea-Japan FTA in a way that can maximize mutual benefit, while addressing these challenging issues.

Table 9.4 Overall economic effects of a Korea-Japan FTA

Unit: US$ billion, %

Economic Indicators(Korea)		Overall Economic Effects
	Welfare (%)	11.24
	Real GDP (%)	2.81
Trade Balance	Changes in Trade Balance with Japan	-6.53
	Changes in Trade Balance with Other Regions	8.01
	Changes in Total Trade Balance	1.48

Source: Sohn (2001b).

Further deterioration of the trade balance

Although Korea and Japan are important trading partners for each other, Korea suffers from a serious chronic trade deficit with Japan.[9] If we examine bilateral trade for the period 1965-2000 Korea's trade balance with Japan steadily deteriorated, peaking at more than US$15 billion dollars in the mid 1990s. Immediately after the Asian financial crisis it dropped sharply to US$4.6 billion in 1998. Yet, with the economic recovery, it is now worsening again, recording a deficit of US$11.4 billion in 2000. In fact, Korea then suffered its largest trade deficit with Japan.[10]

Moreover, the various economic feasibility studies previously mentioned predict that Korea's trade deficit with Japan will increase rather than decrease as a result of a Korea-Japan FTA. Although this negative result of tariff elimination is only a static, short-term effect of an FTA, it is an important issue for the public. The desirability of a Korea-Japan FTA itself may be put into question by this negative public perception.

Of course, an FTA cannot be assessed only in terms of the short-term effects of tariff elimination. The long-term dynamic gains from an integrated market, intensified competition, corporate alliances and attraction of FDI are expected to more than offset the short-term negative effects. However, to realize these dynamic gains, more sophisticated and detailed rules and cooperation mechanisms will be needed in designing a Korea-Japan FTA.

Stagnation of bilateral direct investment

Bilateral direct investment between the two countries has been relatively stagnant compared to the level of trade flows. After record levels in 1994 and 1995, investment has fallen and stagnated since. Of Korea's total FDI, Japan's share peaked at 34.85 per cent in 1994 but, thereafter, dropped drastically, accounting for only between 7.6 per cent and 8.0 per cent since 1997. Although FDI from Japan recently posted a growth rate of more than 200 per cent, recording US$2.4 billion in 2000, its share (15.6 per cent) is still below the level of Korea's other major trading partners such as the US (18.6 per cent) and EU (29.3 per cent). In addition, Japan's share of Korea's total outward direct investment (ODI) has stayed at 2 per cent, recording US$94 million in 2000 (1.95 per cent). The share is insignificant compared to Korea's ODI in the US (24.5 per cent) and China (13.4 per cent). The stagnation of bilateral investment implies that there are significant investment barriers between the two countries, including complex administration procedures, labour inflexibility, unfair business practices and strict investment regulations.

The expansion of bilateral investment is of particular interest for Korea since it will not only increase the benefits of a Korea-Japan FTA by complementing trade, but also has the most efficient complementary method for alleviating the negative impact of tariff elimination on Korea's heavy and chemical industries.

Similarity in production structure: from inter-industry to intra-industry trade

The traditional theory of comparative advantage based on the "two country-two goods" model argues that free inter-industry trade between two countries can be mutually beneficial as they specialize in production and export of sectors that have comparative advantage.

According to the Revealed Comparative Advantage (RCA) analysis, however, Korea and Japan share a similar structure of comparative advantages, indicating that their export structures are assumed to be in a highly competitive relationship.

As a result, a Korea-Japan FTA is not expected to create an effective specialization system due to the similar production and export structures of the two countries. Moreover, if we assume that an FTA reinforces the current system of trade specialization between the two countries, a Korea-Japan FTA will negatively affect some of Korea's competitive sectors such as iron and steel, and electric and electronic products. This is because these sectors, in spite of their comparative advantages, will eventually lose competitiveness in the domestic and Japanese markets, thus resulting in import specialization from Japan. On the other hand, export specialization in some inefficient sectors, including primary and light industries, will reduce general production efficiency due to the absorption of production factors by these industries.

Therefore, the key question will be how to develop intra-industry trade in those sectors where Korea and Japan both have comparative advantage in the world and intensely compete with one another. A fair system of specialization and product differentiation will promote intra-industry trade between the firms of the two countries so that intensified competition promotes the dynamic gains of an FTA rather than develop into a battle for survival.

Need for a comprehensive business initiative

In order to reap the full benefits of the expansion of trade and investment and the stimulation of competition and productivity enhancement, a Korea-Japan FTA should be approached through a comprehensive framework that includes not only increased market access through the elimination of tariff and non-tariff barriers but also the promotion of investment and technical and industrial cooperation, mutual recognition agreements, and the effective implementation of competition policy. In this regard the two governments can work closely together to coordinate their domestic reform policies, such as deregulation and increased transparency in corporate governance, as well as their external policies for promoting bilateral cooperation in investment, industry and technology and the expansion of the exchange of human resources.

In addition, a wide range of discussions on a Korea-Japan FTA should take place within and between the business sectors of the two countries, to foster their role as an integral part of designing an FTA.

Korea-US FTA

Background and current status

Though Korea and the US have been important trading partners for four decades, their trade relationship has often been threatened by serious disputes. Talks on a Korea-US FTA actually began in the late 1980s when, in view of their growing economic interdependency, both countries felt a strong need for deeper bilateral cooperation, particularly in the trade sector. As Korean exports faced severe trade sanctions under Section 301 of the Trade Act of 1974, Korea's main interest lay in securing the US market by avoiding future trade retaliation and discrimination. On the other hand the US hoped that an FTA with Korea would reduce significant trade barriers, thereby facilitating access to the Korean market. With this growing interest in renewing their bilateral partnership, several academic studies have been conducted on the feasibility of a Korea-US FTA.

Real progress, however, came in the late 1990s when the two countries started to actively pursue FTA initiatives as a parallel approach to multilateral trade liberalization. Beyond NAFTA the US has initiated FTA talks with other strategic partners such as Chile and Singapore. Korea, for its part, officially announced an FTA as its main trade policy framework. As a preliminary step to an FTA, in June 1999, the two heads of state agreed to launch talks on a bilateral investment agreement. Although the negotiations reached a stalemate due to screen quota problems, an intensive review is currently being made at the working group level for a breakthrough.

With no formal bilateral FTA initiatives at the government level, the private sector, particularly US and Korean companies, have so far been leading talks on the possibility of an FTA. Also, on the political scene, Democratic Senator Max Baucus submitted a bill, The United States-Korea Free Trade Agreement Act of 1999, that would allow the US government to fast track the launch of FTA negotiations. He reintroduced the bill on May 23, 2001.[11] As a part of this legislative initiative the Senate Finance Committee requested the US International Trade Commission to submit a report in December 2000 on a feasibility study on a Korea-US FTA. In addition, a public hearing was recently held by the trade commission to discuss the issue of a Korea-US FTA from the business community's perspective. The participating US industries - the textile, automobile, cosmetic and footwear industries - expressed a rather reserved approach to a Korea-US FTA, due to Korea's high non-tariff barriers and strong competitiveness.

Although not much progress is expected on Korea-US FTA talks in the short term, the two countries show a preference for each other as potential FTA partners. Therefore, once the need for, and interest in, a bilateral FTA are clearly identified and recognized, Korea-US FTA negotiations will gain momentum.

Analysis of the economic effects

Two important studies conducted on the economic effects of a Korea-US FTA made by KIEP and the Institute for International Economics (IIE) in 1999 and 2001 are as follows. The KIEP study is based on the following different scenarios: a comprehensive liberalization, a partial liberalization with 50 per cent tariff reduction in agriculture and a 100 per cent reduction in all other sectors, and a partial liberalization with 0 per cent tariff reduction in agriculture.[12] As seen in Table 9.5 the greatest welfare increase (1.73 per cent) is expected in the case of comprehensive liberalization. If agriculture is completely excluded from the liberalization scheme, it is estimated that welfare benefits will fall to US$3.3 billion. Real income is expected to increase in all three cases, though in the case of the exclusion of agriculture (0.78 per cent), the growth rate will be only half that of comprehensive liberalization (1.47 per cent).

Table 9.5 Economic effects of a Korea-US FTA on the Korean economy (KIEP)

Unit: US$ billion, %

	Comprehensive Liberalization (100%)	Agriculture	
		Partial Liberalization (50%)	Whole Exclusion
Welfare Index (%)	1.73	1.51	1.19
Equivalent Variation	4.8	4.2	3.3
Real Income (%)	1.47	1.10	0.78
Price Index (%)	-3.11	-0.07	0.22

Source: Cheong and Wang (1999).

On the other hand the IIE study estimates welfare effects of a Korea-US FTA based on two main scenarios: full liberalization and excluding agriculture. For each scenario it also assesses medium-term and long-term effects depending on a fixed or flexible endowment of production factors.

As seen in Table 9.6, according to the IIE analysis, the two scenarios produce welfare benefits. However, the welfare gains are more than double under a comprehensive FTA, with US$4.1 billion in the medium run. If the allocation and the level of capital stock are to adjust in the long run the welfare benefits are expected to be even greater, amounting to US$10.9 billion.[13]

In terms of real income it is estimated that comprehensive liberalization in the long run will result in a growth rate of 2.41 per cent, more than double that of the case of partial liberalization with agriculture excluded (1.09 per cent), which is similar to the KIEP results.

As for bilateral trade volumes, a Korea-US FTA is expected to result in an increase in Korean exports as well as imports from the US. Korea will enjoy an additional trade surplus with the US if agriculture is excluded. It is estimated, however, that under a comprehensive and medium run scenario the growth of Korea's imports from the US (46.1 per cent) will exceed export growth, thereby leading to a deterioration of Korea's trade balance with the US. However, in the IIE report, Korea's trade balance with Japan is expected to improve, and, therefore, its overall trade balance may become positive depending on the magnitude of trade creation and trade diversion.

Table 9.6 Economic effects of a Korea-US FTA on the Korean Economy (IIE) [1]

Unit: US$ million, %

Economic Effects	Comprehensive FTA		Agriculture Excluded	
	Medium Run	Long Run	Medium Run	Long Run
Welfare Effects [2]	4,099.6 (0.91)	10,860.7 (2.41)	1,712.2 (0.38)	4,923.4 (1.09)
Exports to U.S (%)[3]	26.2	30.3	23.8	25.5
Imports from U.S (%)[3]	46.1	49.4	22.1	23.3

Note: [1] The base year for the simulation is 1995.
[2] Mean equivalent variation in millions of 1995 US dollars; per cent of GDP in parentheses
[3] Per cent change.

Source: Choi and Schott (2001).

Future challenges

Although a Korea-US FTA in general is expected to bring economic benefits through the expansion of bilateral trade and investment and efficient allocation of resources, the two countries may face several difficulties in carrying out successful negotiations when different interests are involved.

One important issue is how to cope with the strong opposition from politically sensitive sectors: agriculture in Korea's case; textiles, apparel and automobiles in the US. As we have already seen in the case of a Korea-Chile FTA the main cause of the stalemate in negotiations was Korea's agriculture sector, which is strongly opposed to opening agriculture. Taking into account the high competitiveness of the US in the production and export of agricultural products, even greater opposition is expected from Korea's agricultural sector when pursuing a Korea-US FTA. The US, on the other hand, is expected to receive strong pressure from the textiles, apparel and automobile industries, where Korea is highly competitive (Choi and Schott, 2001). The two countries should, therefore, seek to make mutual concessions in the areas where the most interest is at stake. In this sense a Korea-US FTA, even based on a comprehensive framework, could allow some reservations and exceptions in some specific areas, as was the case with NAFTA.

Another issue is the trade balance. As shown in the analysis of economic effects, Korea's trade balance with the US is expected to shift as a result of a Korea-US FTA. Some may raise the question of the merit of an FTA with the US if it will result in worsening, rather than improving, Korea's trade balance. However, the short-term negative effects could be offset in the long run by strengthening Korea's competitiveness through FDI and technology transfer from the US. Moreover, Korea will enjoy a trade expansion effect by avoiding significant trade barriers in the form of anti-dumping and countervailing measures by the US.[14]

The US is also showing great interest in the opening of the financial and service sectors and trade rules-related areas, such as the elimination of restrictive trade regulations and unfair practices, and the protection of intellectual property rights and raising labour and environmental standards. Another main objective of Korea's FTA policy is the restructuring of the economy through the adoption of rules and standards of developed countries. Therefore, in the case of a Korea-US FTA, Korea should work in closer cooperation with the US to improve its inefficient economic structure, thereby maximizing the potential gains of an FTA.

Korea-China-Japan FTA[15]

Since the Asian financial crisis, Northeast Asian countries have felt a pressing need to strengthen economic cooperation through establishing some kind of regional economic integration. Currently, there are various ongoing talks on possible approaches to materialize cooperation in Northeast Asia.

The first approach is to establish a trilateral FTA among Korea, Japan and China. In this way Japan and Korea can take advantage of the huge market and cheap natural and human resources of China, while China can benefit from technology transfer and FDI from Korea and Japan. Moreover, no one is likely to suffer from a unilateral trade imbalance after tariff elimination as the trade deficit with one will be partly compensated by a trade surplus with the other, according to the current trade structure.

However, this approach seems difficult to achieve in the short term due to several reasons. First, although China joined the WTO by 2001 and is committed to reducing its average tariff rates from 16.8 per cent to 9.44 per cent by 2005, its applied tariff rates for Korea and Japan are expected to be still high, making a Korea-China-Japan FTA unrealizable. Moreover, China currently shows little interest in pursuing Northeast Asian economic integration. On the other hand, China and Korea may fear that economic integration will become another form of Japanese dominance due to their deepening economic dependency on Japan.

The second, and more feasible, approach is two-stage economic integration: form a bilateral FTA between Korea and Japan first and incorporate China at a later stage. As both Korea and Japan have a market economy and the economic gap between them is narrower than with China, relatively lower institutional barriers lie in the way of them forming an FTA. Moreover, the successful launch of a Korea-Japan FTA will motivate China to join as soon as possible in order to avoid serious trade diversion, thereby accelerating the process of Northeast Asian economic integration. However, the second approach also has drawbacks as seen in the previous discussion on a Korea-Japan FTA. In general, Korea, with its higher tariffs and lower level of technology, fears a deterioration of the trade imbalance with Japan and a deepening of economic dependency. On the other hand, China could take a negative position on any preferential trade agreement between Korea and Japan that excludes it.

Discussions have already started on the possibility of establishing Northeast Asian economic cooperation in the form of a Korea-China FTA, Korea-Japan FTA or Korea-China-Japan FTA. Considering the high concentration of intra-regional trade among the three countries, and the complementarity of their industrial structure and geographic proximity, there is a high probability that they will create some kind of economic cooperation in the future. The creation of an FTA between Korea, Japan and China will promote regional trade liberalization and high specialization in relatively competitive industries; therefore, it is expected to bring economic growth and raise the welfare level of the three countries. However, to realize such an FTA, a careful feasibility study based on possible trade and welfare effects should be performed in advance. In addition, as the three economies differ considerably in their trade norms and institutions, they need to harmonize their trade-related rules and procedures before the formation of an FTA. Moreover, overcoming historical animosity and forming public consensus will be another crucial task in addition to economic considerations.

9.4 VARIOUS FTA OPTIONS FACING KOREA

Plurilateral FTA options

There is no doubt that international trade has been, and will remain, an engine of economic growth for Korea (Harvie and Lee, 2003, 2004). Therefore, Korea, and other East Asian countries, should promote further trade liberalization through a number of means. Above all Korea, and other East Asian countries, should regard the multilateral approach as its basic policy option for fostering trade and investment liberalization and therefore commit itself to faithfully abide by the rule-based terms and conditions of GATT/WTO, and take an active role to accelerate the multilateral trade talks of the Doha Development Agenda (DDA) negotiations under the WTO (Harvie and Lee, 2002).

However, in this era of the coexistence of multilateralism and regionalism it is also believed that RTAs, in many cases, have served as stepping stones to integration into the global free trading system, helping industries, sectors and countries adjust to the competitive winds of liberalization. Therefore, acknowledging that regional and multilateral agreements are complementary rather than contradictory in the pursuit of more liberal and open trade, Korea also needs to pursue a parallel approach of multilateral and regional trade initiatives in order to protect and maximize the economic benefits of the continued liberalization process.

There are two different approaches toward promoting trade in the regional context. One is to pursue the formation of a plurilateral trade arrangement involving Korea and other East Asian countries. Another approach for Korea to take is to speed up forming bilateral FTAs with major trading partners. The plurilateral approach is illustrated in this sub-section, while the bilateral approach is illustrated in the next sub-section.

APEC is the only existing regional trade arrangement involving Korea. Thus, for Korea, a more rapid liberalization process under APEC might be an alternative to forming an East Asian regional trade arrangement. However, in its present form, APEC is not expected to show such a rapid liberalization process. This is because APEC is not an RTA in terms of the WTO and does not follow Article XXIV in requiring a plan or schedule of reductions in trade barriers; it has adopted a goal of "free and open trade and investment" for developed member economies by 2010 and for developing member economies by 2020, but to achieve this it relies instead on concerted action by a process of consensus among its member economies.

The main problem with the APEC consensus approach is the absence of a modality to persuade the slow movers to participate in these "concerted" actions. In the GATT/WTO, reciprocity involves all participating countries. APEC leaders and officials have avoided the detailed exchange of offers that characterize the GATT/WTO process, and indeed do not describe the APEC process as "negotiations". APEC introduced a peer review mechanism at the Auckland Meeting in order to try to speed up trade liberalization but it appears to have had little effect to date (Lloyd and Lee, 2001).

One possible way would be for Korea, along with some other major member economies, to propose that APEC become a free trade area. This has been advocated by Fred Bergsten, the Chair of the former Eminent Persons Group of APEC, and more recently by Lloyd (2001). It would be a sharp break with the non-discriminatory style of "open regionalism" that APEC has favoured. However, an RTA provides a well-tested and increasingly popular modality to achieve trade liberalization. It has one additional attraction: only one of the 21 members - Russia - is not involved in an existing or proposed RTA that includes other APEC members. One single APEC RTA would, provided it was for free trade within the area, have one set of preferences replacing many multi-layered sets of preferences in the Asia-Pacific region. It might not replace the sub-regional RTAs themselves, as some of them have harmonization, monetary cooperation and other deepening features that presumably would not be included in an APEC RTA. Under this possibility no APEC member economy would be discriminated against in any of their major markets other than the EU. This RTA would become more attractive as other RTAs in the Asia-Pacific region develop alongside other continental or hemispheric RTAs (Lloyd and Lee, 2001). However, this possibility would be very difficult to negotiate because of the large number of parties that have different levels of economic development.

Another possibility would be for Korea and a subset of countries to form a sub-regional agreement within APEC. This is not a new idea: some scholars and member countries have suggested that a subset of countries that share similar views could form a separate agreement among themselves (see Baldwin, 1993). Specifically, OECD member countries within APEC (such as the US, Japan, Canada, Australia and Korea), and some other advanced, open economies (such as Singapore, New Zealand and Chile) could agree on forming an FTA among themselves. In fact, these leading proponents of the creation of a bilateral/regional free-trade zone are currently negotiating, or have concluded, FTAs with each other and are potential FTA partners for Korea. The trade creation effect these FTA could have is almost as large as an APEC-wide FTA, while negotiations would be a lot less complex.

The third option is that the ASEAN+3 members form an East Asian Free Trade Area (EAFTA), which could promote regional interests and serve as a countervailing force to other dominant trading blocs such as the EU or NAFTA. In fact, China, Japan and Korea are now negotiating or proposing FTAs with ASEAN, respectively, as noted in section 2. If these FTAs are successfully concluded, no country in East Asia would discriminate against another. However, this possibility would be very difficult to negotiate because AFTA (ASEAN FTA) is founded on the basis of the "Enabling Clause" of GATT, being regarded as an exceptional case of preferential trading arrangements among developing countries. The incorporation of Korea, Japan and China to form an ASEAN+3 FTA will not be feasible unless AFTA is transformed into an FTA under GATT XXIV, covering substantially all trade.[16] Thus, the formation of ASEAN+3 would be a time-consuming and complex process, requiring ASEAN countries' full commitment to zero tariffs in almost all sectors. In addition, a practical difficulty facing Korea is that most ASEAN member countries and China have comparative advantages in agriculture and fisheries, which are very politically sensitive industries for Korea.

The fourth option is a variant of the ASEAN+3 FTA. That is, Korea pursues an ASEAN+5 FTA (ASEAN+3 plus Australia and New Zealand). This option is preferred by Japan as well as Australia and New Zealand and has several advantages. First, this would result in a larger trade creation effect than an ASEAN+3 FTA. Second, including Australia and New Zealand would reduce the leadership competition between China and Japan in heading for an East Asian FTA. Third, Australia and New Zealand, which have already concluded several FTAs including their own CER agreement, could render their accumulated experiences in forming an FTA in East Asia. Fourth, including Oceania countries that are English-speaking advanced economies could help East Asian countries reach an FTA that meets global standards. This option would also have similar difficulties in that it would require

ASEAN countries to have full commitment to zero tariffs in almost all sectors, and most ASEAN member countries as well as China, Australia and New Zealand have comparative advantages in agriculture and fisheries (Park and Lee, 2003).

The fifth option is to establish a Northeast Asian Free Trade Area (NEAFTA). As noted in section 3, considering the high concentration of intra-regional trade among the three countries and the complementarity of their industrial structure and geographic proximity, there is a high probability that they will create some kind of economic cooperation in the future. Japan and Korea could take advantage of the huge market and cheap natural and human resources of China, while China could benefit from technology transfer and FDI from Korea and Japan. Moreover, no one would suffer from a unilateral trade imbalance after tariff elimination as the trade deficit with one would be partly compensated by a trade surplus with the other, according to the current trade structure. Discussions have already started on the possibility of establishing Northeast Asian economic cooperation in the form of a Korea-China FTA, Korea-Japan FTA or Korea-China-Japan FTA. This approach also has difficulties. China's applied tariff rates for Korea and Japan are still high, and hence without doubt China currently shows little interest in this option. Moreover, overcoming historical animosity and forming public consensus will be another crucial task in addition to economic considerations. In addition, as the three economies differ considerably in their trade norms and institutions, they need to harmonize their trade-related rules and procedures before the formation of an FTA.

Bilateral FTA Options

Along with the multilateral and plurilateral approach toward trade liberalization, Korea could pursue bilateral FTA agreements with some key countries. However, finding good FTA partners that could maximize the gains of trade liberalization is not a simple proposition. Korea's FTA initiatives, still in their initial stages, lack clear and consistent direction. In order to define and project the future course of Korea's FTA policy, however, some clear selection criteria for choosing desirable FTA partners will be needed.[17]

Therefore, in this section, we first suggest six important selection criteria that could be useful in determining eligible FTA candidates. These are: the structure of comparative advantage, income level, geographical proximity, market size, the level of outstanding trade barriers, and trade-induced adjustment costs.[18]

The structure of comparative advantage

Free trade between the two countries can be mutually beneficial as they specialize in production and exports from sectors with comparative advantage. The structure of comparative advantage, therefore, will be one of the most important criteria for determining eligible FTA partners.

As seen in Table 9.7, according to the revealed comparative advantage (RCA) analysis, Spearman's rank correlation coefficient of the RCA indicator between Korea and the US or Korea and China is relatively low, implying that they have complementary structures of comparative advantage (see also Figure 9.1). Therefore, an FTA with China or the US is expected to foster inter-industry trade based on an efficient system of specialization, bringing trade benefits in the form of economies of scale and efficient allocation of resources. This is also the case for a Korea-Chile FTA.

On the other hand, modern trade theories based on the differentiated products model argue that countries having a similar structure of comparative advantage will trade more through product differentiation based on intra-industry trade. This type of trade is typical among developed countries such as the EU or the US-Canada FTA. In addition, it would be the case of a Korea-Japan FTA as the Spearman's rank correlation coefficient of the RCA indicator between them is 0.5984, which is relatively high. This means that Korea and Japan share similar structures of comparative advantages and maintain a competitive relationship in their export structures. However, a Korea-Japan FTA, if properly designed, has the potential to develop into an advanced form of intra-industry trade, mitigating competition and increasing efficiency and strategic alliances.

Table 9.7 Matrix of Spearman's rank correlation of RCA

	Japan	China	U.S.
Korea	0.5984	0.2852	- 0.0576
Japan	-	0.1754	0.3094
China		-	- 0.3049

Source: Sohn (2001a).

Income level

It is generally known that an FTA between countries at different economic levels will deepen the economic dependency of the lower income country, as the higher income country will monopolize the benefits of free trade by means of abundant capital, efficient markets and advanced technology.

However, Sohn and Yim (2000), in their empirical analysis of the EU, AFTA and ANZER, showed that an FTA will produce economic convergence among its members. Figure 9.2 shows the accelerated income convergence effect of an FTA. If countries A and B form an FTA at time T, the income level of country B is projected to converge with that of A faster (B') than without an FTA (B). For example, in the case of the EU-6, the income convergence indicator almost doubled after the launch of the EEC (European Economic Community) in 1958.[19]

The convergence of income means that the benefits of an FTA with developed countries are realized not only through the increased trade benefit from the elimination of tariff and non-tariff barriers, but also through technology transfer, increased capital productivity and savings rates. Therefore, Korea, by forming an FTA with developed countries such as Japan or the US, is expected to enjoy an accelerated income convergence effect in addition to the potential trade gains from free trade.

Market size[20]

Market size is considered one factor in explaining bilateral trade volumes. From an export perspective it reflects the production capacity, and from an import perspective it implies purchasing capacity. Larger countries with large production capacity are more likely to achieve economies of scale and increase their exports. On the other hand, they have large domestic markets to absorb more imports. Therefore, the larger a trading partner's market size, the more room for trade expansion.

According to the empirical analysis of Korea's trade patterns, based on the gravity model, it is found that the GDP variable as a proxy of market size is the most influential determinant of Korea's bilateral trade volumes, explaining 47 per cent. As one of the main objectives of Korea's FTA policy is to secure export markets and maximize the benefits of market integration and trade expansion, it would therefore be more desirable for Korea to pursue an FTA with large economies such as Japan, China or the US.

Geographical proximity

While traditional international trade theories emphasize the importance of purely economic factors such as comparative advantage and factor endowments in determining bilateral trade volumes, modern theories, in particular the gravity model, pay more attention to the role of geographic elements such as distance, adjacency, population, language and cultural similarities.

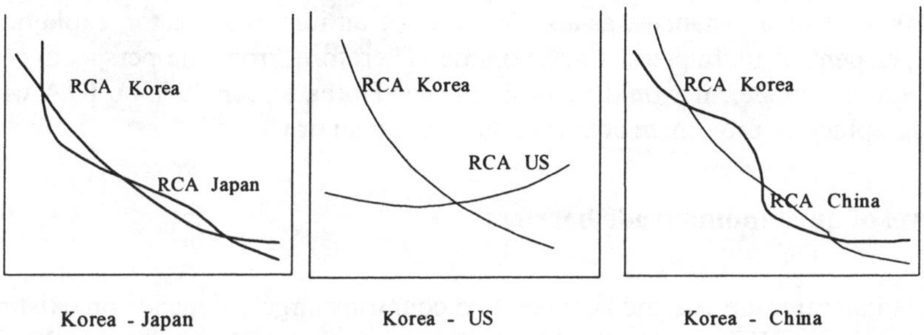

Source: Sohn (2001a).

Figure 9.1 Comparison of Korea's RCA structure with large economies

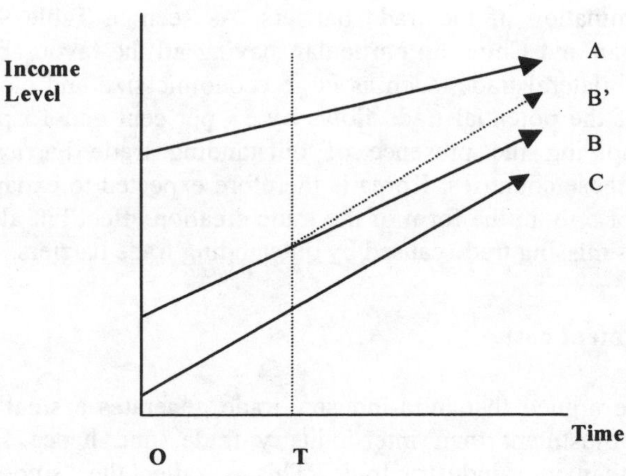

Source: Sohn and Yim (2000).

Figure 9.2 Accelerated income convergence effect of FTAs

Some fundamental reasons why distance can act as a determining factor in international trade can be mentioned.[21] First, short distances will reduce shipping costs and transport times. This, in turn, will lead to regional agglomeration of specific industries across borders, thereby expanding bilateral trade. In addition, countries close to each other have a strong policy preference to increase not only the regional welfare benefit, but also their market power in the world economy by forming a natural trading bloc. In reality, the importance of distance is also evidenced by existing RTAs such as NAFTA, the EU, MERCOSUR, ANZCER, whose members are all closely situated.

As for Korea distance was also found to be an important factor, explaining 17 per cent of its bilateral trade volume. Therefore, from the perspective of the gravity model, it would be desirable for Korea to conclude an FTA with geographically proximate countries such as Japan or China.

Level of outstanding trade barriers

The bilateral trade volume between two countries largely depends on existing trade barriers. If Korea's actual trade volume with a certain country falls far short of the potential value, it implies that a significant level of outstanding trade obstacles exists both in the form of tariff and non-tariff barriers.[22]

The existence of "missing trade" can be a determining factor in choosing a desirable FTA partner for Korea. The wider the gap between the actual and potential trade volume, the greater the trade expansion effect that will take place through the elimination of the trade barriers. As seen in Table 9.8 Korea's trade with Japan and China, in particular, having all the favourable factors for expanding bilateral trade, such as large economic size and close proximity, fall short of the potential trade flows by 33 per cent and 15 per cent, respectively, implying the presence of outstanding trade barriers. Through an FTA with these countries, Korea is therefore expected to expand bilateral trade flows not only in the form of the trade creation effect but also through the recovery of missing trade caused by outstanding trade barriers.

Trade-induced adjustment cost

Many researchers have argued that intra-industry trade generates a smaller inter-industry factor adjustment than inter-industry trade, and hence IIT involves lower costs than inter-industry trade. This is called the "smooth adjustment hypothesis" (SAH).[23]

Therefore, we also attempt to understand the extent and nature of intra-industry trade (IIT) and marginal intra-industry trade (MIIT) in the case of Korea, and help predict the relative degree of adjustment costs that Korea would face as it opens its markets due to the FTA agreements with Chile and others. That is, we will assess the desirability of a regional trade arrangement with different trading partners from the perspective of trade-induced adjustment costs.

Table 9.8 Korea's Actual and Potential Trade: The Size of Missing Trade[1)]

Unit: US$ million, %

Country	Actual Trade (T)	Potential Trade (^T)	T/ ^T (%)
Indonesia	6,118	2.452	249
Chile	1,583	668	237
Singapore	7,617	3,775	202
Germany	10,897	6,328	172
Italy	4,400	3,293	134
France	5,620	4,271	132
Malaysia	5,001	4,105	122
US	50,184	45,845	109
Australia	5,039	4,717	107
England	4,087	3,867	106
Taiwan	6,166	6,123	101
New Zealand	989	1,003	99
China	19,165	22,343	85
Canada	3,830	5,616	68
Japan	46,896	70,059	67
Thailand	3,342	5,231	64
Mexico	1,164	4,004	29

Note: [1)] 1995 as the base year.
Source: Sohn and Yoon (2001a).

By far the most widely used measure of IIT is due to Grubel and Lloyd (1975), who suggested the following formula:

$$GL_i = 1 - \frac{|X_i - M_i|}{(X_i + M_i)}, \tag{9.1}$$

where X_i and M_i refer to a country's exports and imports of goods contained in industry i in one particular year. This measure takes values between zero and one and increases in IIT. The summary GL index over several industries is calculated as a trade-weighted average of the industry indices:

$$GL = \sum_{i=1}^{n} w_i GL_i = \sum_{i=1}^{n} \left(\frac{X_i + M_i}{\sum_{i=1}^{n}(X_i + M_i)}\right) GL_i = 1 - \frac{\sum_{i=1}^{n}|X_i - M_i|}{\sum_{i=1}^{n}(X_i + M_i)}. \tag{9.2}$$

Using the GL index, many researchers uncovered a secular increase in the share of IIT among developing as well as developed economies, and cited this fact as a powerful force for attenuating trade-induced economic frictions within and between countries during the past half-century. However, Hamilton and Kniest (1991) pointed out that the traditional GL index is a static measure in the sense that it describes IIT patterns for one point in time, and hence argued that, in the context of adjustment, dynamic measures of IIT may be more informative than static measures. But they revealed that differencing the GL index (that is, $\Delta GL = GL_t - GL_{t-n}$) was flawed, pointing out that an increase in inter-industry flows will show up an increase in the GL index of IIT when the increase in inter-industry trade acts to reduce the trade imbalance in the sector being measured.

Hamilton and Kniest (1991), Greenaway, Hine, Milner and Elliot (1994), Brülhart (1994) and Dixon and Menon (1997) proposed some alternative indices of MIIT to be used in studies of the SAH. Among these, the so-called 'A' index proposed by Brülhart (1994) is now commonly used by many researchers as a measure of changes in IIT or MIIT. Specifically,

$$B_i^A = 1 - \frac{|\Delta Xi - \Delta Mi|}{|\Delta Xi| + |\Delta Mi|}, \tag{9.3}$$

where Δ is the difference operator. This index, like the GL index, varies between zero and one, where zero indicates marginal trade in the particular industry to be completely of the *inter*-industry type, and one represents marginal trade to be entirely of the *intra*-industry type. The main appeal of the B^A index lies in the fact that it reveals the structure of the *change* in import and export flows.

$B^A{}_i$ can be summed, like the GL index, across industries of the same level of statistical disaggregation, by applying the following formula for a weighted average:

$$B^A = \sum_{i=1}^{k} w_i B^A{}_i \text{ , where } w_i = \frac{|\Delta X_i| + |\Delta M_i|}{\sum_{i=1}^{k}(|\Delta X_i| + |\Delta M_i|)} \qquad (9.4)$$

where B^A is the weighted average of MIIT over several industries, denoted by *i...k*.

Therefore, using the 3-digit SITC data sets (available at the Korea International Trade Association), we first calculated the extent of IIT for the years 1991 and 2001, and MIIT for the period of 1991-2001. IIT is measured using the most widely used Grubel-Lloyd index and MIIT using the "A" index of Brülhart (1994). Estimated results for IIT and MIIT are presented in Table 9.9 and Table 9.10, respectively.

First we focus upon Table 9.9. When measured for all industries (SITC 0-9) in 2001, Singapore, the Philippines, Malaysia, Japan, China, the US, Thailand and Australia are the countries with relatively large GL index values. Among these countries, Singapore is the only country with a large GL index value even when measured only for non-manufactures (SITC 0-4). Interestingly, Japan and China have very similar values of IIT for non-manufactures in 2001, unlike the common perception.

Let us now turn to Table 9.10, which presents the values of the 'A' index for the period 1991-2001 for Korea's FTA candidates. It is interesting to note that countries with high values of the GL index tend to have high values of MIIT. For example, Singapore, the Philippines and Malaysia, which are the countries with the largest GL indices (0.579, 0.526 and 0.525, respectively, for all industries in 2001), also have the largest values of MIIT (0.544, 0.461 and 0.401, respectively, for all industries between 1991 and 2001). The eight countries with large GL index values also rank similarly even when MIIT is measured for all industries between 1991 and 2001.[24] Nevertheless, there are some differences. China has a greater value of MIIT than Japan between 1991 and 2001, regardless of industry group. This is at odds with a common perception that Korea would face greater adjustment costs with China than with Japan. Interestingly, Malaysia, China, the Philippines and Indonesia, considered to have complementary structures of comparative advantage with Korea, have relatively large values of MIIT.

In sum, Singapore, the Philippines, Malaysia, China, Japan, the US, Australia and Thailand are the countries with which Korea would face a relatively lesser degree of adjustment costs when it opens its markets in all industries. Among these countries, Singapore, the Philippines, Indonesia, Japan and China would entail a lesser degree of adjustment costs in non-manufactures on the part of Korea.

Table 9.9 IIT in Korea's trade with major trading partners (1991 and 2001)

	Non-manufactures (SITC 0-4)		Manufactures (SITC 5-8)		All industries (SITC 0-9)	
	1991	2001	1991	2001	1991	2001
Japan	0.323	0.225	0.336	0.431	0.338	0.466
China	0.036	0.193	0.208	0.429	0.271	0.475
ASEAN						
Singapore	0.822	0.788	0.367	0.579	0.273	0.560
Thailand	0.019	0.125	0.163	0.396	0.228	0.457
Malaysia	0.013	0.156	0.227	0.525	0.289	0.547
Indonesia	0.062	0.266	0.123	0.243	0.156	0.226
Philippines	0.305	0.259	0.178	0.526	0.135	0.559
Vietnam	0.000	0.045	0.075	0.124	0.089	0.132
Cambodia	-	0.001	-	0.032	-	0.039
Myanmar	0.000	0.017	0.001	0.039	0.001	0.039
Laos	-	0.000	-	0.004	-	0.006
Brunei	-	-	0.000	0.021	0.000	0.021
Australia	0.039	0.085	0.109	0.242	0.148	0.147
New Zealand	0.008	0.187	0.035	0.154	0.061	0.137
US	0.078	0.137	0.359	0.396	0.402	0.424
Chile	0.035	0.055	0.004	0.008	0.003	0.007
Mexico	0.013	0.109	0.046	0.149	0.049	0.150
Canada	0.058	0.156	0.132	0.229	0.139	0.236
Mean (59)	0.085	0.128	0.131	0.179	0.122	0.179

Notes: 1. Intra-industry trade indices are the weighted average of unadjusted GL indices calculated from three-digit SITC over all (or a subset of) industries. 2. Mean (59) is a simple mean calculated for 59 countries with which Korea traded more than US$1 billion in 1991.

Overall assessment of bilateral FTA partners

Taking into account all six criteria mentioned above, the countries that are the most viable and desirable FTA partners for Korea in the future can be assessed. Overall, from Table 9.11, bilateral FTAs with Japan, China and Singapore seem the most desirable for Korea. However, it should be noted that the six criteria are based on purely economic considerations, but there are a number of important strategic and foreign policy considerations that have not been discussed in this chapter.

Table 9.10 MIIT in Korea's Trade with Major Trading Partners (1991-2001)

	Non-manufactures (SITC 0-4)	Manufactures (SITC 5-8)	All industries (SITC 0-9)
	1991-2001	1991-2001	1991-2001
Japan	0.039	0.283	0.244
China	0.178	0.440	0.399
ASEAN			
Singapore	0.042	0.480	0.461
Thailand	0.033	0.345	0.266
Malaysia	0.092	0.433	0.401
Indonesia	0.372	0.192	0.260
Philippines	0.157	0.577	0.544
Vietnam	0.042	0.131	0.122
Cambodia	0.001	0.039	0.032
Myanmar	0.008	0.038	0.037
Laos	0.000	0.006	0.004
Brunei	-	0.021	0.021
Australia	0.103	0.103	0.260
New Zealand	0.225	0.127	0.151
US	0.085	0.203	0.192
Chile	0.054	0.007	0.009
Mexico	0.049	0.136	0.132
Canada	0.053	0.146	0.137
Mean (59)	0.071	0.137	0.135

Notes: 1. 'MIIT' is the weighted average of Brülhart's (1994) A indices over all industries calculated from three-digit SITC. 2. Mean (59) is a simple mean calculated for 59 countries with which Korea traded more than US$1 billion in 1991.

9.5 CONCLUDING REMARKS

This chapter has reviewed recent movements toward regionalism in East Asia and discussed how Korea, and other countries in East Asia, should respond to these movements. This chapter has argued that in the WTO DDA negotiations, Korea and other East Asian countries have to push toward a non-discriminatory reduction in barriers to global trade in goods and services and work to prevent an increase in RTA trade discrimination. Nevertheless, as with the Uruguay Round, this may not stop the formation of more and larger RTAs. Therefore, Korea, and other countries in East Asia, also has to pay more attention to ways of expanding trade.

Table 9.11 Assessment of selection criteria of Korea's major trading partners

Country Name	Structure of Comparative Advantage	Geographical Proximity	Income Level	Market Size	Level of Missing Trade	Trade-induced Adjustment Costs
Japan	Competitive	Very Close	High	Large	Large	Low
China	Middle	Very Close	Low	Large	Large	Low
ASEAN		Close	Low	Large		High
Singapore	Complementary	Close	High	Middle	None	Very Low
Thailand	Complementary	Close	Middle	Middle	Large	Low
Malaysia	Complementary	Close	Middle	Middle	None	Low
Indonesia	Competitive	Close	Middle	Middle	None	Low
Philippines	Middle	Close	Middle	Middle	Large	Very Low
Vietnam		Close	Low	Small		High
Cambodia		Close	Low	Small		High
Myanmar		Close	Low	Small		High
Laos		Close	Low	Small		High
Brunei		Close	High	Small		High
Australia	Middle	Middle	High	Middle	None	Middle
New Zealand	Middle	Middle	High	Middle	None	Middle
US	Complementary	Far	High	Large	None	Low
EU	Complementary	Far	High	Large	None	High
Chile	Competitive	Far	Middle	Middle	None	High
Mexico	Complementary	Far	Middle	Middle	Very Large	High
Canada	Middle	Far	High	Middle	Large	High

Note: EU represents the simple average value of four major countries: UK, France, Germany and Italy.

This chapter reviewed two different approaches toward promoting trade in the regional context. One is to pursue a formation of plurilateral trade arrangements involving Korea and other East Asian countries. Another approach for Korea to take is to speed up forming bilateral FTAs with major trading partners. Table 9.12 summarizes various plurilateral and bilateral options facing Korea.

Table 9.12 Different FTA options facing Korea

		Positive factors	Negative factors	Evaluation
Plurilateral FTA	APEC FTA	-Largest trade creation effect	- Too many members with different levels of development - Very difficult to negotiate	+
	Sub-regional APEC FTA	- Large trade creation effect - Less difficult	- Negligible	+++
	ASEAN+3 FTA	- Large trade creation effect	- ASEAN developing countries - Politically sensitive industries such as agriculture - Difficult to negotiate	++
	ASEAN+5 FTA	- Large trade creation effect - Several advantages of including Australia and New Zealand (See text.)	- ASEAN developing countries - Politically sensitive industries such as agriculture - Difficult to negotiate	+++
	NEAFTA	- Large trade creation effect - Low trade adjustment costs	- Historical animosity and leadership competition between China and Japan - Politically sensitive industries such as agriculture - Difficult to negotiate	+++
Bilateral FTA	Korea-US	- Large trade creation effect - Advanced country - Relatively low adjustment costs	- Politically sensitive industries such as agriculture - Difficult to negotiate	+++
	Korea-China	- Large trade creation effect - Neighbouring country - Low trade adjustment costs	- Politically sensitive industries such as agriculture - Difficult to negotiate	+++
	Korea-Japan	- Large trade creation effect - Neighbouring country - Advanced country - Low trade adjustment costs	- Enlarging trade deficits - Historical animosity	+++

Table 9.12 (Continued)

	Korea-Singapore	- Corridor to the ASEAN market - Advanced country - Low trade adjustment costs - Easy to negotiate	- Small trade creation effect	+++
	Korea-Thailand	- Corridor to the ASEAN market	- Politically sensitive industries such as agriculture - Small trade creation effect - High trade adjustment costs	+
	Korea-Chile	- Learning from Chile's FTA experiences - Easy to negotiate	- Long distance -High trade adjustment costs	++
	Korea-Mexico	- Corridor to the US market	- Politically sensitive industries such as agriculture - Long distance - High trade adjustment costs	++
	Korea-Australia	- Relative large trade creation effect - Advanced country	- Politically sensitive industries such as agriculture - High trade adjustment costs	++
	Korea-New Zealand	- Advanced country	- Politically sensitive industries such as agriculture - High trade adjustment costs	++

Notes: +++ most preferred, ++ preferred, + less preferred.
1. APEC FTA: 21 members of APEC;
2. APEC Sub-regional FTA: OECD members of APEC (US, Canada, Japan, Korea, Australia, and New Zealand) and other open advanced economies of APEC (Singapore and Chile);
3. ASEAN+3: ASEAN, China, Japan, Korea;
4. ASEAN+5: ASEAN, China, Japan, Korea, Australia, New Zealand;
5. NEAFTA: China, Japan, Korea.

Among the various options for plurilateral trade arrangements, three options are plausible for Korea. The first option is that Korea and a subset of countries form a sub-regional agreement within APEC. Specifically, OECD member countries within APEC (such as the US, Japan, Canada, Australia and Korea), and some other advanced open economies (such as Singapore, New Zealand and Chile) could agree on forming an FTA among themselves. The second option is to pursue an ASEAN+5 FTA. A third option is to establish a Northeast Asian Free Trade Area. On the other hand, Japan, China, and Singapore could be bilateral FTA partners for Korea, entailing large trade creation effects and lesser degrees of trade-induced adjustment costs.

After all, Korea should ensure that FTA initiatives are consistent with multilateral trade rules so that both multilateral and regional approaches can engender a synergic harmonization and accelerate the progress of "freer and fairer trade and investment" in the Korean economy. It should also be noted that the plurilateral and bilateral trade arrangement suggested above should be pursued in the medium-term with a deliberate and sophisticated approach. In the short run, it will be necessary for Korea to restructure its economy and accumulate more experience in operating under a freer trade regime.

NOTES

1 The United States signed FTA agreements with Singapore in May 2003 and with Chile in June 2003. It has also begun negotiating FTAs with Australia; Morocco; Bahrain; the five Central American Common Market nations of Guatemala, Honduras, El Salvador, Nicaragua, and Costa Rica; and the five South African Customs Union nations, Botswana, Namibia, Lesotho and Swaziland (Griswold, 2003). The United States has recently shown its willingness in forging an FTA with the Middle East - an area Washington has tended to neglect economically. Other potential FTA partners proposed by members of Congress include Taiwan, New Zealand, the United Kingdom and Korea.

2 Among the three, each country is one of the largest trading partners of the other two. For China, Japan is its largest trading partner and Korea the third. For Japan, China (including Taiwan) ranks the second and Korea the third. For Korea, Japan and China are the second and the third trading partners, respectively.

3 Nonetheless, the AMF has still not made any tangible progress due to strong opposition from the United States.

4 The CGE model is a computable general equilibrium model that has the advantage of determining the reallocation effects of resources caused by the cross-sectoral transfer of production factors.

5 Frankel (1997) examines how the effect of the formation of free trade agreements on welfare depends on international transportation costs. According to him the formation of natural trading blocs, where each country forms an FTA with its neighbour, will improve welfare, while the formation of unnatural trade blocs has only lower welfare effects due to high intercontinental transport costs.

6 For a more detailed analysis, see Sohn (2001b)

7 A trade diversion effect occurs when country A diverts its imports from a low-cost foreign supplier to the high-cost FTA partner after the elimination of tariffs. This trade diversion brings a deadweight loss measured by the increased cost of procuring imports produced in the partner country.

8 In order to estimate the overall effects of a Korea-Japan FTA we also need to take into account other important factors such as investment expansion and productivity enhancement, in addition to the elimination of trade barriers. The formation of an FTA can stimulate the expansion of FDI from the FTA partner and third countries as firms move their production facilities from nonmember countries to member countries in order to take advantage of zero tariffs within the free trade area. Also, the formation of a Korea-Japan FTA will attract FDI from nonmember countries trying to gain easy access to regional markets after tariff elimination. This increase in FDI, if efficiently reallocated between light industry and the heavy and chemical industries, is estimated to expand the level of output, thus enhancing the total factor productivity as a result of economies of scale.

9 Japan is the second largest exporter and importer for Korea, while Korea is the fourth

largest importer and third largest exporter for Japan.

10 Korea's total trade surplus in 2000 was US$11.8 billion, which almost equals its trade deficit with Japan as a single country. This clearly shows the enormous size of Korea's trade deficit with Japan.

11 Inside US Trade (2001).

12 For simplification, two other scenarios (50 per cent reduction in all sectors with and without agriculture) were excluded from the discussion.

13 The welfare gains for the US, according to IIE analysis, is estimated to be in the range of US$1.5 billion to US$8.9 billion, which means that Korea, as a smaller economy, will enjoy far more welfare gains in proportional terms. Moreover, the IIE analysis points out that the welfare gains of the two countries derive from different effects. In Korea's case most gains come from allocative efficiency, while for the US the effects of improved terms of trade is the largest source of gains.

14 In addition, the IIE report points out that this kind of trade balance problem could still be beneficial to Korea in terms of its trade relations management with the US and Japan. As Korea is under pressure from the US due to its chronic trade surplus on the one hand and suffering a chronic trade deficit with Japan on the other, the trade diversion from Japan to the US as a result of a Korea-US FTA is expected to enable Korea to mitigate the trade imbalances with the US and Japan.

15 For a more detailed explanation, the reader is referred to Sohn (2001a).

16 Paragraph 2(c) of the Enabling Clause allows the formation of preferential trading arrangements among developing countries in goods trade, even though it does not meet the condition of covering "substantially all the trade" stipulated in GATT XXIV.

17 Although many FTAs currently exist in the world, there is little literature that suggests clear criteria for the selection of desirable FTA partners. Multiple factors, not only from economic but also historical and political dimensions, may intervene in the formation of FTAs. However, in this chapter we consider five important criteria taking into account only economic factors.

18 Among the six criteria, the first five criteria were first introduced in Sohn and Yoon (2001b).

19 EU-6 means the six countries that were the first members of the EEC, which later became the EU through a process of enlargement. These include, West Germany, France, Italy, Belgium, the Netherlands and Luxembourg.

20 The next three criteria are mainly based on the gravity model, which aims at explaining the bilateral trade flows and patterns between two economies by regarding them as organic bodies that attract each other in proportion to their economic size (GDP) and inversely to their distance. According to the empirical study of Sohn and Yoon (2001a) it was found that Korea's bilateral trade patterns follow the basic gravity model, implying that bilateral trade flows will increase in proportion to the trading partner's GDP and decrease in proportion to the distance involved. Therefore, in order to expand bilateral trade flows, it appears to be more desirable for Korea to promote bilateral trade with countries in close proximity and having large economies. For a more detailed analysis, see Sohn and Yoon (2001a).

21 Frankel (1997).

22 Here, potential trade volume means the level of bilateral trade volume that could be achieved under normal conditions where a country imposes an average level of trade barriers on its trading partner. If the actual trade volume is much smaller than the potential trade volume, it means that there exist outstanding trade barriers (so-called "missing trade") far beyond the average level.

23 See Lloyd and Lee (2002) for recent developments of research in intra-industry trade.

24 This finding is also evident in the whole sample.

REFERENCES

Baldwin, Robert E. (1993), "Adapting the GATT to a more regionalized world: a political economy perspective", in K. Anderson and R. Blackhurst (eds), *Regional Integration and the Global Trading System*, New York: Harvester Wheatsheaf.

Brülhart, Marius (1994), "Marginal intra-industry trade: measurement and relevance for the pattern of industrial adjustment," *Weltwirtschaftliches Archiv 130*, 600-13.

Cheong, Inkyo and Yunjong Wang. (1999), "Korea-U.S. FTA: prospect and analysis", KIEP Working Paper 99-03, Seoul: KIEP.

Cheong, Inkyo and Kyounghee Yi. (2000), "Korea-Chile FTA: background, economic effects and policy implications", KIEP Policy Analysis 00-07, Seoul: KIEP (In Korean).

Choi, Inbom and Jeffrey J. Schott (2001), *Free Trade between Korea and the United States?* in Policy Analyses in International Economics. Washington, DC: Institute for International Economics.

DIRECON of Chile. (2000), "Current status of progress in FTA negotiation with Korea". Various background materials. Santiago: General Administration of International Economic Relations (in Spanish). [http://www.direcon.cl/acuerdos/index.htm]

Dixon, P. and J. Menon (1997), "Measures of intra-industry trade as indicators of factor market disruption, *Economic Record 73,* 233-27.

Frankel, Jeffrey A. (1997), *Regional Trading Blocs in the World Economy System,* Washington DC: Institute for International Economics.

Greenaway, David, Robert C. Hine, Chris Milner and Robert Elliott (1994), "Adjustment and the measurement of marginal intra-industry trade," *Weltwirtschaftliches Archiv 130,* 418-27.

Griswold, Daniel T. (2003), "Free-trade agreements: steppingstones to a more open world", Trade Briefing Paper, CATO Institute, July.

Grubel, Herbert and Peter Lloyd (1975), *Intra-Industry Trade*, London: Macmillan.

Hamilton, Clive and Paul Kniest (1991), "Trade liberalisation, structural adjustment and intra-industry trade: a note", *Weltwirtschaftliches Archiv 12*, 356-67.

Harvie, and Charles and Hyun-Hoon Lee (2002), "New regionalism in East Asia: how does it relate to the east Asian economic development model?" *ASEAN Economic Bulletin, 19, (2),* 123-40.

Harvie, Charles and Hyun-Hoon Lee, (2003), *Korea's Economic Miracle: Fading or Reviving?*, London: Palgrave Macmillan.

Harvie, Charles and Hyun-Hoon Lee, (2004), "Towards a new economic development model of Korea", in Charles Harvie, Hyun-Hoon Lee and Junggun Oh (eds) *The Korean Economy: Post-Crisis Policies, Issues and Prospects*, Ch13, pp. 286-318, Cheltenham, UK: Edward Elgar.

Helpman, Elhanan (1987), "Imperfect competition and international trade: evidence from fourteen industrial countries", *Journal of Japanese and International Economy.*

IDE. (2000), "Toward closer Japan-Korea economic relations in the 21st century", paper presented on 24 May, 2000 at the International Joint Symposium on "Toward a Korea-Japan FTA: Assessments and Prospects". Seoul, Korea.

Inside US Trade. (2001), "Baucus introduces bills authorizing FTA talks with Korea,

New Zealand, Australia", 23 May [http://www.insidetrade.com] (restricted access).

KIEP (2000), "Economic effects of and policy direction for a Korea-Japan FTA" , paper presented on 24 May, 2000 at the International Joint Symposium on "Toward a Korea-Japan FTA: Assessments and Prospects" Seoul, Korea.

KIET (1999), "Sectoral effects of a Korea-Japan FTA and policy response", KIET Policy Discussion Paper, Seoul: Korea Institute for Industrial Economics and Trade (In Korean).

Lloyd, Peter (2001), "Closer economic relations with East Asia," *Economic Record*, September.

Lloyd, Peter and Hyun-Hoon Lee (2001), "Sub-regionalism in East Asia and its relation with APEC," *The Journal of the Korean Economy 2(2)*, 211-27.

Lloyd, Peter and Hyun-Hoon Lee (eds) (2002), *Frontiers of Research in Intra-industry Trade*, London: Palgrave Macmillan.

Ministry of Foreign Affairs and Trade (1999), *Korea's Mid and Long Term Trade Policy* [www.mofat.go.kr] (In Korean).

OECD. (1995), *Regionalism and its Place in the Multilateral Trading System*, Paris: OECD,

Park, Euijeong and Hyun-Hoon Lee (2003), "Recent trend of regionalism in East Asia and choice of Korea, *International Area Review 7(1),* 257-89 (In Korean).

Sohn, Chan-Hyun (2002), "How FTAs affect income levels of member countries: converge or diverge?" KIEP Working Paper 02-14, Seoul: KIEP.

Sohn, Chan-Hyun, Junsuk Yang and Hyo Sung Yim (1998), Korea's trade and industrial policies: 1948-1998 KIEP Working Paper 98-05. Seoul: KIEP.

Sohn, Chan-Hyun and Hyo Sung Yim (2000), "Free Trade Agreements and the income convergence of member countries: lessons from the EU, NAFTA and ANZCER", *Journal of International Economic Policy Studies, 4(1)*, 3-39.

Sohn, Chan-Hyun, and Jinna Yoon (2001a), "Does the model fit Korea's trade patterns? Implications for Korea's FTA Policy and North-South Korean Trade", KIEP Working Paper 01-01. Seoul: KIEP.

Sohn, Chan-Hyun, and Jinna Yoon (2001b), "Korea's FTA (Free Trade Agreement) policy: current status and future prospects", *KIEP Working Paper* 01-01. Seoul: KIEP.

Sohn, Chan-Hyun (ed.)(2001a), "Analysis of the economic effects of Korea's FTAs with Japan, the U.S. and China", KIEP Policy Reference 01-01. Seoul: KIEP (In Korean).

Sohn, Chan–Hyun (ed.)(2001b), "The Economic Effects of and Policy Direction for a Korea-Japan FTA," *KIEP Policy Reference* 01-03. Seoul: KIEP (In Korean).

WTO. (1995), *Regionalism and the World Trading System*, WTO, Geneva.

WTO. (2001), "Facts and figures: regional trade agreements notified to the GATT/WTO and in force", *Regionalism in the WTO.* [http://www.wto.org/english/tratop_e/region_e/region_e.htm]

10. Some Perspectives on China's Role in the East Asian Economies

Tang Zongming and Tran Van Hoa

10.1 INTRODUCTION

With its fast economic development China has been playing an increasingly important role in the global economy, and especially in the East Asian region. The *New York Times* in mid-2003 even claimed that China would very likely become the engine of growth of Asia instead of the United States. Japan has also reiterated that China is the new force of East Asia's economic development. Will China become the engine of growth or a new force for economic development in this region? What linkages are there between the East Asian nations' economic development and that of China? How will they affect each other in the future? We will discuss all these issues in this chapter.

The chapter consists, after this introduction, of four sections. Section 2 analyses the performance and describes the key features of China's fast economic growth in recent years. In the following two sections, sections 3 and 4, we examine the Chinese economy's impact on the East Asia economies and the influence of East Asia and South East Asian regional integrations, including ASEAN+3 or its subset ASEAN+China, on China's economic development. Finally, section 5 offers some conclusions.

10.2 PERFORMANCE AND FEATURES OF CHINA'S ECONOMIC GROWTH

Since the launching of the reform and open-door-policies programme in 1978 the Chinese economy has achieved continuous and fast growth. According to figures from the Chinese Statistical Yearbook the average annual growth rate for the Chinese economy was 10.75 per cent in the 1980s and 9.71 per cent in the 1990s respectively.[1] Even under the impact of SARS in the first half of 2003 this figure remained at 8.2 per cent (see Figure 10.1). China's fast economic growth is mainly based on robust domestic demand and increasing foreign demand.

Under its fast economic growth, China's domestic demand has had the following four features. First, China has a sizable consumer market. With a population of one-fifth of the global population, China bears a very big consuming capacity. In recent years there has been a continuous increase in household income in China. The total saving amount for Chinese residents is now over 8,000 billion Renminbi (see Figure 10.2). Meanwhile, the Chinese government has been undertaking reform of income and its distribution in order to narrow the gap between the high and low income classes, raising the average marginal propensity of consumption of the whole society. Therefore, China's domestic consumer market will continuously be one of the main forces promoting China's economic growth.

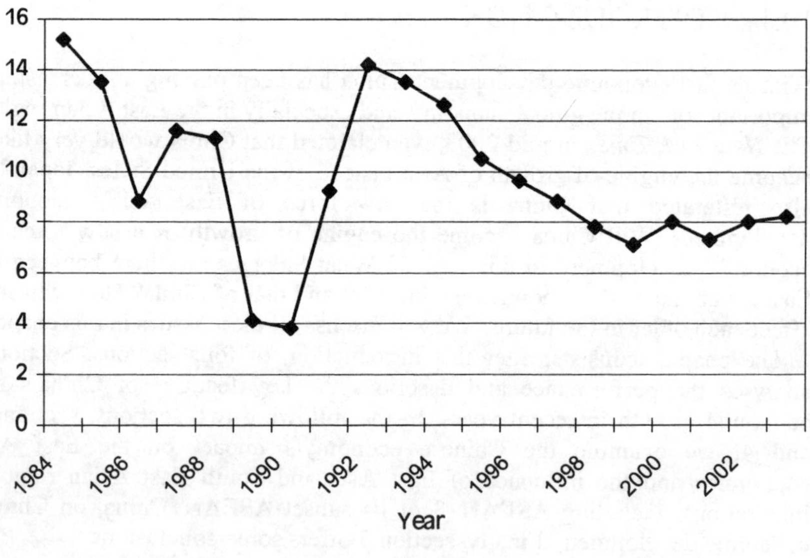

Figure 10.1 China's annual GDP growth rate (%), 1984-2003
Source: China Statistical Yearbook (2003)

Second, new consumer trends emerge and begin to play an important role. Over the past several years, housing expenditure has gained a high percentage of gross expenditure. The real estate industry has become a key force in accelerating China's economic development. Moreover, expenditure on cars, travel, education and communication is also increasing. For example, in 2002, car sales in China exceeded one million units for the first time, and are expected to rise further due to rising domestic demand in the near future.

Third, government investment contributes greatly to China's economic growth. The Chinese government has implemented an expansionary fiscal policy over the past five years. Every year the government issues about 150 billion Renminbi in long-term treasury bonds to finance many important infrastructure projects, such as the Western Areas Development, Technology Modification in Key Enterprises and Transferring Water from the South to the North. Government investment improves national infrastructure, lowers the transaction costs for distributing production factors and expands domestic demand. All these will definitely stimulate economic development in the country.

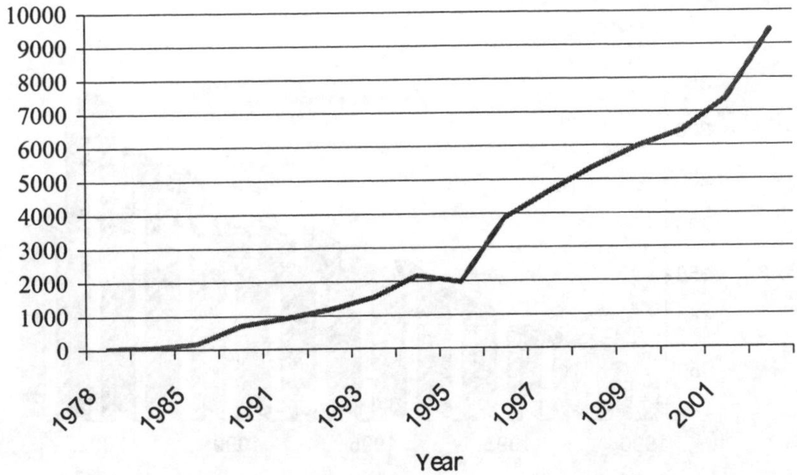

Figure 10.2 Savings deposits in urban and rural areas of China, 1978-2002, (billion yuan)
Source: China Statistical Yearbook (2003)

Finally, private investment has been on the rise. China's private economy is booming although the reform of state-owned enterprises (SOEs) is still experiencing a difficult time. For example, private investment has expanded quickly in recent years and enjoyed an average growth rate of 18 per cent.[2]

In terms of foreign demand, China's demand structure has the following two features. First, the volume and value of China's foreign trade keeps on increasing (see Figure 10.3). From 1991 to 2002 the annual average growth rate for China's total value of imports and exports reached 15.4 per cent. The growth rate of total export value amounted to 15.2 per cent. According to research by Lin Yifu and Li Yongjun (2002), every 10 per cent increase in export growth will give rise to one per cent GDP growth. Therefore, over the past twelve years, China's 15 per cent annual export growth has contributed more than one per cent to its annual GDP growth. Second, FDI flows to China keep rising. Foreign capital continues flowing into China as foreign corporations shift labour-intensive divisions of their production networks to China to take advantage of its low labour costs (see Figure 10.4). In 2002 China overtook the United States to become the number one foreign capital absorbing country, attracting a historical record US$52.7 billion, 37 per cent of the total in-flow of FDI into developing countries, of which 60 per cent flowed into China's manufacturing industries.[3]

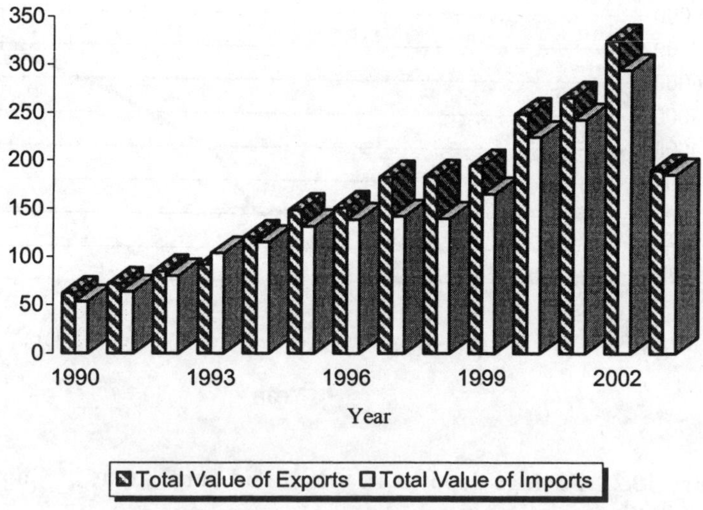

Figure 10.3 China's total value of imports and exports, 1990-2003* (billion US dollars)

Note: * First half of 2003 only

Source: China Statistical Yearbook (2003)

In addition, regional economic growth is also one of the outstanding features in the Chinese economy. In China the economies in the Pearl River

Delta, Yangzi River Delta and the Bohai Gulf grew the fastest, contributing over 60 per cent of the whole Chinese economy. Their total foreign trade value reached more than 80 per cent of China's total value. Meanwhile, they attracted most of the FDI flowing into China (see Table 10.1). Among these three economic areas the Yangzi River Delta is the most active area in China, even in the world. With only 2.2 per cent of the total state area and 10.6 per cent of the whole population, its GDP accounted for about 30 per cent of national income.

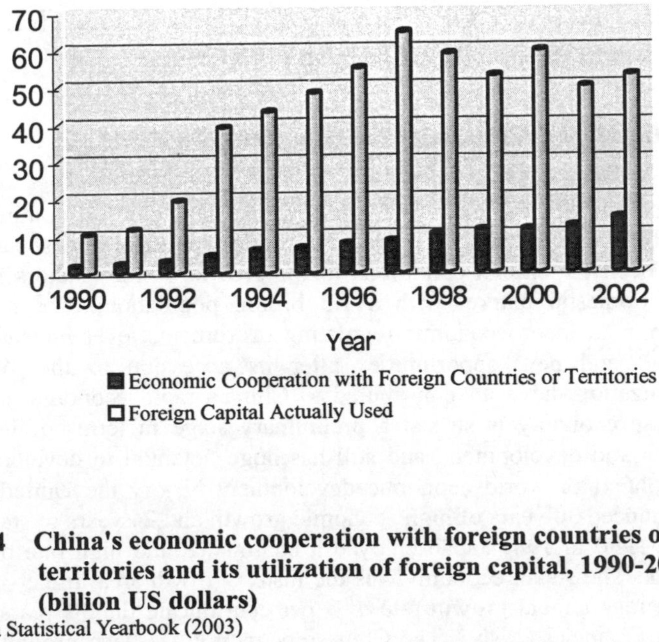

Figure 10.4 China's economic cooperation with foreign countries or territories and its utilization of foreign capital, 1990-2002 (billion US dollars)

Source: China Statistical Yearbook (2003)

In the Yangzi River Delta economy Shanghai plays the most important role. Currently, more than 330 financial institutions from all over the world have set up branches or offices in Shanghai. Half of the Fortune 500 companies have invested in Shanghai. Consequently, Shanghai has gained the reputation of a very high foreign-oriented city. Industries including financial securities, insurance, commercial trade, transportation, communications and real estate have expanded rapidly. Urban and regional linkages have also increased. With the successful bid for the 2010 World Expo, Shanghai has the potential for unprecedented development opportunities. A new investment and construction peak will be approached in the coming years. Shanghai will continue to keep its two-digit growth rate that it has attained for the past eleven years. Benefiting from the radiating growth and development effects from Shanghai, the Jiangsu and Zhejiang provinces have also developed very rapidly in recent years.

In terms of demand structure, China's fast economic growth has mainly come from its considerable domestic market. These three regional economies, especially the Yangzi River Delta, are the *engine* of China's economic development. For this very reason, China can keep its fast growth in spite of the downturn of the world economy. Certainly, increasing foreign demand will also make an important, although more limited, contribution to China's economic growth.

10.3 IMPACT OF CHINA'S ECONOMY ON THE ECONOMIES OF EAST ASIA

The Developing Potentials of the Chinese Economy

Compared with the global economy China has achieved continuing strong growth over a number of years. The State's political and social stabilities have been the crucial conditions for its growth besides factors including: a large domestic market with a 1.3 billion population; ever more mature government macroeconomic regulating instruments; ever increasing foreign capital; and new opportunities after its accession to the World Trade Organization, have all contributed to China's rapid economic growth. The Chinese economy is still at a preliminary stage in terms of its economic growth and development, and still has huge potential to develop further. In the context of world economic development history the United States has experienced 30 years of high economic growth and 24 years of stable growth. From 1950 to 1987 Japan enjoyed a continuous and high rate of economic growth. The Asian economy was the fastest growth area in the world due to its average annual growth rate of 8 per cent during the 30 years before the Asian Financial Crisis.[4] The Chinese economy has been growing at a very high rate for 23 years. Therefore, in the light of this international development record and its own economic power, China can be expected to maintain its fast growth for the next ten to 15 years.

Table 10.1 Major economic indicators of three regional economies and the Yangzi River Delta

Indicators		GDP (billion Yuan)		Total Value of Imports and Exports (Customs Statistics) (billion US dollars)		Total Amount of Foreign Capital Actually Used (billion US dollars)		Revenue of Economic Cooperation with Foreign Countries or Regions (billion US dollars)	
Year		Total Amount	Ratio to China (per cent)	Total Amount	Ratio to China (per cent)	Total Amount	Ratio to China (per cent)	Total Amount	Ratio to China (per cent)
2000	Three regional economies	3529.05	64.21	383.753	82.25	36.195	60.98	3.430	3.028
	Yangtze River Delta	1314.215	29.78	121.88	27.03	12.24	20.62	2.068	18.26
2001	Three regional economies	4584.048	62.15	420.222	82.43	43.497	87.57	4.497	3.703
	Yangtze River Delta	2116.544	28.69	145.045	28.45	16.262	32.74	2.938	24.2
2002	Three regional economies	5109.412	54.18	515.346	83.01	52.575	99.76	5.965	4.141
	Yangtze River Delta	2371.506	25.15	184.964	29.78	20.56	39.01	3.873	26.89

Sources: Statistics of the Yangtzi River Delta are based on that of the Shanghai, Jiangsu and Zhejiang Provinces. Statistics of the Pearl River Delta are based on that of Guangdong Province. Bohai Gulf's statistics are calculated on the basis of that of Beijing, Tianjing, and the Shandong Province.

Impact of China's Growth on the East Asian Economies

According to the *Global Development Finance 2003 Report* released by the World Bank:

'China continued to make strong advances in output - some 8 per cent during 2002 - despite relative stagnation in Japan and volatile US demand. This helped to drive the recovery in East Asia. Together with policy stimulus in other countries, China's performance lifted the region to a growth rate of 6.7 percent in 2002.'

We notice from this that China has helped to stimulate the recovery in East Asia in 2002. Will it continue to play an important role in this area in the near future? First, let us take a look at the economic and trade linkages between China and the East Asian countries.

The Close Economic and Trade Linkages

According to trade value in 2002, Japan, ASEAN and Korea are China's first, fifth and seventh largest trading partners respectively. On the other hand, China is Japan's number two, ASEAN's number six and Korea's number three trading partner respectively. Hence, China has very close trade relations with the East and South East Asian countries. Additionally, from the yearly statistics, China's trade volumes with Japan, Korea and ASEAN keep rising every year, while the trade imbalance between these economies is becoming a serious issue (see Figures 10.5 and 10.6).

From the perspective of FDI, Japan, Korea and Singapore are China's number four, number six and number seven investing countries in terms of FDI inflows in 2002 (see Figure 10.7), respectively. Furthermore, most of the capital from Japan and Korea has been invested in the Yangzi River Delta. On the other hand, China distributed 23.33 per cent of its foreign investment to Asian countries in 2002. The scale of China's investment is expanding in Korea and is at a certain break-through point in Japan. Overall, both China's foreign investment in the East Asian countries and the in-flow of FDI to China from them has been increasing. But China remains a major net in-flow FDI nation.

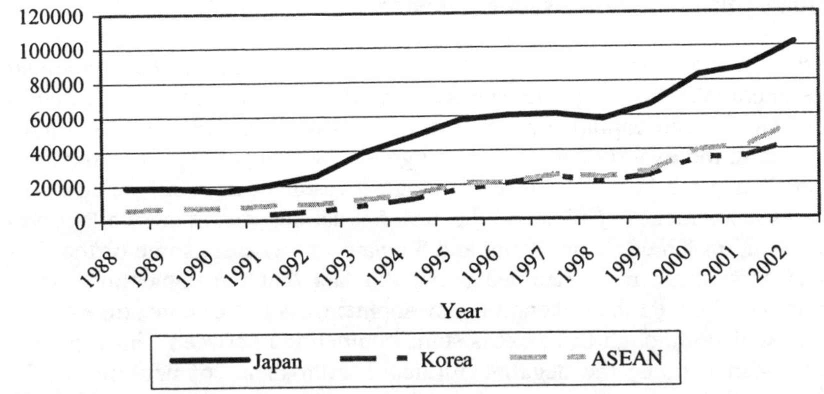

Figure 10.5 China's total value of imports and exports 1988-2002 (US$ million)

Source: China Statistical Yearbook 1989-2003

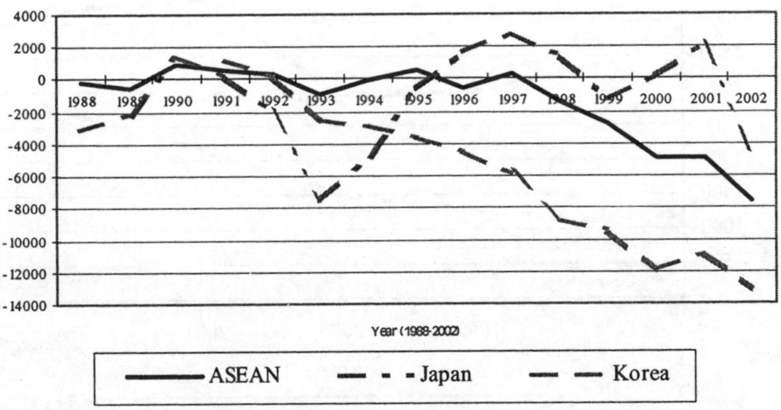

Figure 10.6 China's total value of net exports to Japan, Korea and ASEAN, 1988-2002 (US$ million)

Source: China Statistical Yearbook from 1989 to 2003.

China's role in the East Asian economies

China and the other East Asian nations are important partners in trade and investment. Yet they compete against each other both in foreign trade and in attracting foreign capital. For instance, China and the ASEAN economies compete in the export of manufactured goods. With regard to attracting FDI, by analysing the layout of Japan's foreign investment in 2002, we find that Japan's investment in China and the ASEAN nations was rising while it was decreasing in Korea, Hong Kong and Taiwan. In this case, some of the East Asian economies are concerned about the fact that the competition from China will threaten their economic development. As to this concern, we hold the view that although there exists some competition between China and the East Asian nations, the negative influence from their competition can be offset by the positive influence from the complementary relations between them. China will still be the important partner for these economies in their future development. We base our views on the following reasons:

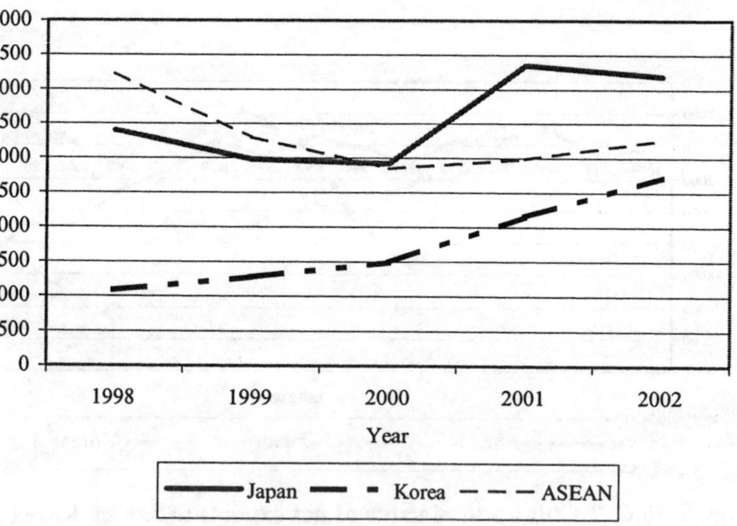

Figure 10.7 Foreign Capital Actually Used 1998-2002 (US$ million)
Source: China Statistical Yearbook from 1999 to 2002.

First, the rise in China's foreign trade has not crowded the East Asian nations out of the international market. Although the annual growth rate for exports reached 15.37 per cent in 2002, China's imports are also increasing. On average, every US$100 in exports will produce 50 to 70 US dollars in imports.[5] Therefore, China not only occupies part of the East Asian market, but it also provides them with access to China's large market. The statistical figures suggest that about half of East Asian exports have been shipped to China and Hong Kong (15.6 per cent), the United States (20.4 per cent) and Japan (13.5 per cent).

Second, China and the East Asian nations compete in terms of attracting FDI, but not seriously. With respect to the sources of China's FDI, two-thirds comes from Hong Kong, Macao and Taiwan, while the remaining one-third is from the United States, Japan and other countries. On the other hand, FDI to ASEAN and other East Asian countries is mainly from Japan and the United States. Thus, China only competes with other East Asian countries in attracting FDI from Japan. Statistical figures also show that FDI from non-Asian economies to China and other Asian countries are both increasing[6] (see Figure 10.8).

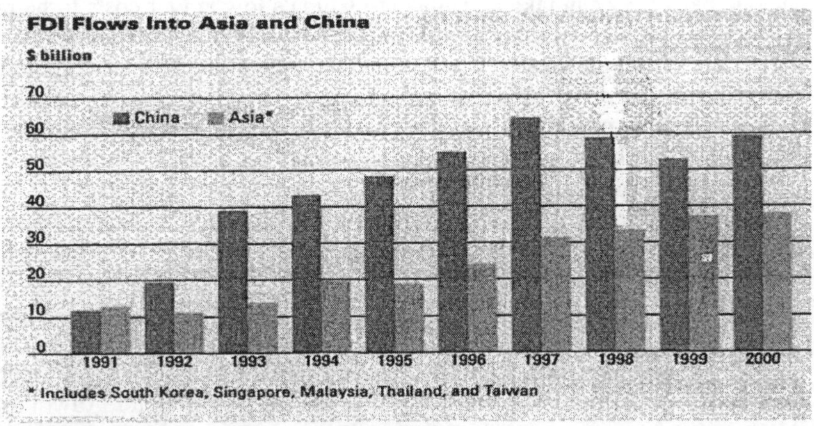

Figure 10.8 FDI flows into Asia and China
Source: Chi Lo (2003).

Third, whoever invests in China first will benefit from China's low labour costs and considerable domestic market size. FDI to China favours both China and its investing countries. China covers one-fifth of the world population, and 70 per cent of its population are in the age group from 15 to 65. This age percentage ranks the highest in the world. China's abundant labour makes its labour costs to be ranked at a low level. By combining China's cheap labour with advanced capital and technologies from developed countries, multinational corporations can achieve very high profits in international and Chinese markets. In fact, Hong Kong and Taiwan have made good use of this combination, and earned considerable returns from their investment in mainland China. Now Japan and Korea are expanding their investment in China to share in this advantage.

Finally, *Made in China* did not dwarf *Made in East Asia*. China's cheap labour costs and ever-favourable investment environment make it an attractive place for increasing FDI, 60 per cent of which flowed into manufacturing industries. However, will this increased manufacturing FDI mean that world manufacturing has shifted to China? Our answer is *No*. We can show this from the following figures. From 1990 to 2000 the share of manufacturing goods produced by developed countries reduced by 11 per cent while it increased by 7.3 per cent in Asia. However, China's growth rate for manufactured goods production was only 2.3 per cent, lower than that of the ASEAN (3.1 per cent).[7] So we say *Made in China* did not dwarf *Made in East Asia*.

Compared with other East Asian economies, China is characterized as a country with low labour costs and a considerable domestic market. In this case if East Asian countries invest in China, they can combine their extant advanced technologies and managerial experience with China's resources. On the one hand they can take advantage of China's low labour costs to be more competitive in the international market. Or, again, on the other hand, they can gain profits from the sizable Chinese market. Accordingly, their corporations will be more competitive.

From the above analysis we conclude that China's fast economic growth has not, and will not, sacrifice its neighbouring economies. On the contrary, China's low labour costs will add to their cost advantage. China's considerable market will enlarge the East Asian nations' domestic markets. In the future, China will continue to be their important partner in terms of trade and investment. China needs the East Asian economies, and vice versa. Both need to develop on the basis of cooperation. However, China, regardless of its fast growth, has a relatively low total output. The size of China's GDP is around one quarter of Japan's GDP or about one-tenth that of the US. Thus, China will not overtake the US or Japan as the leading force for growth in the Asian economies.

10.4 CHINA, THE EAST ASIAN ECONOMIES AND NEW EAST ASIAN REGIONALISM

Taking the lead in the East Asian region

The spectacular progress in regional economic integration in North America has been attributed to the powerful leading role of the United States. The US has spared no effort in promoting regional integration through the North

American Free Trade Agreement (NAFTA). Meanwhile, the European Union, with France and Germany in the driving seat, has been energetically expanding regional integration out from the economic arena and into the political, military and social fields. However, no single nation or leading group has so far emerged in the leading role for regional economic integration in Asia. In the absence of a strong leader, little progress has been made to date in Asia's regional economic integration.

In terms of the current status of East Asia, there are four candidates: ASEAN, Japan, China or a joint Sino-Japanese leadership. Japan has been trying to lead East Asian economic cooperation single-handedly. However, it did not succeed because of the downturn of its domestic economy in the past decade. The relations between China and Japan can be expected to fall short of full mutual trust unless and until Japan's official attitude to Sino-Japanese history is modified and becomes acceptable to China. So joint leadership by China and Japan could not be considered feasible at present.

Regardless of China's fast growth, it has a relatively low total output. As mentioned earlier, China's GDP is around one quarter of the GDP of Japan or about one-tenth of that of the US. Thus, China has been incapable and will not be able to take over from the US or Japan as the leading force for the growth of the Asian economies in the past and also in the near future. Therefore, China, on the other hand, would rather back ASEAN to take the leading role in Asian regional integration than see Japan or other forces dominate economic cooperation in East Asia.

China should continue to endorse the ASEAN+3 as the main channel for future East Asian cooperation in the longer term. However, the reality of circumstances in East Asia means it would be no easy matter to set up the ASEAN+3 cooperative mechanism. Consequently, China should fully support the establishment of the ASEAN-China Free Trade Agreement. This would neither adversely affect common understanding nor present a barrier to eventual progress towards the ASEAN+3 framework.

China and New Asian Regionalism

In 2002 the ratio of China's total value of imports and exports (openness) to its GDP reached nearly 50 per cent. We can say that the foreign dependency of the Chinese economy has been ever increasing during its 20 years of reform and openness, and almost each of its successful miracles has been linked to foreign economies. From the close economic trade relations between China and the East Asian countries, we can also say that the dependency of the Chinese economy on the East Asian countries has ever increased. China's future economic development will continue to rely on its cooperation with its neighbouring nations.

As to Japan and Korea, Japan is at the top step of the industry ladder with abundant capital and sophisticated modern technologies. Korea, as one of the newly-industrialized economies, also has advantages in capital-and technology-intensive industries. Japan, Korea and China have different advantages in industry structure and production factors. So attracting more FDI from Japan and Korea will benefit China in upgrading its industry structure, releasing the pressure from rising unemployment and promoting its economic development.

As far as ASEAN is concerned, China's active attitude toward the establishment of the ASEAN-China FTA implies ASEAN's great importance to China in the near future. China will devote great efforts in forging a close relationship with the ASEAN economies in order to develop its domestic economy.[8] ASEAN's influence on the Chinese economy can, however, be described as follows.

Trade

In the East Asian economies, ASEAN and China have important and rapidly growing trade relations (see Figure 10.9). From the structure of ASEAN-China trade, we can see that the exports of ASEAN do not compete seriously with Chinese exports. On the contrary, they are complementary to each other.

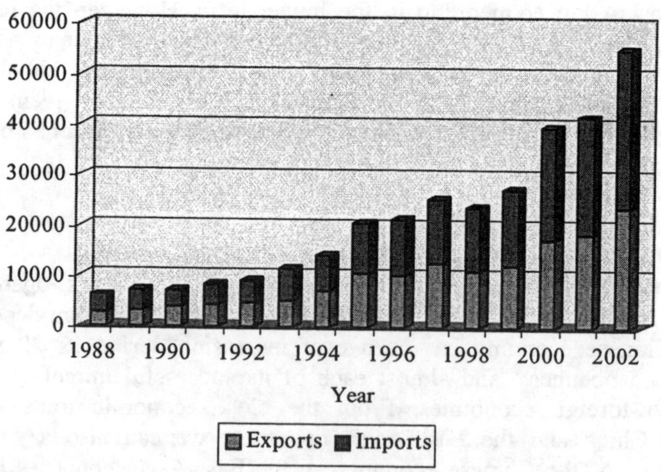

Figure 10.9 China's Total Value of Imports and Exports from/to ASEAN, 1988-2002 (US$ million)

Sources: China Statistical Yearbook from 1989 to 2002, and Chinese Customs Statistics.

The ASEAN region has advantages in such products as mining goods, plastics and rubber goods, wooden goods, paper pulp and paper goods and grease, which cover 42 per cent of China's imports from ASEAN. China also has advantages in products such as metals and metal goods, textiles, apparel and shoes, vegetables and processed food, automobiles, cements and stones, which in all cover 38 per cent of China's exports to ASEAN. In addition, China and ASEAN are partly complementary in the trade of machinery and electrical appliances, chemicals, optical, and precision and musical instruments. Among them, machinery and electrical appliances account for 39 per cent of China's exports to ASEAN and 41 per cent of China's imports from ASEAN.[9]

Over the last decade the strongest rate of growth has been in the trade of manufactured products, with trade in computers/machinery and electrical equipment growing fastest. The fact that these products were the major exports and imports of both ASEAN and China suggests the importance of intra-industry trade, brought about by product differentiation and economies of scale.

The establishment of an FTA between ASEAN and China will create a huge market with 1.7 billion consumers. It will be the biggest FTA in the world in terms of population size. The removal of trade barriers between ASEAN and China will definitely lower transaction costs, increase intra-regional trade and increase economic efficiency. It is well-known that, if protected by trade barriers, domestic enterprises face little competition and pressure. As a result they operate inefficiently. With the formation of an FTA, and with trade barriers among members eliminated, the ensuing fierce competition will further promote specialization, and, as a result, increase productivity and economic welfare.

According to calculations made by ASEAN experts, after the creation of an ASEAN-China FTA China will gain an increase in real GDP of 0.3 per cent equating to a rise of US$2.2 billion. China's exports to ASEAN will increase by US$10.6 billion or by 55.1 per cent. Besides, the establishment of the ASEAN-China FTA will create a sense of community among ASEAN members and China. This will provide another important mechanism for supporting economic stability in East Asia, and allow both ASEAN and China to have a larger voice in international trade affairs on issues of common interest.

Foreign direct investment

Both ASEAN and China are major destinations for foreign direct investment rather than significant investors in each other's economy. With the formation of an ASEAN-China FTA, more investment should be attracted into the region. Not only will more ASEAN and Chinese companies be willing to invest within the integrated market, but US, European and Japanese companies, which are interested in making inroads into the Asian market, will also be attracted to invest in the region since market risk and uncertainty are lowered. The integration of ASEAN with China can entice more foreign corporations, which each market alone cannot otherwise achieve so successfully.

By applying a general computable equilibrium modelling tool known as the Global Trade Analysis Project (GTAP), Chirathivat (2002) came to the assessment that in terms of attracting FDI the impact of tariff and non-tariff liberalization on China is 0.7 per cent and 3.3 per cent respectively. On the other hand, there will be challenges arising from the establishment of an FTA between ASEAN and China. There would be intensifying competition in each region's domestic market given the similarity in industrial structure. A more liberalized environment under the proposed FTA may entail short-run costs in the form of displacement of workers and rationalization of some industries and firms. There would be the need for adjustments to be made by workers and enterprises, particularly the small and medium-sized (SMEs) enterprises. It should also be noted that trade diversion, in terms of a shift from lower-cost non-FTA members to higher-cost FTA members, could occur due to the preferential tariff reduction and elimination among the FTA members. Trade shifting away from producers with natural comparative advantage would incur implicit economic costs. Closely associated with this would be the loss of tariff revenues.

10.5 CONCLUSIONS

In conclusion, from the perspective of China's demand structure, considerable domestic demand and international market opportunities are the forces of China's fast-growing economic development. In terms of regional economic features three big regional economies, especially the Yangzi River Delta, are the engine of China's economic growth, of which Shanghai is the core engine of the Yangzi River Delta development. Based on the major features of the Chinese economy and international economic development experience, we conclude that China will continue with its fast growth in the coming ten to 15 years.

Objectively, in the context of foreign economic trade, China does compete against its neighbouring countries such as ASEAN and Korea in some aspects. Nevertheless, the negative influence of competition would be offset by the benefits that China offers to these nations as their key trading partner.

China's liberalization, as a result of its accession to the WTO and the formation of an ASEAN-China FTA, would provide an important opportunity for expanding current trade and investment activities between the East and South East Asian countries and China.

China will continue to provide East and South East Asian nations with considerable room for furthering their economic development, due to its low labour costs and a sizable domestic market. In the future, China will surely need other East and South Asian nations including the subcontinent, and vice versa.

NOTES

1 According to the World Bank, China's average annual growth rate reached 10.3 per cent over the period 1980-90 and ten per cent over the period from 1991-2001. Source: www.worldbank.org/data/wdi2003.

2 *Beijing Youth Daily*, December 9, 2002.

3 Xiao Geng, "Interaction between global capital flow and Chinese reform", *Finance,* 2003.

4 Cheng Yuansheng, "To develop economic potentials", *People's Daily, 03,July 2000, p.7.*

5 Same as note 4.

6 Lin Yifu, Remarks on China's opportunities, *International Finance*, 4 March, 2003, p. 2.

7 Same as note 3.

8 For further analysis of ASEAN+China in the era of new Asian regionalism, see Tran Van Hoa and Harvie (2003).

9 "Forging Closer ASEAN-China Economic Relations in the Twenty-First Century", A Report submitted by the ASEAN-China Expert Group on Economic Cooperation, October 2001.

REFERENCES

ASEAN-China Expert Group (2001), "Forging closer ASEAN-China economic relation in the twenty-first century", A Report submitted by the ASEAN-China Expert Group on Economic Cooperation, October, Shanghai Giaotong University. Available at http://www.aseansec.org/newdata/asean_chi.pdf, pp.9-10.

Chirathivat, Suthipand (2002), "ASEAN-China Free Trade Area: background, implications and future development", *Journal of Asian Economics, 13(5),* pp. 671-86.

Geng, Xiao (2003), "Interaction between global capital glow and Chinese reform", *Finance, 14*, pp. 60-2.

Lo, Chi (2003), "Asia's competitiveness endgame: life after China's WTO entry", *The China Business Review*, Jan/Feb, p.26.

Tran Van Hoa and C Harvie, (eds.) (2003), *New Asian Regionalism: Responses to Globalisation and Crises,* , London: Palgrave/Macmillan, p. 259.

World Bank (2003), *Global Development Finance Report.*

Yifu Lin, and Yongjun Li (2002), "A Re-examination of International Trade's Contribution to China's Economic Growth", Working Paper, p. 5, Shanghai Giaotong University

11. ASEAN+3 and RTAs and their Impact on Asia-Australia Trade and Growth: Econometric Evidence from an Extended Gravity Theory

Tran Van Hoa

11.1 INTRODUCTION

The recent emergence of various forms of new Asian regionalism (NAR), such as ASEAN+3 (the ten ASEAN countries plus China, Korea and Japan) and other bilateral, plurilateral and multilateral free trade agreements (FTAs) (such as Australia-US, Australia-Japan, Australia-Singapore, Japan-Singapore, Korea-Chile and the proposed ASEAN+5 (ASEAN+3 plus Australia and New Zealand)), as well as the Cotonou-type regional economic integration agreements (EIAs) advocated by the European Union (EU) in order to promote "organic" growth and "normal" opportunities (see Barker, 2002), require new research focusing upon their impact on trade and growth, as well as their viability, sustainability and future expansion.

In the specific case of Australia, its trade with Asia, especially the Asia 3 (China, Japan and Korea), has been substantial both in volume and in share over the past few decades. For example, in 2001, of Australia's total exports of $A122.5 billion 41.1 per cent (or $A50.4 billion) went to North Asia and 12.6 per cent to the countries of ASEAN. By comparison the share to the North American FTA (NAFTA) was only 11.2 per cent and to the EU 12 per cent (Austrade, 2003). In this context the emergence of ASEAN+3 and other FTAs or EIAs or FTAs-EIAs, with expected subsequent trade and services diversion, may have a deep impact on Australia's trade, investment, growth and, through less trade in goods and services, regional economic relations and cooperation in non-trade (such as security and stability) areas. To date, however, not much work in this area has been done and reported on the causal and quantitative significance of the factors giving rise to NARs, and their potential impact in general (see ASEAN, 2002, and also Tran Van Hoa, 2003) or with specific reference to Asia-Australia trade in particular.

While an apparent reason for the emergence of the FTAs and EIAs mentioned above in the Asian region may be the country members' proximity (distance, size and area), other economic (for example, the 'flying geese' pattern and financial crises) and non-economic (for example, social, cultural and religious) factors may regionally and globally also play an important and interdependent part (see below). It would be more appropriate in this case to investigate the impact of NARs (for example, ASEAN+3) on our bilateral focus, Asia-Australia trade, primarily from this new and comprehensive perspective.

The chapter departs from the standard, but restrictive, CGE/GTAP method (which deals statically and only with goods trade in coverage and no econometrics) and proposes instead a new approach, with data-based quantitative and policy outcomes, to empirically validate the *raison d'étre* for recent Asian FTAs, and to comprehensively investigate their potential impact on trading partners' trade. This new approach has four innovative features. First, it proposes to extend the standard gravity theory [1] to construct appropriate simultaneous-equation trade-growth models in flexible functional form (Tran Van Hoa, 1992a) for our three trading blocs of interest, namely, ASEAN, the Asia 3 and Australia, and their relationships. Second, it uses recent World Bank World Tables national accounts and France's CHELEM trade time-series data, and improved 2SHI estimation methodologies (Tran Van Hoa, 1985, 1986b, 1986c, 1997, and Tran Van Hoa and Chaturvedi, 1997, and Namba, 2000 and 2001) to fit these models to provide more reliable empirical evidence on trade-growth causality and historical support (or a lack of it) for the ASEAN, the Asia 3, Australia and their trade linkages. Third, based on these findings, trade and growth policy implications for these three trading blocs will be discussed and the impact of ASEAN+3 on Asia-Australia trade assessed. Finally, applications of our new modelling and impact study approach to, for example, ASEAN+5, ASEAN+India or the recent Australia-China and other regional, plurilateral or multilateral FTAs and EIAs will be briefly suggested.

The structure of the chapter is as follows. Section 2 summarizes the development of new Asian regionalism and ASEAN+3. Section 3 provides a linkage between ASEAN+3 and gravity theory and also a description of our new approach, the extended gravity theory, which will be adopted in our study of ASEAN+3 on Asia-Australia trade and growth. A simple trade-growth model is introduced in section 4 and its estimation reported in section 5. An analysis of the empirical findings is given in section 6 and implications for policy on Asia-Australia trade and growth and economic relations are discussed in section 7. Finally, section 8 summarizes the main findings.

11.2 DEVELOPMENT OF NEW ASIAN REGIONALISMS AND ASEAN+3

The ASEAN+3 proposal, sometimes known as the Young-Ho Kim proposal named after Korea's former Minister of Commerce who strongly supported and put it forward, was discussed in the mid- and especially late-1990s by ASEAN leaders, and implemented notably through the Hanoi Plan of Action in 1998 for ASEAN Vision 2020 (ASEAN, 2002). A number of factors can be attributed to its recent emergence. First, it was the result of decades of fast growth and a number of economic, financial and restructuring developments in North East Asia and in other major trading blocs in the world. Second, it was the result of developments and shifts in focus in North America and the EU in the aftermath of the damaging Asia crisis starting in Thailand in July 1997, and its subsequent contagion to a number of "once miracle" economies in East and South East Asia, the former USSR, and, to a lesser extent, North and South America and the EU (Tran Van Hoa, 2000a). Third, it was the result of a benign neglect from such international organizations as the International Monetary Fund (IMF) or the economic power of North America and the EU on the plight of crisis countries in Asia, and the of lack of interest of the former in seriously helping to solve the economic, financial and social problems arising from the Asia crisis (Tran Van Hoa, 2002d).

In 2001, and early in 2002, other new developments in East and South East Asia gained prominence and assisted in giving rise to a number of new Asian economic integrations or regionalisms and Asian FTAs. These developments included the quick recovery and recurring growth in Korea, the emergence of China as a fast post-Asia crisis growing economy, and the continuing stagnant state of the world's second largest economy (namely Japan). The recent recovery and growth of Korea has also been put forward by some authors as a leader in the post-crisis 'flying geese' theory for ASEAN+3 economies (see Harvie and Lee, 2002).

The NARs and FTAs including customs unions and EIAs (which are accepted exceptions, subject to strict conditions, to the WTO principle of the Most Favoured Nations under Article XXIV of GATT and Article V of GATS) are indeed numerous and proliferating at an amazing speed at the behest of government leaders especially in the Asian region. They include plurilateral and bilateral FTAs such as first ASEAN, ASEAN+3, then ASEAN+5, ASEAN+5+Taiwan, Japan+Singapore, Japan+Korea, Japan+Mexico, Korea+Mexico+Chile, China+Japan+Korea, Singapore+New Zealand, Hong Kong+New Zealand, Australia-Japan (NARA), Australia-Singapore, and last, but not the least, Vietnam+US. Currently there is even a discussion on the setting up of a North Asian FTA in which Japan will play an important part. In mid-2003 a protocol was also being negotiated between Washington and Canberra to address key US complaints about the Australian market and to prepare for the setting up of a sweeping US-Australia FTA, as proposed by the Australian government (Hartcher, 2002). This was to the dismay of New Zealand which wanted, on the other hand, a trilateral US-CER (Closer Economic Relations – an EIA between Australia and New Zealand). In mid-2002 there was a suggestion by New Zealand Prime Minister Helen Clark to set up ANZEC (Australia-New Zealand Economic Cooperation) to boost the low-activity 20-year old CER. An Australia-Thailand CER Agreement – the first between Thailand and a developed country – was also proposed in mid-2003 (DFAT, 2004). The EU has also been strongly advocating regional integration and liberalization for the Pacific nations to create EU-type transnational economic partnerships (an EIA) within the Cotonou framework, to stimulate trade and create growth among them (Barker, 2002).

The main focus and objective of the NARs and Asian FTAs (as separate from currency or customs unions and EIAs) is to promote trade and living standards either among the Asian economies themselves or with the membership of other economies outside Asia such as the US, Mexico and Chile in the Americas, and Australia and New Zealand in Oceania. Prominent among these NARs and Asian FTAs is the ASEAN+3 proposal above and, part of it, the ASEAN+1 or ASEAN+China FTA with a 1,700 million people market, a US$2 trillion GDP, and trade worth US$1.2 trillion. ASEAN+China was endorsed by the ten leaders of ASEAN in Brunei in November 2001, and its details were worked out at a negotiating meeting in Beijing in May 2002.

11.3 ASEAN+3, OTHER FTAs AND GRAVITY THEORY

Since the primary objectives of FTAs are trade liberalization and welfare improvement, as well as economic partnerships generally, for member countries, the FTA premises that directly trade (international and domestic) and indirectly other determinants of trade significantly and causally affect: economic welfare (see Raimondos-Moller and Woodland, 2002); real wages (see Ruffin and Jones, 2003); growth (for developed countries see Frankel and Rose, 1998, Frankel and Romer, 1999); and development (for developing countries, see Harrison (for all countries), 1996, Frankel et al. (for ten East and South East Asian countries), 1996, and Tran Van Hoa (for ASEAN, China, Korea and Japan), 2002a). The outcomes are also mutually beneficial in many other non-economic aspects (e.g. closer regional and international cooperation and collaboration, social harmony, political stability and prosperity), and, in the context of globalisation and enhancing international competitiveness, conducive to regional or international economic integration (ASEAN, 1999).

In view of the expectation that FTAs will enhance trade and produce final outcomes of higher growth and higher real wages or better economic development improvement for trading partners or FTA member countries, a useful causality concept in the form of a gravity theory using geographical, demographic and other common or concurrent attributes (see for example Linneman, 1966 and the specification in Table 3 in Frankel et al., 1996) to explain trade flows (liberalization) between countries may be appropriate in empirical studies of this trade-growth nexus (for another more restrictive justification, see Rose, 2000). Some extensions to this theory's determinants using OECD country data have also been attempted to deal with trade correlations and output fluctuations (see for example, Otto et al., 2002). The data used in these seminal studies of the gravity theory have been singularly cross-sectional.

In the case of Asian economies, especially member countries in the ASEAN+3 FTA, and their impact in a bilateral Asia-Australia trade context, which is the focus of this study, not much research either of a qualitative or quantitative kind has been conducted or reported. Neither has much been done on the validity of the required premises underlying the foundation of this ASEAN+3 FTA (namely, given their regional proximity but diverse culture, history, religion and development components, does more trade cause higher growth in the member countries and over time?) and its trade linkage to Australia's exports and imports of goods and services.

11.4 A TRADE-GROWTH MODEL FOR STUDY OF ASEAN+3 AND ASIA-AUSTRALIA TRADE

Consider, for convenience and without loss of generality, a simple model of two simultaneous implicit functions (extension to more functions is straightforward when more variables are considered and endogenized) comprising and extending the basics of the standard cross-section-data-based gravity theory linking trade and growth between two trading countries or blocs. This extended gravity theory may comprise geographic or demographic attributes (for ASEAN, its neighbouring Asian 3 and Australia), economic factors, and the requirements of a regional FTA or EIA. Since the geographical attributes (such as distance and area) in the ASEAN+3 and Australia region are *a priori* assumed to be a rationale for setting up ASEAN and ASEAN+3, we can then focus on other relevant demographic (e.g, population as a proxy for size – see Frankel and Romer, 1999), economic and non-economic determinants of trade and growth in our model.

In this model, trade (named T) may be defined as exports or imports or openness (exports plus imports) and may include domestic trade (Frankel and Romer, 1999), and growth (Y) may be defined as GNP or, by more popular convention, GDP. The two countries may be comprehensively all possible pairs of the 13 ASEAN+3 members and Australia or, more specifically and within the interest of our present study, as pair-wise (bilateral) combinations of ASEAN-Australia and Asia 3-Australia. Thus

$$F1\ (\alpha, Y, T) = 0 \quad (11.1)$$
$$F2\ (\beta, T, Y, X, W) = 0 \quad (11.2)$$

where F1 and F2 are two arbitrary functionals linking trade and growth and their theoretically plausible determinants, α and β are parameter vectors, X and W denote, respectively, other economic (fiscal, monetary, trade and industry policy – see Sala-i-Martin, 1991) and non-economic (e.g, distance, area, size, policy shifts and external shocks – see Johansen, 1982) variables, relevant to a country or a group of countries' growth or development. Importantly, for our study, in addition to T and Y data for X and W must be available and consistent with published time-series data in a standard Kuznets-type accounting framework (e.g, SNA93), or the accounting system of Stone (1988), or the recent World Bank World Tables.

Taking the total differentials of (11.1) and (11.2), and neglecting terms of second and higher-order (see for example Allen, 1960 and Tran Van Hoa, 1992a), the 2-equation model (11.1)-(11.2) can be written in stochastic form and in terms of the rates of change (Y%, T%, X% and W%) of all the included econometrically exogenous and endogenous variables (Y, T, X and W) as:

$$Y\% = \alpha 1 + \alpha 2T\% + u1 \quad (11.3)$$
$$T\% = \beta 1 + \beta 2Y\% + \beta 3X\% + \beta 4W\% + u2 \quad (11.4)$$

In (11.3)-(11.4), the equations are linear and interdependent in the sense of Marshall or Haavelmo, α's and β's are the elasticities, and u's other unknown factors outside the model (Frankel and Romer, 1999) or disturbances with standard statistical properties. In (11.3)-(11.4) circular and instantaneous causality in the sense of Granger (1969) or Engle-Granger (1987) exists or is regarded as a testable hypothesis. In their non-stochastic forms (in which all disturbances are idealistically zero), these equations form the basic structure of the applied or computable general equilibrium (CGE/GTAP) models of the Johansen class, in which all elasticities are usually assumed to be given or known *a priori* and the impact of endogenous or endogenized variables (say T) on Y is dependent on the exogenous variables and calculated system-wise using such iterative procedures as the Gauss-Euler algorithm with a known sparse matrix of elasticities.

It can be verified that our so-called flexible (or function-free) trade-output growth equation (11.3) in the model above is econometrically identified in the sense of mathematical consistency. An impact study of endogenous trade (or exogenous X and W) on growth can be analysed directly via its 2SLS (or reduced-form adjusted) form structurally given in (11.5) below or indirectly via its reduced form given in (11.6) in terms of all the exogenous economic and non-economic variables in the model. It is well known in the theory of econometrics that the use of OLS to estimate equation (11.3) for example will, in this case, produce biased parameter estimates. These two equations can be written as

$$Y\% = a1 + a2\,\check{T}\% + v1 \tag{11.5}$$

$$Y\% = p1 + p2X\% + p3W\% + v2 \tag{11.6}$$

where $\check{T}$ is T as estimated by the OLS of its reduced form equation (that is (11.6) with T% replacing Y%) and v's the new disturbances with standard statistical properties.

An important feature of our modelling approach is that, contrary to the CGE/GTAP restrictive (goods only) and *a priori* approach, our impact study is data-consistent as all required elasticities are estimated from available data and have asymptotically and statistically desirable and consistent (an important issue in the gravity theory's empirical applications – see Frankel and Romer, 1999) properties when suitable estimation and forecasting methods (e.g. 2SLS or other instrumental variables (IV) methods) are employed. Another important feature is that, contrary to other SNA93-based or Keynesian approaches, our impact study has the general flexibility in modelling specification rationale and implementation in assuming explicitly no *a priori* functional forms for the equations in the model, and it can handle data on trade or budget deficits and real rates of interest when inflation exceeds the nominal interest rate. The usual method of routine log transformations for all variables in an econometric model cannot do this.

To implement the model, equations (11.3)-(11.4) above, to empirically investigate the causal relationship between, for example, trade and growth in the ASEAN, the Asia 3 and Australia, we can use, given fixed geographical components (distance and area) as discussed, and, for time-series data, population (a proxy for size), conventional economic determinants of trade (see for example Frankel and Rose, 1998, Frankel and Romer, 1999, Rose, 2000, and Otto et al., 2002) and/or other relevant factors (e.g, external or internal shocks – Johansen, 1982) when such data are available. One such extended model relevant to our focus of study on the possible causality (impact) between Australia trade and the ASEAN or the Asia 3 may be written in either the reduced-form adjusted equation (11.7), and supplemented by the full reduced-form equation for T (11.8) (and similarly for growth Y) as:

$$Y\% = a1 + a2\,\check{T}\% + a3ST + v1 \tag{11.7}$$

$$T\% = p1 + p2\,YT\% + p3\,FT\% + p4\,MT + p5\,PT + p6ERT + p7IT + p8POT + p9ST + v2 \tag{11.8}$$

In equations (11.7)-(11.8), Australian trade (T%) with its Asian trading partner (ASEAN or the Asia 3 or both) for example is assumed to cause, together with ST (external and internal shocks), Australian growth (Y%) but this trade is also affected by economic activities, trade-related policies and external or internal shocks in Australia and its trading partner (either ASEAN or the Asia 3 or both). Assuming, for convenience, that Australian trade (traditionally defined as its exports (or imports, see Barro and Helpman, 1991)) with its trading partner is affected by this partner's GDP and other major economic activities, trade-related policies (see Coe and Helpman, 1993 for this approach) or external or internal shocks in its trading partner, then Equation 11.8 in its reduced form simply assumes that Australia's partner's trade is affected by the exogenous factors such as GDP (named YT), inflation (PT) – see Romer (1993), fiscal policy (FT), monetary policy (MT), trade policy and exchange rates (ERT) – see Rose (2000), industry structure (IT) – see Otto et al. (2002), population (POT) – see Frankel and Romer (1999), and internal or external shocks (ST) – see Johansen (1982) - of its trading partner.

In deriving equations (11.7) and (11.8) for two trading countries or blocs, we assume that Country 1's trade affecting its growth is a testable hypothesis and this trade itself is essentially a demand equation for either imports (from Country 2) and exports (to Country 2) or vice versa or both. For the economies of the ASEAN and the East Asia 3, geographic attributes (that is, being in the neighbouring region) are assumed to be the *prime facie* reason for setting up the ASEAN+3, and the distance and area characteristics are omitted as all of our variables are expressed in terms of time-series (distance and area may also not be appropriate even for cross-section studies with high-trade countries like Singapore and Brunei in ASEAN+3). All variables in the model, that is, Y, T, YT, FT, MT, PT, ERT, IT and POT are expressed as their rates of change so the units of measurement for the trading countries' variables are irrelevant. ST is a qualitative time-series variable representing shocks having either one-off effects or temporally permanent effects (autoregressive and non-stationary) on trade and growth with discrete values.

The implications of our model above are important for studying the transmission mechanism, or relationship, between trade and growth of the ASEAN, the Asia 3 and Australia, and their trade linkages. This relationship, if empirically substantiated, can provide powerful evidence on the trade, investment and welfare enhancement relationship of these countries as trading partners. It would also lend crucial support for the viability, sustainability and promising prospects of the new Asian regionalism, namely, ASEAN+3 (or other FTAs), as well as providing empirical evidence for quantifying its impact on Asia-Australia trade and suggesting robust and credible trade policy.

11.5 ALTERNATIVE ESTIMATION AND FORECASTING METHODS

The importance of using a suitable estimation method for our model (or similar models) to get more accurate or unbiased results has been emphasized in previous trade-growth studies using standard gravity theory (see for example Frankel and Romer, 1999). These studies deal mainly with the OLS and IV (instrumental-variables) estimation methods. In this section, we briefly survey the various new and improved estimation and forecasting methods that are available. Their appropriate use can produce more accurate econometric outcomes on the trade-growth causal relationship, and subsequently on economic and trade policies and regional integration.

More specifically, in our model, the equations in differential and reduced form as given in equation (11.8) for Y% (or, similarly, for T% to provide $\check{T}$% in equation (11.7)) can be written more generally with a sampling size T and k independent variables (possible causal components) in matrix notation as:

$$\underset{(Tx1)}{y} = \underset{(Txk)}{Z} \; \underset{(kx1)}{ß} + \underset{(Tx1)}{u} \tag{11.9}$$

where y = Y%, Z = the rate of change of the exogenous and predetermined variables (both static and dynamic), ß = the parameters, and u the disturbance satisfying all standard statistical assumptions.

We now define our evaluation criterion (in terms of average MSE or Wald risks) for an arbitrary estimator $\hat{\beta}$ a for β in equation (11.9) as Wald risk ≡ MSE($\hat{\beta}$ a) = ($\hat{\beta}$ a-β)'W($\hat{\beta}$ a-β) where W is a positive definite. Under Wald risks we can estimate equation (11.9), which is essentially a general linear model for structural or behavioural analysis or for direct forecasting and policy studies (see Pindyck and Rubinfeld, 1998), by using OLS or, at a more statistically efficient level, any of the explicit (Baranchik, 1973) Stein or Stein-rule methods as described below.

More specifically, using equation (11.9), the basic and most well-known and used method to produce estimates and forecasts of y (or Y%) is the OLS estimator of ß (denoted by $\hat{\beta}$), and written as

$$\hat{\beta} = (Z'Z)^{-1}Z'y \tag{11.10}$$

A more efficient method is the explicit Stein estimator of ß (Baranchik, 1973) and given by

$$\hat{\beta}s = [1 - c(y\text{-}Zb)'(y\text{-}Zb)/b'Z'Zb]\ \hat{\beta}$$

$$= [1 - c(1\text{-}R^2)/R^2]\ \hat{\beta} \qquad (11.11)$$

where c is a characterizing scalar and defined in the range $0 < c < 2(k\text{-}2)/(T\text{-}k+2)$, and R^2 is the square of the sample multiple correlation coefficient.

A still more efficient method (to avoid, in one respect, implausible results derived from plausible OLS parameter estimates) is the explicit positive-part Stein estimator of ß (Anderson, 1984). This estimator is defined as

$$\hat{\beta}+s = [1 - \min\{1\ ,\ c(y\text{-}Z\hat{\beta})'(y\text{-}Z\hat{\beta})/\hat{\beta}'Z'Z\hat{\beta}\}]\ \hat{\beta}$$

$$= [1 - \min\{1\ ,\ c(1\text{-}R^2)/R^2\}]\ \hat{\beta} \qquad (11.12)$$

A new method to obtain estimates and forecasts of ß in equation (11.9), with better properties in Wald risks, has been proposed (see Tran Van Hoa, 1985, Tran Van Hoa and Chaturvedi, 1988, 1990, 1997). It is in a class of explicit improved Stein-rule or empirical Bayes (also known as the two-stage hierarchical information or 2SHI estimators for linear regression models). This estimator includes the explicit Stein and the double k-class (Ullah and Ullah, 1978) estimators as subsets (Tran Van Hoa, 1993a). Other applications of the Stein, Stein-rule, and 2SHI estimators to linear regression models with non-spherical disturbances and to Zellner's seemingly unrelated regression model have also been made (see Tran Van Hoa et al., 1993, in the case of regressions with non-spherical disturbances, and Tran Van Hoa, 1992b, 1992c, and 1992d, in the case of seemingly unrelated regressions).

The explicit 2SHI estimator is a *bona fide* or fully operational (in statistical theory terminology) estimator, and defined as

$$\hat{\beta}h = [1 - c(1\text{-}R^2)/R^2\} - c(1\text{-}R^2)/\{R^2(1+c(1\text{-}R^2)/R^2)\}]\ \hat{\beta} \qquad (11.13)$$

and its positive-part counterpart (Tran Van Hoa, 1986a) is given by

$$\hat{\beta}+h = [1 - \min\{1\ ,\ c(1\text{-}R^2)/R^2\} - \ \{1/((R^2/c(1\text{-}R^2)) + 1)\}]\ \hat{\beta} \qquad (11.14)$$

While all the estimators given above can be applied to the general linear model equation (11.9) for structural and forecasting analysis, their relative performance in terms of historical, *ex post* or *ex ante* (Pindyck and Rubinfeld, 1998), forecasting of MSE can differ. Thus, it is well known that, in MSE and for $k \geq 3$ and $T \geq k + 2$, $\hat{\beta}s$ dominates (that is, it performs better in forecasting MSE) $\hat{\beta}$, and $\hat{\beta}s$ is dominated by $\hat{\beta}+s$ (Baranchik, 1973,

Anderson, 1984). However, it has also been demonstrated (Tran Van Hoa, 1985, Tran Van Hoa and Chaturvedi, 1988) that, in MSE, $\hat{\beta}$h dominates both $\hat{\beta}$ and $\hat{\beta}$s, and more importantly, $\hat{\beta}$+h dominates $\hat{\beta}$+s (Tran Van Hoa, 1986a).

A further important result of the 2SHI theory has recently been proved (see Tran Van Hoa and Chaturvedi, 1997): *the dominance of the 2SHI over the OLS and Stein exists anywhere in the range* $0 < c < 2(k-1)/(T-k)$. This indicates that the 2SHI produces better (in terms of smaller Wald risk or generalized Pitman nearness) estimates and forecasts even if the estimating and forecasting equation has only one independent variable in it. *The condition for the optimal Stein dominance in the linear equation up to now requires that* $0 < c < 2(k-2)/(T-k+2)$ (see Anderson, 1984). Further, MSE-dominance properties of the 2SHI estimators, and their extensions over the positive-part Stein estimator in regression equations, have been given by Namba (2000, 2001).

Remarks

First, since one of the best known IV estimators, namely the 2SLS, has been demonstrated to be dominated in MSE by the 2SHI in errors-in-variables models and in identified structural equations of simultaneous-equation models (see Tran Van Hoa, 1986b and 1986c) such as equation (11.7), the so-called IV (see Frankel and Romer, 1999) impact of the trading partner's (say ASEAN) trade on Australia growth can be directly studied via the application of the 2SHI to equation (11.7).

Second, while some application of the 2SHI forecasting methods to predictions of economic activities in some developed countries such as Australia (see Tran Van Hoa, 1992d) has been made, these methods have not been investigated explicitly within an open trade-growth theoretical framework and an empirical context using more recent economic data for the major economies in ASEAN and the Asia 3. This issue is taken up in the study below for some of the fastest growth economies, or group of economies, in the world in recent years (even after the Asia crisis of 1997), but with highly fluctuating investment and being very sensitive to foreign trade and capital flows in the region (see Tran Van Hoa and Harvie, 1998).

Third, an interesting feature of our study is that the 2SHI estimators are finite-sample estimators (which converge to the OLS or 2SLS when $T \to \infty$) with optimal MSE properties (see above). Since all time-series data used here are necessarily annual and have, as usual, a small sample size, the study outcomes are therefore finite-sample optimal.

Finally, it has been demonstrated that the 2SHI dominates other conventional estimators when measurement errors exist (Tran Van Hoa,

1986b). Since the poor quality of economic data from the Asian countries and other less developed country economies is well known, one by-product of our study is that the findings are also optimal in errors-in-variables cases.

11.6 SUBSTANTIVE EVIDENCE ON ASEAN, ASIA 3 AND ASEAN+3 TRADE ON AUSTRALIAN GROWTH

This section reports substantive results for a number of trade-growth simultaneous-equation models which are based on several plausible extensions to the standard gravity theory: such as planar approximation to any arbitrary functionals (see below), to time-series data, and incorporating micro/macro factors and shocks, and given in equations (11.7) and (11.8) above. For comparison with the findings of previous studies in standard gravity theory applications, these results are obtained by the OLS, 2SLS and 2SHI for the structural equation of growth, equation (11.7).

Data

Due to data limitations for our studies, especially dealing with developing economies, all original data are obtained as annual and then transformed to their ratios (when appropriate). The ratio variables include trade (exports and imports), government budget, and money supply (M2) all divided by GDP, and labour force divided by population. Other non-ratio variables include exchange rates, population and binary variables representing the occurrence of the economic, financial and other major crises over the period 1961 to 2001. All non-binary variables are then converted to their percentages. The use of this percentage measurement is a main feature of our modelling and impact approach and avoids the problem of *a priori* known functional forms (see above) and also of logarithmic transformations for negative data (such as budget (fiscal) or current account deficits). As the average micro/macroeconomic data for the countries in the ASEAN and the Asia 3 as two regional trading blocs are difficult (if not impossible) to measure, we have reversed the direction of trade below in a "dual ASEAN trade to Australia or, equivalently, Australia trade to ASEAN" context and used Australia as the trading partner of ASEAN and the Asia 3 instead.

The data for regional (e.g, ASEAN and the Asia 3) and national (e.g, Australia) trade (exports (X) to and imports (IM) from, respectively), GDP and estimated mean population (named POP) are retrieved from France's 2001 CHELEM international trade databases. Openness between two trading countries is defined as T=X+IM although the separate effects of either X or IM have been experimented with (see below). All trade and economic data are at current prices. Fiscal, monetary, trade and industry policy data for

Australia was obtained from the 2003 OECD database and approximated, respectively, by government budget/GDP (BUR), M2/GDP (M2R), exchange rates per US dollar (ER), and the unemployment rate (or 1-(employment/labour force)) (UR). In addition to the usual demographic and economic components in our model, we also identified five major world crises that had affected the ASEAN and Asia 3 economies (and other economies) during our sampling period and included them as five dummy variables with persistent effects after their occurrence (one-off effects were postulated but discarded as implausible in the study). These are the first oil crisis of 1975 (named C75), the stock market crash of 1987 (C87), the China turmoil (C89), the Gulf War of 1991 (C91), and the Asia crisis of 1997 (C97). Various modelling experiments in our study also show that these crises all have a permanent or non-decayed effect on growth in ASEAN and the Asia 3.

The Estimated Models

The various bilateral trade-growth models for the ASEAN and the Asia 3 trading with Australia are based on these data. The 2-simultaneous equation trade-growth model for ASEAN and Australia in our studies, for example that based on equations (11.7)-(11.8), can be written fully for estimation and impact analysis as:

$$YA\% = \alpha_1 + \alpha_2 TOZ2A\% + \alpha_3 C75 + \alpha_4 C87 + \alpha_5 C91 + \alpha_6 C97 + v1 \quad (11.15)$$

$$TOZ2A\% = \beta_1 + \beta_{12} YOZ\% + \beta_3 BUR\% + \beta_4 M2R\% + \beta_5 IPD\% + \beta_6 ER\% +$$

$$\beta_7 UR\% + \beta_8 POP\% + \beta_9 C75 + \beta_{10} C87 + \beta_{11} C91 + \beta_{12} C97 + v2 \quad (11.16)$$

where, in percentages, YA = ASEAN's GDP, TOZ2A = Australia's total trade (exports + imports or openness) with ASEAN, and YOZ = Australia's GDP. The variables BUR, M2R, IPD, ER, UR and POP denote, respectively, fiscal, monetary, inflation, exchange rate, industry policy and population in Australia. The v's are the disturbances representing other unknown factors but with effects on YA and TOZ2A respectively (see Frankel and Romer, 1999 for this rationale). The trade-growth models for the Asia 3 and Australia can be similarly constructed.

The Empirical Findings

Two sets of empirical findings for two trade-growth models, based on equations (11.15)-(11.16) above for ASEAN-Australia, Asia 3-Australia and ASEAN+3-Australia, are given in Table 11.1. Since the estimation methods used can provide greatly different results even for the same model (see further detail in Frankel and Romer, 1999), and also for the purpose of statistical efficiency comparison, three types of estimated structural parameters have been calculated for each model. These are the OLS, the 2SLS and the 2SHI (applied on the 2SLS). For testing the hypothesis, the 2SHI has approximately the same asymptotic properties as OLS and 2SLS.

From the results given in Table 11.1, we note three important findings. First, while having high success in modelling output growth is difficult, all three estimated models of Australia growth *vis-à-vis* ASEAN, Asia 3 and ASEAN+3 trade have statistically significant and higher modelling performance (that is, R^2 reaching up to 88 per cent) relative to other trade-growth causality models as reported in previous international studies. A graph of the observed and estimated Australia growth fluctuations in the ASEAN-Australia, Asia 3-Australia and ASEAN+3-Australia models for the period under study (1971-99) also indicate that the peaks, troughs and turning points of Australia growth are accurately predicted for most of the period under study. All estimated models also appear free from serious autocorrelation-induced inefficiency problems. Second, trade, as defined by total trade/GDP between ASEAN, the East Asia 3 and ASEAN+3 *vis-à-vis* Australia, has mixed results. With the Asia 3-Australia model, it has a positive but insignificant impact on Australia growth in terms of the OLS, but it has a negative and also insignificant impact on this growth in terms of the 2SLS and 2SHI. For the ASEAN-Australia model, trade, as defined, has a positive impact on Australia growth, but only the 2SLS and 2SHI show a statistically significant effect (at the 15 per cent significance level for both the 2SLS and 2SHI). For the ASEAN+3-Australia models, trade has no significant positive effect on Australia growth. Third, for all models, the impact of the oil crisis of 1975, the stock market crash of 1987, and the China turmoil in 1989, all have a uniformly and statistically significant negative impact on Australia growth. Surprisingly, the Gulf War and the 1997 Asia economic and financial crisis reveal a large (up to 2.17 per cent), positive but non-significant impact on Australia growth in all three models.

In modelling experiments to verify the use of other definitions of trade (see above), we decomposed total trade into ASEAN, Asia 3 and ASEAN+3 imports from their trading partner (i.e., Australia exports) and Australia's imports from its trading partners (i.e. ASEAN, Asia 3 and ASEAN+3 exports to Australia) separately and included them in the growth-trade equation (11.15). The empirical findings (which are based only on 1971-97 available data) for the impact of these Asian imports and exports on Australia growth

Table 11.1 *Impact of ASEAN, Asia 3 and ASEAN+3 trade on Australia growth and openness extended gravity theory in flexible structural form 1971 to 1999*

	ASEAN-Australia			Asia 3-Australia			ASEAN+3-Australia		
Variables	OLS	2SLS	2SHI	OLS	2SLS	2SHI	OLS	2SLS	2SHI
Constant	16.30**	15.86**	13.83**	16.49**	16.68**	15.55**	16.43**	16.53**	14.57**
Openness/GDP	0.04	0.11@	0.10@	0.01	-0.02	-0.02	0.03	0.01	0.01
Oil Crisis 75	-4.24**	-3.91**	-3.41**	-4.40**	-4.52**	-4.21**	-4.35**	-4.42**	3.90**
Stock Crash 87	-1.30	-2.08	-1.82	-0.80	-0.85	-0.79	-0.84	-0.82	0.72
China Turmoil 89	-7.82**	-7.43**	-6.48**	-8.20	-7.64**	-8.03**	-7.91**	-8.03**	-7.08**
Gulf War 91	1.77	1.50	1.31	1.82	2.14@	2.00	1.72	1.89	1.67
Asia Crisis 97	1.20	2.17	1.89	0.69	0.28	0.26	0.83	0.65	0.57
R^2	0.78	0.76	0.87#	0.77	0.76	0.88#	0.77	0.77	0.88
F	13.12**	12.12**	24.54**	12.50**	11.33**	25.67**	12.58**	12.51**	26.89**
DW	1.96	2.16	1.51	1.77	1.85	1.31	1.77	1.80	1.35

Notes: ** significant at the 5% level, * significant at the 10% level @ significant at the 15% level. # correlation coefficient between Australia growth and its estimate by 2SHI. Tests on 2SHI estimates are based on their asymptotic properties as T -> ∞.

Sources of data: World Bank (2002), CHELEM International Trade Data (2001).

Table 11.2 *Impact of ASEAN, Asia 3 and ASEAN+3 trade on Australia growth export and imports extended gravity theory in flexible structural form 1971 to 1997*

	ASEAN-Australia			Asia 3-Australia			ASEAN+3-Australia		
Variables	OLS	2SLS	2SHI	OLS	2SLS	2SHI	OLS	2SLS	2SHI
Constant	15.82**	15.27**	13.46**	16.05**	16.15**	14.11**	16.35**	16.42**	14.16**
Openness/GDP									
Imports/GDP	-0.01	-0.03	-0.02	0.04	0.01	0.01	0.04	0.01	0.01
Exports/GDP	0.09**	0.16**	0.14**	0.02	0.05	0.05	-0.01	0.01	0.01
Oil Crisis 75	-3.05**	-1.98	-1.74	-3.83**	-3.77**	-3.30**	-4.41**	-4.37**	-3.76**
Stock Crash 87	-3.60*	-5.72**	-5.05**	-1.39	-1.51	-1.32	-0.72	-0.81	-0.70
China Turmoil 89	-8.71**	-9.26**	-8.17**	-7.22**	-7.79**	-6.81**	-7.44**	-7.89**	-6.80**
Gulf War 91	4.15	5.88@	5.18@	1.61	2.05	1.79	1.30	1.72	1.48
Asia Crisis 97									
R^2	0.82	0.79	0.89	0.73	0.78	0.88	0.70	0.76	0.87
F	14.90**	12.74	26.97**	12.44**	11.59**	24.44**	10.90**	10.57**	17.50**
DW	1.84	1.90	1.32	1.88	1.90	1.34	1.83	1.78	1.22

Source: See Table 11.1.

for the three models of ASEAN-Australia, Asia 3-Australia and ASEAN+3-Australia are given in Table 11.2. The findings are reported for OLS, 2SLS and 2SHI.

The first observation from Table 11.2 is that, in terms of the modelling performance (R^2) of the 2SLS estimation, all three estimated models with separate exports and imports are slightly more successful than the models with total trade or openness (with R^2 reaching up to 89 per cent). More specifically, while the predictions of peaks, troughs and turning points are still fairly accurate and serious serial correlation is absent in these models, the impact of Australia imports from the ASEAN, Asia 3 and ASEAN+3 regions is not only small in magnitude but also an insignificant contribution to Australia growth. In contrast, while the impact of Australia exports to the Asia 3 and ASEAN+3 seems again small and insignificant, its exports to the ASEAN contribute a larger and significant impact on Australia growth. The oil shocks of 1975 and the China crisis of 1989 both have negative and significant effects on Australia growth. While the 1987 stock market crash effects are negative for all three models, they are statistically significant only for the ASEAN-Australia case. The impact of the Gulf War on Australia's economic health is surprisingly positive but statistically negligible.

11.7 ECONOMIC AND TRADE POLICY IMPLICATIONS FOR AUSTRALIA FROM AN ASEAN, ASIA 3 AND ASEAN+3 FTAs

While the models we used for study above may be simple in their structure, they contain the main and conventional ingredients of trade-growth analysis and are fairly consistent with similar previous studies for comparative purposes. The empirical findings reported in the preceding section also provide a number of interesting results on trade-growth causation with important international trade or cooperation policy implications for Australia, and with the economies of ASEAN+3 in particular or with other regional and international economic integrations with similar interest and objectives in general. Some of our findings may be useful in providing significant evidence and information for trade-growth analysis, discussions and policy consideration. In addition, while some of the previous trade-growth analysis is based purely on cross-section data or a mix of panel data, our studies are based completely on time-series data due to our interest in economic development in the Asian region and its potential impact on Australia in recent years. These two approaches of gravity analysis are, however, complementary.

Do ASEAN, Asia 3 and ASEAN+3 Trade Cause Australia Growth?

Trade-to-growth is an important causal topic in economics that has attracted some of the best minds in the field over the last ten years or so (see for example Frankel and Romer, 1999, for a survey), and the conclusions have not been finalized for all cases. Our results above show that in the specific case of ASEAN, Asia 3 and ASEAN+3 *vis-a-vis* their trading partner in the Asia Pacific region, namely Australia, their trade, when defined as its relative size of openness or simply their exports to Australia, has at best only weak empirical support as a significant and positive determinant of Australia growth. Australia exports to these three major Asian regions, however, appear to be a significant contribution (especially in the case of exports to the ASEAN) to its growth. Interestingly, this weak contribution is found to be much stronger (by more than 100 per cent) in the case of the methodologically more acceptable 2SLS and 2SHI than the OLS with its well-known Haavelmo or simultaneous-equation bias. The weak evidence may be explained by the fact that advanced countries, such as Australia and the US, are essentially services economies, and they are less likely to be significantly affected by trade in goods only as used in this study. The dominance of exports in Australia growth may also be explained by the fact that Australian exports to Asia are mainly of primary and non-manufactured tradeable goods.

Do Crises Affect Australia Growth?

When openness is used as a proxy for trade between ASEAN, the Asia 3 and ASEAN+3, crises such as the 1975 oil shocks, the stock market crash of 1987, and the China internal turmoil of 1989 all do appear to affect Australia growth. Other major crises such as the Gulf War and the 1997 Asia meltdown have no adverse effect on this growth. When decomposed trade is used, however, the Asia crisis of 1997 and the 1989 China political turmoil are found to be the only factors that have exerted a strong and uniform declining impact on Australia growth in all three models. This finding would support the view of "The Asia crisis. What crisis?" in some sections (for example, the Melbourne Institute) of the Australian economic community (see Tran Van Hoa, 2000b). Another derived conclusion is that a contemporary trade-growth model for ASEAN+3 (or even for other regions or countries) studies, without the inclusion of these recent shock factors (as implied by Frankel and Romer, 1999, or stipulated by Johansen for policy analysis, 1982), may have serious and biased results on the causation being explored.

Are Trade-Growth Causation Results Affected by Estimation Methods?

In previous studies of trade-growth, OLS results of trade-growth models based on the gravity or similar theory seem to indicate an underestimation of the trade effect. IV estimates of the trade effect are usually found to be larger in general than OLS estimates. This is supported in our ASEAN-Australia and Asia 3-Australia models using either openness or imports and exports but not in the ASEAN+3-Australia model. Four reasons have been put forward to support the underestimation of the OLS and two explanations for the overestimation of 2SLS (see Frankel and Romer, 1999, for a brief survey). In our studies using openness, the underestimation of the OLS is found for the trade effect in the ASEAN-Australia and Asia 3-Australia models, but the reverse is found for the ASEAN+3-Australia case. In studies with decomposed trade, however, the 2SLS (and 2SHI) estimated impact is larger than that of the OLS for all three models and only in terms of Australia exports to the ASEAN and Asia 3. For Australia imports from Asia the OLS-based trade elasticities are uniformly larger than their 2SLS (and 2SHI) counterpart in the Asia 3-Australia and ASEAN+3-Australia models.

It is well known from the bias $-\beta Cov(Vu)$ of the OLS in errors-in-variables models (that is, $y = \beta X^{*}+u$, but X^{*} is unobserved and proxied by observed X with $X=X^{*}+V$, where V is measurement errors) or, equivalently, simultaneous-equation models, that the specification of the model or the instruments (as captured through Cov(Xu)) solely determines a downward or upward bias of the OLS. In our view, it is the nature of the model and the characteristics of the instruments and collected data that determine the estimation bias. A general conclusion may not be made in this case.

When we are focused on higher efficiency for the estimates of the models that are subject to misspecification (e.g, omitted relevant variables) or measurement errors or simultaneity bias, then the 2SHI estimates should be used. In this case the impact based on the OLS and 2SLS is overestimated and that on the 2SHI should be used. The smaller MSE estimates of the trade impact as obtained by the 2SHI and compared to the 2SLS, are given for all models in Tables 11.1 and 11.2.

Are Reduced-form Estimates of Trade a Good Proxy for Trade in our Models?

This is a question on the accuracy and reliability of the trade-growth model and the instruments used (a point often raised in the literature, see Frankel and Romer, 1999). The answer, in this case, has to be relative, as different models will have different instruments and therefore different accuracy or reliability outcomes. To answer this question for our models, we have calculated the proxy for T, namely $\check{T}$, from its reduced form for each of the estimations requiring a knowledge of Ť. Standard evaluation criteria such as the correlation coefficient and the Theil-MSE-decomposition Um (bias), Us (variation) and Uc (covariance) are then used to evaluate the proxy performance of Ť as compared to its actual T in each model reported in Table 11.1. The results of this evaluation are given in Table 11.3.

We note first from Table 11.3 that, as in the earlier cases, with Australia growth modelling, the Ť fairly accurately emulates all troughs, peaks and turning points of the actual T in all three models -ASEAN-Australia, Asia 3-Australia and ASEAN+3-Australia. In addition, the results indicate that, according to the evaluation criteria reported in Table 11.3, the Ť seems to be a very good estimated proxy to T in all models. This finding would enhance the robustness of our 2SLS estimation of the impact of Asian trade on Australia growth and related policy recommendations.

Do We Have Empirical Support for the ASEAN+5 FTA Proposal by Australia and New Zealand?

The ASEAN+5 (that is, ASEAN+3 plus Australia and New Zealand) proposal has been strongly supported by Australia and New Zealand within the context of regional economic integration in recent years, but, so far, has been rejected by some members of the ASEAN. As we have mentioned earlier the objectives of setting up an ASEAN+5 FTA are, in addition to better regional cooperation and stability, to enhance trade between its fifteen members and to improve their welfare. These objectives necessarily require that trade does in fact directly and positively affect growth. Our findings reported above (even for Australia only) lend ample support to the hypothesis that trade between the three Asian FTAs and Australia provides only a weak contribution to Australian growth. The implications are, based on our findings, that an ASEAN+5, for example, would therefore serve more a regional political cooperation agenda because of geographical gravity or closeness than a genuine economic and trade objective of mutual benefit.

Implications for Asia-Australia Trade Policy

The above conclusions appear to indicate that Australian trade, and especially crises, are important factors for Australian growth. More specifically, trade (exports) from Australia to the three Asian regions (especially the ASEAN) is the more important contribution. Since the Asia 3 is known to be more competitive, in terms of development stages, advanced technology, comparative advantages, and size, than the majority of the ASEAN, our findings on Australian growth being dependent more on ASEAN trade seems to be an interesting consideration for further study in Asia-Australia trade policy analysis. A good trade or integration policy emanating from ASEAN towards Australia, or vice versa, should take this into account.

Table 11.3 Reliability of the Trade Proxy in 3 Asia-Australia trade growth models - openness (exports+imports)/GDP - 1971 to 1999

Model	ASEAN-Australia (1971-1998)	Asia 3-Australia (1971-1998)	ASEAN+3-Australia (1971-1999)
Correlation Coefficient	0.74	0.74	0.76
RMSE	7.87	4.82	4.64
Mean Error	0.00	0.00	0.00
Um	0.00	0.00	0.00
Uc	0.15	0.15	0.14
Us	0.85	0.85	0.86

Notes: Ub+Us+Uc = 1. See Pindyck and Rubinfeld (1998) for further detail on these evaluation criteria. The estimates are based on TSP.

Implications for Australian Growth and Asian Regional Cooperation

In our earlier study (Tran Van Hoa, 2002a) it was pointed out that while trade between the Asia 3 or ASEAN members and other trading blocs (e.g, NAFTA and EU) reflects an important historical trend in the past thirty years or so, the composition of trade by tradable commodities is also important in promoting growth and development. Since the majority of trade between the Asia 3 or ASEAN and other advanced economies in North America and the EU involve groups of tradable commodities of a hi-tech nature, it was claimed that this technology transfer is essential to growth and development in the Asia 3 or ASEAN.

The implications of this are threefold. First, while showing an interest in improving trade with Australia even though this trade impact may be negligible, the ASEAN+3 FTA members can still cultivate this regional trade and economic cooperation as useful for technology transfer from a developed country with a Western (NAFTA and EU) cultural background in the region. Second, a closer economic cooperation between ASEAN+3 and Australia may have an extra economic benefit in a global context when the major trading blocs such as NAFTA and the EU are seemingly heading more towards regional self-interest or even economic isolationism. Finally, a closer ASEAN+3-Australia relation or even similar bilateral agreements (discussed earlier) would put the country members in a closer framework to promote trade and growth and to avoid crises such as the economic and financial turmoil or terrorist attacks that, on recent experience, have wrought havoc on the "once miracle" economies in the region in the form of economic slowdown and deep recession, political and social unrest, welfare deterioration and regional instability.

11.8 SUMMARY AND CONCLUSIONS

In the preceding sections we have provided a brief description of the emergence of new Asian regionalism including a major FTA, namely the ASEAN+3, and the logical link between it and a novel modelling impact methodology, the extended gravity theory. The resulting trade-growth models for ASEAN-Australia, Asia 3-Australia and ASEAN+3-Australia and their empirical findings appear to support the premise that trade does cause growth in the trading partners, but the evidence is weak statistically and in magnitude. More important to growth, however, are the economic, financial and other external or domestic crises, and trade and economic relations policies that promote regional cooperation to avoid, or to manage better, future similar crises. However, trade and economic relations between the ASEAN+3 and Australia should be encouraged, because this policy is a useful and practical non-treaty arrangement or framework which will strengthen the bilateral cooperation to create mutual benefits for the partner countries.

NOTE

1 For the foundation of this theory, see for example Linneman (1966), Harrison (1996), Frankel and Romer (1999).

REFERENCES

Allen, R.G.D. (1960), *Mathematical Analysis for Economists*, London: Macmillan.

Anderson, T.W. (1984), *An Introduction to Multivariate Statistical Analysis*, 2nd edition, New York: Wiley.

ASEAN (1999), Joint statement on East Asia cooperation, 28 November 1999, www.aseansec.org/, September 2002.

ASEAN (2002), www.aseansec.org/, August 2002.

Austrade (2003), Economic and trade statistics, www.austrade.gov.au/, July 2003.

Baranchik, A.J. (1973), "Inadmissibility of maximum likelihood estimators in some multiple regression problems with three or more independent variables", *Annals of Statistics, 1*, 312-21.

Barker, G. (2002), "Integrate or fail, EU official warns Pacific nations", *Australian Financial Review*, 9 October 2002, p. 10.

Barro, G. and E. Helpman, (1991), "Trade, knowledge spillovers and growth", *European Economic Review*, *35*, 517-36.

CHELEM (2001), *International Trade Databases*, Paris: CEPII.

Coe, D. and E. Helpman, (1993), "International R&D Spillovers", National Bureau of Economic Research Working Paper, Cambridge, MA, No. 4444, August 1993.

DFAT (Department of Foreign Affairs and Trade) (2004), http://www.dfat.gov.au/trade/ftas.html/.

Engle, R.F. and C.W.J. Granger, (1987), "Co-integration and error correction: representation, estimation and testing", *Econometrica, 55*, 251-76.

Frankel, J.A., D. Romer, and T.L. Cyrus (1996), "Trade and growth in East Asian countries: cause and effect", National Buneau of Economic Research Working Paper Cambridge, MA, No. 5732, August 1996.

Frankel, J.A. and A.K. Rose (1998), "The endogeneity of the optimum currency area criteria", *Economic Journal, 108*, 1009-25.

Frankel, J.A. and D. Romer (1999), "Does trade cause growth?", *American Economic Review, 89*, 379-99.

Granger, C.W.J. (1969), "Investigating causal relations by econometric models and cross-spectral methods", *Econometrica, 37*, pp. 424-38.

Harrison, A. (1996), "Openness and growth: a time-series, cross-country analysis for developing countries", *Journal of Development Economics, 48*, 410-47.

Hartcher, P. (2002), "Grape progress on US trade deal", *Australian Financial Review,* 24 May 2002, p. 22.

Harvie, C. and H-H. Lee (2002), "New regionalism in East Asia: how does it relate to the East Asian economic development model?", *ASEAN Economic Bulletin, 19,* 123-40.

Johansen, L. (1982), "Econometric models and economic planning and policy: some trends and problems", in M. Hazewinkle and A.H.G Rinnooy Kan (eds), *Current Developments in the Interface: Economics, Econometrics, Mathematics*, Boston: Reidel.

Linneman, H. (1966), *An Econometric Study of International Trade Flows,* Amsterdam: North-Holland.

Namba, A (2000), "MSE dominance of the PT-2SHI estimator over the positive-part Stein-rule estimator in regression", *Journal of Statistical Planning and Inference. 89,* pp. 175-85.

Namba, A. (2001), "MSE performance of the 2SHI estimator in a regression model with multivariate-t Error terms", *Statistical Papers, 42(1)* 81-96.

Otto, G, G Voss, and L. Willard, (2002), "Understanding OECD output correlations", Seminar Paper, Department of Economics, University of Wollongong, May 2002.

Pindyck, R.S. and D.L. Rubinfeld (1998), *Econometric Models and Economic Forecasts,* Sydney: McGraw-Hill.

Raimondos-Moller, P. and A. D. Woodland, (2002), "A note on two elementary propositions on customs unions", *International Conference on WTO and World Trade, III: Challenges in a New Area,* Gerhard-Mercator University, Duisburg, Germany, 29-30 June 2002.

Romer, D. (1993), "Openness and inflation: theory and evidence", *Quarterly Journal of Economics, 108,* 869-903.

Rose, A.K. (2000), "One money, one market: the effect of common currencies on trade", *Economic Policy, 30*, pp. 9-33.

Ruffin, R J and R. W. Jones (2003), "Real wages and trade: insights from extreme examples", Paper presented at Festschrift Workshop in Honour of Peter Lloyd, Department of Economics, University of Melbourne, 23-24 January 2003.

Sala-I-Martin, X. (1991), "Comment", in O.J. Blanchard, and S. Fischer, (eds), NBER *Macroeconomic Annual 1991*, Cambridge, MA: MIT Press, 368-78.

Stone, R (1988), "Progress in balancing the national accounts", in D. S. Ironmonger, J. O. N. Perkins and Tran Van Hoa (eds), *National Income and Economic Progress: Essays in Honour of Colin Clark,* London: Macmillan.

Tran Van Hoa (1985), "The inadmissibility of the stein estimator in normal multiple regression equations", *Economics Letters, 19*, 39-42.

Tran Van Hoa (1986a), "The inadmissibility of the Stein estimator in normal multiple regression models: analytical and simulation results", 15th Anniversary of the NBER-NSF Seminar on Bayesian Inference in Econometrics, ITAM, Mexico City, 16-18 January 1986.

Tran Van Hoa (1986b), "Improved estimators in some linear errors-in-variables models in finite samples", *Economics Letters, 20,* 355-58.

Tran Van Hoa (1986c), "The inadmissibility of the 2SLS estimator in some linear structural equations", *Economics Letters, 21,* 337-41.

Tran Van Hoa (1992a), "Modelling output growth: a new approach", *Economics Letters, 38*, 279-84.

Tran Van Hoa (1992b) "Energy consumption in Thailand: estimated structure and improved forecasts to 2000" (in Thai), *Thammasat Economic Journal (Thailand), 10,* 55-63.

Tran Van Hoa (1992c), "A multi-equation model of energy consumption in Thailand", *International Journal of Energy Research. 16*, 381-85.

Tran Van Hoa (1992d), "A new and general approach to modelling short-term interest rates: with application to Australian data 1962-1990", *Journal of Economics and Finance: Proceedings, 16.* 327-35.

Tran Van Hoa (1993a), "The mixture properties of the 2SHI estimators in linear regression models", *Statistics and Probability Letters, 16,* 111-15.

Tran Van Hoa (1993b), "Effects of oil on output growth and inflation in developing countries: the case of Thailand 1966:1 to 1991:1", *International Journal of Energy Research17,* pp. 29-33.

Tran Van Hoa (1997), "Improved forecasts of investment and growth in some major ASEAN economies: an economy-wide approach", *Journal of Economics and Finance (Proceedings), 21,* 271-80.

Tran Van Hoa (2000a) (ed.), *The Asia crisis: The Cures, Their Effectiveness and the Prospects After*, London: Macmillan.

Tran Van Hoa (2000b) (ed.), *The Social Impact of the Asia Crisis*, London: Macmillan.

Tran Van Hoa (2002a), "Korea, China and Japan's trade with the world and its impact on new Asian regionalism ASEAN+3", Paper presented at the Joint Conference of the Association of the Korean Economic Studies, Korea Development Institute, and Research Center for International Economics, Yonsei University, Seoul, 21-22 July 2002.

Tran Van Hoa (2002b), "Growth of Asian regional trade and income convergence: evidence from ASEAN+3 based on extended Helpman-Krugman hypothesis and flexible modelling approach", Department of Economics, University of Wollongong, mimeo.

Tran Van Hoa (2002c), "New Asian regionalism: evidence on ASEAN+3 free trade agreement from extended gravity theory and new modelling approach", Department of Economics, University of Wollongong, mimeo.

Tran Van Hoa (2002d) (ed.) *Economic Crisis Management*, Northampton, MA:

Edward Elgar.

Tran Van Hoa (2003), "New Asian regionalism and ASEAN+3 free trade agreement: theoretical and empirical foundation, policy challenges and growth prospects", *Chulalongkorn Journal of Economics* (Thailand), forthcoming.

Tran Van Hoa and A. Chaturvedi (1988), "The necessary and sufficient conditions for the uniform dominance of the two-stage Stein Estimators", *Economics Letters. 28,* 351-55.

Tran Van Hoa and A. Chaturvedi (1990), "Further results on the two-stage hierarchical information (2SHI) estimators in the linear regression models", *Communications in Statistics (Theory and Methods), A19, (12),* 4697-704.

Tran Van Hoa (with A. Chaturvedi, and G. Shukla,) (1993), "Performance of the Stein-rule estimators when the disturbances are misspecified as spherical", *Economic Studies Quarterly (Japan), 44,.* 601-11.

Tran Van Hoa (with A Chaturvedi,) (1997), "Performance of the 2SHI estimator under the generalized Pitman nearness criterion", *Communications in Statistics (Theory and Method), 26(5),* 1227-38.

Tran Van Hoa and C. Harvie (1998*), Causes and Impact of the Asian Financial Crisis,* London: Macmillan.

Ullah and Ullah (1978), "Double k-class estimators of coefficients in linear regression", *Econometrica,. 46,* 705-22.

World Bank, (2002), Washington DC: World Tables, World Bank.

PART FIVE

MONETARY COOPERATION IN EAST ASIA

12. Regional Economic and Monetary Integration – a Modelling and Policy Analysis

Charles Harvie

12.1 INTRODUCTION

This chapter is concerned with developing a two-country model, a large country and a small country, with the objective of identifying the circumstances under which it would be conducive to conduct coordinated macroeconomic policy with the objective of minimizing volatility in terms of key macroeconomic variables such as domestic prices, the exchange rate, the domestic interest rate and domestic output. The analysis is conducted from the perspective of the small country throughout. The analysis is important in providing a starting point for analysing the circumstances under which it would be conducive for a small country to contemplate the coordination of monetary and fiscal policy and those circumstances under which autonomy in these areas would be preferable.

While the approach adopted is a simple one, it does provide a starting point for the development of a more sophisticated two-country model approach that is the ultimate objective of this line of study. Given the increased prevalence of closer regional economic integration in the global economy, the major advances made in terms of economic and monetary union achieved in the European Union, and prospective developments of this in East Asia and the global economy more generally, it would be useful to have a clearer understanding as to what are the key conditions conducive to such closer economic integration and policy coordination.

The remainder of this chapter proceeds as follows. Section 2 presents the simple model to be adopted to explore the issues of external shocks and the desirability or otherwise of closer economic integration of macroeconomic policy between a small and large economy. Section 3 presents some calibrated solutions to the model for some simulation scenarios. Section 4 identifies some of the weaknesses of the modelling framework adopted, and the necessary extensions to it in future work. Finally, section 5 presents a summary of the major conclusions.

12.2 CONCEPTUAL FRAMEWORK

The framework utilized is that of a simple Dornbusch (1976) type rational expectations model. Two versions of this model are adopted, the first of which is based on the assumption of a small open economy with a flexible exchange rate and perfect capital mobility. This is shown by equations (12.1)-(12.4) in Table 12.1. Equation (12.1) describes money (or asset) market equilibrium, where the demand and supply of real money balances are in equilibrium. Real money demand is positively related to real output but negatively related to the nominal interest rate. The money (asset) market is assumed to be in continual equilibrium arising from the instantaneous adjustment of financial variables (in this version of the model the nominal exchange rate and the interest rate). Equation (12.2) describes goods market equilibrium. The demand for real output is positively related to the real exchange rate (equivalent to the domestic price of the imported product to the domestic price of the product), negatively related to the domestic real interest rate (the nominal rate deflated by domestic inflation), positively related to real government expenditure, and positively related to the real output of the large country (or bloc of countries). Small country output is assumed to be identical to that of the output of the large country. Equation (12.2), unlike Equation (12.1), does not remain in equilibrium continuously due to stickiness of adjustment of domestic prices. Hence a key characteristic of the model is that asset markets are in continual equilibrium while there is disequilibrium in non-financial markets during the adjustment process.

Equation (12.3) describes the determination of inflation in the small country, which is based on a very simple (non inflation augmented) Phillips curve relationship, where the price level changes with variations in real output (demand) from its full employment level (y^f) (supply). Note, however, that prices are not perfectly flexible but adjust only gradually to their new equilibrium level, and hence result in disequilibrium in the goods market as previously alluded to. In this version of the model, output is restricted to its full employment level, and any variations in demand simply cause prices to rise or fall. This is a deficiency of the simple Dornbusch (1976) model, but can be amended as discussed below. Finally, Equation (12.4) describes the uncovered interest rate parity condition. Here, the expected nominal exchange rate appreciation/depreciation is fully offset by the small country interest rate being higher than or lower than that available elsewhere to ensure that expected returns on all financial assets are equalized. This is based on the assumption that financial assets in the small country, and elsewhere, including that of the large country, are perfect substitutes. Hence,

Table 12.1 Conceptual framework

Small economy model

$m - p = ky - \lambda r$	(12.1)
$y = \delta_1(e + p^* - p) - \delta_2(r - Dp) + \delta_3 g + \delta_4 y^*$	(12.2)
$Dp = \phi(y - y^f)$	(12.3)
$De = r - r^*$	(12.4)

Large economy model

$m^* - p^* = k^* y^* - \lambda^* r^*$	(12.5)
$y^* = \delta^*_1(e^* - p^*) - \delta^*_2(r^* - Dp^*) + \delta^*_3 g^*$	(12.6)
$Dp^* = \phi^*(y^* - y^{f^*})$	(12.7)
$De^* = r^* - r^{**}$	(12.8)

Definition of variables:

All the variables are in log form, with the exception of r, r* and r**

m –	small country money supply
p –	small country price level
y –	small country real output
r –	small country domestic interest rate
y^f –	small country full employment output
e –	small country nominal exchange rate (the domestic currency price of foreign exchange)
m^* –	large country money supply
p^* –	large country price level
y^* –	large country real output
r^* –	large country domestic interest rate
y^{f*} –	large country full employment output
e^* –	large country nominal exchange rate (the domestic currency price of foreign exchange)
r^{**} –	world interest rate
D –	differential operator

not only is it assumed that there is perfect capital mobility but financial assets in the small and large economies are perceived to be of identical risk (indeed they are riskless).

Economic agents are assumed to possess rational (forward looking) expectations, implying that they do not make consistent forecasting errors. The solution to the model requires the derivation of a stable saddlepath. Any exogenous shock requires the economy to 'jump' on to its new stable saddlepath that will take the economy to its ultimate new equilibrium steady state. In this system there is one 'jump' variable, associated with an unstable eigenvalue (positive characteristic root) and one 'non jump' or predetermined variable associated with a stable eigenvalue (negative characteristic root). Stability can only be attained if this is so. For the small country the unstable root is associated with the nominal exchange rate, which must jump on impact onto the new stable saddlepath. The stable root is associated with domestic prices, which cannot jump on impact. Thereafter, the nominal exchange rate and price level will adjust gradually along the stable saddlepath to long run steady state.

The second version of the model is based on the assumption of a large open economy (or a bloc of countries) with a flexible exchange rate and perfect capital mobility. This is shown by equations (12.5)-(12.8) in Table 12.1. Equation (12.5) describes large country money (or asset) market equilibrium, where the demand and supply of real money balances are in equilibrium. Real money demand is positively related to real large country output but negatively related to the large country's nominal interest rate. The money (asset) market in the large country is assumed to be in continual equilibrium arising from the instantaneous adjustment of financial variables (the nominal exchange rate and the interest rate). Equation (12.6) describes goods market equilibrium in the large country. The demand for real output is positively related to the real exchange rate (equivalent to the domestic price of the imported product to the domestic price of the product), negatively related to the large country domestic real interest rate (the nominal rate deflated by domestic inflation), and positively related to large country real government expenditure. Notice that the small country is too small to exert any substantive influence on the demand for large country production. As for the case of the small country Equation (12.6), unlike Equation (12.5), does not remain in equilibrium continuously due to stickiness of adjustment of large country domestic prices. As for the small country, a key characteristic of the model is that asset markets are in continual equilibrium while there is disequilibrium in non-financial markets during the adjustment process.

Equation (12.7) describes the determination of inflation in the large country, which is based on a very simple (non inflation augmented) Phillips curve relationship, where the price level changes with variations in real output (demand) from its full employment level (y^{f*}) (supply). Note, however, that prices are not perfectly flexible but adjust only gradually to their new equilibrium level, and hence result in disequilibrium in the goods market as previously alluded to. In this version of the model output is restricted to its full employment level in the large country, and any variations in demand simply cause prices to rise or fall. Equation (12.5) describes the uncovered interest rate parity condition. Here, the expected nominal exchange rate appreciation/depreciation for the large country is fully offset by the large country interest rate being higher than or lower than that available elsewhere (globally) to ensure that expected returns on all financial assets are equalized. This is based on the assumption that financial assets, globally, are perfect substitutes.

As for the small country model economic agents are assumed to possess rational (forward looking) expectations, implying that they do not make consistent forecasting errors. The solution to the model requires the derivation of a stable saddlepath. Any exogenous shock requires the economy to 'jump' on to its new stable saddlepath that will take the economy to its ultimate new equilibrium steady state. In this system there is one 'jump' variable, associated with an unstable eigenvalue (positive characteristic root) and one 'non jump' or predetermined variable associated with a stable eigenvalue (negative characteristic root). Stability can only be attained if this is so. As for the small country the unstable root is associated with the nominal exchange rate, which must jump on impact onto the new stable saddlepath. The stable root is associated with domestic prices, which cannot jump on impact. Thereafter, the nominal exchange rate and price level will adjust gradually along the stable saddlepath to long run steady state.

12.3 MODEL SIMULATIONS[1]

In this section a number of numerical simulations are conducted with the objective of identifying, from the perspective of the small country, policy responses in the wake of external disturbances/shocks that will minimize adverse developments in key domestic variables. In this context it will be possible to identify whether closer policy integration, primarily in the form of monetary policy, can dampen the effects from macroeconomic disturbances or will exacerbate such disturbances. In order to conduct this process requires knowledge of the parameter values of the model. The following analysis proceeds on the basis that the parameters of the model have the numerical values as contained in Table 12.2.[2] These parameters are a reasonable approximation of reality and suitable for the purposes of this study. They ensure model stability and result in unambiguous numerical results.

Table 12.2 Assumed parameter values

k	1.0
λ	0.5
δ_1	0.5
δ_2	0.5
δ_3	0.1
ϕ	0.5
k*	1.0
λ*	0.5
δ^*_1	0.5
δ^*_2	0.5
δ^*_3	0.1
ϕ	0.5
r**	0.05

Exogenous Large Country Shocks and the Implications for Small Country Policy

The initial simulation results presented focus upon the impact on the small country from individual disturbances emanating from the large country, specifically relating to large country interest rate shocks, large country output shocks and large country domestic price shocks. For these simulations, the disturbance occurring is in the form of a single exogenous disturbance emanating from the large country. The relevant model simulated is that for the small country only.

Scenario 1 Large country interest rate shock (r)*

In this scenario it is assumed that the interest rate in the large country increases in a way to that identified in Table 12.3; that is, it increases by 1 per cent on impact (0 to 0'), by a further 1 per cent in period 1 (to be 2 per cent above its baseline or starting value), and by a further 1 per cent in period 2. In period 3 it falls by 1 per cent (to be 2 per cent above its baseline value again), falling a further 1 per cent in period 4, and finally returns to its baseline value in period 5. Hence the rise in the large country's interest rate is temporary with no lasting change. Three possible responses, from a number of possible choices, by the small country are focused upon; the first of which is that where there is no response, and the small economy retains its existing macroeconomic policies. The second is that where the small country adjusts its monetary policy settings, conducts an independent policy response, by

Table 12.3 Simulation scenarios

Values are percentage (%) deviations from baseline

Time period	0	0'	1	2	3	4	5
Scenario 1							
Large country interest rate shock (r*)	0	1	2	3	2	1	0
No response	-	-	-	-	-	-	-
Response							
Money supply increase	0	1	2	3	2	1	0
Response							
Money supply decrease	0	-1	-2	-3	-2	-1	0
Scenario 2							
Large country real output shock (y*)	0	1	2	3	2	1	0
No response	-	-	-	-	-	-	-
Response							
Money supply increase	0	1	2	3	2	1	0
Response							
Money supply decrease	0	-1	-2	-3	-2	-1	0
Scenario 3							
Large country price level shock (p*)	0	1	2	3	2	1	0
No response	-	-	-	-	-	-	-
Response							
Money supply	0	1	2	3	2	1	0
Response							
Money supply	0	-1	-2	-3	-2	-1	0

increasing the money supply with the objective of offsetting the adverse interest rate effect coming from the large economy. This could be described as an anti-cyclical adjustment policy, attempting to avoid any deflationary impact upon the domestic economy. The third is where the small country adjusts its monetary policy settings, conducts an independent policy response, by this time decreasing the money supply with the objective of tightening monetary policy in line with the rise in the large economy interest rate. This could be described as a pro-cyclical adjustment policy, exacerbating any deflationary impact upon the domestic economy from the external interest rate shock. Implications for the adjustment of key macroeconomic variables for the small country, for all of these cases, are shown in Figures 12.1 to 12.4. The no response option appears to produce the most stable outcomes for two of the four variables focused upon. The price level and output variables are less volatile where there is no monetary policy response, while the volatility of the small country interest rate is marginally improved if the interest rate shock is met by an increase in the small country money supply. In the output case, this becomes more volatile if the money supply is expanded or contracted, and this is particularly so in the case of a monetary expansion. The volatility of the interest rate is increased if it is met by a monetary contraction. The volatility of the exchange rate is reduced where the money supply is contracted. It is particularly noticeable that the volatility of the small country price level, exchange rate and real output is increased if the money supply is expanded.

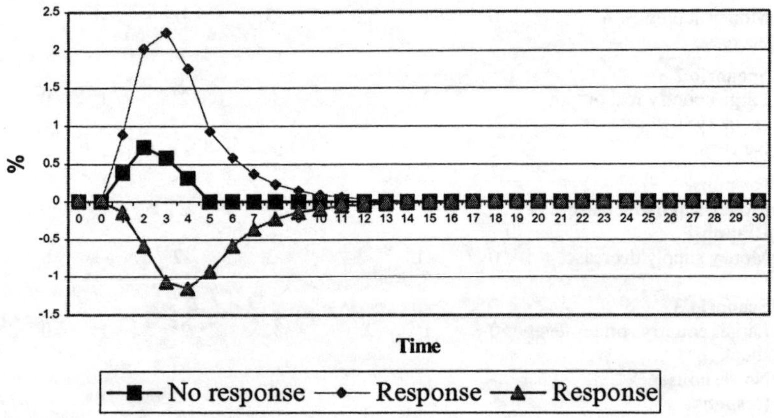

Figure 12.1 Price Level

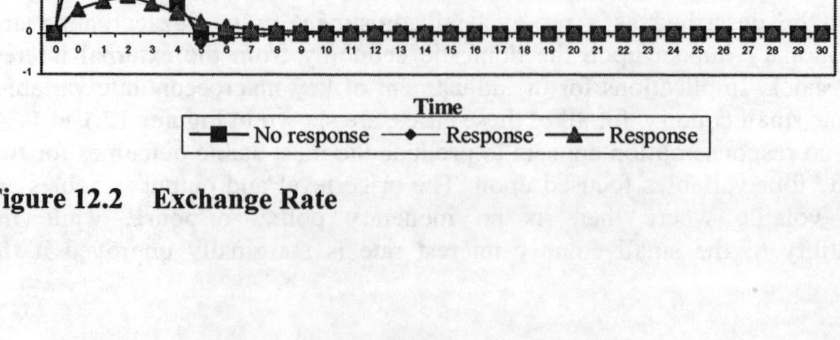

Figure 12.2 Exchange Rate

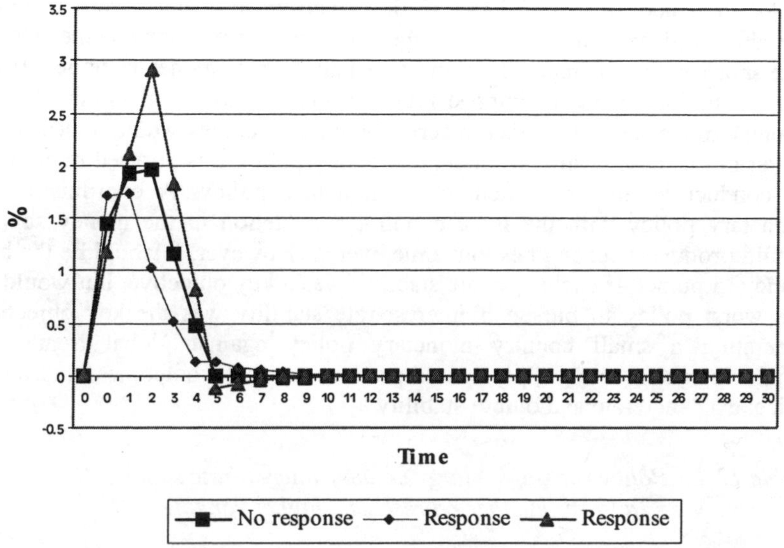

Figure 12.3 Interest rate

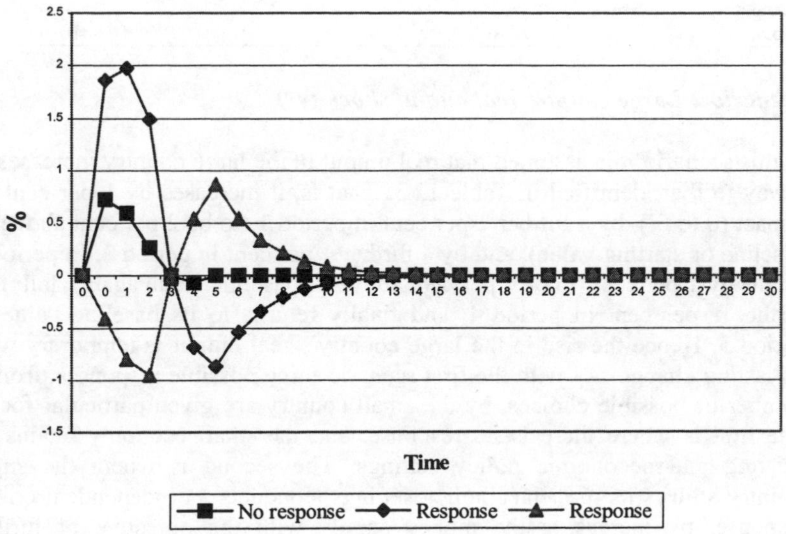

Figure 12.4 Output

As indicated in Table 12.4, if the volatility of each macroeconomic variable is given equal weighting, then the optimal response to the interest rate shock is for no change in domestic small country monetary policy. If the rise in the large country interest rate was induced by a tightening of large country monetary policy, then macroeconomic outcomes would appear to be better in this case if an independent monetary policy was pursued rather than to conduct a similar tightening of monetary policy. A coordination of monetary policy with the large country, a reduction in the money supply, would produce a second best outcome overall. However, it would be the best policy to pursue if exchange rate stability was a key objective, but would be the worst policy to pursue if interest rate stability was the key objective. Operating a small country monetary policy against global trends, by expanding the money supply, would produce the worst outcomes in terms of price, exchange rate and output stability.

Table 12.4 Policy rankings – large country interest rate shock (r) (a lower number represents a higher ranking)*

Volatility	No response	Contract money supply	Expand money supply
Price level	1	2	3
Exchange rate	2	1	3
Interest rate	2	3	1
Output	1	2	3
Total	6	8	10

Scenario 2 Large country real output shock (y*)

In this scenario it is assumed that real output in the large country increases in a way to that identified in Table 12.3. That is, it increases by 1 per cent on impact (0 to 0'), by a further 1 per cent in period 1 (to be 2 per cent above its baseline or starting value), and by a further 1 per cent in period 2. In period 3 it falls by 1 per cent (to be 2 per cent above its baseline value again), falling a further 1 per cent in period 4, and finally returns to its baseline value in period 5. Hence the rise in the large country's real output is temporary with no lasting change. As with the first scenario three possible responses, from a number of possible choices, by the small country are given particular focus. The first is where there is no response, and the small economy retains its existing macroeconomic policy settings. The second is where the small country adjusts its monetary policy settings, conducts an independent policy response, by increasing the money supply with the objective of further enhancing the potential expansionary effects from the increased large country income. This could be described as a pro-cyclical adjustment policy, since it would attempt to further expand the expansionary impact upon the domestic economy. The third is where the small country adjusts its monetary policy settings, conducts an independent policy response, by this time decreasing the money supply with the objective of conducting a tightening of monetary policy to offset the expansionary effects from the higher income of the large country. This could be described as an anti-cyclical adjustment policy, since it would attempt to dampen any expansionary effect of the higher income from the large country upon the domestic economy. The implications for the adjustment of key macroeconomic variables for the small country, for all of these cases, are shown in Figures 12.5 to 12.8.

This scenario produces the most clear-cut outcomes. The no response policy option produces the most stable outcomes for all of the four macroeconomic variables. Exchange rate and interest rate stability is worse in the money contraction case, while output volatility is worse in the case where there is an expansion in the money supply. As indicated in Table 12.5, if the volatility of each macroeconomic variable is given equal weighting, then the optimal response, by far, to the large country income shock is for no change in domestic small country monetary policy. If the rise in large country income originated, say, from an expansionary monetary policy in the large country, then, again, macroeconomic outcomes would appear to be better in the case where an independent monetary policy was pursued rather than to conduct a similar expansion of monetary policy in the small country. A coordination of monetary policy with the large country, through an increase in small country money supply, would produce a second best outcome overall.

Scenario 3 Large country price level shock (p)*

In this scenario it is assumed that the price level in the large country increases in a way to that identified in Table 12.3. That is it increases by 1 per cent on impact (0 to 0'), by a further 1 per cent in period 1 (to be 2 per cent above its baseline or starting value), and by a further 1 per cent in period 2. In period 3 it falls by 1 per cent (to be 2 per cent above its baseline value again), falling a further 1 per cent in period 4, and finally returns to its baseline value in period 5. Hence the rise in the large country's price level is temporary with no lasting change.

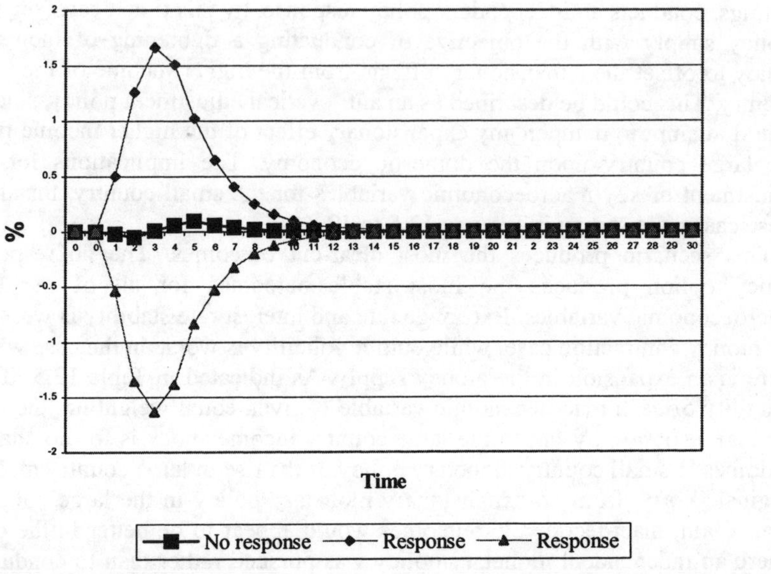

Figure 12.5 Price level

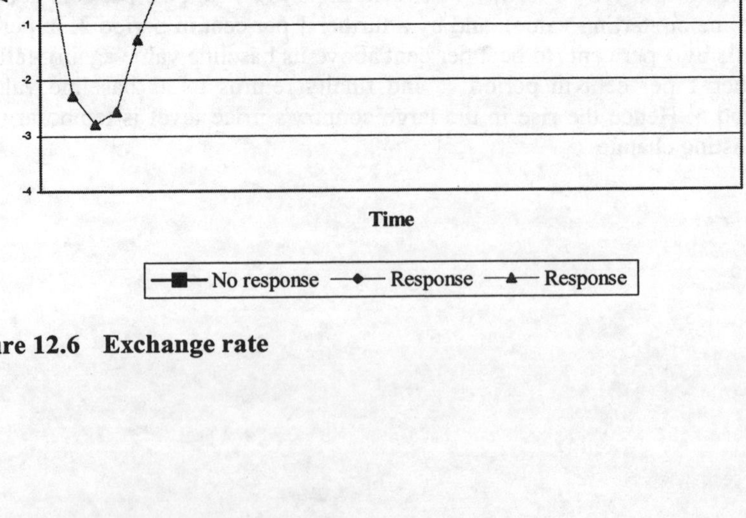

Figure 12.6 Exchange rate

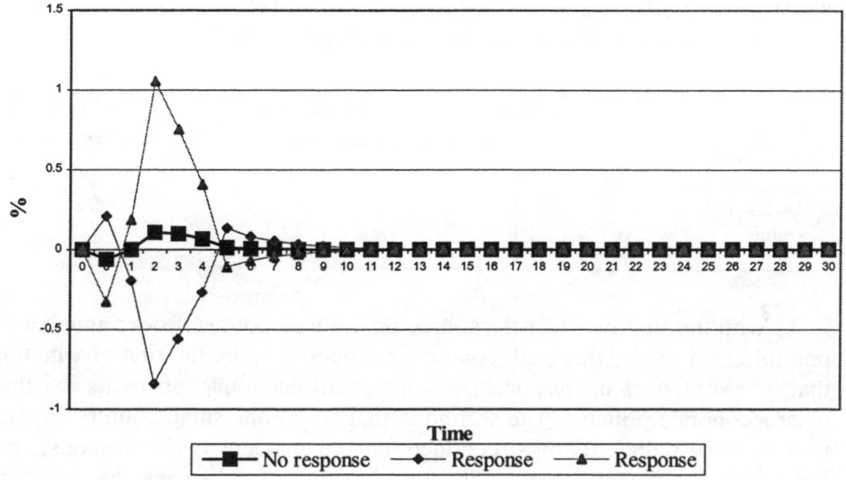

Figure 12.7 Interest rate

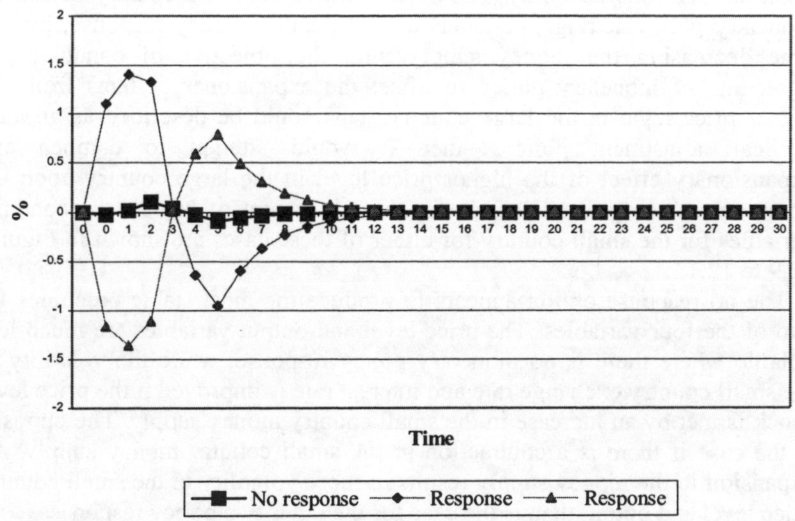

Figure 12.8 Output

Table 12.5 Policy rankings – large country output shock (y) (a lower number represents a higher ranking)*

Volatility	No response	Contract money supply	Expand money supply
Price level	1	2	2
Exchange rate	1	3	2
Interest rate	1	3	2
Output	1	2	3
Total	4	10	9

As with the first two scenarios three possible responses, from a number of possible choices, by the small country are focused upon, the first of which is that where there is no response, and the small economy retains its existing macroeconomic policies. The second is that where the small country adjusts its monetary policy settings, conducts an independent policy response, by increasing the money supply with the objective of enhancing the potential expansionary effects in the small country from the increase in the price level of the large country. This could be described as a pro-cyclical adjustment policy, since it would attempt to further expand the expansionary impact upon the domestic economy. The third is where the small country adjusts its monetary policy settings, conducts an independent policy response, by this time decreasing the money supply with the objective of conducting a tightening of monetary policy to offset the expansionary effects from the higher price level in the large country. This could be described as an anti-cyclical adjustment policy, since it would attempt to dampen any expansionary effect of the higher price level in the large country upon the domestic economy. Implications for the adjustment of key macroeconomic variables for the small country for either of these cases are shown in Figures 12.9 to 12.12.

The no response option appears to produce the most stable outcomes for two of the four variables. The price level and output variables are much less volatile where there is no monetary policy response, while the volatility of the small country exchange rate and interest rate is improved if the price level shock is met by an increase in the small country money supply. The opposite is the case if there is a contraction in the small country money supply. An expansion in the money supply results in more volatility in the small country price level and output than is the case for the other two policy responses.

As indicated in Table 12.6, if the volatility of each macroeconomic variable is given equal weighting, then the optimal response to the large country price shock is for no change in domestic small country monetary policy. If the rise in the large country price level originated, say, from an expansionary monetary policy in the large country, then, again, macroeconomic outcomes would appear to be better in the case where an independent monetary policy was pursued rather than to conduct a similar

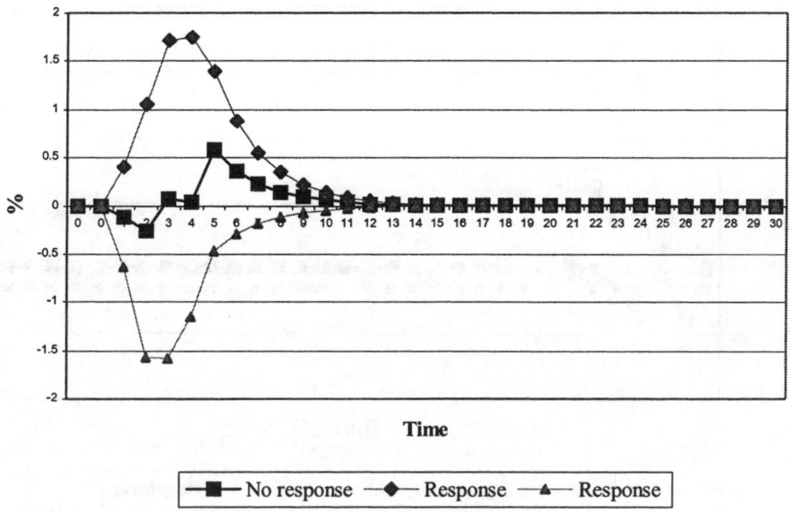

Figure 12.9 Price level

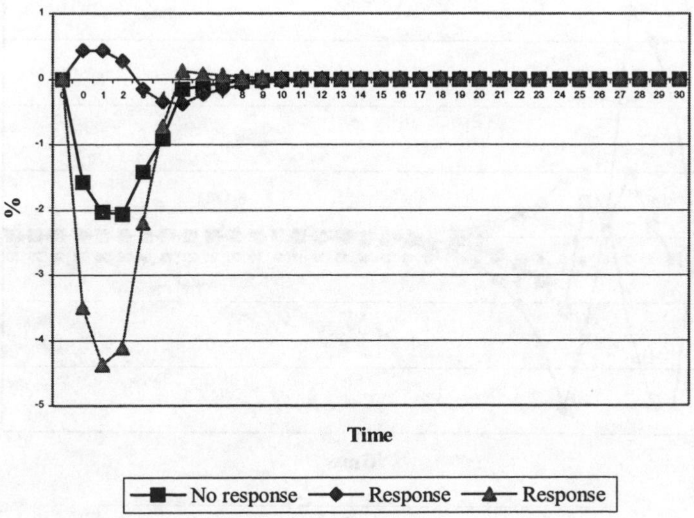

Figure 12.10 Exchange Rate

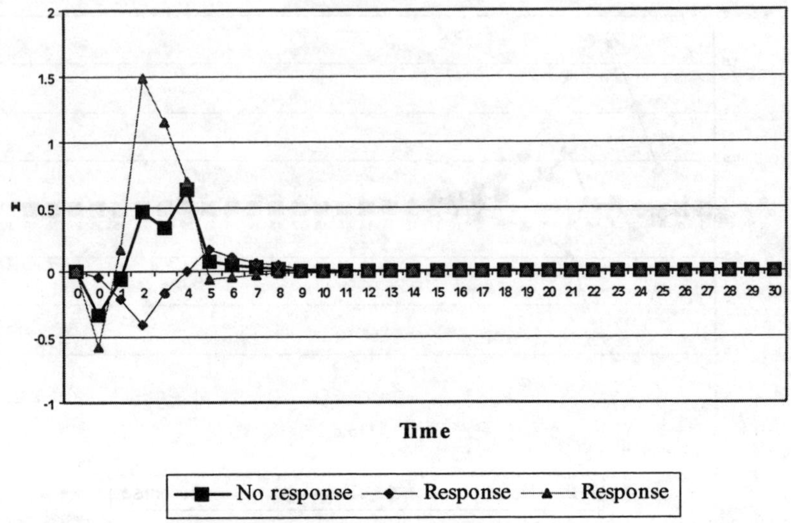

Figure 12.11 Interest rate

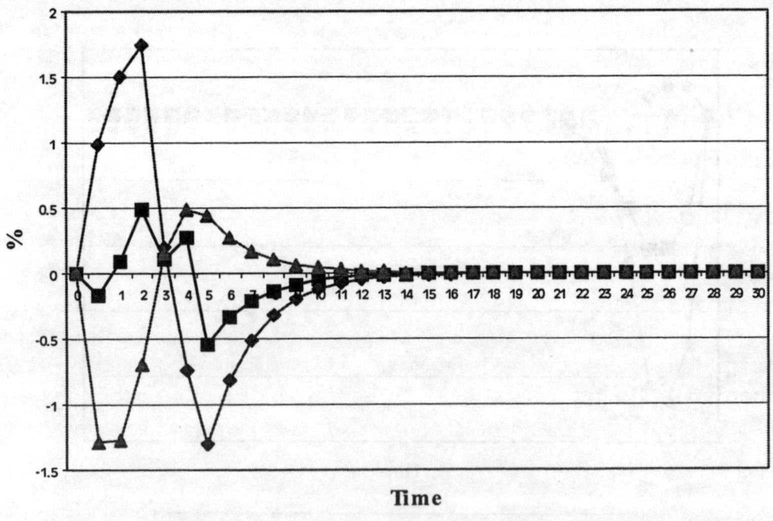

Figure 12.12 Output

Table 12.6 Policy rankings – large country price shock (y) (a lower number represents a higher ranking)*

Volatility	No response	Contract money supply	Expand money supply
Price level	1	2	3
Exchange rate	2	3	1
Interest rate	2	3	1
Output	1	2	3
Total	6	10	8

expansion of monetary policy in the small country. A coordination of monetary policy with the large country, through an increase in small country money supply, would produce, once again, a second best outcome overall.

Exogenous Large Country Monetary Expansion and the Implications for Small Country Policy

In this section a simulation analysis is conducted on the basis that there is an expansion in the large country money supply. Such a monetary expansion contributes to developments in large country output (y*), prices (p*) and interest rate (r*). These changes are then utilized as exogenous changes for the small country model version. The simulation conducted is summarized in Table 12.7. Three possible policy responses to this external disturbance emanating from the large country are then considered. First, where there is no policy response to the external shock. Second, there is a policy response where the small country conducts a coordinated monetary policy involving an equivalent expansion of the money supply to that of the large country. The third involves both a monetary and fiscal policy response to the external shock emanating from the large country. The results from these three scenarios are shown in Figures 12.13 to 12.16. The results suggest some interesting outcomes. In terms of the small country price level (Figure 12.13), a no response to the external shock coming from the large country produces some mild instability, but the price level quickly settles back at its initial level. A coordinated policy response in the form of an expansion in the small country money supply, as well as an increase in government spending, results in an equi-proportional increase in the small country price level to that of the proportional increase in the money supply. Hence the adoption of a coordinated monetary policy by the small country will produce instability and a permanently higher price level. Pursuing a no response policy will stabilize prices at their original level. An expansionary fiscal policy makes no difference to the price level outcome.

Table 12.7 Simulation scenarios – monetary expansion in the large country (values are percentage (%) deviations from baseline)

Time period	0	0'	1	2	3	4	5	10	15	20
External shock										
Money supply expansion (m*)	0	1	2	3	4	5	5	5	5	5
r*	0	0.7	0.5	0.4	0.2	-0.2	-0.1	0	0	0
y*	0	1.3	1.7	1.9	1.8	1.7	1	0.1	0	0
p*	0	0	0.5	1.3	2.2	3.2	3.9	4.8	5	5
Scenario 1										
No response	-	-	-	-	-	-	-	-	-	-
Scenario 2										
Money supply expansion (m)	0	1	2	3	4	5	5	5	5	5
Scenario 3										
Money supply (m) expansion, and	0	1	2	3	4	5	5	5	5	5
Fiscal expansion (g)	0	1	2	3	4	5	5	5	5	5

In terms of stability of the small country exchange rate (Figure 12.14), a no response policy results in a fairly rapid appreciation of the nominal exchange rate and this appreciation is permanent. A coordinated small country monetary expansion results in a depreciation of the nominal exchange rate initially, before it appreciates back to its original level. If the monetary policy is supplemented by an expansionary fiscal expenditure policy the nominal exchange rate also initially depreciates, but by less than that for the monetary policy alone case. It then appreciates to a level below its starting level. Hence, in this latter case, an appreciation of the nominal exchange rate occurs and the exchange rate is mildly volatile.

In terms of stability of the small country interest rate (Figure 12.15), the no policy response option results, initially, in a sharp decline in the small country interest rate. In the other two scenarios the nominal interest rate rises on impact, and more so for the case of a monetary expansion alone policy. Thereafter the interest rate declines, and for all three scenarios there is noticeable volatility of the interest rate. The policy responses appear to produce less volatility, at least initially.

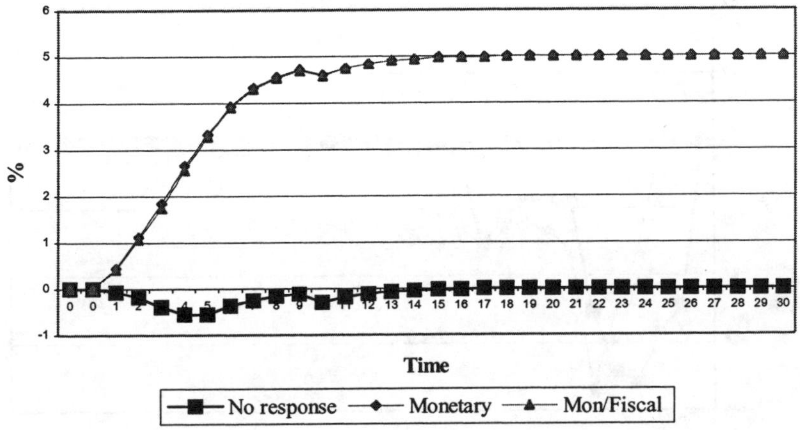

Figure 12.13 Price level

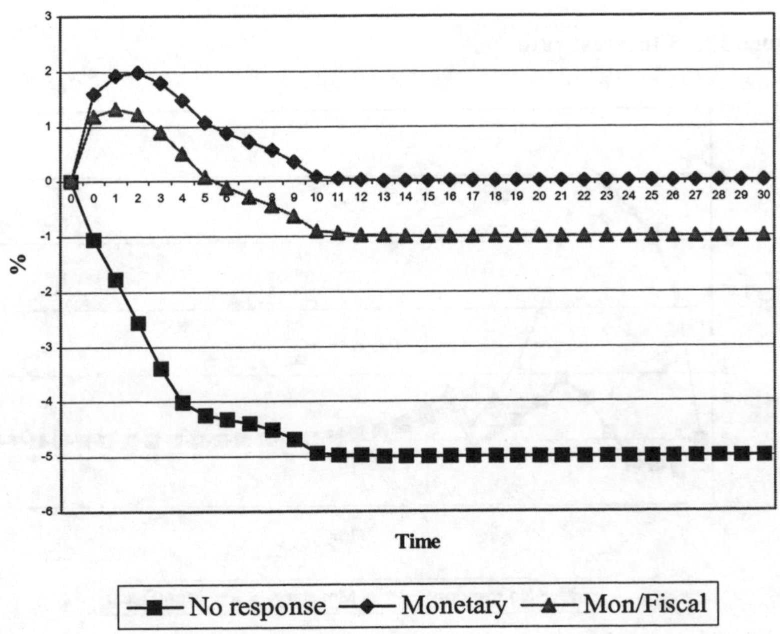

Figure 12.14 Exchange rate

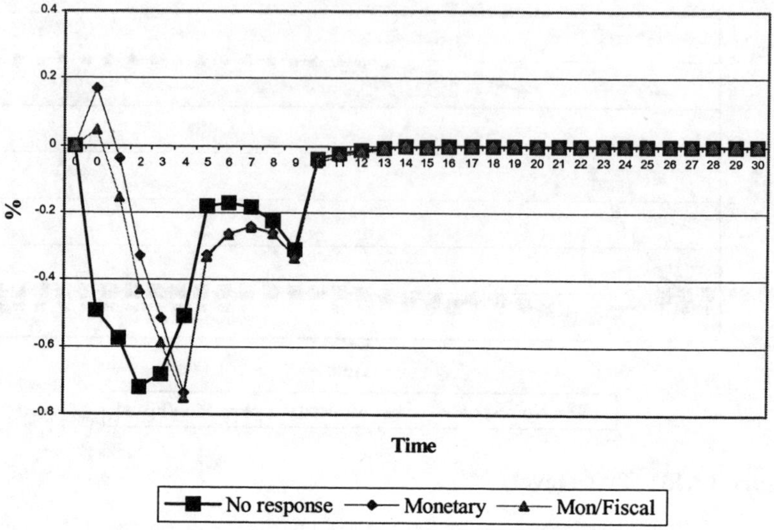

Figure 12.15 Interest rate

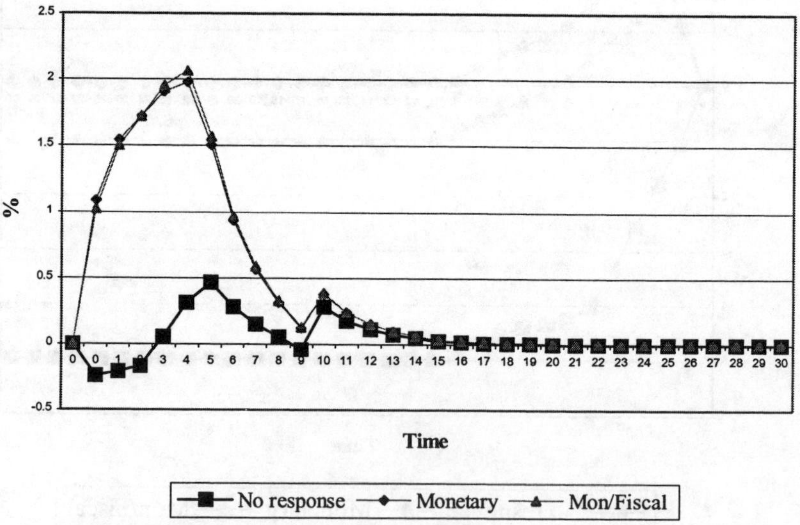

Figure 12.16 Output

Finally, for the case of stability of small country output, the clearly preferred option is to adopt a no policy response approach. In this case the swings of output around its full employment level is noticeably more dampened. The swings in output are larger for the case of an increase in the money supply alone scenario, and intermediate for the case of a monetary and fiscal policy response scenario.

As indicated in Table 12.8, if the volatility of each macroeconomic variable is given equal weighting, then the optimal response to the large country money supply shock is for a coordination of monetary policy, in particular, with that of the large country. On the other hand if the objective of policy is price level and output stability in the small country, an optimal policy response would be to maintain an independent monetary policy (hence no policy response) in the face of an external monetary shock from the large country. On the other hand, if the objective of policy is to maintain financial market stability, specifically in regard to the domestic interest rate and the exchange rate, the adoption of a coordinated monetary policy with that of the large country would appear to be the best option.

Table 12.8 Policy rankings – large country money supply increase (m) (a lower number represents a higher ranking)*

Volatility	No response	Expand money supply	Expand money supply and fiscal spending
Price level	1	2	2
Exchange rate	3	1	2
Interest rate	3	1	2
Output	1	3	2
Total	8	7	8

12.4 WEAKNESSES AND EXTENSIONS OF THE MODEL

The model adopted in this chapter to analyse the issue of policy analysis in the wake of external shocks for a small open economy, is subject to a number of weaknesses. Hence this study should be properly viewed in the context of ongoing research. In particular, the simple Dornbusch model, as presented here, ignores a number of factors that should be incorporated into the macro models for the small and large country. First, the model should incorporate supply side aspects. The model, as it currently stands, only focuses upon the demand side of the economy. The model does not explicitly model the trade and current accounts, nor wealth effects arising from foreign asset stock accumulation and decumulation. Hence stock-flow interactions are ignored in the model. The model assumes a flexible exchange rate for both the small and large countries. It would be useful to develop the model for the case of a fixed exchange rate, where domestic money supplies are endogenously determined, and where the small country can fix its exchange rate to that of the large country currency, and take a further important step towards macroeconomic policy coordination. At this stage it would also be possible to analyse the advantages and disadvantages, for a small country, of moving towards economic and monetary integration with a large country, or bloc of countries.

Also not considered in this chapter is the significance of the parameter values of the models for the determination of the optimal policy response. It would be useful to conduct a sensitivity analysis of the impact of external shocks emanating from the large country on the small country on the basis of different parameter values. It could well be the case that the optimal policy response will be influenced by the size and nature of relevant parameter values.

A three country model may also be useful to analyse, particularly if the small country has a choice of which country, or bloc of countries, to conduct a harmonization of macroeconomic policy with or with which to engage in economic and monetary union. This is a highly pertinent issue in the context of the East Asian economies.

The issue of trade integration, as well as the harmonization of macroeconomic policy, can be developed within the context of the model discussed. In doing so an optimal path towards economic and monetary integration can be considered, starting with trade liberalization, capital account liberalization, macroeconomic policy harmonization, fixing exchange rates, and finally moving towards a single currency. These issues are clearly of profound importance in the global economy arising from the development of regional trading blocs, some of which may have the potential, as with the European Union, to move towards economic and monetary union. What conditions are most essential to make this happen, optimal sequencing of the process, and what countries should these include are important issues and no less so in East Asia.

12.5 SUMMARY AND CONCLUSIONS

This chapter has presented a simple model for analysing the policy coordination benefits and costs for a small country whose macroeconomy is strongly influenced by a large country, or bloc of countries. A simple Dornbusch type model was developed for both the small and large countries. The impact of external shocks, emanating from the large country, and their impact upon the small country were analysed by means of a numerical algorithm. Depending upon the type of shock, it was possible to identify in this framework its impact on key macroeconomic variables in the small country – price level, exchange rate, interest rate and output. Three exogenous shocks were focused upon – large country interest rate, output and price level. In analysing these individually, Tables 12.4, 12.5 and 12.6 tended to suggest that the adoption of an independent policy stance (involving a no policy response) produced more desirable macroeconomic outcomes for the small economy. However, in a simulation scenario involving external shocks to all of these variables arising from a large country money supply increase, the results were less clear-cut. Indeed, taking these shocks as a group, a coordinated monetary response by the small country could be the best option. However, if the aim of the small country is to attain price and output stability, the no response option would still be preferable. Consequently, this chapter raises more questions than it has answered. Further analysis is required regarding the importance of the model itself for the results generated, the need to make the model more general, the need to identify the importance of the parameters of the model, for both the small and large countries, for policy selection, and the need to extend the model to the case where the small country can fix its exchange rate relative to the large country.

NOTES

1 The numerical algorithm utilized is known as "Saddlepoint". This was developed by Austin and Buiter (1982) for solving systems of linear differential equations with constant coefficients, and is based upon the solution provided by Blanchard and Khan (1980) for the case of systems of linear difference equations.

2 A sensitivity analysis can be conducted to identify which of these parameter values are important for model stability and for long run steady state, and for the adjustment process to steady state. Such a procedure is not conducted in this study.

REFERENCES

Austin, G.P. and W.H. Buiter (1982), "Saddlepoint, a programme for solving continuous time linear rational expectations models", London School of Economics discussion paper A.37, November.

Blanchard, O. (1981), "Output, the stock market and interest rates", *American Economic Review*, 71, 132-43.

Blanchard, O. and C.M. Khan (1980), "The solution of linear difference models under rational expectations", *Econometrica, 48*, July, 1305-11.

Dixit, A. (1980), "A solution for rational expectations models with applications to exchange rate and interest rate determination", University of Warwick, UK, November.

Dornbusch, R. (1976), "Exchange rate dynamics", *Journal of Political Economy, 84,* 1161-76.

13. Creating a Common Currency Basket for East Asia: Prospects and Key Issues[1]

Eiji Ogawa and Kentaro Kawasaki

13.1 INTRODUCTION

After the East Asian countries experienced the currency crisis of 1997, regional financial cooperation is perceived as being necessary in order to prevent another crisis in the future. Regional financial cooperation has been realized in the form of the Chiang Mai Initiatives consisting of a network of bilateral currency swap arrangements among the ASEAN + 3 (China, Japan, and Korea) countries. Such a movement has given momentum to the activation of policy dialogues in the field of international monetary arrangements among East Asian countries. This chapter's key objective is to consider a desirable regional currency arrangement in East Asia, which is expected to be an important topic in policy dialogue among East Asian countries in the future.

The Asian currency crisis reminds us of a fact that the *de facto* dollar peg was inadequate for the East Asian countries who have close economic relationships with not only the United States but also Japan, the European countries, and intra-regional countries. It follows that if a regional currency arrangement was to be established in East Asia, regional currencies should have stable linkages with each other and should be stable not just *vis-à-vis* a single major currency but a basket of currencies. The EU created a single common currency, the euro, based on the European Currency Unit (ECU), which had been used as a currency unit in the EU before the euro was introduced. Member countries' currencies were linked with the ECU, a weighted composite among them, while they floated against the US dollar and Japanese yen.

We investigate the possibility of creating a common currency basket in

East Asia according to the optimal currency area theory. Bayoumi, Eichengreen and Mauro (2000) use a structural VAR model to conduct an empirical analysis of an optimal currency area in East Asia. We use a Generalized Purchasing Power Parity (G-PPP) model to analyse this same issue. We investigate which East Asian countries are conducive to the establishment of a common currency area. The analytical results presented suggest that the ASEAN-5 countries, Korea and China will be able to form a common currency area, and that a common currency basket will be more applicable as an anchor currency than the US dollar if these countries form a common currency area.

This chapter consists of five sections. The next section stresses the creation of a common currency basket for the East Asian countries in order to resolve a kind of coordination failure in exchange rate policies among them. In section 3, we empirically investigate, using a G-PPP model, whether part of East Asia will be able to become a common currency area with a currency basket as an anchor currency. In section 4, we report our empirical results. In section 5, we discuss policy implications for a common currency area in East Asia from our empirical results. In conclusion, section 6, we summarize our findings on the possibility of creating a common currency basket for East Asia.

13.2 A COMMON CURRENCY BASKET FOR THE EAST ASIAN COUNTRIES

Some empirical research has found that a currency basket system would contribute to stabilizing trade balances and capital flows in the East Asian countries. Ito, Ogawa and Sasaki (1998) estimated optimal weights on the US dollar and Japanese yen in a currency basket, which would have stabilized trade balances in the East Asian countries before the Asian currency crisis. Results from the estimation showed that the optimal weights on the US dollar were smaller than those estimated by Frankel and Wei (1994) and Kawai and Akiyama (1998). This implies that it was not a *de facto* dollar peg system but a currency basket peg system that would have stabilized their trade balances.

Ogawa and Sun (2001) simulated capital inflows to the three crisis-hit countries, Thailand, Indonesia, and Korea, under a currency basket peg system where weights on the US dollar and Japanese yen were assumed to have been 50 per cent: 50 per cent in a currency basket. Results from the simulation concluded that the *de facto* dollar peg system stimulated capital inflows to the crisis-hit countries before the Asian currency crisis.

We should consider why the monetary authorities of the East Asian countries tended to choose a *de facto* dollar peg system rather than a currency basket peg system. In fact, East Asian currency linkages to the US dollar have recently returned to a similarly high level as they had been before the crisis as McKinnon (2000) and Ogawa (2002a) point out. A reason why the monetary authorities are unwilling to adopt a currency basket peg system is related to a kind of coordination failure in choosing an exchange rate system. The first mover to a currency basket peg system might temporarily destabilize its relations with neighbouring countries that still peg their home currencies to the US dollar, equivalent to a prisoner's dilemma in game theory.[2]

Ogawa and Ito (2002) use a theoretical two-country model to examine an optimal exchange rate system for East Asian countries that export goods to the United States, Japan, and neighbouring countries, in order to minimize the fluctuation of trade balances in the home countries in an environment where the yen-dollar exchange rate fluctuates. They show how an East Asian country's choice of an exchange rate system (or weights in the basket) is dependent on the neighbour country's choice. The dollar's weights in a currency basket of the two countries are determined as a Nash equilibrium. There may be multiple equilibriums, and a "coordination failure" may result.[3]

Under uncertainty about the future movements in the exchange rate of the US dollar *vis-à-vis* the Japanese yen the monetary authorities have a higher possibility of facing coordination failure in choosing an exchange rate system. Suppose that the monetary authorities of a country single-handedly switch their exchange rate policy to a currency basket peg system while the monetary authorities of the neighbouring countries maintain a dollar peg system. The currency of the country that adopted the currency basket peg system would appreciate against the currencies of the neighbouring countries if the US dollar depreciates against the Japanese yen. Therefore, under such uncertainty, the monetary authorities would tend to adopt a "wait-and-see" strategy if they are averse to risk.

All of the monetary authorities are likely to take such a "wait-and-see" strategy if they are all risk averse. The situation is a so-called prisoner's dilemma in game theory. All of the monetary authorities cannot help but choose to keep the dollar peg system, which means a Nash equilibrium, even though they do know that there is a better cooperative solution. Coordination among some of the monetary authorities in the East Asian countries is necessary for shifting the situation from a Nash equilibrium to a cooperative solution.

A possible form of solution is an international policy coordination for arrangements of a regional monetary system. For example, all of the monetary authorities of the countries in a region might agree on an arrangement that they create a common currency basket. Or they might make references to the virtual common currency in conducting their exchange rate policy. A rigid arrangement is that all of the monetary authorities in the region peg their home currencies to a common currency basket. On one hand, a more flexible arrangement is that they target the home currencies in a wider band around a central exchange rate of the home currencies *vis-à-vis* a common currency basket.

In either case it is necessary to create a common currency basket to which the monetary authorities of the countries make reference when they conduct their exchange rate policies. Such regional currency arrangements might help to prevent competitive devaluations among the related currencies in a region. If the monetary authorities of a country devalue its home currency the devaluation worsens the price competitiveness of products made in neighbouring countries. For that reason the monetary authorities of the other countries would have an incentive to devalue their home currencies, following the first country's devaluation. The regional currency arrangements that the monetary authorities in a region make require a commitment to a coordinated exchange rate policy by making references to a common currency basket that would prevent a possible competitive devaluation.

We should now consider the possibility of introducing a common currency basket in East Asia. What conditions are required to make use of a common currency basket among a group of countries? It is clear that optimal weights on currencies in a currency basket should be almost the same among the countries. Thus, an area where a common currency basket is used is related to a common currency area.

According to optimal currency area theory the possibility of establishing a common currency area in a region depends on whether the region is an optimal currency area or not. The literature nominates a group of factors that determine an optimal currency area. Mundell (1961) regarded labour mobility as a necessity for a common currency area while McKinnon (1963) regarded openness of the economy as another necessity. Moreover, symmetry of shocks was pointed out as a factor for an optimal currency area (Bayoumi and Eichengreen (1993)). It is possible to form an optimal currency area, because it is unnecessary to make intra-regional adjustments in a region where symmetric shocks happen. Symmetry of supply shocks is focused on because supply shocks have long run effects on GDP while demand shocks have no long run effects on GDP in a situation where the natural rate of unemployment hypothesis holds. Supply shocks, such as productivity shocks and oil price shocks, have effects on an economy's production function.

Bayoumi, Eichengreen and Mauro (2000) conducted an empirical analysis on an optimal currency area in the East Asian region.[4] Their results show that correlations are relatively higher among Malaysia, Indonesia, and Singapore. Also, correlation is higher between Singapore and Thailand. Therefore, these four ASEAN countries might be able to form an optimal currency area. Moreover, supply shocks in Japan, while having a lower correlation with ASEAN countries except Thailand, have a positive correlation with those in Taiwan, Korea, and Australia.

13.3 AN OPTIMUM CURRENCY AREA FOR EAST ASIA

In this section we extend the works of Kawasaki (2000) and Ogawa and Kawasaki (2001) to empirically analyse an optimum currency area for East Asia. In doing so we use a Generalized Purchasing Power Parity (G-PPP) model. We use a common currency basket as well as the US dollar as the anchor currency. We define the common currency basket as one that is composed of the three major currencies: the US dollar, the Deutsche mark, and the Japanese yen. We assume that each of the three currencies has the same weight in the currency basket.

The G-PPP model is extended from a simple PPP model by taking into account difficulties in maintaining PPP because frequently occurring nominal and real shocks continuously have effects on macro fundamentals. Even in the long run changes in a bilateral exchange rate depend not only on changes in the relative prices between the related two countries, but also on those in relative prices among the two countries and other countries. Price levels in other countries may have effects on domestic price levels in the two countries because prices of intermediate goods imported from abroad may have effects on prices of domestic products. Therefore, it is assumed in the G-PPP model that there are common factors among some bilateral real exchange rates of the home currency *vis-à-vis* currencies of foreign countries with which the home country has strong economic relationships. Thus, the real exchange rates have a stable equilibrium in the long run if they have strong economic relationships with each other.

The G-PPP model explains that PPP holds if a linear combination of some bilateral real exchange rate series have an equilibrium in the long run, even though each of the bilateral rate series is non-stationary. Therefore, we investigate such stable linear combinations in the long run composed of some bilateral real exchange rate series based on the cointegration analysis of Johansen and Juserius (1990). Using this econometric method, we can find the optimal members in the common currency area.

Data

The sample for our empirical tests with the G-PPP model covers the period between October 1985 and June 1997. Seven East Asian countries are included; Korea, Singapore, Malaysia, Thailand, the Philippines, Indonesia, and China. Real exchange rates were based on the monthly data of nominal exchange rates and consumer price indices of the related countries.[5] The rest of the data are from the IMF, *International Financial Statistics* (CD-ROM).

Anchor Currencies and Common Currency Areas

We regarded either the US dollar or the common currency basket that was composed of the US dollar, the Deutsche mark, and the Japanese yen as an anchor currency. Since we supposed that each of the three major currencies had the same weights in the currency basket, the real exchange rate between each of the seven East Asian currencies and the currency basket could be defined as follows,

$$RE_{i,CB} = \left(RE_{i,US}\right)^{(1/3)} \cdot \left(RE_{i,JP}\right)^{(1/3)} \cdot \left(RE_{i,DM}\right)^{(1/3)}. \qquad (13.1)$$

where $RE_{i,j}$ is the real exchange rate between country i and country j.

We analysed which of the seven East Asian countries (Korea, Singapore, Malaysia, Thailand, the Philippines, Indonesia, and China) could form a common currency area with either the currency basket or the US dollar as an anchor currency. In this study, we focused on the cases in which more than two countries are included in the linear combinations, therefore each combination consisting of either three, four, five, six, or seven countries was examined as a possible optimal currency area. Then, we conducted a "Johansen test" for the 198 possible linear combinations. Since the G-PPP model assumed that all real exchange rates in a common currency area must be non-stationary, we conducted unit root tests: the Augmented Dickey-Fuller (ADF) test, and the Kwiatkowski, Phillips, and Shmidt and Shin (KPSS) type unit root test, for each real exchange rate series, and confirmed all series have a unit root.

Cointegration Analysis

We used the Johansen method (Johansen and Juselius (1990)) to test whether a long run relationship can exist in the vector auto regressive (VAR) model. In the case that there is a long run relationship in the VAR model, we can recognize that variables in the model are cointegrated, and that equilibrium errors from the long run relationship must be corrected in the long run. Assuming that variables in the model are cointegrated, we can rewrite the VAR model as the error correction model (ECM) as follows:

$$\Delta R_t = \sum_{l=1}^{k-1} \Gamma_l \Delta R_{t-l} + \Pi R_{t-1} + \mu + \varepsilon_t, \quad \Pi = \alpha \cdot \beta' \tag{13.2}$$

where the elements of the vector R are the real exchange rates and μ is the linear trend in the data.

We tested whether products of the non-stationary vector R_t and the matrix Π, which contains the cointegration vector, are stationary or not at the 5 per cent or less significance level.

We have to consider the robustness problems in conducting the Johansen test. One problem is related to the choice of the lag length in the VAR or the ECM. It is usual to choose the lag length of the VAR model or the ECM according to the fitting criteria, e.g. the Schwartz information criterion or others. It is true that these criteria are useful, but may not determine the degree of lag-order uniquely. Unfortunately, the two models with different lag lengths produce different results. It means that we may have two opposite implications for our investigations. Another problem in conducting the cointegration analysis is related to difficulties in identifying the proper rank of the matrix Π, and the appropriate equilibrium in the matrix β. When the Johansen test indicates the possibility of plural cointegration vectors in the matrix β, meaning that the number of ranks r of the matrix Π can be more than one, we may face the identification problem in choosing the long run equilibrium.

In our empirical test it is also important to investigate which error correction model with lags is better for the data generating processes, and can bring each variable into an appropriate long run equilibrium. Therefore, our attempts to improve the robustness are to carefully conduct the Johansen test with the following eight additional tests.

First, we assume the maximum lag-effect of the data generating process is 12 lags and conducted the Johansen test for each model containing two to 12 lags. We varied the sample period to equalize the degrees of freedom in each of the 11 models. Second, we calculated the statistics of two information criteria: the Schwartz information criterion and the Hannan-Queen information criterion. Third, we conducted three kinds of tests for autocorrelations in the residuals of the ECM: the Ljung-Box test on the estimated auto- and cross-correlations, and the LM-type test for the first and fourth order autocorrelations. These calculations and test statistics enable us to choose the proper lag order. Fourth, we conducted three additional chi-square-based tests for each alpha or beta in the matrix Π to avoid identification problems about the appropriate equilibrium. The first chi-square-based test will show whether each variable is excluded from the vector. The second one is to test whether the individual series are stationary by themselves. The final one is to test whether each variable can be considered weakly exogenous or not. These three tests will be helpful for us not only in identifying the long run equilibrium but also in choosing proper lag lengths in the ECM. If we choose proper lag-orders of the ECM, the null hypothesis of the second test must be rejected. If the second test shows the acceptance of the null hypothesis of stationarity, it conflicts with the fact that each variable has a unit root since we had already confirmed the non-stationarity of each variable with two kinds of unit-root tests. Therefore, the second test would help us to choose the proper lag lengths in the ECM. The other two tests also help to indicate the possibility of over-identification or under-identification. The first test will show the lack of needed variables in the model. The third test can indicate the existence of extra variables if we inappropriately increase the lag-orders of the model.

In our arbitrary strategy of improving robustness, the point is that we should choose a lag length by taking into account whether the equilibrium of that model is adequate for the cointegration relationship or not. In other words, we investigated models that have an appropriate equilibrium in the data, and compared the fitness of these models in terms of lag-orders. Our first step of choosing the ECM with proper lag-orders and an appropriate long run equilibrium is that we select the cases in which the assumption of no serial correlation about residuals holds. The next step is that we select the cases in which the chi-square-based tests show significances in the alternative hypotheses of long run exclusion, stationarity, and weak exogeneity. The final step is to make a comparison among all the possible models using the two information criterions. When we have more than two different results, we should compare the information criteria. Following these steps, we can uniquely define each ECM that included proper lag-orders and an appropriate equilibrium. We show details of our strategy to define the unique model in the Appendix.

Based on our strategy, we carefully chose the optimal error correction model with lags according to our strategy. We had several cointegration relationships: 70 combinations for the US dollar as an anchor currency and 49 combinations for the common currency basket as an anchor currency. Here, we should only focus on the combinations in which all countries in a linear combination have significant results on those three tests, because we need to specify the minimal combination of currency areas including all of the seven East Asian countries.

13.4 EMPIRICAL RESULTS

Table 13.1 shows the combinations where all countries in a linear combination have one stable relationship at least in the long run, and showed significant results on the three chi-square-based tests. For the US dollar, we found only one combination in which all countries in a linear combination showed significant results on the three tests. This combination included

Singapore, Malaysia, Thailand, and Indonesia in a currency area. For the common currency basket, we found 12 combinations in which all countries in a linear combination showed significant results on the three tests. Seven of the 12 combinations included three East Asian countries in a currency area: Korea, Singapore, and Indonesia; Singapore, Malaysia, and the Philippines; Korea, Singapore, and Thailand; Singapore, Malaysia, and Thailand; Indonesia, Malaysia, and Thailand; Singapore, Thailand, and China; and Korea, Singapore, and China. The other five combinations include four East Asian countries in a currency area: Korea, Malaysia, the Philippines, and Indonesia; Korea, Singapore, Thailand, and Indonesia; Korea, Malaysia, Indonesia, and China; Korea, Singapore, Thailand, and China; and Singapore, Thailand, Indonesia, and China.

Table 13.1 Summary of the empirical analysis

Currency Basket

Number of Countries in the Currency Area	Korea (Won)	Singapore ($SG)	Indonesia (Rupiah)	Malaysia (Ringgit)	The Philippines (Peso)	Thailand (Baht)	China (Yuan)
	O	O	O				
		O		O	O		
	O	O				O	
3		O		O		O	
			O	O		O	
		O				O	O
	O	O					O
	O		O	O	O		
	O	O	O			O	
4	O		O	O			O
	O	O				O	O
		O	O			O	O

US dollar

Number of Countries in the Currency Area	Korea (Won)	Singapore ($SG)	Indonesia (Rupiah)	Malaysia (Ringgit)	The Philippines (Peso)	Thailand (Baht)	China (Yuan)
4		O	O	O		O	

We now show the results of a cointegrating analysis for these combinations in Tables 13.2, 13.3 and 13.4.[6] Table 13.2 shows maximum ranks of the cointegrating vector, two kinds of information criteria, and three tests for residuals from two to 12 lags for each of the nine combinations. Table 13.3 shows the result of the Johansen test; λ-trace and λ-max tests after selecting the correct lag-order of all ECMs of each of the nine combinations. Table 13.4 shows the results of the three chi-square-based tests identified as the optimal model.

Our empirical results show three features in comparing the US dollar with the currency basket as an anchor currency. First, while the common currency area evaluated by the US dollar as an anchor currency has only one combination, the common currency area evaluated by the currency basket as an anchor currency has several varieties of combinations. Second, some ASEAN countries can form a common currency area together with Korea or China with the currency basket as an anchor currency, while the common currency area with the US dollar as an anchor currency is limited to four ASEAN countries. Third, for the currency basket as an anchor currency, we could find two different groups, which include all of the East Asian countries, but their membership does not overlap; these combinations are, first, Korea, Malaysia, the Philippines, and Indonesia, and, second, the combination of Singapore, Thailand, and China. We could not find any two complementary groups when we tested for the possibility of a common currency area by adopting the US dollar as an anchor currency. From these features, our empirical results suggest that the common currency basket is more applicable for an anchor currency than the US dollar when East Asian countries form a common currency area in the region.

13.5 POLICY IMPLICATIONS

Among the findings, the third one implies that the two non-overlapping groups will be able to form a larger common currency area by their inter-group policy coordination. Adjustment speeds toward the long run equilibrium are different between the two groups, although the two groups can share the same basket weights. The equilibrium, defined by our G-PPP model, can be interpreted as a balance of payments equilibrium for the total common currency area countries. If the two groups have different adjustment speeds toward the long run equilibrium, there is the possibility that one group may run a consolidated current account surplus in total while the other may run a current account deficit as a group during the process. Our empirical results suggest that a combination that includes all seven countries would not be stable in the long run, while the two non-overlapping

Table 13.2 Maximum number of ranks, 2 information criteria, and Residual Analysis: p-value

Combination †1		lags2	lags3	lags4	lags5	lags6	lags7	lags8	lags9	lags10	lags11	lags12 †2
CB301	Rank(s)	0	1	1	0	1	0	0	2	1	1	1
	SBC	-26.221	-25.929	-25.497	-25.178	-25.003	-24.759	-24.501	-22.009	-21.620	-21.343	-21.198
	HQC	-26.526	-26.357	-26.044	-25.840	-25.777	-25.641	-25.489	-23.098	-22.808	-22.628	-22.576
	LB	199.094 0.89 *	189.365 0.96 *	191.876 0.95 *	183.16 0.98	192.827 0.87 *	202.961 0.73 *	229.026 0.26 *	204.552 0.70 *	196.343 0.69 *	204.07 0.54 *	217.734 0.29 *
	LM(1)	10.503 0.31 *	7.92 0.54 *	12.526 0.19 *	15.883 0.07 *	4.974 0.84 *	4.654 0.86 *	17.631 0.04 *	24.052 0.00	15.532 0.08 *	7.54 0.58 *	5.24 0.81 *
	LM(4)	7.324 0.60 *	6.892 0.65 *	7.073 0.63 *	5.294 0.81 *	6.247 0.72 *	2.676 0.98	3.868 0.92 *	15.687 0.07 *	14.058 0.12 *	12.538 0.18 *	11.35 0.25 *
CB309	Rank(s)	0	0	0	0	0	0	1	3	3	1	1
	SBC	-24.105	-23.819	-23.541	-23.326	-23.108	-22.906	-22.756	-22.641	-22.377	-21.978	-21.736
	HQC	-24.410	-24.247	-24.088	-23.988	-23.882	-23.788	-23.743	-23.730	-23.565	-23.263	-23.114
	LB	219.076 0.60 *	229.702 0.40 *	237.113 0.28 *	231.397 0.37 *	235.05 0.18 *	246.093 0.08 *	250.795 0.05 *	242.167 0.11 *	237.813 0.07 *	244.402 0.04 *	253.936 0.01
	LM(1)	2.807 0.97 *	4.924 0.84 *	11.477 0.24 *	8.845 0.45 *	7.499 0.59 *	6.418 0.70 *	16.642 0.05 *	8.277 0.51 *	8.594 0.48 *	6.99 0.64 *	4.111 0.90 *
	LM(4)	12.711 0.18 *	11.034 0.27 *	8.72 0.46 *	14.009 0.12 *	7.321 0.60 *	12.054 0.21 *	13.41 0.14 *	11.815 0.22 *	13.678 0.13 *	5.506 0.79 *	9.108 0.43 *
CB311	Rank(s)	0	1	0	0	1	1	1	3	2	2	3
	SBC	-26.761	-26.513	-26.134	-25.839	-25.720	-25.504	-25.285	-25.129	-24.785	-24.501	-24.261
	HQC	-27.066	-26.941	-26.681	-26.501	-26.494	-26.386	-26.273	-26.218	-25.973	-25.785	-25.639
	LB	235.204 0.31 *	239.556 0.24 *	230.204 0.39 *	234.394 0.32 *	220.597 0.40 *	234.775 0.18 *	243.663 0.10 *	241.182 0.12 *	234.102 0.10 *	234.651 0.09 *	243.636 0.04 *
	LM(1)	5.491 0.79 *	6.112 0.73 *	6.648 0.67 *	16.228 0.06 *	11.35 0.25 *	5.672 0.77 *	11.678 0.23 *	5.921 0.75 *	13.731 0.13 *	16.939 0.05 *	8.186 0.52 *
	LM(4)	8.936 0.44 *	6.987 0.64 *	6.006 0.74 *	6.075 0.73 *	9.57 0.39 *	5.044 0.83 *	4.564 0.87 *	7.87 0.55 *	8.037 0.53 *	10.535 0.31 *	19.888 0.02
CB315	Rank(s)	0	0	0	0	0	0	0	1	1	1	1
	SBC	-26.402	-26.222	-25.930	-25.682	-25.552	-25.314	-25.111	-24.922	-24.596	-24.395	-24.014
	HQC	-26.706	-26.650	-26.477	-26.345	-26.326	-26.196	-26.099	-26.011	-25.784	-25.680	-25.392
	LB	243.391 0.19 *	228.338 0.43 *	225.717 0.47 *	233.758 0.33 *	226.055 0.31 *	228.627 0.27 *	236.705 0.16 *	239.59 0.13 *	234.684 0.09 *	241.327 0.05 *	248.266 0.03 *
	LM(1)	7.697 0.56 *	6.507 0.69 *	10.717 0.30 *	17.261 0.04 *	10.003 0.35 *	11.923 0.22 *	3.953 0.91 *	8.189 0.52 *	21.378 0.01	8.377 0.50 *	11.295 0.26 *
	LM(4)	15.676 0.07 *	10.742 0.29 *	10.876 0.28 *	9.634 0.38 *	5.087 0.83 *	11.129 0.27 *	13.078 0.16 *	4.584 0.87 *	9.627 0.38 *	11.25 0.26 *	19.676 0.02
CB316	Rank(s)	0	0	0	0	0	0	2	1	1	1	2
	SBC	-26.408	-26.220	-25.944	-25.668	-25.617	-25.354	-25.059	-22.484	-22.119	-21.840	-21.593
	HQC	-26.712	-26.648	-26.491	-26.331	-26.391	-26.236	-26.046	-23.574	-23.307	-23.125	-22.971
	LB	252.489 0.10 *	249.142 0.13 *	246.533 0.15 *	245.72 0.16 *	241.156 0.12 *	231.852 0.22 *	257.461 0.03 *	220.102 0.41 *	219.389 0.26 *	189.68 0.80 *	200.097 0.62 *
	LM(1)	14.265 0.11 *	11.251 0.26 *	11.88 0.22 *	24.153 0.00	17.941 0.04 *	11.495 0.24 *	11.059 0.27 *	12.731 0.18 *	16.435 0.06 *	4.493 0.88 *	7.089 0.63 *
	LM(4)	11.643 0.23 *	9.142 0.42 *	7.642 0.57 *	6.781 0.66 *	12.114 0.21 *	12.706 0.18 *	16.328 0.06 *	24.006 0.00	24.259 0.00	10.916 0.28 *	10.098 0.34 *
CB324	Rank(s)	0	0	0	0	0	0	0	0	0	1	1
	SBC	-24.464	-24.220	-23.873	-23.616	-23.444	-23.204	-23.046	-22.770	-22.390	-22.231	-21.889
	HQC	-24.769	-24.648	-24.420	-24.278	-24.218	-24.086	-24.033	-23.859	-23.578	-23.515	-23.267
	LB	192.243 0.94 *	196.347 0.92 *	193.318 0.94 *	205.251 0.82 *	197.796 0.81 *	199.855 0.78 *	202.638 0.73 *	218.801 0.43 *	215.6 0.33 *	225.89 0.18 *	244.467 0.04 *
	LM(1)	7.4 0.60 *	4.025 0.91 *	8.907 0.45 *	8.878 0.45 *	5.436 0.79 *	13.616 0.14 *	7.75 0.56 *	5.34 0.80 *	20.908 0.01	6.975 0.64 *	12.085 0.21 *
	LM(4)	10.05 0.35 *	10.16 0.34 *	7.992 0.53 *	3.321 0.95 *	6.595 0.68 *	12.72 0.18 *	10.064 0.35 *	14.385 0.11 *	14.282 0.11 *	11.976 0.21 *	17.229 0.05 *

Table 13.2 Maximum number of ranks, 2 information criteria, and Residual Analysis: p-value (Continued)

Combination †1		lags2	lags3	lags4	lags5	lags6	lags7	lags8	lags9	lags10	lags11	lags12 †2
CB335	Rank(s)	0	1	1	0	1	1	0	2	2	2	2
	SBC	-23.520	-23.246	-22.848	-22.538	-22.355	-22.105	-21.902	-21.655	-21.380	-21.193	-20.979
	HQC	-23.825	-23.674	-23.395	-23.200	-23.129	-22.987	-22.889	-22.744	-22.568	-22.477	-22.357
	LB	208.317 0.78 *	199.966 0.88 *	216.458 0.65 *	217.007 0.64 *	211.349 0.58 *	217.618 0.46 *	225.313 0.32 *	210.932 0.58 *	212.575 0.38 *	237.893 0.07 *	252.006 0.02
	LM(1)	3.645 0.93 *	2.9 0.97 *	10.207 0.33 *	10.114 0.34 *	5.045 0.83 *	10.427 0.32 *	9.009 0.44 *	4.478 0.88 *	13.49 0.14 *	5.662 0.77 *	4.088 0.91 *
	LM(4)	6.256 0.71 *	5.559 0.78 *	6.854 0.65 *	12.517 0.19 *	7.276 0.61 *	13.38 0.15 *	11.564 0.24 *	12.998 0.16 *	12.147 0.21 *	10.702 0.30 *	16.405 0.06 *
CB404	Rank(s)	0	0	0	1	1	1	1	1	1	1	2
	SBC	-32.510	-32.222	-31.812	-31.378	-30.935	-30.621	-30.257	-29.751	-27.385	-26.607	-26.353
	HQC	-33.065	-33.004	-32.810	-32.583	-32.337	-32.213	-32.030	-31.699	-29.501	-28.884	-28.786
	LB	388.281 0.22 *	398.022 0.14 *	415.058 0.05 *	413.7 0.05 *	433.99 0.01	417.817 0.04 *	437.315 0.01	461.483 0.00	476.589 0.00	391.433 0.19 *	417.9 0.04 *
	LM(1)	26.237 0.05 *	16.498 0.42 *	19.196 0.26 *	17.526 0.35 *	23.044 0.11 *	13.822 0.61 *	13.402 0.64 *	27.373 0.04 *	23.567 0.10 *	26.176 0.05 *	18.801 0.28 *
	LM(4)	13.731 0.62 *	9.515 0.89 *	10.349 0.85 *	10.189 0.86 *	12.809 0.69 *	20.965 0.18 *	18.934 0.27 *	30.895 0.01	57.934 0.00	11.012 0.81 *	22.356 0.13 *
CB406	Rank(s)	0	0	1	2	1	1	1	1	2	2	1
	SBC	-36.037	-35.548	-35.111	-34.624	-34.272	-33.954	-33.445	-33.129	-30.177	-29.576	-29.140
	HQC	-36.592	-36.330	-36.110	-35.828	-35.674	-35.545	-35.218	-35.077	-32.292	-31.854	-31.573
	LB	393.878 0.17 *	386.792 0.24 *	377.151 0.36 *	382.389 0.29 *	395.247 0.16 *	417.277 0.04 *	431.68 0.01	466.06 0.00	411.765 0.06 *	418.594 0.04 *	408.983 0.07 *
	LM(1)	11.058 0.81 *	17.206 0.37 *	11.442 0.78 *	21.019 0.18 *	20.167 0.21 *	5.766 0.99	25.131 0.07 *	16.505 0.42 *	17.521 0.35 *	10.426 0.84 *	19.774 0.23 *
	LM(4)	12.037 0.74 *	6.683 0.98	9.977 0.87 *	12.546 0.71 *	24.746 0.07 *	13.105 0.67 *	17.817 0.33 *	5.888 0.99	26.113 0.05 *	25.411 0.06 *	30.958 0.01
CB418	Rank(s)	0	0	0	0	1	0	0	1	1	2	2
	SBC	-31.925	-31.547	-31.125	-30.652	-30.257	-29.857	-29.442	-28.930	-26.269	-25.852	-25.585
	HQC	-32.480	-32.329	-32.123	-31.856	-31.660	-31.449	-31.215	-30.878	-28.385	-28.130	-28.018
	LB	358.433 0.63 *	371.943 0.43 *	379.408 0.33 *	396.615 0.15 *	389.363 0.21 *	397.603 0.14 *	418.941 0.03 *	437.971 0.01	375.113 0.39 *	394.744 0.16 *	405.687 0.09 *
	LM(1)	19.262 0.26 *	18.302 0.31 *	14.75 0.54 *	27.895 0.03 *	6.872 0.98	7.636 0.96 *	13.442 0.64 *	24.497 0.08 *	21.953 0.14 *	9.127 0.91 *	9.821 0.88 *
	LM(4)	15.764 0.47 *	12.445 0.71 *	12.722 0.69 *	8.751 0.92 *	10.977 0.81 *	13.182 0.66 *	14.963 0.53 *	24.621 0.08 *	42.841 0.00	14.349 0.57 *	15.763 0.47 *
CB426	Rank(s)	0	0	0	1	1	1	2	2	1	1	1
	SBC	-33.112	-32.624	-32.147	-31.704	-31.285	-30.988	-30.729	-30.438	-29.985	-29.667	-29.052
	HQC	-33.667	-33.406	-33.145	-32.909	-32.688	-32.580	-32.503	-32.386	-32.101	-31.944	-31.485
	LB	347.686 0.77 *	360.157 0.61 *	351.86 0.72 *	365.732 0.52 *	369.02 0.48 *	378.127 0.35 *	399.916 0.12 *	414.104 0.05 *	412.402 0.05 *	440.608 0.01	455.948 0.00
	LM(1)	9.592 0.89 *	11.035 0.81 *	13.419 0.64 *	17.829 0.33 *	18.029 0.32 *	17.055 0.38 *	9.248 0.90 *	9.089 0.91 *	16.788 0.40 *	4.651 1.00	11.265 0.79 *
	LM(4)	13.281 0.65 *	7.931 0.95 *	11.205 0.80 *	6.879 0.98	14.147 0.59 *	7.658 0.96 *	4.813 1.00	7.85 0.95 *	18.862 0.28 *	17.846 0.33 *	21.139 0.17 *
CB428	Rank(s)	0	1	1	0	0	0	1	0	1	0	1
	SBC	-33.604	-33.165	-32.724	-32.298	-32.029	-31.685	-31.301	-30.745	-27.783	-27.275	-26.822
	HQC	-34.159	-33.946	-33.722	-33.503	-33.431	-33.277	-33.075	-32.693	-29.899	-29.552	-29.256
	LB	390.143 0.20 *	396.407 0.15 *	388.234 0.22 *	391.558 0.19 *	373.738 0.41 *	377.589 0.35 *	399.653 0.12 *	477.017 0.00	388.266 0.22 *	377.983 0.35 *	393.898 0.17 *
	LM(1)	11.249 0.79 *	18.926 0.27 *	14.797 0.54 *	25.65 0.06 *	11.185 0.80 *	13.059 0.67 *	12.13 0.73 *	21.214 0.17 *	23.916 0.09 *	9.153 0.91 *	21.119 0.17 *
	LM(4)	18.147 0.32 *	11.664 0.77 *	11.007 0.81 *	11.494 0.78 *	11.284 0.79 *	16.213 0.44 *	10.034 0.86 *	12.701 0.69 *	17.175 0.37 *	15.145 0.51 *	24.463 0.08 *

Table 13.2 Maximum number of ranks, 2 information criteria, and Residual Analysis: p-value (Continued)

Combination †1		lags2		lags3		lags4		lags5		lags6		lags7		lags8		lags9		lags10		lags11		lags12 †2	
US409	Rank(s)	0		1		2		2		4		2		2		2		2		2		2	
	SBC	-37.252		-36.847		-36.549		-36.190		-35.698		-35.425		-35.021		-34.741		-31.339		-30.880		-30.446	
	HQC	-37.806		-37.628		-37.547		-37.395		-37.100		-37.017		-36.794		-36.689		-33.455		-33.157		-32.879	
	LB	446.074	0.00	447.708	0.00	414.458	0.05 *	418.45	0.04 *	413.542	0.05 *	425.809	0.02	446.847	0.00	483.86	0.00	475.517	0.00	480.122	0.00	494.301	0.00
	LM(1)	15.999	0.45 *	25.992	0.05 *	25.731	0.06 *	22.083	0.14 *	19.258	0.26 *	13.431	0.64 *	18.805	0.28 *	19.634	0.24 *	27.033	0.04 *	15.24	0.51 *	16.588	0.41 *
	LM(4)	26.658	0.05 *	24.256	0.08 *	24.091	0.09 *	11.401	0.78 *	4.84	1.00	16.479	0.42 *	18.936	0.27 *	8.296	0.94 *	35.223	0.00	23.802	0.09 *	29.056	0.02

†1: Combination

CB/US301: Korea + Singapore + Indonesia, , CB/US302: Korea + Singapore + Malaysia, , CB/US303: Korea + Indonesia + Malaysia, , CB/US304: Singapore + Indonesia + Malaysia, CB/US305: Korea + Singapore + The Philippines, CB/US306: Korea + Indonesia + The Philippines, CB/US307: Singapore + Indonesia + The Philippines, CB/US308: Korea + Malaysia + The Philippines, CB/US309: Singapore + Malaysia + The Philippines, CB/US310: Indonesia + Malaysia + The Philippines, CB/US311: Korea + Singapore + Thailand, CB/US312: Korea + Indonesia + Thailand, CB/US313: Singapore + Indonesia + Thailand, CB/US314: Korea + Malaysia + Thailand, CB/US315: Singapore + Malaysia + Thailand, CB/US316: Indonesia + Malaysia + Thailand, CB/US317: Korea + The Philippines + Thailand, CB/US318: Singapore + The Philippines + Thailand, CB/US319: Indonesia + The Philippines + Thailand, CB/US320: Malaysia + The Philippines + Thailand, CB/US321: The Philippines + Thailand + China, CB/US322: Malaysia + Thailand + China, CB/US323: Indonesia + Thailand + China, CB/US324: Singapore + Thailand + China, CB/US325: Korea + Thailand + China, CB/US326: Malaysia + The Philippines + China, CB/US327: Indonesia + The Philippines + China, CB/US328: Singapore + The Philippines + China, CB/US330: Indonesia + Malaysia + China, CB/US330: Indonesia + Malaysia + China, CB/US331: Singapore + Malaysia + China, CB/US332: Korea + Malaysia + China, CB/US333: Singapore + Indonesia + China, CB/US334: Korea + Indonesia + China, CB/US335: Korea + Singapore + China, CB/US401: Korea + Singapore + Indonesia + Malaysia, CB/US402: Korea + Singapore + Indonesia + The Philippines, CB/US403: Korea + Singapore + Malaysia + The Philippines, CB/US404: Korea + Indonesia + Malaysia + The Philippines, CB/US405: Singapore + Indonesia + Malaysia + The Philippines, CB/US406: Korea + Singapore + Indonesia + Thailand, CB/US407: Korea + Singapore + Malaysia + Thailand, CB/US408: Korea + Indonesia + Malaysia + Thailand, CB/US409: Singapore + Indonesia + Malaysia + Thailand, CB/US410: Korea + Singapore + The Philippines + Thailand, CB/US411: Korea + Indonesia + The Philippines + Thailand, CB/US412: Singapore + Indonesia + The Philippines + Thailand, CB/US413: Korea + Malaysia + The Philippines + Thailand, CB/US414: Singapore + Malaysia + The Philippines + Thailand, CB/US415: Indonesia + Malaysia + The Philippines + Thailand. CB/US416: Korea + Singapore + Indonesia + China. CB/US417: Korea + Singapore + Malaysia + China. CB/US418: Korea + Indonesia + Malaysia + China. CB/US419: Singapore + Indonesia + Malaysia + China
CB/US420:Korea + Singapore + The Philippines + China, CB/US421:Korea + Indonesia + The Philippines + China, CB/US422:Singapore + Indonesia + The Philippines + China, CB/US423:Korea + Malaysia + The Philippines + China, CB/US424:Singapore + Malaysia + The Philippines + China, CB/US425:Indonesia + Malaysia + The Philippines + China, CB/US426:Korea + Singapore + Thailand + China, CB/US427:Korea + Indonesia + Thailand + China, CB/US428:Singapore + Indonesia + Thailand + China, CB/US429:Korea + Malaysia + Thailand + China, CB/US430:Singapore + Malaysia + Thailand + China, CB/US431:Indonesia + Malaysia + Thailand + China, CB/US432:Korea + The Philippines + Thailand + China, CB/US433:Singapore + The Philippines + Thailand + China, CB/US434:Indonesia + The Philippines + Thailand + China, CB/US435:Malaysia + The Philippines + Thailand + China, CB/US501:Korea + Singapore + Indonesia + Malaysia + The Philippines, CB/US502:Korea + Singapore + Indonesia + Malaysia + Thailand, CB/US503:Korea + Singapore + Indonesia + The Philippines + Thailand, CB/US504:Korea + Singapore + Malaysia + The Philippines + Thailand. CB/US505:Korea + Indonesia + Malaysia + The Philippines + Thailand. CB/US506:Singapore + Indonesia + Malaysia + The Philippines + Thailand. CB/US507:Korea + Singapore + Ir
CB/US509:Korea + Singapore + Malaysia + The Philippines + China, CB/US510:Korea + Indonesia + Malaysia + The Philippines + China, CB/US511:Singapore + Indonesia + Malaysia + The Philippines + China, CB/US512:Korea + Singapore + Indonesia + Thailand + China, CB/US513:Korea + Singapore + Malaysia + Thailand + China, CB/US514:Korea + Indonesia + Malaysia + Thailand + China, CB/US515:Singapore + Indonesia + Malaysia + Thailand + China, CB/US516:Korea + Singapore + The Philippines + Thailand + China, CB/US517:Korea + Indonesia + The Philippines + Thailand + China, CB/US518:Singapore + Indonesia + The Philippines + Thailand + China, CB/US519:Korea + Malaysia + The Philippines + Thailand + China, CB/US520:Singapore + Malaysia + The Philippines + Thailand + China, CB/US521:Indonesia + Malaysia + The Philippines + Thailand + China, CB/US601:Korea + Singapore + Indonesia + Malaysia + The Philippines + Thailand, CB/US602:Korea + Singapore + Indonesia + Malaysia + The Philippines + China, CB/US603:Korea + Singapore + Indonesia + Malaysia + Thailand + China, CB/US604:Korea + Singapore + Indonesia + The Philippines + Thailand + China. CB/US605:Korea + Singapore + Malaysia + The Philippines + Thailand + China. CB/US606:Korea + Indonesia + Malaysia + The Philippines + Thailand + China. CB/US607:

†2 Since we set that DGF are equalized from lags 2 to lags12, the starting point of the sample period for all estimations are valid.

CB/US301-335; DGF=105, Lags2=1988:04, Lags3=1988:01, Lags4=1987:10, Lags5=1987:07, Lags6=1987:04, Lags7=1987:01, Lags8=1986:10, Lags9=1986:07, Lags10=1986:04, Lags11=1986:01, Lags 12=1985:10.
CB/US401-435; DGF=93, Lags2=1989:02, Lags3=1988:10, Lags4=1988:06, Lags5=1988:02, Lags6=1987:10, Lags7=1987:06, Lags8=1987:02, Lags9=1986:10, Lags10=1986:06, Lags11=1986:02, Lags 12=1985:10.
CB/US501-521; DGF=81, Lags2=1989:12, Lags3=1989:07, Lags4=1989:02, Lags5=1988:09, Lags6=1988:04, Lags7=1987:11, Lags8=1987:06, Lags9=1987:01, Lags10=1986:08, Lags11=1986:03, Lags 12=1985:10.
CB/US601-607; DGF=69, Lags2=1991:10, Lags3=1990:04, Lags4=1989:10, Lags5=1989:04, Lags6=1988:10, Lags7=1988:04, Lags8=1987:10, Lags9=1987:04, Lags10=1986:10, Lags11=1986:04, Lags 12=1985:10.
CB/US701; DGF=57, Lags2=1991:08, Lags3=1991:01, Lags4=1990:06, Lags5=1989:11, Lags6=1989:04, Lags7=1988:09, Lags8=1988:02, Lags9=1987:07, Lags10=1986:12, Lags11=1986:05, Lags 12=1985:10.

Table 13.3 Johansen tests

	Combination	k	H_0	Eigen Vector	L-Max	L-Trace
				Currency Basket		
301	Korea + Singapore + Indonesia	11	0	0.197	30.270 ***	41.280 ***
			1	0.069	9.890	11.010
			2	0.008	1.120	1.120
309	Singapore + Malaysia + The Philippines	11	0	0.242	38.320 ***	54.130 ***
			1	0.069	9.900	15.810 *
			2	0.042	5.910 **	5.910 **
311	Korea + Singapore + Thailand	10	0	0.175	25.990 ***	44.300 ***
			1	0.106	15.070 ***	18.310 **
			2	0.024	3.240	3.240
315	Singapore + Malaysia + Thailand	11	0	0.321	53.510 ***	65.200 ***
			1	0.060	8.560	11.690
			2	0.022	3.120	3.120
316	Indonesia + Malaysia + Thailand	8	0	0.131	18.040 ***	34.730 **
			1	0.113	15.480 ***	16.690 *
			2	0.009	1.210	1.210
324	Singapore + Thailand + China	11	0	0.220	34.300 ***	39.260 ***
			1	0.034	4.760	4.960
			2	0.002	0.200	0.200
335	Korea + Singapore + China	9	0	0.171	24.690 ***	41.910 ***
			1	0.110	15.380 ***	17.220 *
			2	0.014	1.840	1.840
404	Korea + Indonesia + Malaysia + The Philippines	12	0	0.239	38.530 ***	77.400 ***
			1	0.155	23.720 ***	38.860 ***
			2	0.087	12.840 **	15.140
			3	0.016	2.300	2.300
406	Korea + Singapore + Indonesia + Thailand	4	0	0.204	24.890 ***	51.090 **
			1	0.168	20.060 ***	26.200
			2	0.055	6.130	6.130
			3	0.000	0.000	0.000
418	Korea + Indonesia + Malaysia + China	11	0	0.219	33.940 ***	67.740 ***
			1	0.145	21.470 ***	33.800 **
			2	0.070	9.880	12.330
			3	0.018	2.450	2.450
426	Korea + Singapore + Thailand + China	9	0	0.259	39.850 ***	68.720 ***
			1	0.156	22.600 ***	28.870
			2	0.041	5.490	6.270
			3	0.006	0.780	0.780
428	Singapore + Indonesia + Thailand + China	10	0	0.218	32.730 ***	47.820 *
			1	0.065	8.920	15.090
			2	0.044	5.990	6.170
			3	0.001	0.170	0.170

	Combination	k	H_0	Eigen Vector	L-Max	L-Trace
				US Dollar		
409	Singapore + Indonesia + Malaysia + Thailand	4	0	0.226	27.960 ***	62.010 ***
			1	0.188	22.730 ***	34.050 **
			2	0.067	7.530	11.330
			3	0.034	3.800	3.800

Notes: k: lag length *95%, **97.5%, ***99.0%

Table 13.4 Chi-square based tests

Combination	k	r	DGF	CHISQ 10%	5%	2.5%	1%	Korea (Won)	Singapore ($SG)	Indonesia (Rupiah)	Malaysia (Ringgit)	The Philippines	Thailand (Baht)	China (Yuan)
CB301	11	1	1	2.71	3.84	5.02	6.63	10.42 ****	3.42 *	19.92 ****				
		1	2	4.61	5.99	7.38	9.21	23.27 ****	25.60 ****	10.66 ****				
		1	1	2.71	3.84	5.02	6.63	3.52 *	15.93 ****	7.07 ****				
CB309	11	1	1	2.71	3.84	5.02	6.63		13.81 ****		24.57 ****	13.12 ****		
		1	2	4.61	5.99	7.38	9.21		24.75 ****		15.52 ****	27.47 ****		
		1	1	2.71	3.84	5.02	6.63		26.23 ****		15.25 ****	3.54 *		
CB311	11	2	2	4.61	5.99	7.38	9.21	10.07 ****	11.30 ****				15.05 ****	
		2	1	2.71	3.84	5.02	6.63	6.87 ****	7.00 ****				7.13 ****	
		2	2	4.61	5.99	7.38	9.21	8.19 ***	16.41 ****				5.41 *	
CB315	11	1	1	2.71	3.84	5.02	6.63		12.48 ****		31.48 ****		7.90 ****	
		1	2	4.61	5.99	7.38	9.21		39.22 ****		12.54 ****		31.67 ****	
		1	1	2.71	3.84	5.02	6.63		28.05 ****		15.12 ****		5.87 ***	
CB316	8	2	2	4.61	5.99	7.38	9.21			16.67 ****	13.82 ****		10.71 ****	
		2	1	2.71	3.84	5.02	6.63			10.42 ****	8.77 ****		11.77 ****	
		2	2	4.61	5.99	7.38	9.21			15.12 ****	12.91 ****		8.18 ***	
CB324	11	1	1	2.71	3.84	5.02	6.63		10.79 ****				3.20 *	9.41 ****
		1	2	4.61	5.99	7.38	9.21		19.13 ****				10.91 ****	29.23 ****
		1	1	2.71	3.84	5.02	6.63		22.01 ****				6.87 ****	4.04 **
CB335	9	2	2	4.61	5.99	7.38	9.21	18.50 ****	12.21 ****					13.71 ****
		2	1	2.71	3.84	5.02	6.63	7.90 ****	11.31 ****					11.58 ****
		2	2	4.61	5.99	7.38	9.21	13.53 ****	14.11 ****					6.78 **

Table 13.4 Chi-square based tests (Continued)

Combination	k	r	DGF	CHISQ 10%	5%	2.5%	1%	Korea (Won)	Singapore ($SG)	Indonesia (Rupiah)	Malaysia (Ringgit)	The Philippines (Peso)	Thailand (Baht)	China (Yuan)
CB404	12	2	2	4.61	5.99	7.38	9.21	18.15 ****		22.46 ****	15.58 ****	14.94 ****		
		2	2	4.61	5.99	7.38	9.21	11.33 ****		8.02 ***	7.57 ***	17.46 ****		
		2	2	4.61	5.99	7.38	9.21	6.76 **		12.70 ****	14.87 ****	5.26 *		
CB406	4	2	2	4.61	5.99	7.38	9.21	12.15 ****	12.74 ****	15.92 ****			13.73 ****	
		2	2	4.61	5.99	7.38	9.21	11.45 ****	8.40 ***	13.89 ****			15.45 ****	
		2	2	4.61	5.99	7.38	9.21	11.99 ****	6.34 **	15.03 ****			5.32 *	
CB418	11	1	1	2.71	3.84	5.02	6.63	11.28 ****		10.36 ****	8.41 ****			7.22 ****
		1	3	6.25	7.81	9.35	11.34	26.23 ****		13.84 ****	14.49 ****			19.81 ****
		1	1	2.71	3.84	5.02	6.63	4.36 **		12.42 ****	3.66 *			11.86 ****
CB426	9	2	2	4.61	5.99	7.38	9.21	30.98 ****	29.00 ****				14.86 ****	25.57 ****
		2	2	4.61	5.99	7.38	9.21	16.43 ****	15.55 ****				29.09 ****	26.05 ****
		2	2	4.61	5.99	7.38	9.21	17.00 ****	32.61 ****				12.55 ****	4.85 *
CB428	10	1	1	2.71	3.84	5.02	6.63		4.82 **	13.57 ****			5.41 ***	3.08 *
		1	3	6.25	7.81	9.35	11.34		28.57 ****	6.52 *			19.20 ****	24.46 ****
		1	1	2.71	3.84	5.02	6.63		16.51 ****	17.02 ****			13.07 ****	12.49 ****
US409	4	2	2	4.61	5.99	7.38	9.21		18.10 ****	15.29 ****	9.83 ****		13.55 ****	
		2	2	4.61	5.99	7.38	9.21		10.91 ****	18.37 ****	13.22 ****		14.41 ****	
		2	2	4.61	5.99	7.38	9.21		8.21 ***	9.42 ****	13.35 ****		14.61 ****	

Notes: Test statistics indicate for "long-run exclusion"(top), "stationarity"(middle), and "weak exogeneity"(bottom) respectively.

†Significance level: *90%, **95%, ***97.5%, ****99%, k is lag-order of ECM, r is row of matrix beta

combinations had cointegration relationships when both of the two combinations used the common currency basket as an anchor currency. This means that each of the two groups will be able to create a different common currency area by using a common currency basket and the same basket weights simultaneously. However, in the adjustment process toward the long run equilibrium the two groups may face current account deficits or surpluses. In this case, governments included in the two common currency areas need to conduct policy coordination between the two groups, which can be called "inter-group policy coordination". We suggest that the key feature of this "inter-group policy coordination" should be the employment of macroeconomic policies, including fiscal spending or transfers, to adjust the transitional asymmetry in the balance of payments between the two groups during the adjustment process. In addition to inter-group policy coordination we also suggest that the deepening of financial integration or structural economic integration in East Asia, may help to equalize the different adjustment speeds between the two groups.

13.6 CONCLUSIONS

This chapter has suggested that it is necessary to create a common currency basket in order to resolve a coordination failure in choosing a desirable exchange rate system for the East Asian countries. From this point of view, it is natural that a future regional currency arrangement in East Asia should be related with a common currency basket. The European experience of the ECU should provide the region with useful information in considering a common currency unit in East Asia. East Asian countries have international trade relationships with a variety of regions that include the intra-region, Japan, the United States, and European countries. Therefore, a possible common currency unit in East Asia would consist of the US dollar, the Japanese yen, and the euro and so on. This is in contrast to the ECU which consisted of intra-regional currencies.

The Generalized Purchasing Power Parity (G-PPP) model was used to investigate the possibility of a common currency area for some of the East Asian countries, in terms of a long run stable linear combination among some regional currencies. The analytical results imply that the ASEAN-5 countries, China, and Korea will be candidates for a common currency area with a common currency basket as an anchor currency. Also, we conclude that a common currency basket is more applicable as an anchor currency than the US dollar, in forming a common currency area in the region.

However, the establishment of a currency union in the East Asian region in the near future may be questionable. The possibility of regional policy coordination depends on a consensus of policy objectives among the governments of the East Asian countries. Needless to say, if the monetary authorities of the East Asian countries intend to implement regional policy coordination, as a premise they need to create a common currency area. It is difficult for them to conduct regional policy coordination unless they have common policy objectives. It is important, especially, that they have common objectives in monetary and exchange rate policies, in order to create a common currency area.

APPENDIX

A cointegration analysis is a very useful tool to investigate the dynamic paths of multiple economic variables. However, it is susceptible to criticism regarding the robustness of the test results. Namely, the number of cointegration relationships (the cointegration rank) sometimes varies with the lag order of the underlying vector-autoregressive model. If the rank condition is variable, a number of possibilities exist to identify equilibrium among the variables. There are two key issues. First, whether or not the long run relationship among the variables is present in the data and, second, which equilibrium has more important economic implications depends on the choice of the lag order. Therefore, we need to carefully identify the appropriate error correction model before conducting the Johansen test.

In this study, we provisionally introduce eight additional tests into the Johansen cointegration analysis to solve "the dilemma" problem. The point is that we choose the lag order of the error correction model considering the appropriate equilibriums and elements in the matrix Π. In other words, we first investigate an appropriate equilibrium of those variables, and then test whether that equilibrium and the resultant error correction model satisfy the several assumptions of the Johansen test. Our assumptions are that (1) there is no serial correlation among the residuals of the VAR models, (2) each variable could be included in the long run relationship, (3) each variable is non-stationary, and (4) each variable is an endogenous variable in their relationship. If we can find the true data generating process between variables, and it has a long run equilibrium to converge to, that model must fulfill all our assumptions of the cointegration analysis. In the case where there is no equilibrium that meets our assumptions we can recognize that there is no long run relationship at all among the variables, and the cointegration rank must be zero. Depending upon the lag order, we may encounter conflicting results: one result is that there is at least one cointegration and the other is that there is no cointegration, but in both instances the assumptions of the Johansen procedure are satisfied. To choose between the two, we examine the fitness of the alternative models by applying the conventional information criteria. Our empirical strategy is as follows.

Prior to a cointegration analysis, we have to confirm whether or not each variable has a unit root and is non-stationary. In some cases, stationary series can be included in the cointegration relationships or the error correction models. But in our G-PPP model, we assume all variables to be non-stationary.

(Step 1) We conduct the Johansen test for VAR models. Here, we conduct the tests for the 11 sets of error correction models with the lag order of two to 12 per one linear combination of variables, and varied the sample period to equalize the degrees of freedom in each of the 11 models. We assume that the maximum lag order affecting the equilibrium is 12 in the true data generating process. This assumption can easily be changed.

(Step 2) Next, we calculate three test statistics for residuals: the multivariate Ljung-Box test based on the estimated auto- and cross-correlations of the first quarter number of lags of all the sample periods, the Lagrange-Multiplier type tests for first and fourth order autocorrelations. The residuals of the VAR or the error correction model are assumed to have no serial correlation. Therefore, we exclude the cases where the assumption is not met regardless of whether the cointegration rank is zero or not.

Here, we gather the cases that validate the assumption of no serial correlation in residuals. We can divide those models into a group of no cointegration rank and that of more than one. If there are some cases that the cointegration rank is more than one, which means there are more equilibria between variables, we have to conduct further tests for these cases.

(Step 3) We conduct three kinds of chi-square-based tests for the cases that have an equilibrium. Usually, these tests are used for identifying the equilibrium. We use these tests not only to identify the equilibrium but also to choose a proper lag order. The first test is to find variables that can be excluded from the long run relationship in the cointegrating vector R. The null hypothesis in this test is $\beta_{ij} = 0$. If the null is accepted and the test statistic is asymptotically distributed as the chi-square with r degrees of freedom, it might mean the possibility that some relevant variables are missing from the cointegration relationship. In the case of strong multicollinearity, we will also get an insignificant test value. The second test is about stationarity. This test is to check whether the individual series can be stationary by themselves. The null is $\beta = (H_i, \varphi)$. If the null is accepted and the test statistic is asymptotically distributed as the chi-square with r degrees of freedom, it might mean the possibility that the variable will be excluded from the cointegration relationship; therefore we can identify the minimal set of variables that comprise the long run equilibrium relationship. The last is to test whether any of the elements in the vector R can be considered as weakly exogenous for the long run equilibrium. The null hypothesis is $\alpha_{ij} = 0$. In the case of accepting the null as asymptotically distributed as chi-square with r degrees of freedom, that variable might be a weakly exogenous series for the long run equilibrium. Therefore, we can exclude such cases.

If all the three tests are passed we can find the minimum set of variables in the long run equilibrium. Therefore, for most cases, we can identify an optimal error correction model with proper lags and appropriate equilibrium to converge to. We can call this the "Best fitting model". If we cannot find any cases that satisfy the three tests, we should focus on the second best case. We regard the second best cases to be those which meet the stationarity test, but fail to pass the other two tests. We should not jump to a conclusion of no linear long run equilibrium. The first and third tests are very helpful for us because these tests can detect the possibilities of over-identification or under-identification of the model, not only for the minimum set of variables but also for the proper lag length. When we wrongly increase the lag length, or erroneously determine the rank, the test statistics suddenly show the possibility of accepting the null. On the other hand, we may be able to find some other exogenous variables to form a long run equilibrium relationship as an exogenous variable. Therefore, we have to carefully look into a second best case. Here, we only focus on the cases in which at least two variables in the vector can be rejected, the null of long run exclusion and weak exogeneity, because it is not important to think that only one endogenous variable with several exogenous variables can converge to a long run equilibrium in a common currency area or Generalized Purchasing Power Parity (G-PPP) model.

(Step 4) We compare all possible models in terms of the fitness of the true data generating process. This step is helpful in avoiding the arbitrariness in choosing a model in the final step. In step 3, we may not be able to find the best case and may have to look for second best cases. It is true that the first and third test indicate the possibility of over- or under-identification of the model, but we cannot fully identify it. This means that we cannot recognize whether or not that model is more suitable than the others. Therefore, in the final step, we use an information criterion to choose proper or fitting models for the data generating process. According to these steps, we can identify the unique model and equilibrium.

Table 13.1A Choosing the lag order of ECM

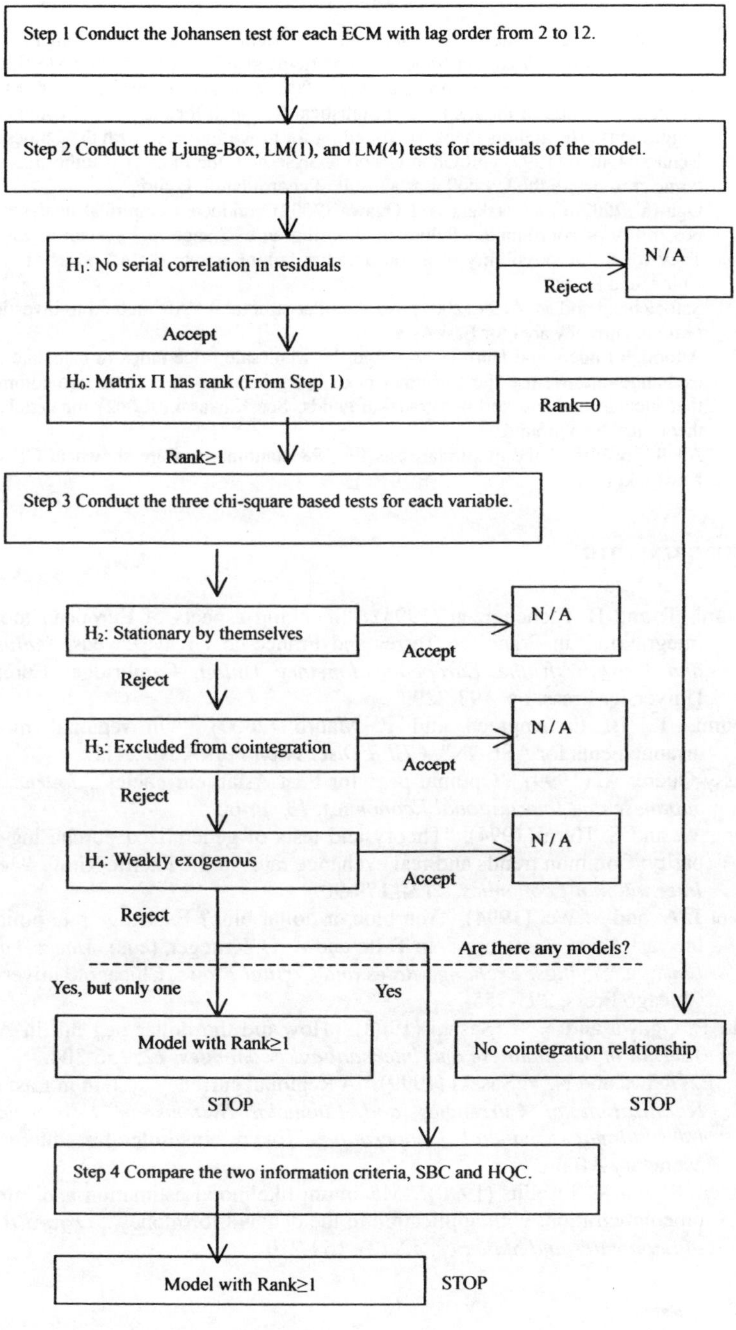

NOTES

1 The authors are grateful to Takatoshi Ito, Kenjiro Hirayama, Shinichi Fukuda, Munehisa Kasuya, Yuko Hashimoto and participants of the 2002 Spring Meeting of the Japan Economic Association and the 2002 Summer Conference of Monetary Economics Group of the Institute of Statistical Research for their useful comments and suggestions. The authors thank Yu Yongding for providing them with the Chinese data.

2 Bénassy-Quéré (1999) and Ohno (1999) analyse how the monetary authorities peg the home currency to the US dollar as a result of coordination failure.

3 Ogawa (2002b) and Nakata and Ogawa (2002) conducted empirical analyses of the possibility of coordination failure in choosing an exchange rate system in East Asia. They found the possibility of a coordination failure among the countries of ASEAN, China, and Korea.

4 Sato, Zhang and McAleer (2001) use a similar structural VAR method to investigate an optimal currency area for East Asia.

5 Although Enders and Hurn (1994) used the wholesale price index to calculate the real exchange rate, we use the consumer price index because we assume two commodities that include tradable and non-tradable goods. See Kawasaki (2002) for details of the theoretical background.

6 All the results of the empirical tests for 198 combinations are shown in Ogawa and Kawasaki (2003).

REFERENCES

Bayoumi, T. and B. Eichengreen (1993), "Shocking aspects of European monetary integration", in Francisco Torres and Francesco Givavazzi eds., *Adjustment and Growth in the European Monetary Union*, Cambridge: Cambridge University Press, pp. 193-229.

Bayoumi, T., B. Eichengreen and P. Mauro (2000), "On regional monetary arrangements for ASEAN", *CEPR Discussion Paper*, No.2411.

Bénassy-Quéré, A. (1999), "Optimal pegs for East Asian currencies", *Journal of the Japanese and International Economies, 13,* 44-60.

Enders, W. and S. Hurn (1994), "Theory and tests of generalized purchasing-power parity: Common trends and real exchange rates in the Pacific Rim", *Review of International Economics*, *2* (2), 179-90.

Frankel J. A. and S. Wei (1994), "Yen bloc or dollar bloc? Exchange rate policies of the east Asian economies", in T. Ito and A. O. Krueger, (eds), *Macroeconomic Linkage: Savings, Exchange Rates and Capital Flows*, Chicago: University of Chicago Press, 295-355.

Ito, T., E. Ogawa and N. Y. Sasaki (1998), "How did the dollar peg fail in Asia?", *Journal of the Japanese and International Economies*, *12*, 256-304.

Ito, T., E. Ogawa and N. Y. Sasaki (1999), "A Regional currency system in East Asia", *Stabilization of Currencies and Financial Systems in East Asia and International Financial Cooperation*, Tokyo: Institute for International Monetary Affairs.

Johansen, S. and K. Juselius (1990), "Maximum likelihood estimation and inference on cointegration; with application to the demand for money", *Oxford Bulletin of Economics and Statistics*, *52*, (2), 169-210.

Kawai, M. and S. Akiyama (1998), "The role of nominal anchors currencies in exchange arrangements", *Journal of the Japanese and International Economies, 12,* pp.334-87.

Kawasaki, K. (2000), "A test of OCA in Asian currency area: Empirical analysis based on G-PPP Theory", *The Hitotsubashi Review, 124,* (6), 127-46 (in Japanese).

Kawasaki, K., (2002) "Give a New Life to the PPP Theory: Modifying the Generalized PPP Model", (mimeo).

Kim, T., J. Ryou, and Y. Wang, (2000), *Regional Arrangements to Borrow: A Scheme for Preventing Future Asian Liquidity Crises*, Seoul:.Korea Institute for International Economic Policy.

McKinnon, R. I. (1963), "Optimum currency area", *American Economic Review, 53,* 717-25.

McKinnon, R. I. (2000), "After the crisis, the East Asian dollar standard resurrected: An interpretation of high-frequency exchange rate pegging", August.

Mundell, R. A. (1961), "A theory of optimum currency areas," *American Economic Review, 51,* 657-65.

Nakata, H and E. Ogawa (2002), "Necessity and scope of coordination for currency system in East Asia", Hitotsubashi University Faculty of Commerce, Working Paper Series, No. 80 (in Japanese).

Ogawa, E. (2002a), "Should East Asian countries return to dollar peg again?", P. Drysdale and K. Ishigaki eds., *East Asian Trade and Financial Integration: New Issues*, Canberra: Asia Pacific Press.

Ogawa, E. (2002b), "Economic interdependence and international coordination in East Asia", in *Exchange Rate Regimes for Asia* (Kobe Research Project), Ministry of Finance.
(http://www.mof.go.jp/jouhou/kokkin/tyousa/tyou042.pdf)

Ogawa, E. and T. Ito (2002), "On the desirability of a regional basket currency arrangement", *Journal of the Japanese and International Economies, 16*, 317-34.

Ogawa, E. and K. Kawasaki (2001), "Toward an Asian Currency Union," a paper prepared for the 2001 KIEP/NEAEF Conference on Strengthening Economic Cooperation in Northeast Asia held in Honolulu, Hawaii, on 16-17 August 2001.

Ogawa, E. and K. Kawasaki (2003), "Possibility of creating a common currency basket for East Asia", Discussion Paper No. 5, JBIC Institute Tokyo, Japan.

Ogawa, E. and L. Sun (2001), "How were capital inflows stimulated under the dollar peg system?" in T. Ito and A. O. Krueger (eds), *Regional and Global Capital Flows: Macroeconomic Causes and Consequences*, Chicago:.University of Chicago Press.

Ohno, K. (1999), "Exchange rate management in developing Asia: Reassessment of the pre-crisis soft dollar zone", ADB Institute, Working Paper Series, No. 1, January 1999.

Sato, K., Z. Zhang, and M. Mcaleer (2001), "Is East Asian optimum currency area?" a paper prepared for 2001 Far Eastern Meeting of the Econometric Society in Kobe.

Stock, J., and M. Watson (1988), "Testing for common trends", *Journal of the American Statistical Association, 83*, 1097- 107.

Index